Contents

List of Maps

About the Authors

Pauline Frommer is the creator of the *Pauline Frommer Guidebooks,* an award-winning new series aimed at adult budget travelers. There are now 13 titles in the series, with four more in the works. *Pauline Frommer's New York City* and *Pauline Frommer's London* were both named Guidebook of the Year (in 2006 and 2007, respectively) by the North American Travel Journalists Association. In addition, Pauline was awarded a Lowell Thomas Medal from the Society of American Travel Writers for her magazine work. She was the founding editor of Frommers.com, and won a People's Voice Webby Award for her work there. Pauline's byline has appeared on hundreds of articles for such publications as *Budget Travel Magazine, Marie Claire, Nick Jr.,* MSN.com, MSNBC.com and the *Dallas Morning News.* She spent two years as the editor of the travel section for MSNBC.com, one of the largest news sites on the web. Her column, "The Vacation Doc," appears twice monthly on MSN.com. Currently, along with her writing work, Pauline co-hosts *The Travel Show* with her father, travel legend Arthur Frommer. The show is broadcast to over 100 radio stations nationwide. Every Wednesday, she appears on CNNOnline to talk about the latest travel trends. She's also made appearances on *The Today Show, Good Morning America, Live with Regis and Kelly, The O'Reilly Factor, The Early Show, The CBS Evening News,* CNN, FOX, MSNBC, CNN Headline News, NPR's *Talk of the Nation* and just about every local news station you can name. Pauline is happily married to physical therapist Mahlon Stewart and the mother of two wonderfully well-traveled daughters, Beatrix (age 5) and Veronica (age 9). She's a graduate of Wesleyan University.

Kate Silver intended to live in Las Vegas for just a year, but she took to Sin City like a dauber-wielding Bingo buff. She has spent nine years getting to know and often love the city, paying special interest to the offbeat people who call Las Vegas home. An award-winning journalist, she extols the eccentricities and intricacies of the city. Her adventurous nature and writing experience were assets when she was invited to pen three chapters in this book (gambling, shopping and side trips), in which the R & D involved competing in a slot tournament, visiting a "top secret" government base, and shopping. While on staff at *Las Vegas Weekly* newspaper, Silver won awards from the Nevada Press Association for Outstanding Journalist in 2003 and Journalist in 2001. A former editor at *Las Vegas Life* magazine, she received a "gold" from the City Regional Magazines Association for a city guide published in 2006. She's now a freelance writer, and her work has appeared in *Playboy, People,* and *Spirit* magazines.

Acknowledgments

It takes a village to write a travel guide—especially when you're trying to raise two young daughters at the same time. So I must thank Joy Joseph for the loving care she gave to my daughters as we all ran around Vegas together (and during the weeks I was in Vegas alone). To my remarkably patient and insightful daughters: I apologize for writing about you in the book. I know that embarrasses you right now, but seeing Vegas through your eyes was immensely instructive for me. For my friends Joan Fernald, Sasha Carrera and Lael Lowenstein: without your help and companionship, this book wouldn't have been half as much fun to write (I can't thank you enough). I also thank Kathleen Silver for generously sharing her insider's point of view with me. I want to thank my father, Arthur Frommer, whose unstinting support (and unsparing red pen), have helped me shape this book and grow as a writer. I owe a debt of gratitude to my terrifically supportive publisher Ensley Eikenburg, and my editor Kathleen Warnock. I dedicate this book to the love of my life, my husband Mahlon, who I missed dreadfully lo those many months spent in Vegas researching this tome. Next time, you're coming with me!

The editor wishes to thank fellow Frommer's editors Naomi Kraus, Ian Skinnari and Marc Nadeau for their help and guidance on this edition.

An Invitation to the Reader

In researching this book, we discovered many wonderful places—hotels, restaurants, shops, and more. We're sure you'll find others. Please tell us about them, so we can share the information with your fellow travelers in upcoming editions. If you were disappointed with a recommendation, we'd love to know that, too. Please write to:

Pauline Frommer's Las Vegas, 2nd Edition
Wiley Publishing, Inc. • 111 River St. • Hoboken, NJ 07030-5774

An Additional Note

Please be advised that travel information is subject to change at any time—and this is especially true of prices. We therefore suggest that you write or call ahead for confirmation when making your travel plans. The authors, editors, and publisher cannot be held responsible for the experiences of readers while traveling. Your safety is important to us, however, so we encourage you to stay alert and be aware of your surroundings. Keep a close eye on cameras, purses, and wallets, all favorite targets of thieves and pickpockets.

Star Ratings, Icons & Abbreviations

Every restaurant, hotel and attraction is rated with stars ★, indicating our opinion of that facility's desirability; this relates not to price, but to the value you receive for the price you pay. The stars mean:

No stars: Good
★ Very good
★★ Great
★★★ Outstanding! A must!

Accommodations within each neighborhood are listed in ascending order of cost, starting with the cheapest and increasing to the occasional "splurge." Each hotel review is preceded by one, two, three or four dollar signs, indicating the price range per double room. Restaurants work on a similar system, with dollar signs indicating the price range per three-course meal.

Accommodations
$ Up to $100/night
$$ $101–$135
$$$ $136–$175
$$$$ Over $176 per night

Dining
$ Meals for $7 or less
$$ $8–$12
$$$ $12–$17
$$$$ $18 and up

In addition, we've included a kids icon 🧒 to denote attractions, restaurants, and lodgings that are particularly child friendly.

Frommers.com

Now that you have this guidebook to help you plan a great trip, visit our website at **www.frommers.com** for additional travel information on more than 4,000 destinations. We update features regularly to give you instant access to the most current trip-planning information available. At Frommers.com, you'll find scoops on the best airfares, lodging rates, and car rental bargains. You can even book your travel online through our reliable travel booking partners. Other popular features include:

- Online updates of our most popular guidebooks
- Vacation sweepstakes and contest giveaways
- Newsletters highlighting the hottest travel trends
- Podcasts, interactive maps, and up-to-the-minute events listings
- Opinionated blog entries by Arthur Frommer himself
- Online travel message boards with featured travel discussions

I started traveling with my guidebook-writing parents, Arthur Frommer and Hope Arthur, when I was just 4 months old. To avoid lugging around a crib, they would simply swaddle me and stick me in an open drawer for the night. For half of my childhood, my home was a succession of hotels and B&Bs throughout Europe, as we dashed around every year to update *Europe on $5 a Day* (and then $10 a day, and then $20 . . .).

We always traveled on a budget, staying at the mom-and-pop joints Dad featured in the guide, getting around by public transportation, eating where the locals ate. And that's still the way I travel today, because I learned—from the master—that these types of vacations not only save money but offer a richer, deeper experience of the culture. You spend time in local neighborhoods, meeting and talking with the people who live there. For me, making friends and having meaningful exchanges is always the highlight of my journeys—and the main reason I decided to become a travel writer and editor as well.

I've conceived these books as budget guides for a new generation. They have all the outspoken commentary and detailed pricing information of the Frommer's guides, but they take bargain hunting into the 21st century, with more information on using the Internet and air/hotel packages to save money. Most important, we stress "alternative accommodations"—apartment rentals, private B&Bs, and more—not simply to save you money, but to give you a more authentic experience in the places you visit.

A highlight of each guide is the chapter that deals with the "other" side of the destinations, the one visitors rarely see. These sections will actively immerse you in the life that residents enjoy. The result, I hope, is a valuable new addition to the world of guidebooks. Please let us know how we've done! E-mail me at editor@frommers.com.

Happy traveling!

Pauline Frommer

Pauline Frommer

1 Losing It in Las Vegas

Sin City will rob you of your time, your money, and your waistline (but not your desire to vacation here again)

LAS VEGAS NOW RECEIVES THREE TIMES AS MANY VISITORS PER YEAR AS Mecca and Vatican City put together. Pilgrims of a, well, different sort, these conventioneers, vacationers, gamblers, and gawkers come here not to be saved but—let's be blunt—to sin. Or at least to engage in behavior that previous generations would have found slightly immoral at best.

What sort of behavior? There's the wanton **gluttony** of Vegas, with its chocolate fountains, meals that cost more than a month's rent, endless buffets groaning under the weight of their fat content.

Lust is as big a moneymaker, with a third of the casinos on the Strip supporting some sort of T&A show, and cocktail waitresses squeezed into costumes that wouldn't have been seen outside a bordello up until about, oh, 1955 or so.

Sloth is celebrated with architecture and attractions that are proudly plagiarized from other cities, huge mountains of cash that substitute for genuine creativity or (in many cases) good taste, and kitsch that runs rampant in every fake pyramid and Eiffel Tower.

And then there's **greed,** the driving engine of the city; that happy sin that puts the spring into crap players' wrists and circumvents the super ego, allowing players to forget their mortgages as they wager their earnings away.

It is, in short, a place to dip your toe into that undercurrent of nihilism, of derring-do, of the unadulterated sensuality that courses through most of our veins but perhaps hasn't been given free rein since our teenage, or maybe even, toddler years.

> **❝** Vegas is everything that's right about America. You can do whatever you want, 24 hours a day. They've effectively legalized everything here. **❞**
>
> —Drew Carey

And yet it's all great fun. The sins of Sin City are what 40 million mostly ethical, upstanding travelers pursue each year. They come to this never-never land of fantasy piled upon fantasy to let off steam, stop watching the clock (just try to find one in Vegas!), forget their inner lives, and simply act in ways that give them pleasure. In short, to do the things these upstanding citizens might be shy about doing publicly at home (there's a reason the slogan "What Happens in Vegas, Stays in Vegas" has been so popular). It can be a hell of a lot of fun to visit Vegas.

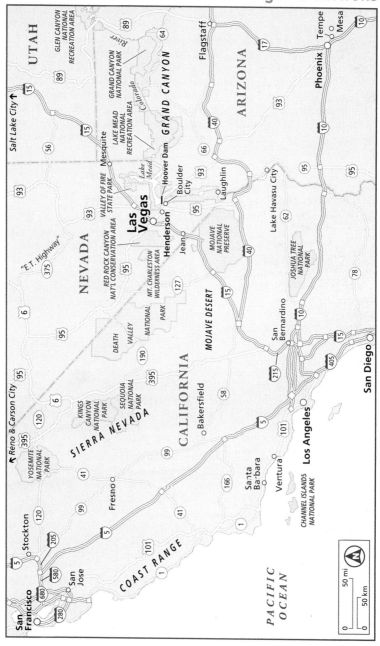

As an added bonus, Las Vegas, which means "The Meadows" in Spanish, is also set in one of the most starkly beautiful areas of the United States, an oasis (the springs here formed those meadows) in the heart of the Mojave Desert. As such, it is a superb hopping-off point for excursions into the arid region, whether you decide on a day of hiking in nearby Red Rock Canyon or Valley of Fire National Park, or make a car or copter trip all the way to that exquisite, unearthly, hole in the ground, the Grand Canyon. For information on all of the exceptional day trips one can take from Vegas, turn to the "Get Out of Town" chapter (p. 275).

I'll do my best in this chapter to sort through a book's worth of options, selecting those attractions that, in my view, are sure to turn your vacation from standard into a first-rate bacchanal.

SIGHTS YOU'VE GOTTA SEE, THINGS YOU'VE GOTTA DO

Novelist Chuck Palahniuk once wrote that "Las Vegas looks the way you'd imagine heaven must look at night." I can only assume he was describing a stroll down the **Strip** (p. 114) after the sun had set. During the day, this famous stretch of roadway, flanked by monolithic hotels and tacky souvenir shops, shows its cracks and seams, looking somewhat like Wayne Newton must look before he's donned his tux and shellacked his face. But at night, it's a glittering, glowing spectacle, each silly/splendid monument lit up and framed just so against the black desert sky. A stroll or a slow drive down the Strip at night is, to my mind, the absolute "can't-miss" activity on a Vegas vacation.

During that stroll, it's imperative to stop for one of the **Fountain Shows at the Bellagio** (p. 118). Absolutely mesmerizing, the precision jets arc through the air like laser beams, shooting up waves of water as tall as the massive building the fountain fronts. Set to dozens of different tunes, the show is constantly changing, so you may want to make several stops here over the course of your visit. Be sure also to head to **The Venetian** (p. 120), the most beautifully realized and just plain beautiful, of the faked environments on the Strip (with **Caesars Palace** [p. 120] running a close second).

Las Vegas boasts one of the most talented populations in the United States, so you'll want to see a live performance of some sort while you're here. If you can afford it, go with a **Cirque du Soleil** show (my favorites are *O* [p. 184] and *Mystère* [p. 184]). Surreal circuses, with awe-inspiring stage effects, costumes, and performances, they've redefined entertainment in Vegas. Or go see one of the Vegas headliners. Once you do, you'll understand why **Mac King** (p. 195), **Wayne Brady** (p. 181), **Lance Burton** (p. 189), and **Anthony Cools** (p. 189), have their names above the marquee (the same can be said for pricier performers too, especially Barry Manilow and Bette Midler).

You should also challenge yourself to step out of your everyday life while in Vegas and try something new. This might mean entrusting yourself with $100 to lose at **blackjack** (I recommend it as it's one of the more social games and has the best odds for players); or, for a real rush, trying **Indoor Skydiving** (p. 146).

A Word About the Current Economics of Vegas

It seems like overkill in a chapter about the "sinfulness" of Sin City to point out that recently, the town's economy has been going to hell in a handbasket. But that seems like the only phrase appropriate to the current recession, which has been hitting Las Vegas with a far stronger punch than most other cities around the United States. As I wrote and researched this book, I found prices to be spiraling downwards on an almost daily basis. So my advice to you, dear reader, is to take the prices in this book as markers, knowing that you may be able to do better. So wheel and deal, bargain and beg. The powers that be *want* you to come visit and you'll find that for once, you'll probably be able to do it on your own terms (and on a low, low budget).

THE FINEST MUSEUMS

Vegas doesn't have to be all mindless entertainment. At the world-class **Atomic Testing Museum** (p. 125), you'll learn everything you ever wanted to know about the bomb . . . but were really too afraid to ask. The physics behind nuclear energy, the innovations that came out of the testing, how the government is using the site today, and much more make up the engrossing, often interactive exhibits at this Smithsonian Institution–affiliate museum.

Also off-Strip, but worth the commute, the **Springs Preserve** (p. 126) is a cutting-edge exegesis of desert living with well-done exhibits on the history of Vegas as an oasis in the desert, plus thought-provoking exhibits on the light topic of how civilization will be able to survive in this era of dwindling water supplies (not only in Vegas, but across the planet). Not the typically mindless entertainment you tend to find in Vegas.

Competition in the world of high culture is the **Bellagio Gallery of Fine Art** (p. 123) which has an excellent track records, bringing the works of such masters as Vermeer, Van Gogh, Georgia O'Keefe, and Calder into the pleasure dome that is the Bellagio Hotel.

Not to be ignored in the museum category is that temple of kitsch, the **Liberace Museum** (p. 129). Even if you have little interest in the man himself, you'll want to see this over-the-top collection of wacky cars, historic pianos, and clothing so exuberantly sparkly and gaudy, it will bring a glow to your kitsch-loving heart.

UNCOMMON LODGINGS

You don't have to stay on the Strip to enjoy Vegas. One of the most comfortable ways to vacation here is to rent your own little house, which will likely boast flatscreen TVs, a private pool, a pool table, and a fully equipped kitchen—all standard features of Vegas vacation rentals, and all for the cost of a hotel room! Read up on this alternative to hotels on p. 18.

For those who simply want a clean place to sleep—so they can gamble away all the money they save—the **Silverton** (p. 64), **Sam's Town** (p. 54), the **Gold Coast** (p. 61), and **Palace Station** (p. 61), offer beautifully furnished, oversized rooms in hotels that boast large casinos, multiple restaurants, bowling alleys, and other forms of entertainment, yet often cost half of what you'd pay on the Strip.

And then there are the Strip hotels themselves, whether you decide on a Hollywood memorabilia-laden room at **Planet Hollywood** (p. 33), a froufrou-laden French Empire–style room at **Paris Las Vegas** (p. 39), or cheap, but ultra comfy digs—once you get through the crowded, tacky casino—at **Circus Circus** (p. 41).

All of these options—and more (see chapter 3)—should bring you a comfortable bed at night, and a wealth of entertainment options during the day.

DINING FOR ALL TASTES

Though you'll have traveled only to Vegas, your stomach can travel the world, odd as that may sound, at the many excellent ethnic restaurants that dot the city. For the Thai meal of a lifetime, head to **Lotus of Siam** (p. 100), and let the waiter order for you. (The owner heads to Thailand many times a year to bring back unusual spices and ingredients, so the meals you get here are unlike anything you're likely to have tried in your hometown Thai joint.) Or head to the restaurant where Vegas' large Mexican population goes when it has a special event to celebrate. At **Lindo Michoacan** (p. 100), the meal is always a party, and the mole sauce is to die for. Festive food, plus lots of beer, is the focus at the delightful **Hofbräuhaus** (p. 103), a perfect replica of that famous Munich beer garden. Innovative Japanese food is the thing at **Raku** (p. 109), and you'll find just as high a level of creativity where Spanish tapas are concerned at **Firefly** (p. 106).

Of course you'll want to try a buffet while you're here (it's the thing to do) and for that you have a multiplicity of options. You could indulge your sweet tooth with freshly made cotton candy and all sorts of luscious fruits dipped in chocolate at the **Buffet at Treasure Island** (p. 88); try top-notch Middle Eastern fare (along with other types of foods in a glitzy, newly renovated eating area) at the **Palms** (p. 107); or confine yourself to just sushi—loads and loads and loads of sushi—at **Makino** (p. 98).

THE FINEST "OTHER" EXPERIENCES

Get off the tourist treadmill and take part in one of the activities performed by actual Las Vegans each day. Go **discuss philosophy** in a casino (p. 163) or **learn how to become a dealer** (p. 160) or even a stripper at a **Stripper 101 class** (p. 162). **Meet a showgirl** and take a backstage tour of the long-running show *Jubilee!* (p. 165). Take a **cooking class from a top Vegas chef** (p. 161), or spend a day experiencing what it would have been like to work at the nearby **Atomic Testing Site** (p. 173), on an insider's tour. Hang out with magicians at a **magical karaoke** night (p. 171) or quaff **Martinis with the Mayor** (p. 169). These and many more activities discussed in chapter 7 allow visitors to see sides of the city that visitors usually miss, gain a new skill, and meet actual residents.

2 The Lay of the Land

A quick description of where everything is and some important tips on how to get around

AS CITIES GO, THERE'S NOTHING OVERLY COMPLEX ABOUT THE TRANSportation to and within Vegas. It's served by a number of air carriers, has speedy highways darting straight into its heart, and is laid out in a rough grid, making navigation fairly easy. That said, actually getting from point A to point B, especially if you have to cross the Strip, is about as much fun as having a root canal on your birthday. Traffic is horrendous, few sights are within easy walking distance of one another, and the public transportation system is improving but still has its flaws.

My job is to take the pain out of getting around, supply you with the various ways to do so, and help you figure out how to get where you're going a bit easier.

THE VEGAS GRID

We'll start with the simple stuff: The most famous thoroughfare in Las Vegas is the so-called **Strip,** which is the stretch of Las Vegas Boulevard South that leads from the Mandalay Bay all the way north to the Stratosphere. Keep going further north and you'll be in **Downtown,** which has as its heart Fremont Street, home to the famous light show, the Fremont Street Experience.

Caesars Palace, the Bellagio, Treasure Island, Circus Circus, and the Luxor (among others) lie on the west side of the Strip, with Highway I-15 right behind them, and behind that is the area we'll call **West Las Vegas.** To the east of the Strip (and you'll know you're looking east if you see Paris Las Vegas, Wynn Las Vegas, Harrah's, and Bally's, among others) lies **East Las Vegas.** The airport is also to the east of the Strip, just a 5- to 10-minute drive away. (See p. 310 for info on transportation to and from the airport.)

While Las Vegas Boulevard (the Strip) is the major artery running north to south, there are a number of major east–west roads that are fairly easy to remember, as some are named for the casinos that abut these roads, or once abutted them. At the northern end of the Strip, for example, you have **Sahara Avenue** (named for the Sahara); in the center, **Flamingo Road** is a major artery (at the Flamingo); and just next to the Tropicana you'll find—drum roll, please— **Tropicana Avenue.** I find that whenever I am lost when wandering in the outlying areas of Vegas, I simply look for one of these three roads (or Charleston Blvd., Spring Mountain Rd., and Desert Inn Rd., other major ones) to eventually find my way back to the Strip. You'll be amazed at how long these streets are, so be careful when you're looking at freeway exits, as sometimes the listed exit for, say, Flamingo, will be nowhere near the Strip.

Because Las Vegas is a young city, it doesn't have too many of the twisty, unusual roads of older towns, at least when it comes to major thoroughfares (get into one of the larger gated communities and you may need a compass). The city's layout is mostly a grid, which makes it not too, too difficult to navigate when you're driving off the Strip.

AVOIDING TRAFFIC JAMS

How do you escape traffic gridlock when you drive on these major roads? Locals tend to avoid driving on the Strip when they can, especially at the intersection of Flamingo and Las Vegas Boulevard South, which turns into a noisy parking lot between roughly 5pm and 9pm most days. But really, you can spend a lot of time stuck in your car anywhere between Spring Mountain Road and Tropicana Avenue at those times—there are just too many cars for too little boulevard.

Savvy drivers detour to the service roads and back roads that often run parallel to the Strip and serve as back entrances to a number of casinos. See the list below for a rundown of these secret streets and which hotels they access:

Harmon Avenue: Planet Hollywood; Bally's (via Audrie St., off Harmon); Paris (via Audrie Lane, off Harmon)

Koval Lane: Flamingo (you'll ultimately turn onto Audrie St.); Harrah's (you'll ultimately turn onto Audrie St.); Imperial Palace (you'll ultimately turn onto Audrie St.); Tropicana (for Trop, turn right from Koval onto Reno Ave.); Venetian

Convention Center Drive: Wynn Las Vegas

Flamingo Road: Bellagio

Frank Sinatra Drive: Caesars Palace; Excalibur; Luxor; Mandalay Bay; New York–New York

Industrial Road: Circus Circus

Spring Mountain Road: Mirage; Treasure Island

Paradise Road: Sahara; Riviera (you'll turn onto Riviera Blvd. from Paradise)

As for the vehicles, modes, and facilities for moving about, you have several options. Which is the cheapest or most time efficient will really depend on the location of your hotel and the amount of gadding about you plan to do. Consider the following:

RENTING A CAR

Despite Strip traffic, I think renting a car is a great strategy. It gives you the freedom to explore beyond the Strip and may allow you to save in food costs what you pay for rental and gasoline, by eating where the locals do. In contrast to visiting other cities, you won't have the added expense of parking. With few exceptions, Vegas parking garages are free, as is valet parking (though you'll have to tip, of course).

Finding a good rental-car rate is part art and part luck. Like hotel rates, they shift by the day and if you have the misfortune to visit when one of those 100,000-plus attendee conventions is in town, you could easily pay triple what

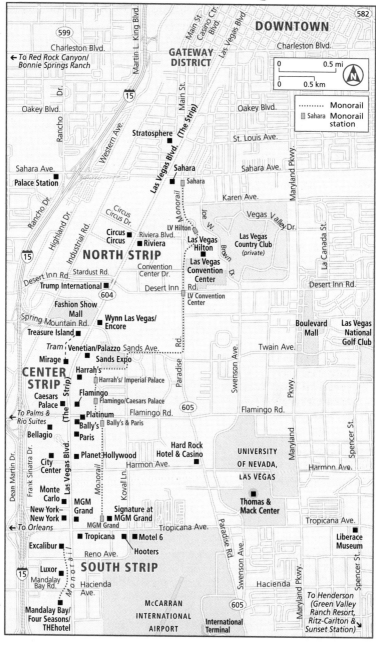

582

599

DOWNTOWN

Charleston Blvd.

Charleston Blvd.

← To Red Rock Canyon/
Bonnie Springs Ranch

GATEWAY
DISTRICT

0   0.5 mi
0   0.5 km

Oakey Blvd.

Oakey Blvd.

Main St.

Casino Ctr. Blvd.

Las Vegas Blvd.

Maryland Pkwy.

········· Monorail
◻ Sahara Monorail
            station

Western Ave.

Rancho Dr.

Stratosphere

St. Louis Ave.

Sahara Ave.

Sahara

Sahara Ave.

Palace Station

◻ Sahara

Karen Ave.

La Canada St.

Rancho Dr.

Highland Dr.

Industrial Rd.

Circus
Circus Dr.

Vegas Valley Dr.

Circus
Circus

Riviera Blvd.

LV Hilton

■ Riviera

Las Vegas
Hilton

Las Vegas
Country Club
(private)

Joe W.

Brown Dr.

NORTH STRIP

Stardust Rd.

Convention
Center Dr.

Las Vegas
Convention
Center

Desert Inn Rd.

Trump International

Desert Inn Rd.

Desert Inn Rd.

604

LV Convention
Center

Fashion Show
Mall

Wynn Las Vegas/
Encore

Paradise Rd.

Boulevard
Mall

Las Vegas
National
Golf Club

Spring
Mountain Rd.

Treasure Island

Twain Ave.

Swenson Ave.

Tram Venetian/Palazzo   Sands Ave.

Mirage

Sands Expo

CENTER
STRIP

Harrah's

Harrah's/ Imperial Palace

Caesars
Palace

Flamingo

Flamingo/Caesars Palace

605

Flamingo Rd.

Flamingo Rd.

← To Palms &
Rio Suites

Platinum

Flamingo Rd.

Bally's

Bally's & Paris

Bellagio

Paris

Maryland Pkwy.

Planet Hollywood

Hard Rock
Hotel & Casino

UNIVERSITY
OF NEVADA,
LAS VEGAS

City
Center

Harmon Ave.

Harmon Ave.

Dean Martin Dr.

Frank Sinatra Dr.

Las Vegas Blvd.

Monte
Carlo

New York–
New York

MGM
Grand

Signature at
MGM Grand

Thomas &
Mack Center

Spencer St.

← To Orleans

MGM Grand

Tropicana Ave.

Tropicana Ave.

Excalibur

Tropicana ■ Motel 6

Liberace
Museum

Reno Ave.

Hooters

Paradise Rd.

Swenson Ave.

Maryland Pkwy.

Spencer St.

Luxor

SOUTH STRIP

Mandalay
Bay Rd.

Hacienda
Ave.

Hacienda

To Henderson
(Green Valley
Ranch Resort,
Ritz-Carlton &
Sunset Station)→

Mandalay Bay/
Four Seasons/
THEhotel

McCARRAN
INTERNATIONAL
AIRPORT

605

International
Terminal

you would during a slow period. (See our chart on p. 302 for dates of the big conventions.) Beyond hitting town at the right time, strategies for saving on car rentals include:

◆ **Bidding for cars:** Companies such as **Priceline** (www.priceline.com) and **Hotwire** (www.hotwire.com) work only with the major, national car-rental chains. So, bidding on a rental is no more risky than going to a car-rental company direct, though you might have to accept a Pontiac Grand Prix rather than a Chevrolet Monte Carlo. You never want to bid blind, though, because during heavy periods these "opaque" sites may not have better rates than the regular companies. To quickly survey the rental options, do a search on one of the following "aggregator" sites: BNM.com, Kayak.com, Sidestep.com, or Mobissimo.com. Each searches many websites for car-rental rates, giving you an impartial result and one without the booking fees of, say, Expedia. Be aware, though, that reservations made through Priceline or Hotwire cannot be cancelled. You'll be asked to pay upfront and you will lose your money if, for some reason, you end up not being able to use the car.

◆ **Go local:** By avoiding the chains, you can sometimes save a bundle on car rentals . . . or you could be left sitting on the curb, as I was once, having rented from Savmor Rent a Car. When I showed up, there were no cars left on the lot. Those that were supposed to have been returned were still out, and because Savmor has just one outlet rather than Enterprise's or Avis's dozens, I was out of luck and had to scramble, running from counter to counter at the airport to secure another car. To be fair, there might have been a car for me the next morning, and the agency offered to transport me to my hotel that night and back in the morning, but I had early morning appointments that I needed to get to. If you're more flexible than I am, you can check the following reputable local agencies for deals:

  ◆ **Savmor Rent a Car** (5101 Rent A Car Rd.; ☎ 702/736-1234; http://reserve.savmorrac.com/frontdesk/reserve/index.asp at the airport rental center as well)
  ◆ **US Rent a Car** (4700 Paradise Rd.; ☎ 800/777-9377 or 702/798-6100; counter at airport with its new owner, Advantage Rent a Car)
  ◆ **Brooks Rent a Car** (3041 Las Vegas Blvd.; ☎ 702/735-3344; www.brooksrentalcar.com; no airport counter but free airport pick-up)

One final word about local agencies: With so many planes arriving in Vegas in the wee hours of the morning, airport rental agencies tend to stay open quite late. This is not always so with the local agencies (Brooks, for one, closes at 5pm, though the others are open all hours). So if you go beyond this list, make sure that you'll be able to pick up your car when you want it.

◆ **Book off-airport:** Airport taxes and usage fees can add a whopping 27.5%, plus a $3 per day "consumer facility charge," to the final cost of a rental car. For long-term rentals especially, the savings that come from simply renting off-airport can be substantial. Rental car agencies located outside the terminal add a less ugly (but still hefty) 17% in local and state taxes, and have no facility charge. Suppose you find a car rental for $35 a day. Renting at an airport counter with all the additional taxes and fees would cost you $330 a week; that same rental elsewhere in Vegas could cost just $286. Occasionally,

A Word on Parking . . .

Free, but far from hassle-free, parking garages in Vegas range from the standard three- and four-story concrete boxes to dizzyingly huge, multi-level, multicolored, and multicoded labyrinths. That's why some are patrolled by men on bicycles; according to one guard with whom I've spoken, 80% of his job consists of helping people find the cars they parked and then lost. Here are some tips on making parking more of a pleasant experience:

- **Only valet park if you have a 15- to 25-minute cushion when you leave:** Valet parking may seem the quickest and easiest way to go, but in reality, it can be a huge hassle. Waits are particularly long if you try and retrieve your car after a show or even after the dinner hour in some of the plusher casinos. You'll be competing with the, oh, 150 to 300 people who also valet-parked that night, and they're just as eager as you are to get out.
- **Write down the name, number, color, or code of your parking space:** The reason I got to know that nice patrol-fellow so well is that I once lost my car for a good hour at the MGM Grand parking lot. For half an hour of that time, two patrol guys on bikes were searching for it with my license plate number. This is a long way of saying it's very easy to lose your car in these places, especially if it's a rental or if you've had a drink or two.
- **Head to the casino parking if you're downtown:** The public lots here are about the only ones in town that charge for parking. At the casinos you may have to validate your ticket, but that's usually quite easily done (and won't even require a purchase on your part).

off-airport agencies charge a higher base price, but for the most part I've found the opposite to be true, and lower rates plus lower taxes can add up to bigger savings. Doing a survey of Avis prices for a 1-day midsized rental, I was quoted a final price of $99 at the airport and $61 at a Strip rental counter.

- **Shop around:** Considering the different charges for on-airport vs. off-airport bookings, I also ran numbers for a number of different companies and came up with very different prices. As I mentioned, Avis was $61 (at a Strip rental counter), but Thrifty and Enterprise came in at just $30 (including all taxes and fees) on the same day. The websites I listed above in our "Bidding" section will work best for these sweeping searches. You'll also want to shop around in terms of car sizes. Every once in a while, companies sell out compacts first and then offer lower prices on midsized or full-sized vehicles (this is particularly true when fuel costs are high).

- **Use your VIP status:** Yes, you are a VIP—you just might not know it. But if you're a member of AAA or AARP, make that known . . . after you get your quote (do it before and you might not get as good a deal). If you work for a large corporation or are a member of a union, see if it has arranged benefits at the car-rental counter. If you're going to be using a credit card, go to the site of the rental company you've picked first and see if there are any printable coupons there for credit card discounts (sorry, just using the credit card won't usually get you the discount, you have to hand in the darn coupon!). And if you shop at Sam's Club, Costco, or BJ's Wholesale, see if they have any rental coupons at their travel counters—often they do, and these can save you between 5% and 30%.
- **Check, check, and recheck:** If you book a car rental directly from a company, revisit its site before you get to the airport. Sometimes prices do drop. Simply rebook yourself at the lower rate (I've saved as much as $60 this way) and bring a copy of your confirmation letter so that the counter-folks are clear on the cost. Carrying paper confirmation is a must any time you rent a car, as you don't want to be confronted with a much higher price than the one you thought you booked.

TAKING TAXIS

You'll meet some very interesting people when you take a cab in Vegas. Many drivers come from all parts of the U.S.—and the world—simply to work as cabdrivers for 6 months and then take the next 6 months off (more common than you'd imagine). Which might tell you a bit about how costly cabs are. This is the most expensive way to get around town, and often not the most convenient.

It'll cost you $3.30 just to get into the cab and then 53¢ for every ⅛ of a mile thereafter. Add a $1.80 fee if you're being picked up from the airport. Riders wait for cabs at the taxi lines at various major hotels around town, as it's illegal for a cab to stop when hailed (and the cops are stringent about this, especially on the crowded Strip); I've waited up to 30 minutes in these lines. While you're in line, see if anyone else would like to share the cab with you; you can squeeze up to five people in a cab and there's no extra charge as long as you're all going to the same destination.

Major cab companies in town are: **Desert Cab Company** (☎ 702/386-9102), **Whittlesea Blue Cab** (☎ 702/384-6111), and **Yellow/Checker Cab Company** (☎ 702/873-2000).

USING THE MONORAIL

Remember *The Simpsons* episode where a scam artist comes to town hoping to bamboozle the city into building a monorail? Many in Vegas are wondering if the same sort of thing happened in their city. Widely touted as being the answer to Vegas' traffic problems, the **Monorail** (☎ 702/699-8299; www.lvmonorail.com), built at a cost of $650 million and opened in 2004, has been an unmitigated bust so far. Officials had predicted that 50,000 riders a day would use this 4-mile track down the Strip from the MGM Grand to the Sahara (it also loops off the Strip to stop at the Convention Center). In summer of 2008, the number of actual riders was a scant 23,700 a day, slightly up from 2007, but well below what it needs to carry to be profitable.

Public Transportation Fares

Single ride: $1.25 off the Strip, $2 on it and for the Deuce everywhere it travels
Single ride, seniors and kids 6–17: 60¢ on all
Single ride, kids 5 and under: Free
Day pass: $5, usable on all three systems

Why so unpopular? Ah, there's a litany of reasons. I'd love to meet the geniuses who decided to stick the monorail stations in the most difficult-to-find area of each casino, from obscure basement malls (at Bally's) to spots a good 20-minute walk from the Strip (at MGM Grand). They also don't run as frequently as they should. While the monorail folks claim that the cars depart every 5 to 6 minutes during peak periods and every 5 to 12 minutes otherwise, I've ridden it a number of times and have only once had less than a 10-minute wait on the platform. Once you're on, the unrelenting commercial announcements, disguised as a "tour" of Vegas, are beyond annoying, especially if you're hearing the monologue for the third or fourth time. Finally, rides and passes are just too darn expensive.

On the bright side—and there always must be a bright side, right?—once you're aboard, there are no traffic jams to deal with, and you know that the ride itself will be relatively speedy. It takes a quick 18 minutes to get from one end to the next (not counting waiting-on-the-platform time). And if you use it enough to buy a daily pass it can be cost effective, especially now that they've lowered the prices.

THE DEUCE, CAT & MAX

Cute names, huh? Sounds kind of like a gang you'd want to play poker with. Marketing savvy even comes into play when naming the public bus systems in Vegas. But just because they're named smart doesn't mean their prices are upscale. Using these buses is a penny pincher's way to get around town. What they lack in speed and efficiency, they make up for in savings.

The Deuce (☎ **702/228-RIDE** [7433]; www.rtcsouthernnevada.com/transit) are double-decker buses—get it?—that traverse the most popular swath of Las Vegas Boulevard South from the Downtown area (where the bus briefly veers off Las Vegas Blvd. to stop at the Fremont Street Experience), all the way to the

The Monorail in a Nutshell

Hours: Mon–Thurs 7am–2am, Fri–Sun 7am–3am
Prices: Single ride $5, 1-day pass $12, 3-day pass $28
Stations: MGM Grand, Bally's, the Flamingo, Harrah's, Convention Center, Hilton

Mandalay Bay, and then several blocks past that, south to a transfer terminal between Sunset Road and Hidden Hills Road. Operating 24 hours a day, it's on its most frequent rotations (leaving every 6 min.) between 11am and 11:30pm, but even at 5am in the morning, you probably won't wait more than 15 or 20 minutes for the Deuce. Each bus has 97 seats, but it's sometimes standing room only, especially for those hoping to take in the Strip from a second-floor perch. All in all, though, it ain't a bad way to get around.

CAT (☎ 702/228-RIDE [7433]; www.rtcsouthernnevada.com/transit) is the acronym for the Soviet-sounding Citizens Area Transit. Unlike newbie The Deuce (which debuted in fall of 2005 and is technically part of CAT), it has been sending regular buses to all areas of the city since 1992. It has 51 routes served by 365 buses, so if you have the patience to wait at a bus stop and possibly make transfers, you can literally get most anywhere you want to go on the back of the CAT. Most routes operate from 5am to 1am, with 14 going 24 hours a day. Be prepared for a wait; on certain routes the buses can be mighty slow. Wheelchair lifts and bicycle racks make the buses accessible to all.

Max (☎ 702/228-RIDE [7433]; www.rtcsouthernnevada.com/transit) is Vegas' own bionic bus. Looking like a cross between a bullet train and a bus, it uses a new "optical guidance system" that directs it along lines painted on the street. A very "green" transportation system, its fuel source is a hybrid of electric and diesel power.

The Max goes only to a limited number of stops on a limited number of routes at the moment, but because it has a dedicated driving lane, it gets around quickly. As it serves a mostly residential neighborhood, running primarily along Las Vegas Boulevard North, it's unlikely that you, the visitor, will ever ride it, but it's such a cool development I had to add it here.

ENJOYING FREE TRANSPORTATION

Several free shuttles, and the power of your own two feet, are your other options for getting around Vegas. In terms of shuttles and trams, there are several that run between partnering casinos, including the ones between:

- The Barbary Coast, the Gold Coast, and the Orleans
- The Bellagio and the Monte Carlo
- Excalibur, Luxor, Mandalay Bay, Four Seasons, and THEhotel
- The Mirage and Treasure Island
- The Palms and Bally's
- The Rio and Paris Las Vegas
- Sam's Town, Harrah's, and Main Street Station
- Terrible's and the airport (not a casino, but useful nonetheless)

You don't have to stay at any of these hotels to take advantage of their shuttle services, nor is there ever a charge.

WALKING

If you're considering walking as your main form of transportation, more power to you. You'll need to stay on or very near the Strip, however, or you'll be miserable. Also take into account the heat; in the summer months, when the temperatures reach 105°F (41°C) in the shade, walking can be agony at best, and dangerous at worst. You should budget for other forms of transportation during June, July, and August.

Moreover, remember that you're hiking in the desert. I'm not only talking about the heat, but about distance perception. There's something about the quality of the air, and the outsize proportions of the casinos, that make distances look much shorter than they actually are along the Strip. Like that clichéd fellow crawling through the desert, thinking he's going to reach the mirage shimmering in the distance, you'll probably find that what you thought would be a quick stroll from, say, Excalibur to the Venetian, is in reality quite a trek. Trust maps, and not your eyes, in this desert oasis.

3 Accommodations, Both Standard & Not

Many of the "usual suspects," plus excellent other options you may not have considered

To strip or not to strip? That is the question and it's an important one.

No, I'm not recommending that your Vegas vacation include a career change. I'm saying that where you decide to stay will shape your experience of the city and determine how much you're likely to spend.

Though other guidebooks will recommend otherwise, I don't think it's a given that one MUST stay on the Strip to enjoy Vegas. Just like any other decision you make, it has its advantages and disadvantages. So before we go any further, I'm going to list the pluses and minuses, which should help you evaluate the options listed in this chapter.

REASONS FOR STAYING ON THE STRIP

Reason #1: I'll start with the obvious: Because it's the *Las Vegas Strip,* the most important sightseeing attraction in the city, and when you roll out of bed in the morning you'll be in the center of all that glorious insanity.

Reason #2: You won't need a car. Though distances on the Strip are deceptive, if you're smart enough to bring sneakers and fit enough for 20- to 30-minute walks, you can hoof it to a number of sights without having to bother about the price of gasoline.

Reason #3: The hotel you're staying in is likely to be as big a tourist attraction as, say, the Liberace Museum (p. 129) or nearby Lake Mead (p. 280). So staying at the Luxor or New York–New York will give you more of a chance to experience all that fake stuff, in-depth. Spend the time and you'll quickly become an expert in *trompe l'oeil* ceilings, fiberglass statues, and the gravity-defying voodoo that allows those skimpily clad cocktail waitresses to avoid "Janet Jackson moments."

REASONS FOR NOT STAYING ON THE STRIP

Reason #1: Okay, think this one through: Do you actually want to be in the midst of all that "glorious insanity"? Are you really into dodging weaving drunks in the hallway at 2am; hiking that mile and a half from your parking space to your bed at night; trying to get to bed early (or sleep late) and being rudely woken every 15 minutes by the eruption of a "volcano," or the screams from the roller coaster outside your window? And staying at a Strip property guarantees that

16

you'll spend a sizable chunk of your vacation in line: standing in long lines to check in, then standing in line for your coffee shop breakfast, then standing in line for the bathrooms in the casino, then . . . you get the picture. Crowds are inevitable, even when the town is quiet, so if you're the type of person who likes to relax on vacation . . . well, the Strip may not be the place for you.

Reason #2: MONEY! Not to shout, but you'll often pay far less for far nicer digs off-Strip (not always, it will depend on the season, but we'll go into that on p. 23). You'll always pay more, however, for the items that the Strip hotels sell beyond beds: meals, minibar items, toothpaste from the on-site convenience store, you name it. The Strip hotels revel in the fact that their audience may be too drunk or attached to a particular slot machine to venture far and up the price of everything. (Don't believe me? Stroll over to that Strip casino ATM and shell out $4.50 to make a withdrawal. Can you say "pillaged"?)

Reason #3: Because you may be forced to rent a car. Now, this may seem like a bizarre selling point, but the truth is many of the great attractions in Vegas can't be reached on foot and are too pricey by taxi. With a car you're more likely to get out of town and take in the wonders of the area, with jaunts to Red Rock Canyon (p. 284), the Valley of Fire (p. 286), or Hoover Dam (p. 275). Whenever I've talked with people who have visited Vegas, they mention these sights as the highlight of their visits, not the time spent on the Strip. Wheels will also allow you to explore eating and shopping options beyond the Strip, particularly important for budget travelers. On the subject of eating, you'll notice that the majority of my three-star restaurants in my dining chapter are not on the Strip; I go into more depth on this subject there, but I'm firmly convinced that you often eat better off the Strip, especially if you're looking for top-quality, low-cost meals.

Reason #4: It's not a kid-friendly place to stay. Most Strip hotels charge an extra fee for children over the age of 2, a fee that's not levied at properties off the Strip. Strip hotels are also making it clearer and clearer that they don't really want kids there. Wynn Las Vegas will not allow strollers, the Bellagio only allows kids to enter who can prove that they're staying there, and there's not one wading pool the length of that entire long street. I can't speak for your children, but my young ones really didn't like the atmosphere in the big casinos. They wilted on the long treks from the parking garage to the restaurant (or from the restaurant to the pool, or the pool to the elevators . . .); they complained endlessly about the smoke; and, at one point, my then 7-year-old took to huffing through the casino with her fingers in her ears to protest the incessant-jangling of the slot machines. I can't remember another trip where they've complained as much. For more on bringing kids to Vegas, see p. 314.

Reason #5: Having a place to call your own. This is a corollary to avoiding the madness of the Strip. When you rent a condo or a house you have a place where you can really kick back. Though the values aren't as great for couples and singles, families and other groups can save a lot of money with rentals, often paying half as much per night for three times the amount of space. An on-site kitchen allows you to snack at will, or prepare meals at times, cutting down on the expense of dining out. And you'll get a tiny glimpse into the everyday life of this extraordinarily popular city.

RENTING A HOME OR CONDO OF YOUR OWN

Because point #5 (about renting a condo or home) is such an important one, we're going to discuss it in full ahead of hotels.

Please note, first, that there are very few on-Strip condos and those that do exist (with one exception; see MGM Signature p. 22) are monstrously pricey. So if you MUST stay on the Strip, you can skip this section, as the companies I profile deal with affordable and/or small splurge properties. (By the way, don't fall for it if some fellow on VRBO.com claims to have a reasonably priced Strip-accessible property just because it's near Las Vegas Boulevard. That's a mighty long street and the actual Strip only runs from the Stratosphere to Mandalay Bay.)

But if you're the type who enjoys having a patch of grass all to yourself to lounge on regardless of whether it's on the Strip . . . if what you mainly crave is a separate room for the kids, should the romance of the desert make you and your spouse eager to do more than renew your vows . . . if your chief desire is a kitchen to call your own—then a condo or private home rental should be just your speed. Though not as quirky or original as you'll find in other cities—in Vegas, 99% of vacation rental properties are never lived in by their owners and were purchased simply as investments (which may be why Las Vegas had the largest foreclosure problem in the country in 2009)—every one I've seen or stayed in has been spacious, clean, comfortable, and competitively priced. Yes, by and large, the decor is bland in the extreme (the common look: innumerable shades of tan for the furniture, carpets, drapes, and walls), but the privacy rentals afford, and their overall amenities, more than make up for their appearance.

So what do you get with a Vegas condo stay? Pitched to the sporting, gambling, and convention crowd, many come with private pools, Jacuzzis, pool tables, and access to adjoining golf courses. (I have even visited one that had a mini-putting green in the backyard!) As these are often used by groups of traveling businesspeople, high-tech touches are common and I have yet to see a unit without flatscreen or oversized TVs; multi-disc CD and DVD players; and either Wi-Fi or high-speed cable Internet access. Also common are cutting-edge video-game systems, microwave ovens (along with full kitchens), washers and dryers, and for some reason, really snazzy blenders.

My only real disappointment about condo stays in Vegas (and I say this as someone who's now visited dozens of condos) is how difficult it can be to find the right one. Because the casinos have a stranglehold on the accommodations market, you won't find information about condo rentals in any of the tourist literature or even from the Las Vegas Convention and Visitor's Center, a real anomaly; in other cities these are prime sources of information on condos. Arcane laws (with residency requirements for rentals) penned by casino lobbyists, have also been successful in discouraging agents from getting into the biz.

Not all have been discouraged, however,

The folks behind **Las Vegas Retreats** (☎ 888/887-0951 or 702/966-2761; www.lasvegasretreats.com) have long been in the forefront for those seeking top quality rental homes. "We've gotten extremely selective," says Linda Logan, co-owner. "Our homes are not a mishmash of second hand furniture. We work with a professional decorator to ensure that when you walk in, you're going to say 'Wow, this is great.'" And if you think Pottery Barn and West Elm are the be-all and end-all in home goods, you'll probably agree.

Rental Home Costs

Size, location, amenities: These will shape the price of the vacation home you're considering. But unlike hotel prices, condo rental rates don't soar up and down as drastically when a big convention hits town or when it's Super Bowl weekend. To give you an idea of what you might pay, I've pulled the following examples from various rental-by-owner websites. But remember that these are just sample prices; they were correct when I wrote this but may have changed by the time you read it:

1-bedroom/1-bath suite: $75–$125 per night

2-bedroom/2-bath: $85–$165 per night

3-bedroom/3-bath: $120–$200 per night

5-bedroom/3-bath: $300 per night

One example, a two-bedroom condo with private pool, deep pile carpets, flatscreen TVs in each room and such niceties as microfiber (suedelike) couches which comes piled high with silk pillows. Nearby is a public park with tennis courts and a children's playground. The condo rents for $249 per night ($169 Sun–Wed), but you might pay less for it if you're willing to leave the choice up to Logan. To get business moving in these tough economic times, Logan and her partner have worked out a deal whereby if you reserve a place with a set number of bedrooms and you allow the firm to place you in what they have available 2 days before your arrival, you'll save between 50% and 70% off the nightly rate.

This helps the firm keep their apartments full; and it's not all that much of a risk for you as all of Retreats' homes are darn nice. Pillow-top mattresses are de rigueur, as are sheets that always have a thread count of 250 or more, top-of-the-line kitchen appliances, combination locks on the door (ideal for large groups), pools in every backyard, and a thorough inspection of each property before use. Free local and long-distance phone service is also included. Upon arrival you'll find the bathrooms fully stocked with soaps and shampoos.

"It's just so people don't get off the plane and get to the house and have nothing," Logan explained.

And if you think that Frank Sinatra would probably have been very happy with the home you're renting, you'd probably be right . . . if you went with **Las Vegas Luxury Home Rentals** (☎ 702/871-9727; www.lasvegasluxuryhome rentals.com). Run by a former back-up singer for Old Blue Eyes himself, Marlene Ricce was inspired to get into the biz by all the rental homes she and the band stayed in while touring from city to city. So she not only rents homes but acts as their decorator, swathing kitchens and bathrooms with Corian and marble, and bedrooms with jewel-toned bedding, deep-pile carpets, and handsome pieces of art. They're at one and the same time quite luxe and comfortable. All in all, Ricce reps nine large homes with rates starting at $299 a night for multi-bedded digs. She's a bit pricier than the other two, but certainly has some lovely properties on offer.

Many Vegas visitors also turn to the Internet's direct-from-owner sites such as:

- Vacation Rental By Owner (www.vrbo.com)
- Cyberrentals (www.cyberrentals.com)
- Zonder (www.zonder.com)
- A1 Vacations (www.a1vacations.com)
- Rentalo (www.rentalo.com)

Though prices will often be lower at these sites (as there's no commission involved) and the variety of choices is infinitely greater, there are some risks to booking over the Web in this way. The homes will not be vetted or inspected. So you could arrive at a home, as I once did, only to find that one of the bedrooms didn't have any light source in it (the lamp had been broken and thrown out by the previous tenant; I made do with a lamp I moved in from the living room, making that room dimmer than it should have been). Usually the maintenance issues aren't too bad, but sometimes you'll be confronted by threadbare towels, squeaky garage doors, and poorly groomed lawns. And there's no "out" if you have a big problem with the home; the owner takes your money well before you arrive (whereas most agencies will try to move you if you're unhappy).

If you still want to use one of these sites—and I wouldn't dissuade you, you can find great deals this way—be sure to ask the following questions before putting any money down:

1. **Does the owner live in the state?** It's preferable that she does, as she'll be better able to help you should you have a problem with the house. I've also found that the closer the owner is to his property, the better the maintenance tends to be. If the owner isn't in-state but you like the look of the property, make sure that there's at least some type of caretaker nearby whom the owner can call on to come over if necessary.
2. **What's included in the rental fee?** You don't want to show up at a rental place for 3 days and find that there's no dishwashing soap, garbage bags, toilet paper, or other basic household goods. Most rentals do include them, but it's important to ask. If the house is adjacent to a golf course (many will be), find out what additional fees there will be to use it. Free local calls and Wi-Fi or high-speed Internet access can save you a lot of money and are standard in many rental homes but not all, so be sure to ask about that as well.
3. **Where is it?** Sounds like a basic question, but many owners can be vague about the actual location of a home, knowing that the closer to the Strip it is, the more in demand it will be. So be sure to get cross-streets, don't be shy about asking if it's in a gated community (many are), how close the nearest police precinct is, and what county it's located in. Henderson and Green Valley, while lovely residential areas, can be a good 30-minute drive from the Strip; stay in Summerlin and you're looking at about a 20-minute drive.
4. **What's the square footage of the home?** The more space you have, the more privacy each member of your party gets.

If you can combine the right answers to the questions above with the right prices, I say go for it. As with the homes rented by the agencies (which are, in some cases, the same ones being offered on such sites as VRBO.com), you're

Hidden Costs of Rental Homes

Whether you rent directly from an owner or from an agency, calculate the following costs into the price of your stay before committing:

- **Cleaning fee:** Most homes charge between $50 and $270, depending on the size of the home, for someone to come in and scrub after you've left.
- **Taxes:** As with hotels, you'll pay 9% in taxes on top of the cost of the rental.
- **Commissions:** Agencies charge a fee for their services of between 10% and 25% of the cost of the rental.
- **Car rental:** Most rentals are in gated communities, and none at this stage are within walking distance of the Strip, or any other major Vegas attraction. Taxis are too costly, so be sure to factor in the price of a rental car into your overall budget.

obtaining the lodgings for a less expensive, more relaxing vacation. Let me repeat for emphasis: private swimming pools and Jacuzzis, golf courses right next door, lots of space and privacy, a fully usable kitchen complete with all the flatware and cutlery you need to avoid busting your budget eating every meal on the Strip. I think these are the elements for a great Vegas vacation, particularly for parents who might want their kids to have a respite from all the neon and naughtiness of the Strip.

TWO CONDO COMPLEXES YOU MIGHT CONSIDER

Las Vegas now boasts several buildings right near or on the Strip that are chock-full of privately owned vacation condos. While some, such as the City Center properties, are ridiculously expensive, there are two that I think offer extremely good value. Since these may be booked directly with the property, I've listed them separately (although you may also find them represented through an agency or on a direct to owner website, so you should comparison shop your quote). Much like hotels, they both have a front desk offering standard hotel services (concierge, for example), a pool, some sort of food option, and pretty much everyone staying there is a temporary resident. So choosing one is not a good way to meet locals. However, you'll have privacy, a kitchen, and more space than a normal hotel room provides. Though newly introduced, both properties have proven to be extremely popular, so book well in advance if you decide you want this kind of stay.

Platinum Hotel Las Vegas ✮✮✮ (211 E. Flamingo Rd. at Koval Lane; ☎ 877/211-9211 or 702/365-5000; www.theplatinumhotel.com; AE, DC, MC, V) certainly delivers on the promises of a condo rental, offering guests an abundance of space (smallest rooms are 950 sq. ft. with two bedrooms up to 2,200 sq. ft.), cushy beds, deep tubs with whirlpool jets, whip-up-a-Thanksgiving-dinner-ready full kitchens and even washer/dryers tucked away in one of the closets. (Though these are individually owned condos, management requires all owners to buy them furnished, so they all have the same, hotel-like look.) Because the building was originally meant to be long-term apartments, the sound-baffling is better than

Liberace Slept Here . . . & You Can, Too

If you assumed that staying at one of the Strip's large "theme resorts" was as over-the-top as you could get in Vegas, think again. Liberace's former home is now a rental, and those willing to spend $275 a night can swim in his piano-shaped pool, gaze at his 6-foot-tall painting of Valentino, and lounge in rooms once frequented by Elvis, Frank Sinatra, Diana Ross, and other friends of the original "piano man." At night, guests pull the gold lamé drapes closed and climb into Mr. Showmanship's own bed, waving goodnight to themselves in the mirrored ceiling above. Set in a pricey neighborhood, the home can sleep up to 10 people in five bedrooms and tends to book up months in advance, so if you're interested, contact current owner **Cyril K. Bennett** (www.cyberrentals.com/rental/p318118) as early as you can. Later in the chapter, I'll also list a fabulous B&B operated by Liberace's former personal chef (p. 53).

usual (meaning, even if your neighbors are partying, you're unlikely to hear it) and the Plat also has the unusual-for-Vegas feature of a sweet little balcony attached to each room (I guess with digs this nice, management ain't worried about suicides). On an upper floor is an indoor/outdoor all-weather pool (another Vegas anomaly) and a full spa/gym; the lobby features a sexy lounge. Best of all, there's no charge for extra people in the rooms or even extra rollaway beds, so if you're trying to save as much as possible by bunking a group together, well, here's where you can do it easily. Prices will vary by how and where you book your room. Book direct with the Platinum, for example, and you could pay between $119 and $159 (up to $199 when a convention's in town) for their smallest one-bedroom; at VRBO, I've seen these units drop to $89 a night. For two-bedroom units, add about $50 to those ranges (and the two-bedrooms are definitely shareable by two couples as each has their own bathroom, with the living room/kitchen in the middle).

I give **Signature at MGM Grand** ✪✪ (145 E. Harmon Ave. off Koval Lane; ☎ 877/612-2121 or 702/797-6000; www.signaturemgmgrand.com; AE, DC, MC, V) one fewer star because though its units are truly lovely (textured heavy fabrics with chic pops of color, all the amenities of home and then some), they are significantly smaller than Platinum's. Here junior suites, not true one-bedrooms, are the lowest-priced option; they come in at about 550 square feet. But because of the tie-in with a bigger name, they go for about the same rate as Platinum's true one-bedrooms (I've seen them sell on VRBO for as little as $89 a night; the starting rate through Signature itself is $149). Yes, they arguably do have a better location, attached by walkways to the MGM Casino with its many restaurants and attractions, but the Platinum is just 1 long block's walk from the Strip—not bad at all. And the Signature won't provide rollaways at any cost, though each suite has a fold-out bed (so they might be less useful for groups). The Signature consists of three towers, each of which has its own pool (though only two towers have gyms).

HOTEL & B&B STAYS

The current economic crisis has literally decimated the hotel industry in Las Vegas. As I write this, nightly rates have dropped a good 20%, a reflection of the decline in occupancy rates. What this means for the consumer are unprecedented bargains for even the cushiest of Strip properties. Of course, the drop in pricing has also led to a drop in disposable income for many travelers, so I'll still be focusing on the very best of the bargains in this chapter. But should you see, say, the new Wynn Encore hotel going for just $59 (unlikely, but not impossible) grab it. Just because it, and such usually pricey places as Caesars Palace, Bellagio, Pallazzo, and Venetian, aren't reviewed in this book doesn't mean they wouldn't be swell places to stay. I simply made the decision to concentrate on the places where you're most likely to get a great deal. But in this topsy-turvy time, well, anything's possible, especially considering that Sin City has more hotel rooms than any other place in the U.S. to fill (some 153,000 rooms which is 4% of the total in all of the U.S. and enough to house the entire population of Iceland).

Since prices can soar when the town's filled with conventioneers, I'll assess the best ways to save on rooms before getting to the reviews of the hotels.

SIX WAYS TO SAVE BIG ON A HOTEL ROOM

Nothing is ever guaranteed, of course, but by following the suggestions below you should save enough money to more than justify the purchase of this book.

1. Go at the right time

If you can figure out how to do this, ditch all other methods. There's simply no better way to save money in Vegas than to go when the town is slow, as prices in this mathematically savvy city are set by supply and demand. And Vegas' planners are getting more sophisticated by the hour at calibrating just when the town's going to be busy. Which means that if you're able to travel during a convention-free week, when the temperature's pushing 115°F (46°C), and no major sports teams are playing anywhere, you could very well find yourself center Strip, in a luxe room, for just $39 a night. Vacation at a time when all of those factors are against you (great weather, loads of gadget-pushing conventioneers, and every seat taken in the Sports Book) and that same room, and I mean that very same room—same hotel, same floor, same number—might top $229. I've seen prices flip-flop between those extremes in the course of 1 day.

How can you tell, then, if you're visiting at an advantageous moment? Follow these rules of thumb. In general, December and January are slow, with the exception of the time of the National Finals Rodeo (early Dec), New Year's Week, Super Bowl weekend, and the week of the Consumer Electronics show. Beastly weather keeps July and August affordable, except when the World Series of Poker is in town or there's a large convention. And, of course, weekdays are always cheaper than weekends.

But dates can also vary significantly within the fall and spring months as well. For more specific information, go online. The **Las Vegas Convention and Visitors Authority** (www.visitlasvegas.com) offers a free listing of every convention up to 36 months out, with their dates. As it may be difficult for an outsider to tell which of these will really paralyze the town, it's also useful to visit the Strip casino hotels' websites directly—really, any will do—and search for their pricing calendar. It will list starting rates for each day of the month up to 5 months ahead. On most websites, you'll click on the "Special Offers" section of that site to access the calendar. (Often, but not always, if one hotel's calendar shows it to be a busy period, prices will be up at its competitors as well. Be careful, however, with such hotels as the Riviera or the Hilton, which book a lot of convention business. Because they often hold conventions on-site, they may well have periods of outrageously high pricing that the others will not match.)

One last tip on timing: Occasionally a hotel will lower the weekend price for someone who checks in Monday through Thursday. So if you can be flexible with your dates, try to improvise the sequence of your stay and see where it gets you.

2. Book an air/hotel package or contact a wholesaler

Not all hotel rooms are sold directly by the hotels themselves. Tour operators (who put together air/hotel packages) and "wholesalers" (who simply sell hotel rooms) buy up blocks of rooms in advance and at a discount, which they then resell to the public with a small mark-up. This benefits the hotels, as they're guaranteed occupied rooms throughout the year; and it benefits travelers as the prices these companies charge will often be lower than those quoted by the hotels themselves.

When these sorts of deals are good, they can be stellar. On the package front, I've seen wonder-bargains from such companies as Southwest Airlines Vacations, which charge vacationers just $99 for 2 nights at an older Strip property and airfare from California (other Western gateways tend to cost between $20–$60 more a night, with the Midwest coming in at $100 more and the Eastern states for about $120–$200 more). Please take a look at the box on p. 25 for a listing of recommended air/hotel packagers.

Because nothing is ever that easy, you'll need to pull out your calculator before you pull out a credit card, as not all packages will be good deals. Do a quick Web search to find out what the actual costs for hotel and airfares are (see p. 25 on how to do that), and then compare those numbers to what you'll be getting with the package. Calculate the base cost first, by which I mean the cost of your airfare and hotel room, times two (as these packages are always based on double occupancy). If it's less than you would have paid booking these elements separately, as Bob Barker would say—book that package! If you think you can get a better price on the airfare, check to see if the company will sell you the hotel only. If none of this works, move on to the next suggestion below. **One warning:** Be careful when estimating the value of other items that might be included in the package, such as shopping coupons, two-for-one show or attraction tickets, discounts on tours, and so forth. Often these items are easily picked up on-site and for free in the tourist literature handed out around town. The only additional items that you can take at face value are free meals (such as included breakfasts), casino credits, and free shows.

Wholesalers are like packagers in that they buy up rooms in bulk, but these folks don't tend to handle the transportation side of the vacation, just hotel rooms. They're also known in some circles as "Reservations Services." You'll find my recommendations for the best wholesalers in the "Top Tour Ops & Reservations Services" box on p. 25.

3. Call up and bargain

Never haggled? It's easier than you think and can lead to big savings in Vegas . . . if you do it intelligently. By that I mean don't try it if it's Super Bowl weekend or New Year's Eve—in fact, if the prices seem to be high across the boards, it's a good sign that something's going on in town and all of your bargaining won't get you a bargain.

Just as important—do your research first: Visit one of the top "aggregator" sites (websites that are not selling travel, but instead simply searching for and categorizing travel information, much as Google does for general information). I always recommend **Hotels Combined** (www.hotelscombined.com) for this purpose, as it's a mighty powerful engine; you can also turn to such worthy alternatives as **Sidestep** (www.sidestep.com), **Mobissimo** (www.mobissimo.com), or **Kayak** (www.kayak.com).

If you're feeling really sneaky, surf over to **Biddingfortravel.com.** Normally used by those planning to bid for hotel nights on Priceline.com, the site is not affiliated with that company. Instead average Joes post what their "winning bid" was for a room on a particular date, to help others who might be bidding. It will tell you which big hotels are accepting low bids and which dates are most fruitful for bargaining. The site also posts many of the discounted rate codes for the major casino-hotels, which can sometimes net visitors serious discounts and/or freebies.

Once you figure out how much the going rate online is, call the hotel directly. You can use the toll-free number if you've chosen one of the big Strip casinos, but if you're going for one of the chains in town (Motel 6, Travelodge, Marriott), call

Top Tour Ops & Reservations Services

There are more, but to my mind these companies have offered the most consistent values over the years:

For air/hotel packages:

- **Southwest Airlines Vacations** (www.swavacations.com; ☎ 800/243-2372)
- **Funjet Vacations** (www.funjet.com; ☎ 888/558-6654)
- **Worry Free Vacations** (best from Midwest and Western states; www.worryfreevacations.com; ☎ 888/225-5658)
- **Leisure Link** (best from Eastern and Southern states; www.eleisurelink.com; ☎ 888/801-8808)

For hotels only:

- **Hotels.com** (www.hotels.com; ☎ 800/246-8357)
- **Travelworm** (www.travelworm.com; ☎ 888/700-8342)
- **Reserve Travel** (www.reservetravel.com; ☎ 866/914-8917)
- **Accommodations Express** (www.accommodationsexpress.com; ☎ 800/444-7666)

the local number, as only the managers on-property will have the authority to play "let's make a deal." Be nice, be friendly, be downright charming, but don't beat around the bush. Tell them that you'd sure like to give your business to hotel X, but you can't pay more than such and such a price. Stand firm and see what happens. If you're traveling with a group of people or staying for longer than 5 nights, use those facts as well when making your case. You could end up with a group discount or a "long stay" rate.

I once found an $89 room rate at Expedia for Harrah's. So I went to the Harrah's site and found a $59 rate. I then called the hotel directly and got the room for $39 a night . . . and all I did was ask, with a smile in my voice.

4. Join the club

You'll find complete information on the joys of slot clubs on p. 225, but just to reiterate here: You want to join them. Even if you're not a high roller. You'll give up some personal information, but then for the rest of your life, you'll receive coupons and sale announcements from the casino you've joined, allowing you to stay at the property you joined for half the regular rate (sometimes less). In the depths of January, it's not unheard-of for casinos to give away free rooms to club members just to get those fannies into those slot-facing seats. For first-timers to Vegas: Some hotels allow you to join the clubs before you get to town, and they don't seem to distinguish between those who've actually gambled in the casino and those who haven't; they send out those coupons to just about anyone.

5. Patronize a "dinosaur"

The older the hotel, the lower the room rate (usually). This is particularly true for those hotels on "death row." It takes a while to put into place the plans to implode a hotel and just as long to draw up the design for the next mega-resort that will replace it. In that 9- to 18-month-long goodbye period, prices will often hit rock bottom at these goners. So, unfortunately, will service and upkeep, as long-term employees scramble to find new jobs; but if price is the priority you can't beat this method. To find out which hotels are slated for the ax, visit the **Casino Death Watch** site (www.jetcafe.org/~npc/gambling/casino_death_watch.html).

6. Gamble for freebies

I have left for last this final recommendation, as it's actually a rather dangerous way to save on accommodations. But if you gamble enough or say you'll gamble enough, you could end up in a "free" room. Problem is: That $79 room could cost you $7,900 in blackjack losses when all is said and done. Don't try to be cute either, and talk your way into a freebie by promising to gamble more than you will. Big Brother is alive and well in Vegas, and the casino will be watching you and your wagers. Big talkers who don't put enough chips on the table or quarters in the slots will be confronted by a full-price bill at check-out time. Though I've read that some people have managed to get freebies at some of the higher priced spots in town, your best bets for pursuing this option are the locals' casinos and the small casino chains (such as the Coast and Station casinos).

CHOOSING THE RIGHT HOTEL

Hopefully at this point, you have some idea whether you'd like to stay on the Strip or off. But what about the differences between the properties in those areas? Are they significant?

Well yes . . . and no. The truth is, if you're going to be staying at a major casino resort, you'll be staying in a room designed by committee, created for easy maintenance, which will look like the 2,000 other rooms in that hotel . . . and often will look similar to the rooms in the other casinos owned by that parent company. Remember: Most of the casinos in Vegas are owned by either MGM MIRAGE, Boyd Gaming, or Harrah's—big corporations all, so you're not going to find the same kinds of quirky, personal touches you'll encounter in smaller hotels in other cities (for the most part). And if you're constantly having to squint to read the paper in bed, don't call your optometrist. Dim lighting in guest rooms is the norm. It's a way of getting customers back onto the casino floor— the longer you stay in your room, the less the casino is making, after all.

> *Casinos and prostitutes have the same thing in common; they are both trying to screw you out of your money and send you home with a smile on your face.*
>
> —VP Pappy

Some differences that will hit you, and which I'll discuss below, will be in the overall ambience and decor of the public areas; what types of customers each hotel attracts; how opulent their pool areas are; and their eating, shopping, and entertainment options. With the exception of the swimming pools, which can only be used by guests of the resort (they do check for room keys), I'm conflicted as to how important the other options actually are. Savvy budget travelers simply choose the cheapest hotel in the area they wish to stay and then hang out in the cushier places. But when the mercury breaks 100°F (38°C), it sure can be tempting to stay put within the icily air-conditioned confines of your home hotel. It's your call.

Our pricing symbols for accommodations:

$: $50 a night or less
$$: $50–$100
$$$: $101–$150
$$$$: $151 and up

In addition, many hotel listings also carry a cluster of stars ✮, indicating our opinion of the hotel's desirability (this does not have anything to do with price, but with the value you receive for the price you pay). The stars mean:

No star: Good
✮ Very good
✮✮ Great
✮✮✮ Outstanding! A must!

SOUTH STRIP HOTELS

Alternately chichi and run-down, the South Strip is arguably the most polyglot portion of this famous boulevard. At one end you have the ultra-exclusive THEhotel at Mandalay and the Four Seasons; just a short hop away are such old warhorses as the Tropicana and Excalibur. There's Prada at the first two, JCPenney at the latter, and everything in between for those who choose other properties in this section of the Strip. Though this area doesn't have the outdoor spectacles (dancing fountains, pirate battles) that the Center Strip does, it does offer a wide range of eating, shopping, and entertainment choices in all price ranges, from frugal to obscene.

$–$$ Your cheapest option on the South Strip is not on the Strip itself, but a very walkable three-quarters of a block away (I promise!). Fronted by a huge, Vegas-glitzy sign, it's the largest **Motel 6** (195 E. Tropicana Ave., at Koval Lane; ☎ 800/4-MOTEL-6 [466-8356] or 702/798-0728; www.motel6.com; AE, DC, DISC, MC, V) in the country, so massive that another small (and not as nice) motel is wedged into the center of it. I last stayed here during one of those major sports events that periodically paralyze the town, and it was the only decently located Vegas lodging I could find at that time with a bed for under $70 a night (most of the other "budget" hotels had rates in the $200s for that time period!). You'll likely pay between $29 and $62, depending on whether it's a weekday or weekend and the season. Other than the blankets on the beds—which could have been issued by the army, they were that rough to the touch—the decor was quite spiffy, with a multi-colored advertisement-cum-comforter over that rough blanket (it had pictures of different sorts of Motel 6s printed on it) and newly painted white walls. A sink sits at the back of the room, but the tub/shower and toilet are closed off by a door. Other pluses: The mattress was a good one, local phone calls were free, there's a small, uncrowded on-site pool, and the TV came with HBO. It wasn't the most spacious or the quietest of digs—I could hear the TV next door and the folks outside who brought a flatbed truck filled with beer cases for their tailgate party in the motel's parking lot—but for the money . . . hey, I've done much worse.

$$–$$$ A step up, both in comfort and cost, the **Hooters Casino Hotel** ★ (115 E. Tropicana Ave., near Las Vegas Blvd.; ☎ 866/LVHOOTS; www.hooterscasino hotel.com; AE, DC, DISC, MC, V) next door—it's about half a block closer to the Strip—is the next stage in a mammary-ogling empire that now includes over 450 restaurants. Ironically set in the former San Remo Hotel (which had been the casino hangout for Las Vegas' gay population—guess they're going elsewhere now), it's actually a swell place to stay. As a woman, I haven't found it to be any more prurient than any of the other Vegas hotels—compared to the camel-toe costumes those poor Mandalay Bay cocktail waitresses are required to squeeze into, the Hooters girls who inhabit the place (it holds the distinction of having over 250 of these comely maidens on hand to entertain customers, more than any other place in the world) in their Farrah Fawcett–esque mix of gym shorts and tight Ts, seem downright innocent. One note to the guys: Sorry, the Hooters girls are only on duty on the casino floor and entrance; they don't perform massages or do maid service.

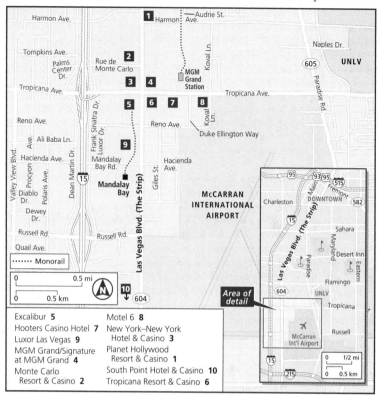

Excalibur **5**	Motel 6 **8**
Hooters Casino Hotel **7**	New York–New York
Luxor Las Vegas **9**	Hotel & Casino **3**
MGM Grand/Signature	Planet Hollywood
at MGM Grand **4**	Resort & Casino **1**
Monte Carlo	South Point Hotel & Casino **10**
Resort & Casino **2**	Tropicana Resort & Casino **6**

As for Hooters' settings, plywood and bright orange paint have always been the "we're rednecks and proud of it" aesthetic of the original chain restaurants, and it carries into the decor here, which I'd call Daytona Beach tropical (lots of fake palm fronds, palm-patterned bedspreads, surfboards as wall art). Each room comes with one king or two double platform beds, with extremely comfortable pillow-top mattresses. While there's no desk in many of the rooms, there is a kind of tall bar table with stools that you can perch on to write or type, and high-speed Internet access is available for an extra fee (though the outlets are inconveniently placed behind the beds). Prices can range from $39 a night up to $127 with the best rates usually on the hotel's own website.

On the ground floor, Hooters has a human-sized casino (as big as one football field rather than six), a decent-sized pool area out back, four low-key restaurants, two bars, and a spa.

$–$$$ Excalibur 🧒 (3850 Las Vegas Blvd., at Tropicana Ave.; ☎ 800/ 937-7777 or 702/597-7700; www.excalibur.com; AE, DC, DISC, MC, V) is the place most likely on the South Strip to be throwing a sale. As well it should: If you paid more than $49 per night here, you'd feel ripped off once you got to your depressing, dark room with its mud-colored decor. To be fair, the rooms are not nearly as bad as they were 2 years ago, when stained carpets and chipped bathtubs were the norm. They've put in better mattresses and replaced all of the soft goods in the room. But they're still grim and the walls are thinner than an Olsen twin (you'll hear everything your neighbor is saying . . . and perhaps thinking, too!). I've seen prices range from $36 to $141, but I think I've made it clear that I don't think you should pay beyond the bare minimum to stay here.

And this is one of those cavernous casinos where if you take the wrong turn, it could be half an hour before you find your way back to your car or room (so leave a trail of bread crumbs). Speaking of cars, Excalibur doesn't handle them well: The valet parking seems to be full most of the time, and if you self-park it's a long and uncovered walk from the garage to your room (hell on a really hot day).

Beyond the casino, there's the second-floor Castle Walk, a medieval version of a mall where you "shoppe 'til you droppe," picking up such items as dragon stat-uettes, conical princess hats, crystals, T-shirts, handbags, and more. It's not great for top-end gear, but kids will love it. They'll also dig the basement Midway that combines video games and a "magic motion film ride" with those classic carnival games (fishing with magnets, knocking over milk bottles). The pool is particularly kid-friendly, too—no, there's no wading pool but it's large enough so that over-enthusiastic splashing won't disturb anyone. Pools are NOT heated, though, as management claims. Also on-site is one of the worst buffets in Vegas, a standard food court, four restaurants, a fine spa, and surprisingly, one of the nicest wed-ding chapels on the Strip (p. 159).

$–$$$ Just across the street from Excalibur, the **Tropicana Resort & Casino** (3801 Las Vegas Blvd. S., at Tropicana Ave.; ☎ 888/826-8767 or 702/739-2222; www.tropicanalv.com; AE, DC, DISC, MC, V) was a record-breaker when it opened in 1957, a princely $15 million of mob and Teamster smackeroos poured into its construction. Known as the "Tiffany's of the Strip," it was the last word in ele-gance, with its Czechoslovakian crystal chandeliers, classy *Folies Bergeres* show, and mahogany walls. Today, it's generally referred to as one of the last examples of "classic" Las Vegas, which is a polite way of saying that it's old. And unfortunately, because it's been on "death row" so many times, it hasn't done the necessary main-tenance on certain parts of the hotel (most particularly the old motel unit which,

Staying in Touch

Internet: Every hotel in Vegas supplies either Wi-Fi or high-speed Internet access via cables. That's a given. Hotels commonly charge $9.95 to $12 a day for this service; in the cases where Internet access is free, I've noted that in the text. When there's no mention, you can assume that the above charges apply.

Phone: Bring your own! Phone charges are obscene in Vegas hotels; if you're not careful, you could spend more on phone calls than on the cost of the room. Avoid hotel room phones except in cases of extreme emergencies.

while cheapest, may not be worth the savings thanks to dripping faucets that will keep you up all night, grungy carpets, and sagging mattresses).

The Trop does have its merits, though: its gardens are dandy, tropical, and no longer filled with noisy birds; and it boasts the only swim-up blackjack table on the Strip at its large outdoor pool. There's also a small indoor pool (an anomaly in Vegas), seven restaurants, two lounges, and three weekly shows. And of your three lodgings options (the motel unit and the two towers), the middle-priced Island Tower is a hoot. It's retained its tropical theme, and it's here you can act out any of your Tom Jones–Vegas fantasies—many of the beds come with bamboo and mirror backboards and "viewing ceilings," and the tubs are pentagon shaped. They're not chichi—the carpeting's too old for that, and the ceiling's too low— but they certainly are a giggle. The newer tower has no theme whatsoever, but those travelers looking for a bit more comfort may want to choose it, as these rooms come with a couch and chair, an empty fridge, new carpeting, and a hair more space. In general, you'll get the better rates on rooms by skipping the reservations center here and going through such services as TripRes.com or Vegas.com. Using those services, I've seen rates plunge to between $38 and $45 ballooning up to between $79 and $109 at other times of the year (for the cheapest rooms; add $10 for the Island tower and $20 for the other tower).

$$–$$$$ Now for something a bit more glamorous, though sometimes you can't judge a casino by its cover. I'll be the first to admit that the exterior view of **New York–New York Hotel & Casino** ✪ (3790 Las Vegas Blvd. S., at Tropicana Ave.; ☎ 800/693-6763 or 702/740-6969; www.nynyhotelcasino.com; AE, DC, DISC, MC, V), with its simulation of the New York skyline, is a thrilling sight, one of the most exciting in this visual Candyland of a city. Bristling with skyscrapers built to one-third the size of the originals, it merrily jumbles together the city's famous landmarks from the Chrysler Building to the Statue of Liberty to the Empire State Building. That there's a roller coaster zooming in front of these icons, its cars painted taxi-cab yellow, seems only appropriate—if you've ridden in a New York taxi, you'll know what I mean.

And then you go inside. And everything that was witty, sharply observed, and fresh in the exterior becomes sepia toned, Disney-fied, and dull. Maybe I'm being a curmudgeon, since I'm a native New Yorker, but this re-creation, mired in the Art Deco New York of the 1920s and 1930s, doesn't come close to capturing the gritty vitality of the city itself. There are too many fake trees for starters, making New York look like a city in the Garden State (hey, that's next door); the "streets" of Greenwich Village—now a food court—are so cobblestoney and winding, you'll feel like you're on the set for a traveling show of *Annie*. On the mezzanine level is "Coney Island," which is supposed to channel the amusement park of the early 1900s. Who knew that they had laser tag and video games back then? (The idea's nice, but this "midway" ends up looking almost exactly like the ones in other casinos.) There are a few New York–based restaurants—America, Gallagher's Steakhouse, Gonzalez y Gonzalez—but tellingly, these are the tourist traps that native New Yorkers avoid when home (and America closed long ago in the Big Apple).

I know, I know, this was a landmark in theming when it opened in 1997, but today, it needs a rethink, a de-hokifying, if you will. I'm probably in the minority in this view, I admit, as there's no other casino on the Strip that feels as crowded as this one, with legions of gawkers simply wandering around staring.

So what's it like to stay here? Well, that's a mixed bag, too. Elbowing through the lobby crowds each morning is no picnic, nor is finding your room in the correct tower (there are 12) and along their confusing, endless corridors. I'm embarrassed to admit this, but on my last stay here, I had to call the hotel operator one night to give me directions to my room (and in case you were wondering, I was sober). Once you finally get into your room, however, it ain't bad at all. What you get will depend on what you pay, as there are different sized rooms, and themes vary slightly from tower to tower. On my last stay here, I was in a '30s Deco-themed room and though I found the colors of it a bit murky, the bed was quite sleepable, the headboard nicely padded, and the entertainment center was enclosed in a pretty, inlaid wood armoire. While the rooms and bathrooms at the cheapest level are not the roomiest on the Strip, they're laid out well, so they don't feel cramped. The large number of rooms here keeps prices relatively decent; I've seen them range from $59 to $139 midweek, up to $220 on busy weekends. **Two warnings:** If you're a late sleeper ask for a room that faces away from the roller coaster. And if you have mobility issues, request a room fairly close to the elevator as hallway distances can be long.

Other amenities include a choice-ripe food court (see my review on p. 70); some eight other restaurants, and four lounge/bars (including Coyote Ugly, p. 209); a poorly designed and cramped pool area; a nice spa and fitness room; and, of course, all the gambling your pocketbook can handle in the 84,000-square-foot casino.

$$–$$$$ I very much doubt there are two casino resorts as opposite in every way as the neighboring New York–New York and the **Monte Carlo Resort & Casino** ✹✹ (3770 Las Vegas Blvd. S., between Flamingo Rd. and Tropicana Ave.; ☎ 800/311-8999 or 702/730-7777; www.montecarlo.com; AE, DC, DISC, MC, V). Whereas the former is crowded at all hours, has a disappointing pool area, and is a caricature of its subject, the Monte Carlo has . . . well, much of the ambience of the real Monte Carlo, which is both its charm and its curse. Somehow, it feels European, not "pretend European." It's an illusion that's aided by the design, certainly—you gotta love the massive Renaissance statues out front backed by their Corinthian colonnade and the all-marble lobby with its exquisite crystal chandeliers. But it's just as much the slightly formal service at the check-in desk and the fact that they don't force you to tramp through the casino to the elevator for your room (a Vegas custom I've grown to hate). While no Vegas casino-hotel could be called "serene," the Monte Carlo certainly has a less frenetic energy than the others, the crowds absorbed seamlessly into its 102,000-square-foot casino, that despite its size is blessedly easy to navigate and seems ever-so-slightly quieter than most.

But this all begs the question: Do the folks want all of this refinement in a midrange Strip casino? And how many of those who visit the Strip can actually conjure up a picture in their minds of what "Monte Carlo" is supposed to be like? Blessedly few, I'd guess, and this being a huge hotel, with over 3,000 guest rooms, that translates into trouble for the owners and fair pricing for guests. I've seen nightly rates for standard rooms drop to as little as $56, though you're more likely to get them ranging from $69 to $129 and up. Those are darn decent prices for this location and for a hotel with its amenities, which include a veritable wonderland out back: The first wave pool brought to Vegas, a lazy river, and three night-lit tennis courts. While the pools may no longer be as cutting edge as some of the newer hotels' aquatic offerings, they're tops in this price range. Inside are a bevy of good and, for the most part, reasonably priced restaurants (including the excellent Market City Caffe, p. 78); a food court; a top quality salon; and the kid-friendly Lance Burton show (p. 189).

As for the rooms: That's a bit of a mystery at this point, as they were in the midst of a massive overhaul when I last visited, and I wasn't able to see the new model. I can tell you that they have good "bones" in that they were larger than the norm, and I doubt they've gone down in quality from the primo pillow-top mattresses they used to have. Beyond that, your guess is as good as mine.

$$–$$$$ Though this may be more information than you need, dear reader, I have to tell you that there are few things I enjoy more in the world than a good, hot bath. And that's one of the reasons I so enjoy **Planet Hollywood Resort & Casino** ★★ (3667 Las Vegas Blvd. S.; ☎ 877/333-WISH [333-9474] or 702/785-5555; www.planethollywood.com; AE, DC, DISC, MC, V). Each room is blessed with a deep soaking tub, where the water gets plenty hot and the pressure is good. Since I know that not everyone shares my obsessions, I'll also tell you that the room design is a handsome, modern take on Art Deco, with cloudlike beds (really, they have just the right mix of support and cushioning). The gimmick here is to have celebrity-themed memorabilia in each room so on my last stay, I slept below the lustful gazes of Leonardo DiCaprio and Kate Winslet in a *Titanic*-themed room; in wall boxes and set into a glass-topped coffee table were china pieces and other memorabilia from the movie set. Maybe I'm a geek, but I thought that was pretty cool.

The rest of the property is also much improved since its Aladdin days. Well, there wasn't all that much they could do about the rooftop pools (which are fine, but nowhere near as glamorous or large as other pools on the Strip), but the casino is pretty swell, its tall ceilings making it less boxed-in feeling than others on the Strip, its boxes of glittering strands of crystals (they look like something Marilyn Monroe might have worn), giving it a welcome touch of classy glitz. Its central location, access to the Miracle Mile Mall (which envelops the hotel), and plethora of good eating choices makes it quite the buy when it goes for $69 a night (try the site booking.com to get that rate); but even when it's pricier ($99–$129 seems to be the rate from other sources, though I have seen it inflate to $259 when the town's busy), I'd still say it's worth it.

Soaking vs. Showering

Don't assume that you'll have a tub to soak in when you crash at your hotel after that 10-hour poker session. Even the swank Strip hotels have some shower-only rooms, so if it's important to you, make sure to ask for a room with a tub.

$$–$$$$ While Planet Hollywood improved with its makeover, the geniuses in charge of the **Luxor Las Vegas** ✦ (3900 Las Vegas Blvd. S., between Reno and Hacienda aves.; ☎ 888/777-0188 or 702/262-4000; www.luxor.com; AE, DC, MC, V) pretty much killed it with theirs. They took a delightfully kitschy icon and transformed it into one of the blandest in town in their desperate attempt to make this giant pyramid, get this: less Egyptian (!). Gone are the fabulous statuary, the fun King Tut Museum, the hieroglyphic-laden wallpaper. Yes, the outside is still a lollapalooza of a sight, gleaming gold during the day, at night almost disappearing into the sky, invisible except for a 135,000-watt beam shooting from its tip (the most powerful on earth . . . or so claim the not-shy staff here). But once you're inside, well, you might as well be in Akron, Ohio. No, that would insult Akron. I'm sure it has places less generic looking than this.

So rooms have a bland, corporate feel, though those in the pyramid all still have one slanted wall (the higher you are, the deeper the angle). Unless you really want to try the "inclinator" (the diagonal elevator that takes guests in the pyramid to their floors) you'll probably want to go for the tower: rooms are significantly bigger, with deeper tubs and higher ceilings.

A 100,000-square-foot casino, *Bodies . . . The Exhibition* (see p. 116), and 5 acres of pools (including outdoor hot tubs) round out the amenities here. Luxor is connected to Mandalay Bay via the Mandalay Place mall which has loads of stores and better restaurants than you'll find in the Luxor itself. Room rates tend to range from $70 to $90, up to $180 when Vegas is busy.

$$–$$$$ Why is the **MGM Grand** ✦✦ (3799 Las Vegas Blvd. S., at Tropicana Ave.; ☎ 800/929-1111 or 702/891-7777; www.mgmgrand.com; AE, DC, DISC, MC, V) lizard green? Despite rumors to the contrary, it has nothing to do with how much green stuff you'll fork over to stay here. When it was first erected in 1993, it was supposed to look like the "Emerald City" of MGM's famous movie musical, *The Wizard of Oz*. No joke, inside were animatronic representations of the characters, a yellow brick road, a "Wizard of Oz on Ice" show, and when it was time to go to sleep at night, you put your nose right up to your poppy-field print bedspread and inhaled. Well, that theme is gone, and the 33-acre amusement park that used to be out back has also been dismantled, but no one seems to have figured out what to do with what's left. It's a sometimes bland, sometimes grand hodgepodge of elements that don't really add up. Does its menagerie of celebrity chefs and pricey eateries put it in the high-roller category? Or are the low ceilings and chaotic look of its massive casino (a whopping 170,000 sq. ft.) reason enough to say it's slipping into "grind joint" territory? This is a tough place to get a handle on.

The problem is magnified by the size of the darn thing. Once the largest hotel in the world, it has 5,044 guest rooms in four 30-story towers, dozens of elevators, 50 shops and eateries, four first-class theaters, and one of the largest pool areas on the Strip. And for some visitors, especially anyone with a mobility impairment, that makes it an intimidating choice. At most casinos you must hike from the restaurant to the showroom to your car; here it's a marathon. But other visitors will find the size and variety of choices exhilarating. Obvious but true, you could have a swell 4-day vacation here, doing different things each day and eating in different restaurants for each meal, without ever leaving the property.

That said, I'm sad to report that guest rooms don't have the old-fashioned Hollywood glamour that they had just 2 years ago. Now the look's more executive brown, with jute wallpaper and heavy wood furnishings. They're still plush looking (and feeling; the beds are great), but they're inescapably faceless.

The pool complex is snazzy though, with five distinct pools (one with slides and a waterfall) and a lazy river. For this fab pool area alone I give the MGM a thumbs up for families. (Kids will also groove on visiting the Lion Habitat [p. 141] and the on-site TV rating facility [p. 142], and seeing *KÀ* [p. 186]).

So what's the verdict? It will all depend on when you hit it. Recently the MGM has been pricing itself at just $59 a night, which is a terrific buy. If it's going for the low $200s you can probably look elsewhere, but if you can snag it in the low $100s it might be worth it. Prices here are truly all over the map, with the best rates usually scored through Hotels.com.

CENTER STRIP HOTELS

This is it, the area most visitors would choose if money were no concern. Dancing fountains, lurid volcanoes, pirates, sirens, gondoliers—it's entertainment 24/7. Right? Well, sure, but it's also packed with crowds, the highest overall accommodation costs in the city, and an ever-gridlocked Boulevard where The Venetian waves to Treasure Island. If you want to really be at the heart of the Strip, this is your first choice. But if budget is a concern, skip this section.

$–$$$　　Or go directly to the **Imperial Palace Hotel & Casino** ✸ (3535 Las Vegas Blvd. S., between Sands Ave. and Flamingo Rd.; ☎ 800/634-6441 or 702/731-3311; www.imperialpalace.com; AE, DC, DISC, MC, V), the rock-bottom cheap option in this neck of the woods. Its greatest selling point is, well, the low point at which it sells; it has no other bells and whistles. Family-owned until 2006 (when it was sold to Harrah's), it was given a bit of an overhaul with the sale, though some of its guest rooms still hark back to the 1970s, when bright orange, flowered bedspreads were the height of groovy, especially if you added ceiling trim to match. Ask for a "Luv Tub" room and the look gets downright *Newlywed Game,* with mirrors above the bed and surrounding the large, sunken, in-room tub. The other rooms now feature dignified wicker furniture and a bright cream-on-white color scheme; thankfully the granite-hard mattresses have been replaced throughout.

And the staff sure is trying to do right by its customers. The furnishings in some of the rooms may be old, but they're kept white-glove clean. Down in the casino are the hardest-working dealers in town, many doubling as entertainment, dressed as "Stevie Wonder," "Cher," "Michael Jackson," "Elvis," or "Madonna"; at regular intervals, they ascend the stairs to a tiny stage to belt out a song. The program's called "dealertainment," and it doesn't get campier than this—it's a hoot, even if most of the impersonators look and sound nothing like the folks they're imitating. And to be fair to the place, there's a decent pool out back that doubles as a luau spot; a very basic spa and fitness room; the Imperial Palace Automobile Collection (p. 132); a handful of bars and cheap restaurants; and the best tribute show on the Strip (p. 198). But the biggest draw, as I said, is the location and price: from $35 going up only to about $90, even on weekends in high season (usually; this being Vegas, well, it's all a crapshoot).

Monorail Hotels

If you're not planning on renting a car, staying in a hotel with a monorail stop does give you more transportation options. For info on monorail pricing and policies, go to p. 12.

Hotels/sites with monorail stops are: The MGM Grand, Bally's, the Flamingo, Harrah's, the Las Vegas Convention Center, the Las Vegas Hilton, the Sahara.

$$–$$$$ Bill's Gamblin' Hall ★★ (3595 Las Vegas Blvd. S., at Flamingo Rd.; ☎ 866/BILLS-45 or 702/737-2100; www.billslasvegas.com; AE, DC, DISC, MC, V) is the former Barbary Coast, and despite the name change, it's still the charmer it's always been. Originally built in 1978, it boasts a beautifully realized Victorian theme. As you stroll through the not-too-sprawling, 30,000-square-foot casino there are elegant touches everywhere, from the brass fixtures, to the crystal chandeliers, to the rich oak of the wainscoting. The casino's stained glass is as magnificent as what you'd see in many churches. Rooms are just as lovely, many boasting views of the Bellagio fountains, and decorated in high Victorian style with dark wood headboards and oh-so-authentic striped maroon-and-white wallpaper. Modern touches include excellent Serta mattresses topped with fluffy white duvets and 42-inch plasma TVs. Bathrooms are a bit cramped, and the rooms aren't the largest on the Strip, but I think their well-thought-out design camouflages much of this.

Bill's is also a great place to hang out. "Big Elvis," a plus-sized Elvis impersonator, jams the lounge area most afternoons, and when the Strip's other nightspots close at around 2am, Drai's (see p. 206) becomes the town's go-to after-hours club. And the prices are certainly right, averaging $50 midweek and about $80 to $110 weekends, up to $163 only when the town's at its most crowded.

The downside? Because of its small size, there's no swimming pool, just a handful of restaurants and shops, and possibly the tightest parking lot on the Strip.

$$–$$$$ Large rooms and competitive pricing are the main reasons to choose **Bally's Las Vegas** 🧒 (645 Las Vegas Blvd. S., at Flamingo Rd.; ☎ 800/634-3434 or 702/739-4111; www.ballyslv.com; AE, DC, MC, V). Obviously, it's not the cheapest option on the Center Strip, but of the midpriced properties—by which I mean Treasure Island, Paris, the Flamingo, and Harrah's—it's usually, if not always, at the lower end of the price range. (What does that mean? Good question. I've tracked prices for the last few months and have come up with a range for Bally's of $62–$89 at slow times and $120–$180 at other times.) And you'll get a good sleep here: beds made ultracushy by the addition of extra pillowbeds between the mattress and sheet. There's even a handy oversized mirror in the all-marble bathroom, perfect for a last-minute hem check. As for the decor: It could use some rethinking. A number of the rooms just look out of date at this point with strange prefab furnishings (and avoid those that are right next to the elevators as they get a lot of mechanical grinding sounds). Families take note: Rooms here are among the biggest on the Strip; if you're willing to pay extra to have Junior in the room

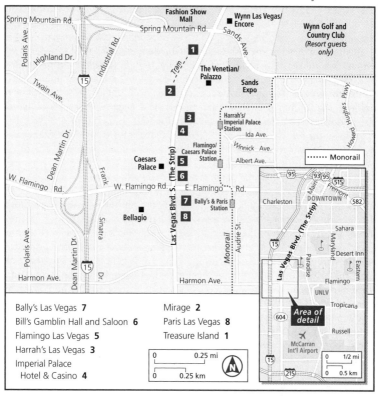

Bally's Las Vegas **7**

Bill's Gamblin Hall and Saloon **6**

Flamingo Las Vegas **5**

Harrah's Las Vegas **3**

Imperial Palace
  Hotel & Casino **4**

Mirage **2**

Paris Las Vegas **8**

Treasure Island **1**

with you (a terrible policy that holds at most Strip properties; see box on p. 56), at least here, you won't be on top of each other.

As for the ambience outside the guest rooms: It's equally forgettable. Bally's is themeless (which in Vegas is a little like forgetting to wear your pants to a cocktail party), and I really wish they had embellished it in some way. That's not to say the large casino isn't perfectly pleasant or the eight tennis courts and the lushly planted pool complex out back aren't up to snuff. They are. But I somehow always find myself stifling a yawn at Bally's.

Along with all the usual gaming tables and slot machines, Bally's is home to the famed *Jubilee!* show (p. 187) and the live version of *The Price Is Right* (p. 191). It attaches to Paris Las Vegas, shares a parking lot with that property (if you self-park, you'll park in Paris, so follow the correct signs), and features eight restaurants (including the terrific steakhouse, see p. 79), one of which hosts the most expensive brunch in town and a fab 15,000-square-foot full-service health club. In the basement are a slew of shops and the entrance to the monorail.

$$–$$$$ How Vegas is this? When it came time to name what was in 1946 the most glamorous and expensive Vegas casino ever built, gangster Bugsy Siegel chose the nickname he had for his long-legged, starlet girlfriend. The **Flamingo**

Las Vegas (3555 Las Vegas Blvd. S., between Sands Ave. and Flamingo Rd.; ☎ 800/732-2111 or 702/733-3111; www.flamingolasvegas.com; AE, DC, MC, V), the original, was razed in 1993—what you see today are a series of towers built from the '70s through the '90s—but it still commemorates that leggy lady with actual Chilean, pink flamingos strutting through the back gardens. They're joined by swans, quails, cranes, pheasants, guinea fowls, ducks, macaws, and all sorts of fish in the 15-acre Wildlife Habitat at the back of the resort, to my mind one of the loveliest outdoor spaces in Vegas. Alongside this mini-zoo are two Olympic-sized pools, water slides, and one dedicated kiddie pool; and though you didn't hear this from me, this is one of the few pool areas on the Strip where they don't make a fuss about room keys (so dive right in, it's one of the top five pool areas on the Strip and just delightful).

If only the interior of the hotel were as nice as its gardens. While some of the rooms have been upgraded recently (and now look a bit like candy boxes with brown and pink striped walls, hot pink colorboxes, and shiny white patent leather headboards—it's almost a *Clockwork Orange* look), the majority feature old-fashioned, scruffy but clean chain-motel type furnishings. When I asked at the front desk I was told the upgrade wouldn't be touching most of the rooms for the foreseeable future, so ask to see your room before you accept it. And I've always disliked the low ceilings and cramped layout of the casino. I will point out that the Flamingo is known for its showroom (currently hosting Donny and Marie and the comedian George Wallace; see p. 181 and 182), has eight on-site restaurants, and hosts wonderful weddings in its gardens (p. 159).

As for pricing: It mirrors pretty closely what you'll find at its sister property, Bally's ($62–$89 at slow times, and $120–$180 otherwise; hotels.com consistently gets better rates here than the competition).

$$–$$$$ Though its prices are often reasonable, I find **Harrah's Las Vegas** (3475 Las Vegas Blvd. S., between Flamingo and Spring Mountain roads; ☎ 800/HARRAHS [427-7247] or 702/369-5000; AE, DC, MC, V) a bit hard to take. It boasts one of the most frenetic, loud casinos on the Strip topped by a ceiling so low in places that Michael Jordan would be in danger of serious bruising if he ever came in (or at least it feels that way). Where there's statuary or art of any sort, it's of the gaudy Biloxi Mardi Gras variety, as disposable looking as the beads they throw from floats. Rooms have been gussied up, with a new pseudo–Art Deco design, wooden headboards, and marble countertops, but many standard rooms still are oddly shaped, somewhat like an arrow, and thus still feel cramped. I do like the showroom here, and am an apostle for magician Mac King (p. 195), who everyone should see—he's that good. But he's the best thing Harrah's has going: The pool area is functional and large, but nothing special; the same could be said about the on-site restaurants and spa. And keep your wits about you: Harrah's hosts some of the most aggressive timeshare sellers on the Strip and they pounce when you least expect it (they roam around, gosh darn it!).

Expect to pay anywhere between $35 and $150 a night here, though lately the prices most nights have seemed to settle in the $55 range (and at really dead times, Harrah's has even floated a $1 Tuesday deal when 3 nights are booked).

The Starbucks Test

As I said at the top, sometimes the total cost of your vacation is not influenced so much by how much you paid for your room—especially right now in this period of declining room rates—but by how much you pay for the other elements of your trip. Let's take that cup of morning Joe for example. I started comparing Starbucks' pricing at different casinos around Vegas and found that my decaf mocha cost 50¢ more at the Mandalay Bay than it did at New York–New York and that coffee in the "Big Apple" was a good 30¢ more than the Starbucks on Fremont Street. That in turn was about 50¢ more than I paid outside of the tourist areas altogether in Vegas.

These differences may seem puny, but they're reflective of an overall rise in pricing at the Strip's pricier properties for everything from restaurant meals to boxes of tampons in the in-casino convenience store and can really start eating into your vacation budget if you're not careful.

$$–$$$$ Paris Las Vegas ★★ (3655 Las Vegas Blvd. S.; ☎ 888/BONJOUR [266-5687] or 702/946-7000; www.parislv.com; AE, DC, DISC, MC, V) by contrast, is downright pretty and has a pleasant expansiveness to it, from its slate gray *trompe l'oeil* sky, which arches high above the casino, to the meandering cobblestone country lanes back where the buffets, restaurants, lounges, and shops are. It gets crowded, too, but somehow the height of the ceiling makes that less problematic. And though it's a caricature of the City of Light, with its Eiffel Tower sticking up the top (you see three of its legs on the casino floor), and its myriad of Beaux Arts street lamps lining the path through the casino, it doesn't offend. It's nowhere near as beautiful as the real Paris—*sacre bleu,* what could be?—but this charlatan has a dignity and charm that some of the other mock-ups lack.

Guest rooms feel small at the lowest price level, but are so bursting with overstuffed, colorful Empire-style furnishings—settees, armoires, carved wooden headboards—that they'll charm away any disappointment. The pink marble bathrooms, I should say, are positively divine. All is not perfect at the Paris—the pool ain't so hot, restaurants are of varying quality, and the spa's not what it used to be—but on the whole it outclasses many of the other midpriced properties on this stretch by a mile. And a half. Prices seem to veer between $90 and $169 a night here, though I have seen them drop to $79 at hotels.com.

$$–$$$$ After an attempt at "detheming" and calling itself "TI at the Mirage," **Treasure Island** ★ (3300 Las Vegas Blvd. S., at Spring Mountain Rd.; ☎ 800/944-7444 or 702/894-7111; www.treasureisland.com; AE, DC, MC, V) is back to its old name after an attempt to distance itself from the pirate theme. The swashbuckling element—the outdoor pirate battle show—is now fought between open-shirted hunks and bootylicious *Playboy* models, er, I mean "sirens." The focus within the casino has shifted from all-ages fun to burlesque shows, chic restaurants (including the terrific Isla, p. 87), and hot lounges. Hey, I'm not judging—that's the direction the entire town is moving in, and I think it's appropriate (my kids have told me in no uncertain terms that they never want to return to Vegas after the 2 weeks they spent here with me).

The rooms too, have recently been redone which is a shame. They used to have subtle, very pretty Victorian elements (such as the swooping curtains at the head of the bed and the pretty gold-flecked comforters) that gave them real character. Today the ambience is totally indistinguishable from a dozen other hotels on the Strip (sigh). It's not unpleasant—bits of art here and there, a faux suede armchair, a pillow-piled bed, lots of neutrals accented by bright swatches of orange—just so . . . expected. Rates have stayed fairly stable at $79 to $89 when the crowds have thinned, up to whatever the market may bear otherwise (which, in this case, seems to be $138–$209 a night, occasionally up to $299). The pools are fine too; again, there are better, much better in fact, but the pool area's large and has slides and will suffice.

A tram connects Treasure Island with The Mirage next door; it's free and runs all hours. Behind the pirate stage is a "Caribbean Village," really an outdoor mall, with a good number of fun window-shopping ops. Do I even need to mention that there's a spa and a very large and well-stocked gym, or would you have guessed that?

$$-$$$$ In another sign of how bad the economy currently is—or perhaps how quickly "au courant" becomes "old hat" in Vegas—I'm adding the once fabled **Mirage** ✹✹ (3400 Las Vegas Blvd. S; ☎ 702/791-7111; www.mirage.com; AE, DC, MC, V) to this edition of the book as their prices have recently dropped into the realm of the doable ($99 a night during slow periods, though $119–$229 may well be the going rate when you check—roll the dice, as they say here). The first casino built using Wall Street money (junk bonds, actually) it marked a new day in the then-declining Vegas when it opened in 1989. Instead of neon and showgirls, it had gold windows tinted with actual gold, white tigers (as the home of Siegfried and Roy), and a classiness that was always lacking in the places where ring kissing and pistol packing among top management were de rigueur. And thanks to the publicity surrounding its construction costs ($630 million, a record back then), it helped make Vegas chic again, inspiring a whole new style of casinos . . . which eventually overshadowed poor old Mirage.

I think it's still a swell place and one that's improved recently thanks to a renovation that's brought with it high-quality hardwood furnishings, flatscreen TVs, and, in some rooms, a purple and pink color scheme that seems like a bad idea on paper, but in person looks darn swank and not at all "Barbie Dreamhouse" (no mean feat). Other perks of staying here: 11 quality restaurants; cool entertainment choices, helmed today by Cirque's *LOVE* (p. 186); and the nice pools out back with their slides, waterfalls, and tropical landscaping. And you can't beat the lovely and soothing oasis in the desert that is the lush rainforest area under its 110-foot atrium (between the lobby and casino). Heck, even the signature volcano (p. 118) has recently been given a pyrotechnic makeover. Bottom line: If The Mirage is in the affordable range, scoop it up. This is still one of the coolest addresses on the Center Strip.

HOTELS ON THE NORTH STRIP

Welcome to the low rent end of the Strip! The North Strip is home to such classic (and always affordable) casinos as the Riviera, Circus Circus, and the Sahara; in between are budget motels, downscale eateries, and fenced off lots where the rubble of recently imploded casinos billows with dust. Sure, in some spots the Trumps of this world have moved in—Donald Trump himself has a new 1,282-condo tower here now and Steve Wynn's eponymous casino and its sibling Encore grace the southern tip (his plans apparently include more towers so that he can spell out a big "W" with high-rises). But on the whole this area features an unvarnished (if sometimes seedy) view of '60s and '70s Vegas. If you want the "Super Casino" experience, the free outdoor spectacles, and ultragourmet eateries, move southward. If you're looking for a good deal on the Strip, here's where you stay.

$ And the rock-bottom cheapest places you'll stay on the Strip, or anywhere in Las Vegas for that matter, are at the **Sin City Hostel** (1208 Las Vegas Blvd. S.; ☎ 702/868-0222; www.sincityhostel.com; AE, DISC, MC, V) or the **Tod Hotel & Hostel** (1508 Las Vegas Blvd. S.; ☎ 702/477-0022; www.todlasvegas.com; AE, DC, MC,V) which features one of those fab Googie architecture signs out front spelling out TOD (these were the initials for the real estate developer who built the original motel here in 1962). Let me say right off the bat that I'm going to be very un-budget and recommend that you splurge the $2 a night to stay at the Tod (which is $20 a night in a dorm room) over Sin City ($18 a night dorm). Let me put it this way: It'll be quieter, your bed will be a brand new, sturdy bunk (as opposed to a rectangle of foam covered in plastic atop a wooden board), and you're less likely to feel that your body is covered in a film of grime when you wake in the morning. Yeah, Sin City's that grungy. Comparatively, Tod is quite spiffy, having opened up in 2007 and featuring such niceties as a swimming pool, a common room with free Internet service and snacks for sale (plus a usable kitchen), and even a fun hang-out area in the large parking lot with barbecues and swing benches. Don't go for a private room here, though ($39–$149 a night) as they're actually much drearier than the dorm rooms, furnished with battered dressers, beds, and chairs that were salvaged from the Stardust before it was imploded.

$–$$$ Children are banned from these hostels, but it probably doesn't matter as most of them seem to be staying at **Circus Circus Hotel & Casino** ★ 🎪 (2880 Las Vegas Blvd. S., between Circus Circus Dr. and Convention Center Dr.; ☎ 800/444-CIRC [444-2472] or 800/634-3450; www.circuscircus.com; AE, DISC, MC, V). In fact, you may feel like every child in the state of Nevada is staying at Circus Circus, especially when you're plowing your way through the lobby, desperately sidestepping careening toddlers, and the massive, bouncing furry basketballs that seem to be the souvenir of choice here.

Circus Circus was originally conceived for adults who wanted to act like kids. When it opened in 1968, it had midway games and circus acts, yes, but with a twist—in one game you threw a ball at a target and if you hit it, a gust of wind would blow the sheet off a semi-nude showgirl who would then dance. The original Big Top was so over-the-top, in fact, that one of its star performers was Tanya "the first gambling elephant," who would amble through the casino pulling slot levers for guests, her trainer following with a bucket. It's all much more G-rated now, but there are still live circus acts entertaining guests throughout the day and evening; a huge midway with carnival games; and the massive glass Adventuredome, an indoor amusement park with flume rides, roller coasters, 3-D movies, bumper cars, and the like. (Read all about this on p. 131.) If your kids are anything like mine, this will be their favorite place in Vegas.

The sheer mass of all those children dropping wrappers, spilling drinks, and generally making a mess keeps the public areas of the resort pretty scruffy looking. I get the feeling that the staff has given up on trying to keep the place in order, a thought confirmed by the graffiti in the elevator leading to the pool, the bleak concrete pool area itself, and the sloppy way in which huge racks of soiled linens are simply left standing in the hallways. Even the areas where the kids aren't supposed to wander feel dingy: The labyrinthine casino is noisy, low-ceilinged, and a tad depressing.

So it's a shock to find that the guest rooms are actually lovely—clean, comfortable, in a word, great. I stayed and visited rooms in all the towers and the motel extension and I can report that they're all high quality with fine bathrooms, soft carpets, firm beds, and pretty circus pictures on the walls in some (the motel suites are a bit more bland looking but just fine). Considering that rates are among the lowest on the Strip, starting as low as $28 (try HotelClub.com) and rarely going far above $100 (for standard rooms), even when the town is jam-packed, this actually turns out to be one of the best values on the Strip. In addition to regular rooms, Circus Circus also has an RV park out back, with its own pool, for folks who bring their own accommodations when they travel.

$–$$$ I'm fudging it a bit, I admit, placing the **Aruba Hotel** (1215 Las Vegas Blvd. S; ☎ 866/383-3150 or 702/383-3100; www.arubalasvegas.com; AE, DC, MC, V) on the North Strip as it's actually 4 long blocks north of the Stratosphere. Still, it's too far away from Downtown to be categorized there, and the Aruba is the latest incarnation of the legendary Thunderbird Resort, which was the fourth Strip resort to open (in 1948) and once played host to the likes of Mae West, George Burns, and Bob Hope, giving it an important place in Sin City history. You'd never know, of course, from the looks of it, as this seems like just one of the many old-fashioned motels in town. When I once asked the staff what they felt their appeal is, one of the friendly staffers answered bluntly, "we're the only motel in the Arts District that isn't a flophouse." And so it is. Tucked away behind a high fence and an odd mottled wall, it's well-screened from the seedier joints that surround it, and the tremendously sweet staff goes out of their way to pamper the guests (as you'll see from the big baskets of towels they leave in each room, topped with tubes of toothpaste and disposable razors). But if you're wary about staying in this part of town, you may want to look elsewhere.

That being said, rooms are extremely clean, fairly modern, and large—though so bland in appearance you'll forget what they look like the moment you leave. A decent pool in the back and tiny workout room for active guests are other good signs. For all of this you'll pay between $28 and $35 most nights (try hotels.com), though when Vegas is jumping prices have been known to jump too, to about $65 to $100 a night. The legendary Thunderbird Lounge has been revived at the front

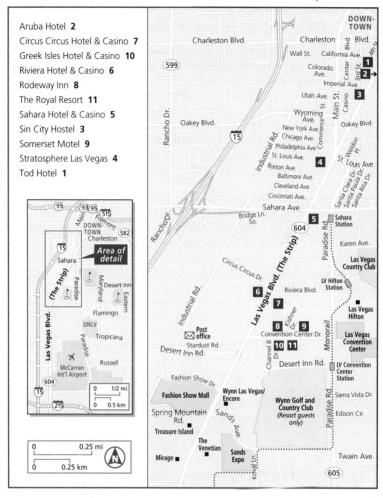

Aruba Hotel **2**
Circus Circus Hotel & Casino **7**
Greek Isles Hotel & Casino **10**
Riviera Hotel & Casino **6**
Rodeway Inn **8**
The Royal Resort **11**
Sahara Hotel & Casino **5**
Sin City Hostel **3**
Somerset Motel **9**
Stratosphere Las Vegas **4**
Tod Hotel **1**

of the motel; it's a fun place to have a drink, grab breakfast (cheaply), listen to a local band, and occasionally watch a local theatrical production.

Two words of warning: You may want to avoid the Aruba on the first Friday of each month as the hotel is part of the First Friday celebrations (p. 170) and it can get LOUD. As well, ask for a room away from the generator room, another noisy problem.

$–$$$$ Pricewise, **Stratosphere Las Vegas** (2000 Las Vegas Blvd. S., between St. Louis Ave. and Baltimore Ave.; ☎ 800/99-TOWER [998-6937] or 702/380-7777; www.stratospherehotel.com; AE, DC, DISC, MC, V), that tall needle at the very northern tip of the Strip, is in the same league as Circus Circus. When it's slow,

Convenience on Convention Center Drive

Who knew? Convention Center Drive, that somewhat dreary street abutting Las Vegas Boulevard, doesn't look like much, but it's a hidden oasis for genuinely friendly, well-maintained budget accommodations. Because the street ain't all that long, it's easy to stroll from your room to the Strip itself, meaning you don't need a car to stay here. In fact, it's convenient to all areas of the Strip via the monorail at the nearby Convention Center station.

My favorite along the block is the **Somerset Motel** ★★ (294 Convention Center Dr., between Las Vegas Blvd. and Paradise Rd.; ☎ 888/336-4280 or 702/735-4411; AE, DC, V, MC; $-$$). No it's not fancy, and it's pretty old-fashioned—they don't even have e-mail or a website!—but you gotta love that great Googie (aka doo-wop or populuxe style) architecture, with the vintage star-speckled sign out front. Also adorable, really, are the prices, which are among the lowest in town and don't jump up precipitously when there's a convention nearby. Instead, you'll always pay $42 to $52 for a Sunday through Thursday stay, and up to $72 on weekends; those with a AAA card can shave $7 off those prices. Call direct to get the best rates.

So what do you get for those sums? First up is a warm, warm welcome from the grandmotherly women who run the place and keep it feeling like that proverbial home away from home. Most of the rooms were recently renovated, and about half have kitchenettes (for which there's no extra charge; ask if you want one). They're pretty nifty now, with quality mattresses, new TVs, huge closets, and cheerful royal blue and gold curtains and bedspreads. Free in-room movies are offered on the TVs on a daily basis; you'll be handed a schedule of what's showing when you arrive (it's usually a mix of vintage and current releases). There's only a small pool on property and no casino, spa, or fitness room, but for those who simply want a cheap, nice place to stay, it's a real find.

Next door, the **Rodeway Inn** ★ (220 Convention Center Dr., between Las Vegas Blvd. and Paradise Rd.; ☎ 702/735-4151; AE, DC, V, MC; $-$$) is another solid value, with oversized rooms, quality beds, free Wi-Fi, and free coffee. I'd rank it well below the Somerset because the service isn't quite as sweet (it's hard to compete with those swell ladies), and the rooms are a bit more generic looking now that its no longer the Villa Roma Motel (when it had pretensions to artsiness). Again there's a small pool, but no casino or fitness room. Its nightly rate seems to hold steady at $60,

you can stay at this soaring tower, the tallest building in the West, for as little as $29 to $35 a night on weekdays, up to $89 weekends. I'm a bit surprised at the parity in prices as I think the rooms are nicer, in general, at Circus Circus. I guess in most conventioneer's minds, staying in an inconvenient spot—which to be blunt, describes the Stratosphere's lousy location (you can't walk from here to, which is a bit high for a weekday, but decent for what you get here on a weekend.

Have a thing for pilots? Here's where to meet one. Airline crews make up the majority of the guests at the **Greek Isles Hotel and Casino** (305 Convention Center Dr.; ☎ 800/633-1777 or 702/752-9000; www.greekisles vegas.com; AE, DC, MC, V; $-$$). In fact, they occupy floors two through eight (of a 10-story building), have their own gym (the only one in the building), and even have their own lounge to cook and party in. But sometimes they come out of their sanctuary to sing karaoke in the little lounge/casino here, or hit the slots. You might also see them working off the jet lag by doing laps in the heated pool out back. I'm thinking that their rooms may be a bit less odd than the ones given to the rest of us, otherwise why would they keep returning? If you're not among the flying class you'll be put in a spic and span, quite large (400–500 sq. ft.) room, decorated in a jarring blend of stripes and checks. It's a bit dizzying, which may be why, instead of giving guests a regular chair, you get a genuine Barcalounger (woo hoo!). A fridge and a good-sized bathroom up the ante, as do the prices which seem to pop between $59 and $69 a night, sometimes sticking at $59 on weekends (because the hotel doesn't list its prices online anywhere, its rates stay more stable than most, so this is a good option to pick during crowded periods).

Half timeshare, half resort, **The Royal Resort** ✮✮ (99 Convention Center Dr., between Las Vegas Blvd. and Paradise Rd.; ☎ 800/634-6118; www.royalhotelvegas.com; AE, DC, V, MC; $-$$$) is the splashiest choice on the block but still a pretty good deal. There's no casino, but it does have many of the same amenities as the Strip resorts, including a nice pool with cabanas, a cocktail/piano lounge, room service, and a small but modern and quite usable fitness center. Chic rooms, with heather green velvet armchairs, swish pillow-top mattresses, purple and gold coverlets, and actual balconies (a rarity in Vegas) are why so many business travelers choose the joint. (The nice business center is also a lure.) And the Royal is now home to some fun and very affordable shows (see p. 192). Average rates here: $65 on weekdays, $99 on weekends, but at the last minute it's not at all unusual to find it for $35 a night. Try Hotels.com when looking for rates, as it seems to have some kind of in when it comes to discounts here (from the searches I've done).

well, *anywhere*)—is preferable to dealing with swarms of youngsters. Here the digs are a bit more dreary, at least at the bottom of the price range, featuring particle board furnishings and brown everything—curtains, quilts, mood. Views from the higher floors, to be fair, will cheer you up (so ask to stay above the 10th floor, if possible).

And adrenaline junkies will enjoy the Stratosphere. Though it closed its rooftop roller coaster in 2006, it still has a number of other rides at the top that dangle thrillingly off the edge (p. 131; I found myself worrying about my will when I last rode these). It also boasts a huge and unusually friendly casino that's one of the few in town to feature crapless craps and video poker with 100% + pay (the Holy Grail of VP). A rooftop pool has terrific views of the Strip, and the hotel has seven restaurants, including one of my favorite diners in the city (p. 91). The shows here aren't worth recommending, but if the price is right and you have wheels (you really don't want to stay all the way out here without a car), it's certainly a decent option.

$–$$$$ The first high-rise in Vegas at nine stories in 1952, the **Riviera Hotel & Casino** (2901 Las Vegas Blvd. S., at Riviera Blvd.; ☎ 800/634-6753 or 702/734-5110; www.rivierahotel.com; AE, DC, MC, V) still feels mighty big. That's not a good thing. In this town of mazelike, endless casinos, it wins the prize for poorest layout. Couple that with public areas that have seen better days, and dull food and shopping options and you have . . . well, a casino you may want to avoid.

Unless . . . Well, unless you get a deal on one of the rooms, which come in two varieties right now. The unrenovated ones are perfectly tidy, somewhat old-fashioned motel-like rooms (the mattresses are very good, though, I'll give them that). And the renovated ones are quite pleasing, with pristine white duvets, solid dark wood furnishings, pretty textured rugs and curtains, and the nice extra of a padded tray to hold your laptop in bed. Prices run the gamut from $42 up to about $142 (it gets a lot of conventions which skew prices up), with best rates usually found on Travelworm.com. Guest rooms in the Mediterranean Tower are the largest, so ask for one of those. If you're a diver, you'll like the pool, which is the deepest in town and is quite large, though with none of the slides, lush landscaping, and other bells and whistles that have become so common here. Tennis players will appreciate the fact that there are two night-lit courts on the property. There's also a wide choice of shows here, some of which, like the skating spectacle *ICE* (p. 188), are definitely worth seeing.

$$–$$$$ The **Sahara Hotel & Casino** ★ (2535 Las Vegas Blvd. S., at E. Sahara Ave.; ☎ 888/696-2121 or 702/737-2111; www.saharavegas.com; AE, DC, DISC, MC, V) has more *va-va-voom* than the city's other older casinos, thanks in part to $100 million in renovations over the last decade which have, interestingly, been used not to remake the hotel (though there's been a bit of that), but to restore much of its original beauty. The chandeliers glisten again with fine crystals, though these aren't the originals from 1952, these are new, if old-fashioned looking beauties. The kitschy Arabian carpeting and Islamic detailing have been restored, and while the place doesn't look swank, you feel like you get a better sense here than at the Strip's other oldsters what it might have been like to visit when Sinatra and Sammy Davis, Jr. owned the town. Guest rooms, too, are not fancy by any means, but cute and comfortable with '60s-style furniture and fun, campy touches such as camel lamps and Aladdin chairs. They're kept spotlessly clean and constitute a good buy at between $32 and $142 per night for a standard room (to be fair, they rarely break $110 anymore if you use a discounter site).

And who are their customers? The Sahara seems to be guessing they're NASCAR fans; those areas of the casino that aren't Arabian Nights–themed, are filled with race cars, black checkered flags, and NASCAR memorabilia. There's a NASCAR Café, a NASCAR roller coaster out front, and in the back arcade a highly realistic NASCAR simulator ride where you compete against other guests after watching a 5-minute training video (p. 133). A usable pool (nothing to write home about), two theaters, a bad buffet, and a handful of other restaurants complete the offerings here.

DOWNTOWN HOTELS

Remember how I wrote that the North Strip was a good, if sometimes down at the heels, example of '60s and '70s Vegas? The same thing could be said of Downtown . . . times 10. This is where Vegas began, an area originally called "Glitter Gulch" for all of the glamorous neon signs that fronted the casinos on Fremont Street.

The glamour has evaporated, but for visitors seriously into gambling, who enjoy being able to walk from casino to casino, and who need to adhere to a strict budget, Downtown is an excellent choice. At many times of the year, rooms will be half as expensive, though they're just as nice as what you'll find on the Strip. While the casino areas can be claustrophobic and well, seedy, the slots have a reputation for being looser, and the minimums on the table games are often far lower.

Safety-wise it's advisable to stay on or as near to the Fremont Street Experience as possible. A downtown revitalization is in the works—or so Mayor Goodman says—but right now, the areas away from the heavily trafficked Fremont Street area have a skid row vibe that's less than appealing.

$–$$ The farthest I'd go east of the Fremont Street Experience canopy would be to the **El Cortez Hotel and Casino** ✪ (600 Fremont St., between 6th and 7th sts.; ☎ 800/634-6703 or 702/385-5200; www.elcortezhotelcasino.com; AE, MC, V). Though it's 3 slummy-looking blocks away, it has the low prices, great rooms, and classic Vegas vibe to justify the trek. Much of "El Cheapo" (its loving local nickname) was renovated in the past few years; stay here and your $28 to $45 a night price tag—a common rate here for much of the year—will buy you a slightly larger than normal room, with sleep-enhancing beds (they're brand new and topped with lovely white duvets), handsome heavy wood beds, flatscreen TVs, and a small but spotless bathroom. In effect, you're paying a third of what you'd likely pay at Bally's or the Flamingo for a nicer, newer room. I can't say the same about the casino, which is smoky, crowded, and filled with characters out of a Tim Burton movie. And you're not going to get a pool or a spa (hey, they've got a barber shop though!), but at these prices are you going to complain? Be sure to take a good look at the outside of the casino—it has the largest number of original neon signs of any casino in Vegas (and they're pretty cool looking, too).

$–$$ The second cheapest decent option is the **Vegas Club** (18 E. Fremont St.; ☎ 800/634-6532 or 702/385-1664; www.vegasclubcasino.net; AE, DC, MC, V), a sprawling casino right on Fremont Street that's as close as you get to a theme hotel in Glitter Gulch. In case you can't guess from the decor—and to be honest, it will take a while for the theme to emerge—it's sports, and there are some nice pieces of memorabilia here (signed baseball bats and the like) as well as a mural or two

The Hotel Spread

Nonsensical pricing that's based on whatever the market will bear is the norm in Vegas. But it's not a total free-for-all. Yes, rates on the same hotel room can sometimes jump $200 in the course of a day, but . . . well, they're always jumping in tandem with others in their price category. So if you know which hotels are traditionally cheapest, traditionally in the midrange, and traditionally the priciest, you can tell into which category you're going to need to jump when the town is busy. And when it's slow, you just may be able to upgrade.

I've created the chart below using real prices culled from extensive searches performed over the course of several months. I can't guarantee that you'll be able to get these rates, nor do I have the space to include every property, but I thought this would give readers a Rosetta stone, so to speak, to help untangle the mysteries of nightly rates in Sin City:

	Midweek, Low Season	Midweek, High Season	Weekend, Low Season	Weekend, High Season
Rock Bottom: Arizona Charlies, El Cortez, Wild Wild West	$24	$36	$45	$74
Cheap: Circus Circus, Stratosphere, Imperial Palace	$28	$40	$55	$93
Midrange: Harrah's, Bally's, Rio	$58	$124	$122	$155
High End: Palazzo, Bellagio, Wynn	$128	$276	$239	$320

Please note that the rates above are averages, and there are times when they have dipped slightly higher and lower; I've excluded New Year's Eve and other insanely pricey dates from this chart.

with cheerleaders and other sporting types. Other than those touches, this is the usual dimly lit, low-ceilinged, cramped downtown casino. But guest rooms are quite roomy, ranging in price from averaging just $25 to $35 much of the time, though they can go up to $96 when a convention's in town. I should point out that though it's often pricier than El Cortez, the rooms here aren't nearly as nice. The older ones look like they still have the same furniture and carpeting from the '70s and the "newer" ones have a distinctly '80s vibe. They're all clean, but pretty threadbare at this point, and are missing items that you take for granted at other hotels around town (like ice-buckets and alarm clocks). No pool on-site, but guests can use the one a block away at the Plaza Hotel.

$–$$ The main draw of **The Four Queens Hotel & Casino** (202 Fremont St., at Casino Center Blvd.; ☎ 800/634-6045 or 702/385-4011; www.fourqueens.com; AE, DC, MC, V) is its location at the center of the Fremont Street Experience. That means that those guests who get even-numbered rooms on the sixth floor or below, will have a view from their windows of the swirling lights and sounds of

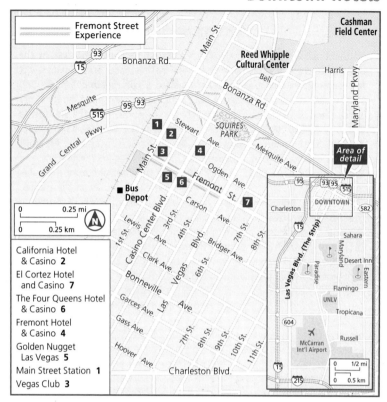

California Hotel
& Casino **2**

El Cortez Hotel
and Casino **7**

The Four Queens Hotel
& Casino **6**

Fremont Hotel
& Casino **4**

Golden Nugget
Las Vegas **5**

Main Street Station **1**

Vegas Club **3**

that hourly show. Come to think of it, I guess I should state this as a warning as well: If you stay at The Four Queens, you're probably going to be dealing with the soundtrack and swirling lights of the Fremont Street Experience, which may be a negative if you're an early to bed type. (But heck, if you're an early-to-bed type, why have you chosen to vacation in Vegas?)

Rooms are tidy and much more pleasant than they were 2 years ago, with brightly colored bedspreads and art on the walls (plus new mattresses, gotta love that); those in the North Tower are a bit smaller, but the elevator in the South Tower is slower, so you'll have to choose your poison. Average rates run $39 to $49 when it's slow, up to $120 otherwise. As at the majority of other downtown casinos, there's no pool, fitness room, or chapel on-site, but The Four Queens does have swimming rights at the nearby Binions, where the rooftop pool has swell views. Also convenient is the on-site half-price tickets booth for shows. The casino itself is large and friendly, more brightly lit than other casinos along Glitter Gulch with a faded but classy decor.

$–$$$$ Downtown's answer to the Strip, the spiffy **Golden Nugget Las Vegas** ★★★ (129 E. Fremont St., at Casino Center Blvd.; ☎ 800/634-3454 or 702/385-7111; www.goldennugget.com; AE, DC, MC, V) has gotten even more,

Betting on Boyd

With the exception of the Golden Nugget (p. 49), the classiest of the downtown properties all come from one mother ship, Boyd Gaming. It's this corporation that's responsible for **Main Street Station** ✪✪✪ (200 N. Main St., between Fremont St. and I-95; ☎800/465-0711 or 702/387-1896; www.mainstreetcasino.com; AE, DC, DISC, MC, V), the **California Hotel & Casino** ✪✪ (12 Ogden Ave., at 1st St.; ☎ 800/634-6255 or 702/385-1222; www.thecal.com; AE, DC, DISC, MC, V), and the **Fremont Hotel & Casino** ✪ (200 E. Fremont St., between Casino Center Blvd. and 3rd St.; ☎ 800/634-6182 or 702/385-3232; www.fremontcasino.com; AE, DC, DISC, MC, V). And while they're far from cookie cutter in their looks, they share a common pricing scheme—on weekdays, you'll likely pay in the mid- to upper $40s for a room, with weekend pricing hopping between $65 and $100. They also share a common clientele, as Boyd Gaming owns Vacations Hawaii, which brings thousands of Hawaiians into Vegas every year on air/hotel packages, bunking most of them at these three hotels. For those of us outside the Aloha State, this is bad news because it means that it can often be near impossible to find a room at these properties at certain times of the year. Very, very bad news actually, as these three are real gems.

Most impressive of the bunch, **Main Street Station** was originally opened in 1992 as a fee-for-entry, casino-cum-museum, designed with high Victorian panache and filled with exquisite antiques and artifacts from the era. When Boyd came in, they renovated, added rooms, and dropped the fee, but you can still take a self-guided tour (ask for the brochure) of all the pretty antiques. Stop first outside and peek into Private Car 92, the 1903 Pullman Rail Car, which was originally built for a railroad prez but was eventually bought by Buffalo Bill Cody to use as his home on wheels while touring the country with his Wild West show (car 100 next door is just as ornate). The wonders continue inside: A massive mahogany apothecary cabinet, with its hammered tin relief panels, beveled glass, and labeled drawers, gives the front check-in area the look of an Old West hotel. Go into the center of the casino and into the buffet area, look up, and you'll see elaborate chandeliers, some taken from opera houses in Paris and San Francisco; the stained glass windows have similarly impressive pedigrees. You'll also enjoy dining here, as Main Street houses one of the best buffets in Vegas (p. 96).

Renovated in 2006, the guest rooms are the most modern part of the hotel, but still give off the air of refined pampering you'll get downstairs, with striped celadon green, navy, and light blue bedspreads so pretty

I coveted them for my own home, large gilt-framed mirrors opposite the cushy beds (for that voyeuristic Vegas touch), excellent mattresses, and thick carpets. Bathrooms are older, but spotless, with those new curved shower curtain rods that are becoming so popular. Can you tell, I really, really like this hotel? (Though if swimming pools, fitness rooms, and shopping arcades matter to you, you'd best stay elsewhere.)

The Aloha shirts worn by the largely Hawaiian staff is the first give-away that the **California Hotel & Casino** is the most popular resort in Vegas for the 808 state. Walk through the small second-floor mall with its Aloha eatery (p. 94), its Lapperts Ice Cream stand (part of the biggest ice cream chain in Hawaii), and its convenience store selling Spam and it becomes even clearer—you're never going to be able to get a reservation here because the entire state of Hawaii has gotten here before you. According to the management, the clientele here is about 90% Hawaiian (as opposed to 70% at Main Street Station), and the place is often taken over fully by high school reunions (family reunions are big, too). After staying here, it'll be clear why the place is so popular. It's not the casino— built in 1975 it has that gloomy, "two million cigarettes smoked down to the nub here" ambience. But the laid-back, convivial staff are extraordinarily friendly (at the blackjack table, I met a return visitor who had just gotten a ride in from the airport from a porter he's friendly with—at no cost); and the newly renovated rooms with their calming creams and tans are swell. (Tip: Avoid the older East Tower, which has smaller rooms and louder plumbing.) On the roof is a postage-stamp-sized pool that's shared with guests from the Fremont and Main Street Station.

The **Fremont** celebrated its 50th anniversary in 1996. In its day, it was the place downtown; the first high-rise here, its former showroom served as a stage for Wayne Newton, Liberace, Lou Rawls, and others. It also was instrumental in introducing gambling as a pastime to female customers, opening up the first all-female card room in Vegas. All that said, it's my least favorite of the three Boyd properties (though I'd still take it over most of the other downtown properties any day). It has a similar casino to the California's but minus dealers that remember your name when you come back 6 months later. Somehow, it is just a bit less friendly and the rooms are smaller, though they too have been re-done, here in a mod palette of ice blue and midnight brown that's so chic, you might feel like you're in some fancy Hollywood hotel. Though it had the first roof pool downtown, that's since been closed; guests use the one next door at the Cal.

well, "Stripified" thanks to a giant upgrade, which added an Olympic-sized outdoor pool to the hotel, complete with water slide and, set behind the pool, an aquarium filled with sharks through which the enclosed slide zips. (Funny that no one in this town ever thought of swimming with sharks before.) It's just the latest salvo for the Golden Nugget, which since its opening in 1946 has always managed to outglitz its neighbors. Frank Sinatra opened its showroom, its spa was designed to look like the Garden Room at NYC's Frick Museum (the fitness room is superb as well), and on display in the lobby is the "Hand of Faith," the largest known gold nugget in the world (all of 61 lb., 11 oz.).

The Nugget was helped along in its glam quest over the years by no less than Vegas' golden boy himself, Steve Wynn, who was once chairman of the board here. You'll see his touch in the awning-laden casino (which looks a bit like the ones at Bellagio and Wynn Las Vegas), the marbled lobby, the richly patterned fabrics and carpeting, and unfortunately in the pricing policies—this is the only Downtown hotel that charges extra for children to stay in a room.

Sleeping here is also a honeymoon-worthy experience, as the guest rooms are positively imperial in design, with richly patterned bedspreads and curtains (of the type you'd see at a fine Parisian hotel); thick, soft carpeting; marble bathrooms with deep tubs and lighted vanities; and large flatscreen TVs. It's the equivalent of what you'd find at such glam Strip properties as The Mirage and yet you'll always pay at least $30 less to stay here, and sometimes as much as $100 less (lately prices have been swinging between $63 and $150). Granted, the on-site eating options aren't as good as at The Mirage, and when you walk out of the hotel, you'll probably be confronted by someone urgently wanting to inscribe your name on a grain of rice (or sell you a personalized T-shirt, or some other such Fremont St. antic). But if you want deluxe accommodations for less, this is not a bad choice.

HOTELS EAST OF THE STRIP

When you go off the Strip and outside of Downtown, you're confronted with Vegas' true character: an endlessly repeating mix of gated communities, low-rise apartment buildings and hotels, and strip malls. Mostly strip malls. All that said, the area directly east of the Strip contains some of the best eating options in town; and a handful of swell casinos to hang out in, including the ultrahip Hard Rock Hotel and the geek-chic Hilton (home to Barry Manilow).

$–$$ For budgeteers, it may be most notable as the area holding the Boulder Highway. Half as glamorous but twice as affordable as the Strip, Vegas' second Strip is home to half a dozen large, bustling casino resorts. It's a hot spot among local gamblers, for slots that are reportedly loosey-goosey, and though it's a 15-minute drive east of the Strip, there's so much here to keep visitors busy that many end up spending the majority of their time here. That's certainly the case for **Arizona Charlie's** (4575 Boulder Hwy.; ☎ 888/236-9066; www.arizonacharlies.com; AE, DC, MC, V)— it's so far out on Boulder that you could as well be in, well, Arizona. But with the money you're going to save here you could take a taxi each day to neighboring casinos and the Strip. When I last visited, the lowest priced rooms were going for a jaw-dropping $16 a night. Now, that's not the norm, even here, but what is usual is to find Charlie's consistently offering the lowest rates in town, usually tied with Wild, Wild West (see p. 60)—even at the busiest of times, I've never seen Charlie's break

Vegas' Only B&B

In this topsy-turvy city where hotels routinely bed 2,000 guests a night, where ceilings are painted to look like the sky, and hotel staff walk around dressed like gladiators and gondoliers, the most idiosyncratic, unusual lodging is a stand-alone nonconformist that would be considered garden-variety anywhere else: a simple little B&B. Draconian zoning laws have conspired to make **Lucky You Bed & Breakfast** ✰✰✰ (☎ 702/384-1129; no credit cards; $–$$) the only lodging of its kind in all of Las Vegas. And because of its small size (it has only three rooms for rent) and the charm of its host, it offers something that no other lodging in town can: intimacy, a personal touch, and a peek into the real life of Las Vegas. Well, sorta. Because your host here is none other than Ole, once the personal chef of Liberace, which makes him a minor celebrity; and in his low-key, Austrian way, he's as much of a showman as Mr. Showmanship. You'll see that when entering his antique-jammed ranch house, in which there's nary an inch of wall not covered by an oil painting, or a corner without some rococo bronze or stone statue. Some of the grand art pieces and furniture were a gift from Liberace; Ole will show you around if you ask. Out back is a pool, a hot tub, and a fabulous garden lushly blooming with orchids, other flowers, and lemon and almond trees. The three guest rooms all have ornate beds, TVs, VCRs, and one has a working fireplace. Like his former employer, Ole is gay, and so is most of his clientele, though all are welcome here (you'll need to be tolerant of nudity, though, as guests are free to go au naturel in the pool area). Gourmet breakfasts are included in the rates, which come to $59 for a single, $79 for a double (add $12 to make the room a triple). If you're up for something unusual, terrifically festive, yet homey, this is the place to pick.

$60 and most of the year, you can snag a bed for between $25 and $35 a night. So what's wrong with the place, you may be thinking suspiciously? Well, it's an older casino with afterthought motel units in eight buildings behind the casino (300 rooms total). But really, the rooms here are okay, with new, if industrial carpeting, and pre-fab furnishings (though you might encounter a concave bed here or a scuff mark there). On-site is a swimming pool and five different dining options (all in the casino), plus a lounge with live acts. When it comes down to it, I think the extreme discounting here has more to do with the amount of competition and the bad economy than any serious flaws at Charlie's. **Tip:** Ask for a garden-facing unit to avoid noise from the parking lot/highway.

$–$$$ Let's get this out of the way first: **Terrible's Hotel & Casino** ✰ 🧒 (4100 Paradise Rd., at Flamingo Rd.; ☎ 800/640-9777 or 702/733-7000; www.terrible-herbst.com; AE, DC, MC, V) is not actually terrible. That moniker comes from the nickname of the owner, Ed "Terrible" Herbst who made part of his fortune with a chain of local gas station (and often gives gamblers free gas as an enticement for playing and/or staying). Though its prices are no longer the lowest in town, Terrible's is famous for its innovative discounts, packages, and giveaways which range from free shuttles to and from the airports to six-packs of beer for gamblers during slow periods. My favorite? The packet of coupons the "gambling fairy" leaves under your pillow each night (no need to leave a tooth). Speaking of the pillows, they're nicely stuffed here which reflects the quality of the bed and bedding overall (high). And since a recent renovation you'll find the rooms to be quite conducive to sleep in, as they're quiet, done up in soothing tans and greens, and altogether dignified (a statement which couldn't have been made before they gussied the place up). An on-site pool is open year-round and pared with, glory be!, a wading pool for kids; a medium-sized fitness room (with two treadmills and free weights) is nearby. Best of all, once you've stayed here you can brag to your friends that you stayed in the most "Terrible" hotel in town. **Booking tip:** Never reserve a room here directly. You'll almost always pay less by going through such companies as Travelworm or Hotels.com (p. 25).

$–$$$$ Back to the Boulder Highway and one of my favorite properties in Vegas, **Sam's Town Hotel & Gambling Hall** ★★★ (5111 Boulder Hwy., at Flamingo Rd.; ☎ 800/634-6371 or 702/456-7777; www.samstownlv.com; AE, DC, DISC, MC, V) is a perfect marriage of Strip-like glitz with amenities you normally don't get on that famous boulevard. In the "just as fun as the Strip" category, the centerpiece of the place is a huge atrium designed to look like an old Western town . . . where the town square is actually the Rocky Mountains (or at least a campy version of said mountains). On each side are fake Western buildings, eight stories tall, the windows of which are actually the windows of the guest rooms; in the middle is a Vegasized, mini-national park, with real trees and bushes, and fake little mountains on which animatronic beavers and bears cavort. You'll hear it before you see it, as the sound of rushing water from the small falls here is overpowering . . . but still pleasant. This being Vegas, this little wilderness area erupts into a laser and water show four times a day. Off the atrium are six restaurants, two showrooms, a food court, and a fab buffet (p. 106), as good as most on the Strip but cheaper.

Just as good, but cheaper, also describes the lovely guest rooms, which continue the Old West theme with plaid bedspreads and curtains and lots of wood furniture. These rooms are much comfier than anything they ever had in Dodge City, with soft-to-the-touch carpets, beds you sink into at night, and lots of space, even in the standard rooms. Rates usually run between $38 and $52, up to $108 when the town's gone nuts. There's also an RV park, and a good-sized pool.

So what do you get at Sam's that you may not on the Strip?

♦ A spiffy casino spread across three levels, the top level of which actually gets (gasp!) natural light via a series of skylights. Sounds like a small thing, but it's a really nice change from the usual dark casino. The lounge act here gets talented performers (always a plus).
♦ A child-care center with all kinds of things for the wee ones to clamber on while you gamble away their college fund.
♦ A 56-lane state-of-the-art bowling alley and an 18-screen movie theater.

Not enough to keep you happy? If you're still yearning to get to the Strip, there's a regular, free shuttle back and forth. Can you tell I really like this place?

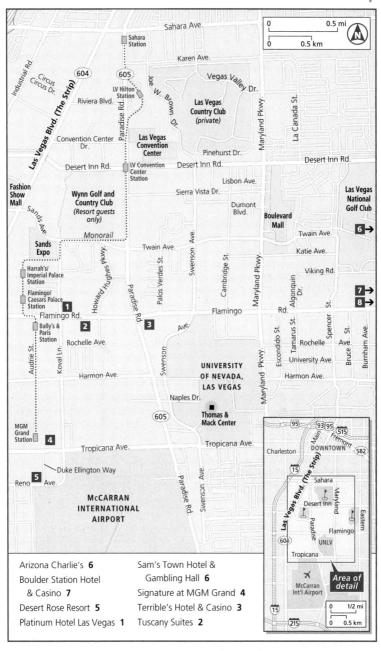

0   0.5 mi
0   0.5 km

Sahara Ave.

Sahara Station

Karen Ave.

Vegas Valley Dr.

604   605

LV Hilton Station

Riviera Blvd.

Las Vegas Country Club (private)

Convention Center Dr.

Paradise Rd.

Las Vegas Convention Center

Pinehurst Dr.

Desert Inn Rd.

Desert Inn Rd.

Desert Inn Rd.

LV Convention Center Station

Lisbon Ave.

Wynn Golf and Country Club (Resort guests only)

Sierra Vista Dr.

Dumont Blvd.

Boulevard Mall

Las Vegas National Golf Club

Fashion Show Mall

Sands Ave.

Monorail

Twain Ave.

Twain Ave.

Katie Ave.

6 →

Sands Expo

Howard Hughes Pkwy.

Swenson Ave.

Palos Verdes St.

Cambridge St.

Maryland Pkwy.

Viking Rd.

Algonquin Dr.

7 →

Harrah's/ Imperial Palace Station

Flamingo/ Caesars Palace Station

1

Flamingo Rd.

Paradise Rd.

Flamingo   Rd.

8 →

Bally's & Paris Station

2

Rochelle Ave.

Audrie St.

Koval Ln.

3

Ave.

Swenson

Escondido St.

Tamarus St.

Spencer   St.

Rochelle   Ave.

Bunham Ave.

University Ave.

Bruce   St.

Harmon Ave.

Harmon Ave.

UNIVERSITY OF NEVADA, LAS VEGAS

Naples Dr.

Maryland Pkwy.

605

Thomas & Mack Center

MGM Grand Station

4

Tropicana Ave.

Tropicana Ave.

Duke Ellington Way

Reno   Ave.

5

McCARRAN INTERNATIONAL AIRPORT

Paradise Rd.

Swenson Ave.

95   93/95   515

Charleston   DOWNTOWN   582

Main

Fremont

15

Sahara

Las Vegas Blvd. (The Strip)

Maryland

Desert Inn

Paradise

Flamingo

Eastern

604   UNLV

Tropicana

McCarran Int'l Airport

Area of detail

15

215

0   1/2 mi
0   0.5 km

Arizona Charlie's **6**	Sam's Town Hotel & Gambling Hall **6**
Boulder Station Hotel & Casino **7**	Signature at MGM Grand **4**
Desert Rose Resort **5**	Terrible's Hotel & Casino **3**
Platinum Hotel Las Vegas **1**	Tuscany Suites **2**

Child-Friendly Hotels

Here's the big quandary for parents: Should you book your family into a Strip resort, knowing you'll have to pay an additional amount for each child, though the resort may have more kid-thrills on-site, such as elaborate pools and game rooms? Or should you choose off-Strip properties, as the kids will be able to stay free—a big issue, especially for larger families, as Strip properties charge between $10 and $20 a night for each extra person over the age of 2? I don't think there's an easy answer, and other factors come into play as well:

- **Will the children have to walk through the casino to get to their hotel rooms?** Adults act in raunchy, sometimes depressing ways in casinos. Do you really want your 8-year-old seeing drunk 60-year-olds, crying and yelling at slot machines; or working girls trolling for customers? In even the fanciest casinos, you'll see these sad scenarios and others playing out.
- **Will the staff make you feel comfortable with junior in tow?** Bellagio and Wynn Las Vegas have made it abundantly clear they don't want little dears about by requiring the presentation of room keys or theater tickets for admission in the former, and banning strollers in the latter. And they aren't the only hotels that extend a less than warm welcome to kids, though others are a bit more subtle with their sneers (never mind the annoyed reception they'll get from other guests).
- **Mile-long hikes:** Maybe my 5-year-old's a wuss, but she really hated all the walking she had to do in the larger casinos. Getting from the car to the restaurant was cause for a meltdown; trudging from the restaurant to the pool brought on the sniffles. Off-Strip properties tend to be smaller, and thus more friendly to little feet.

I have strong opinions on whether you should bring your kids to Vegas at all (which you can read on p. 314), but for those planning to bring 'em, here's a list of reasonably kid-tolerant places:

$–$$$$ Just next door, **Boulder Station Hotel & Casino** ✪ (4111 Boulder Hwy.; ☎ 702/683-7777; www.boulderstation.com; AE, DC, MC, V), a large, bustling casino with an attached smaller hotel of just 300 rooms, isn't quite as bright and shiny, but still pleases. Rooms are generously proportioned, spotlessly maintained, dignified, and because the hotel part of the enterprise is relatively small, service is a bit warmer and more personal than you'll find at many of the large casino resorts. There's the usual complement of restaurants, an 11-screen movie theater, a Kids Quest child-care facility (love those!), a small swimming pool, gift shop, and an impressive live music venue that focuses on country and

Circus Circus: Low prices, free circus acts, nice and roomy rooms, and an on-site amusement park—need I say more? It may not be all that classy, but there's no better place in town for high-energy kids to blow off steam. See p. 41.

MGM Grand: What's outside is the lure here for families, and it's terrific: water slides, lazy rivers, and big swimming pools. See p. 34.

Monte Carlo: Also gives good pool. And if its pools aren't quite as whiz-bang as those at the MGM Grand, it makes up for it in lower room rates, and a layout that allows you to get to your hotel room without having to tramp through the casino. See p. 32.

Sam's Town: Kids will love this place, with its Disney-esque animatronic animals, its bowling alley, nice pool, and movie theater. Good on-site short-term day care and reasonable rates are what's going to get the grown-ups to agree. See p. 54.

South Point: Cowboy and Indian time. Children will enjoy the on-site equestrian arena and wading pool. Day care, large rooms, a movie theater, and bowling alley add to the appeal, despite its distant location. See p. 64.

Any rental home: And because I feel it's important to get my kids away from those demon casinos when we're here, I tend to go the rental home route. With rental homes, you get a kitchen so you don't have to spend too much on restaurant meals (that finicky youngsters end up leaving on their plates). For the price of one hotel room, you can often rent a house with several bedrooms, allowing you to shut your door at day's end for some quiet time with your spouse. And you'll often have private access to all kinds of amusements, such as pool tables, private pools, board games (yup, many rental homes stock 'em), VCRs, DVDs, and even, sometimes, Nintendo systems. See p. 18 for more on why you might want to consider a rental.

blues. Rates here are also reasonable, sliding between $29 and $59 per night most of the year, occasionally ascending into the $159 range on really hot weekends.

$–$$$$ Closer to the Strip, on the stretch of East Las Vegas that's become known as the gourmet corridor for the large number of fine restaurants here, the **Tuscany Suites** ★ (255 E. Flamingo Rd.; ☎ 877/887-2261 or 702/893-8933; www.tuscanylasvegas.com; AE, DC, MC, V) is big among the business travelers who like its proximity to the convention center, its usable business center, elegant lobby, and generous on-site convention space. But you won't feel out of place if you arrive without a laptop; many families stay here as well, drawn to the low-key comfort of this complex of 15 low-rise buildings (none over three stories), which house large rooms that each have that top family amenity: a working kitchen, with a usable fridge and a table and chairs so you don't have to squat on a bed to eat. Many also have foldout couches; ask. I personally like the fact that the knotted wood furniture is just one step shy of chic and the bathrooms are huge. Two pools (a regular and a lap pool), a medium-sized casino in a separate building away from the hotel, and a usable fitness room are also part of the deal. Prices are even more all over the map than usual here; I've seen them range from just $36 all the way up to $160 (and will sometimes swing between $100 and $160 depending on which firm you go to, so do shop around if you decide to stay here). For those disappointed not to be directly on the Strip: It is walkable from here, though it will take a good 10 minutes to reach the back end of Bally's.

$–$$$$ Even better for families and for, really anyone, is **Desert Rose Resort** ✪✪✪ (5051 Duke Ellington Way; ☎ 800/811-2450 or 702/739-7000; www.shell hospitality.com; AE, DC, MC, V) which is, quite truthfully, the only hotel in Vegas that I've ever walked into and thought "hmmm . . . I wouldn't mind living here for a while." Really, I wouldn't even be tempted to redecorate; all the apartments (and you have full apartments here with separate seating areas, kitchens, and balconies) are exquisitely fitted with chichi pillow-laden couches (a pullout for extra guests); a usable dining table plus a counter at the kitchen area with bar stools for more casual dining; plush carpeting and even plusher feeling beds. Rooms are awash in a Southwestern spectrum of colors—rosy ochres, mustard yellows, heathered greens—which really lift the mood as does the large pool, fitness room, and on-site basketball court. Rates start at about $89 a night for a one-bedroom, about $110 a night for a two-bedroom, which I think is fair for a place this shareable; prices include a filling, hot breakfast buffet. Some of the units are now timeshares, so if you're hooked into that world, see if you can trade your way in.

The neighborhood in the direct vicinity of the hotel is in transition, with a new luxury apartment building going up, surrounded by older condos. Though not well lit, it's reasonably safe for those walking back from the Strip at night (though you should still take the precautions you'd take in any large city).

HOTELS WEST OF THE STRIP

How does the area west of the Strip differ from the area east of the Strip? Umm . . . it's on the other side of town? For most visitors there's no significant difference between the two, beyond the fact that you can possibly get away with not having a car if you're staying on the east side of town off the Strip. That's not an option on the west side, thanks to the massive highway that bifurcates the city (yes, you could cross the highway on foot, but it's not a pleasant prospect). Some hotels do offer shuttles, as I've noted, but in reality you'll be better off on the east side without a car.

Other than that, you'll find the same lineup of chain restaurants, strip malls, motels, and gas stations east as you will west. Of the big casinos here, there are the same types of appeal. For hipsters, simply substitute the Palms Hotel for the Hard Rock; for geek chic, look to the Rio (hey, it's got *Chippendales* and a goofy "Mardi Gras in the Sky" parade over the casino, nerd pursuits at their most basic). And as we said before, at many times of year, you'll pay less staying off the Strip than you will on it.

Hotels West of the Strip

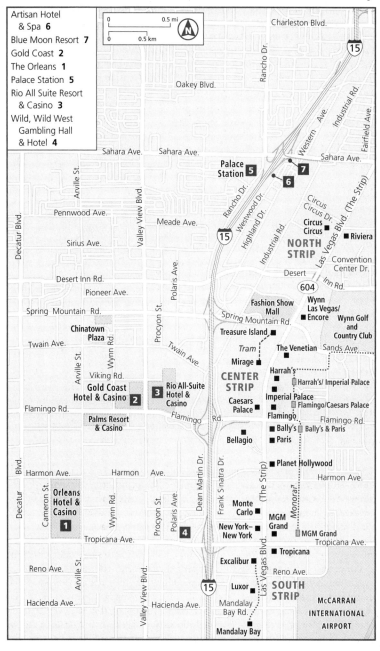

Artisan Hotel
  & Spa **6**
Blue Moon Resort **7**
Gold Coast **2**
The Orleans **1**
Palace Station **5**
Rio All Suite Resort
  & Casino **3**
Wild, Wild West
  Gambling Hall
  & Hotel **4**

0   0.5 mi
0   0.5 km

Charleston Blvd.

Rancho Dr.

Oakey Blvd.

Western Ave.

Industrial Rd.

Fairfield Ave.

Sahara Ave.   Sahara Ave.   Sahara Ave.

Palace
Station **5**

7

6

Arville St.

Valley View Blvd.

Rancho Dr.

Westwood Dr.

Highland Dr.

Industrial Rd.

Circus
Circus Dr.

Las Vegas Blvd. (The Strip)

Decatur Blvd.

Pennwood Ave.

Meade Ave.

Circus
Circus

**NORTH
STRIP**

Riviera

Sirius Ave.

Convention
Center Dr.

Desert Inn Rd.

Polaris Ave.

Desert Inn Rd.

604

Pioneer Ave.

Spring Mountain Rd.

Procyon St.

Spring Mountain Rd.

Fashion Show
Mall

Wynn
Las Vegas/
Encore

Wynn Golf
and
Country Club

Chinatown
Plaza

Treasure Island

Twain Ave.

Wynn Rd.

Twain Ave.

Tram

The Venetian   Sands Ave.

Arville St.

Viking Rd.

Mirage

Gold Coast
Hotel & Casino **2**

Rio All-Suite
3 Hotel &
Casino

**CENTER
STRIP**

Harrah's

Harrah's/ Imperial Palace

Flamingo Rd.

Flamingo   Rd.

Caesars
Palace

Imperial Palace

Flamingo/Caesars Palace

Palms Resort
& Casino

Flamingo

Flamingo Rd.

Bally's   Bally's & Paris

Bellagio

Paris

Decatur   Blvd.

Harmon Ave.

Cameron St.

Harmon   Ave.

Wynn Rd.

Dean Martin Dr.

Frank S.natra Dr.

Procyon St.

Polaris Ave.

(The Strip)

Planet Hollywood

Harmon Ave.

Monorail

Orleans
Hotel &
Casino
1

4

Monte
Carlo

New York–
New York

MGM
Grand

MGM Grand

Tropicana Ave.

Tropicana Ave.

Tropicana

Reno Ave.

Arville St.

Valley View Blvd.

Excalibur

Las Vegas Blvd.

Reno Ave.

15

Luxor

**SOUTH
STRIP**

Hacienda Ave.

Hacienda Ave.

Mandalay
Bay Rd.

McCARRAN
INTERNATIONAL
AIRPORT

Mandalay Bay

15

59

$–$$ In fact at any time of year, you're going to save by choosing the **Wild, Wild West Gambling Hall & Hotel** (3330 W. Tropicana Ave.; ☎ 702/740-0000; http://wwwesthotelcasino.com; AE, DC, MC, V). Rate-wise it's the brethren of Arizona Charlie's and El Cortez in that it consistently offers the lowest nightly prices in town. I'll admit, though, that it has tested my travel writing code of ethics. Taking a look at the windswept, 15-acre big rig–filled parking lot in which the hotel is marooned, I had the urge to pass it by without a look. But my vow to let no hotel bed go untested won out, and I'm glad I accepted the challenge. The semis were the first clue: This is a major truck stop hotel, meaning that the rooms are going to not only be cheap, but reasonably clean—truckers don't return to places that aren't decent. Which they are, looking like slightly downscale versions (smaller rooms but with framed prints on the walls, colorful carpets, and good mattresses) of the cushier Station Casinos properties, which isn't surprising as they share the same owner. A postage stamp–sized pool sits in the center of one of the unit blocks. And don't believe the maps—though it may look it, this place is NOT walkable to the Strip. Bottom line: When prices all over town have reached unreasonable levels, this is a reasonable alternative. Otherwise, stay somewhere else (extreme budgeters should pick El Cortez or Terrible's first) as the casino here is depressing and it really is out of the way. I include the Wild, Wild West as another arrow in your quiver of options.

$–$$ My next two recommendations are more than mere options, they're actually darn good choices, part of the Boyd Gaming family of resorts, which means that you can depend on the quality of the offerings here. My theory: Because Boyd is coming up in the world and doesn't yet have the name recognition of say, Harrah's or MGM MIRAGE, it's at the stage where it just tries harder. That may be why there are flatscreen TVs in all of the 1,800-plus rooms at **The Orleans** ★ 🎯 (500 W. Tropicana Ave.; ☎ 800/ORLEANS or 702/365-7111; www.orleans casino.com; AE, DC, MC, V), its massive "French Quarter"–themed casino. Or why each of the rooms is blessed with a back-coddling mattress, designed exclusively for Boyd by Serta, and they enhance their quality by making up the bed with three sheets, which give them a cushioned feel. Rooms vary in decor from those that have out and out N'Awlins looks with brass beds, fleur-de-lis coverlets, and marble-topped tables; to more standard looking, smaller modern rooms (guess which are pricier? You'll usually pay about $20 more for NOLA theming). Other niceties here include the spaciousness of the casino, its high ceiling, bright lighting, and bouncy zydeco and Cajun music soundtrack making it a place where you actually don't mind losing money (well . . . you'll probably still mind, but at least you won't feel like the walls are caving in on you at the same time your finances are). Six unpretentious restaurants, a video arcade, and a day-care center for kids make it a fine choice for families. Entertainment comes in the form of a large jellyfish-shaped heated pool, a massive bowling alley, a movie theater, and an arena where hockey matches, concerts, and monster truck–type shows take place. Massages, manicures, and more are available at the polished spa. To escape it all— and the location is not great, as there's literally nothing within walking distance except a large strip club—there's a free shuttle that makes a loop from here to the Gold Coast Hotel and Bill's Gamblin' Hall right on the Strip.

$-$$$ Speaking of the **Gold Coast** ✪ (4000 W. Flamingo Rd.; ☎ 800/331-5334 or 702/367-7111; www.goldcoastcasino.com; AE, DC, MC, V), that's Boyd's other eastern property. It only joined the Boyd group in 2005 so it's not quite as plush as the Orleans in terms of amenities (the pool and fitness room are smaller). Still, you can see why Boyd bought it. The central room of the casino features a high, stained glass ceiling that's quite attractive. The staff are delightful, genuinely friendly, and caring. And the rooms are quite large, with unusually thick walls, meaning that you're less likely to hear your neighbor here than in other hotels. Recently Boyd renovated them all, giving them a downright groovy look as hip as anything on the Strip with large and darn cool abstract photos on the walls, cut glass square mirrors, those same customized Serta beds *(ahhh!),* and a vibe that's as hip as anything on the Strip. Its location, next to the Palms, is also a plus for those who like to casino hop (guests also have more shuttle options as they can hitch a ride on the Palms shuttle from Bally's as well as the one that goes direct to the Gold Coast from Bill's Gamblin' Hall on the Strip). In terms of its demo-graphics, the Gold Coast could be nicknamed the "Golden Age," as it seems to attract the oldest crowd in Vegas (the median age looked to be about 70 when I was last here). I'd guess that they're drawn here by the Big Band and Dixieland jazz groups who play here live daily from 1 to 6:30pm in the free lounge; the new look of the rooms may start attracting younger clientele as well. Bingo is a big attraction here, along with bowling.

At both the Gold Coast and the Orleans, expect to pay between $25 and $60 midweek (depending on season), up to $129 if the town is full. But as a staffer told me "Our rates are more likely to be low and stay low, rather than just dip-ping low a few times a year." Truly, these two hotels are among the best deals in town, despite their isolated locales.

$-$$$ If you're retired and coming to town with your Bingo buddies, **Palace Station** (2411 W. Sahara Ave.; ☎ 800/634-3101; www.palacestation.com; AE, DC, MC, V) is not a bad choice, about a 10-minute drive from the northern end of the Strip. A shuttle for both the Strip (with stops at Fashion Show Mall, Tropicana, and Excalibur) and the airport leaves every hour throughout the day. Like the Gold Coast, it tends to attract an older crowd, though younger people won't feel out of place here, especially if they're on a budget. A staffer whispered in my ear that a certain number of rooms are always set aside to sell at $29 a night, a fact I haven't been able to confirm. Still, you'll often be able to get the rooms for a reliably rea-sonable amount, usually between $29 and $59 midweek, up to $120 on weekends (but often less than that). In the new tower, rooms come with Ethan Allen–type furniture, brass lamps, and fancy wooden headboards. Medium-sized, they feel a bit cramped with two queens in them so if you can, go for a king-bedded room. The lowest prices are usually to be had in the motor lodge section of the property, which is a good 20 years older than the tower, with even smaller rooms and only stall showers (no tubs). Still it's comfortable in a Motel 6 kind of way. Two small-ish pools and a functional fitness room are also available for guest use.

The casino itself has a cute turn-of-the-20th-century railroad theme, with actual historic cars out front. It's not as cutting edge as some of the other Station Casinos (such as Sunset Station, Green Valley Ranch, and Texas station), but I don't recommend those as they're even farther from the Strip—a good half-hour as opposed to 10 minutes. Lots of video poker and an impressive range of talent in the lounge make this a local's favorite, so if you're hoping to meet some of the folks who actually live in town, this is a good place to bunk.

$$–$$$$ Love it or hate it, it's impossible to feel neutral about the **Artisan Hotel & Spa** ✫✫ (1501 W. Sahara Ave.; ☎ 800/544-7092 or 702/214-4000; www.the artisanhotel.com; AE, DC, MC, V), which to my mind wins the prize for most genuinely creative, artistic, and just plain funky hotel in Vegas. You'll know as soon as you enter its romantic cave of a lobby, in which flickering candles are the main source of light, that this place is different. And it's startlingly beautiful, with every inch of wall space, and ceiling space for that matter, covered with reproduced art works of the world's great masters—Rembrandt, Picasso, Rivera, Manet—displayed in ornate, gilded frames. The air is dense with flamenco guitar music (or throbbing house music—what's playing will depend on the time of day), a grand Belle Epoque fountain (all lightly draped maidens on swirling rocks) bubbles in one corner, and throughout the room overstuffed sofas and chairs of velvet, leather, or French Empire–styling crouch, await the lounging hipsters who crowd the space, and its popular bar/restaurant come evening.

This infatuation with great art is carried into the guest rooms, each of which is devoted to a different artist—Frida Kahlo, Klimt, Sargent, or more obscure choices such as Kazimir or Malevich—and covered with their works exclusively. Now, all of this art has a practical purpose, too—it's meant to conceal the fact that this is a converted Econolodge, so the 64 rooms here are fairly small and the exterior is nothing to crow about. But despite their size, guest rooms are chicly appointed, the beds covered in duvets, throws, and decorative pillow. As in the lobby, the walls are colored a chocolate brown or deep purple and the lighting is dim, for a womblike . . . or dank cave effect . . . depending on your point of view. Bathrooms are tiled all in black and are among the smallest in the city. There's also a teeny tiny workout room; and a reasonably spacious pool out back, around which large, white mattresses are placed for sunbathing or perhaps boogying, as the soundtrack in the lobby is blasted into this groovy pool area as well.

All sounds good, right? Well, to my mind it is, but there are a lot of things here that many travelers will hate. First off, all that great art means a lot of frontal nudity and in some cases, racy subject matter, so this ain't the place to take your kids (or your Born Again cousin for that matter). As I keep repeating, everything is dark here, which some find relaxing, but if you want to read a newspaper or apply mascara . . . fuggedabout it—those simple tasks are near impossible. Some of the elements in the rooms were not up to date when I last visited, like the older TVs and the free Wi-Fi, which seems to flicker in and out. And the location isn't the greatest, across from a power station and a strip club. The freeway also zooms right by here, so make sure you request a room on the other side of the building if you're a light sleeper. In spite of the name, there was no spa when I most recently visited (apparently, that's in the works). Most annoying are the extra charges: Tacked on to each bill is a $3.50 power surcharge (what, the massive power station next door won't cut them a deal?); and this is one of the only places in Vegas that charges guests extra for parking ($12), which is valet only, so you'll also have to tip. Before you shell out the $99 to $130 that it generally seems to cost here (up to $170 at times), factor in these expenses. The resort also offers an all-inclusive meal plan, the only one in Vegas; but that seems like an odd entice-ment in a town with many great restaurants (binge drinkers might find it appeal-ing as unlimited beverages are included; see the website for pricing).

Booking tip: Don't book with the hotel directly; you'll usually get better rates with Hotels.com or such opaque agencies as Priceline.com and Hotwire.com.

$$–$$$$ If you're a gay man, and you want to stay in a not just gay-friendly, but gay-welcoming hotel, you have, surprisingly for a city this size, only one real choice: The party-happy **Blue Moon Resort** (2651 Westwood Dr.; ☎ 702/361-9099; www.bluemoonlv.com; AE, DC, MC, V). Because it's the only one of its kind in town, prices are higher than they should be for digs that are, to be blunt, not the most luxurious (chipped furniture, scuffed walls, too-soft beds). Expect to pay $119 a night most of the year, with prices occasionally dipping to $79 and soaring to $139 for standard rooms. Negatives aside, the Blue Moon has one of the most gracious staffs in town, a large pool area with a waterfall, and a club-house feel that's fun and warm. There are weekly BBQs, periodic parties, and all sorts of other social occasions, making it a good choice for solo travelers. And though the majority of the guests will be gay, it's straight-friendly, too, though everyone should be comfortable in their own skin (and nothing else), as the pool is clothing-optional, and what goes on around the pool . . . well, it's a partying scene. Also on-site is a small snack bar and fitness room. One note: The hotel is very hard to find, tucked into the middle of a faceless, confusingly laid out indus-trial neighborhood, so ask for exact directions when you book.

$$-$$$$ The **Rio All Suite Hotel and Casino** ✮✮ (3700 W. Flamingo Rd.; ☎ 866/756-7671; www.riolasvegas.com; AE, DC, MC, V) often gets overshadowed by the too-cool-for-school Palms nearby but I think it has a kind of Austin Powers–like charm—bucktoothed and goofy—particularly in its entertainment offerings. Along with *Chippendales* (p. 194) and Penn & Teller (p. 188) there's a several-times-weekly free floor show, complete with showgirl-bearing "floats" that move on a track above the casino floor (see p. 119); and smaller stages where, with startling randomness, cocktail servers hop up and go-go dance or belt out a tune. Yeah, it's kind of weird, but it certainly adds character.

Rooms have no such surprises but, perhaps in keeping with the hotel's theme, seem as big as Brazil itself. Really, even the cheapest rooms here are huge, I'm talk-ing twice as big as others in Vegas (with massive bathrooms as well), so if you make a lot of buddies down in the casino, you could conceivably spread out five or six sleeping bags for them on the floor with no one feeling all too crowded. Their size is accentuated by floor to ceiling windows (ask for a Strip-view room). Other luxe touches: duvets, free fridges (empty, hooray!), dataports, and lots of nice bathroom products.

I wish I could be specific on pricing, but for Rio suites I've seen rates run any-where from $60 to $230 a night. Despite this price uncertainty, there are smart rea-sons to pick the Rio for your stay, including an appealing choice of restaurants (highlighted by BBQ mecca RUB, see p. 110), a well-equipped gym, and the fun in its "backyard" which includes a highly rated golf course and several pools (includ-ing one with a sandy beach that hosts an infamous party, see p. 207). Up top of the Rio tower is a throbbing dance club called Voodoo with swell Strip views.

SOUTH OF THE STRIP

Keep going south from the Mandalay Bay and you'll encounter the following two top value lodgings, along with a lot of mall shopping opportunities and a burgeoning area of new condos and gated communities.

$$–$$$ The **South Point Hotel & Casino** ✦ (9777 Las Vegas Blvd. S.; ☎ 866/796-7111 or 702/796-7111; www.southcoastcasino.com; AE, DC, MC, V) was supposed to be the gambling den for this newish community, but it's been underperforming so severely that it was sold by Boyd Gaming back to Michael Gaughan, the original developer, in 2007. What's bad for the casino is good for the consumer, of course, as that means that you'll have plenty of table space and slot machine time in this massive casino, as well as less of a wait to get into the restaurants here than on the Strip. The other targeted audience for the South Point is cowboys, and they're quite a presence, lounging in front of the slot machines, their deep tans the same shade as their cowboy hats. They're not just here to gamble, but to attend and appear in shows in the South Point's 4,400-seat state-of-the-art Equestrian Center, one of the finest of its kind in the nation, and the only one anywhere attached to a hotel. The horses get their hay in one of 120 climate-controlled stalls located in the back of the property. Just so their riders don't get jealous, the hotel rooms are individually climate-controlled, too, and unusually large, with a lot of deluxe accouterments such as 42-inch plasma TVs, custom-made mattresses, free Wi-Fi, and big bathrooms with good soaking tubs (perfect after hours in the saddle . . . or at the slot machines, for that matter). I'd say the third group this hotel will appeal to is families, for its good-sized squiggly pool and wading pool (a rarity in Vegas), its 64-lane bowling alley, 16-screen movie theater, volleyball court, and day-care center. As I write this, standard rates are toggling between $30 and $70 a night (and every once in a while go up to $120).

Cowboys, or really the state of Texas, are the inspiration for the **Silverton** ✦✦ (3333 Blue Diamond Rd; ☎ 866/946-8373 or 702/263-7777; www.silverton casino.com), probably because President Craig Cavalier is from the Lone Star State and he's been quite "hands on" in shaping its look. It was he who chose the paisley leather headboards, the massive Western art pieces on the walls of the bedrooms (cows, lots of cows), the wide-boarded rough-hewn side tables, the lamps shaped like metal logs, and the fact that each guest room gets a copy of *Cowboys and Indians* magazine. (Rooms come in different configurations, so they won't each have those elements, but they all have an ambience that literally yodels *"yee haw!"*). Cavalier also took care of the physical "feel" of the place. After staying one night at the Bellagio he was so impressed by the quality of the mattresses he bought the same exact brand for the Silverton!

Hotels are much more than just their guest rooms, of course, and the Silverton is blessed with some quirky attractions. Most famous are the "mermaids" who swim most days in the massive tank at the front of the lobby; one is a former Olympic medalist (in synchronized swimming). At feeding time (for the fish not the mermaids!), a scuba divers enters the tank with food while a hotel staffer talks about the various small sharks, clownfish, and rays in the tank and answers questions. One of the casino's six restaurants, the Mermaid Bar and Grill, overlooks all the fishy action. The second biggest draw, believe it or not, is the massive Bass Pro Shop, one of the largest in the country and as interactive, in some areas, as an arcade (yup they let you try the equipment). My personal go-to area of the casino is the bar with the Airstream trailer; inside it, believe it or not: duckpin bowling! (no joke; there are often lines to play a game). When I last visited, the powers-that-be were busy expanding the casino and adding a showroom for touring acts. They should both be operational by the time you pick up this book.

Nightly rates have recently dipped to just $39 a night though their previous norm had been $67 and they can pop to $159 at busy times; best rates live on the "hot deals" page of the Silverton website. Those prices include the use of a free shuttle bus (11am–10:25 pm) to and from the airport and Strip.

4 Eating Better for Less

A new Vegas emphasis on meals as a profit center calls for smart tactics on your part

DON'T BELIEVE THE HYPE WHEN IT COMES TO LAS VEGAS CUISINE. SURE, chefs here are treated like rock stars, and you'll see their toque-topped faces smiling at you from billboards around town. And yes, these are the same fellows—Bobby Flay, Emeril Lagasse, Wolfgang Puck, Bradley Ogden, and others—who spend their downtime whipping up soufflés on the Food Network. But that doesn't mean you're missing out because you can't stomach paying more for meals than the cost of your airfare. Frankly, these glamorous, celebrity-driven offshoot restaurants just aren't as good as they are in the cities in which they originated. I personally don't think they're worth the nausea-inducing checks, and I'm no lonely curmudgeon in holding that view. Mark Bittman, the PBS food critic and author of *How to Cook Everything* (Wiley Publishing, Inc.), wrote in the *New York Times:* "After sampling the cooking at the satellite restaurants of the world's greatest chefs . . . after seeing prices triple (there was a time we considered a $30 dish extravagant), after trying to learn where the greatness had gone, I must report that we've lost something. Betting on name-brand restaurants with absentee chefs is often a gamble that doesn't pay off."

I'm not saying you'll never have a great meal at one of these brand name "temples of gastronomy," but I've found places where you'll pay half as much, and have a meal that's often just as tasty (albeit without the parade of waiters, dress code, and free extra pastries at the end of the meal).

Ironically, we can thank the celebrity chefs for improving the cuisine throughout Vegas—not only for raising the bar, but for bringing into town higher quality ingredients. I've heard from smaller restaurateurs that they're able to get better prices on produce, fish, and fine meats by hopping on the coattails of the superstar chefs and negotiating for a small portion of the load that's coming into town anyway.

And as in many cities, diners' own standards have gotten higher, their palates more complex. This has led to a flowering of "ethnic" restaurants both on and off the Strip, and at all price levels. Sushi and tacos are now de rigueur on most buffet lines in town; a generation ago, the fare would have been strictly roasts, mashed potatoes, fried chicken, and other "all-American" classics. And if you've got a hankering for Vietnamese, Malaysian, Cuban, Hawaiian, Persian, or Indian food, you've come to the right place.

66

SO HOW CAN DINERS SAVE MONEY & STILL HAVE A QUALITY MEAL?

By reading this book, first of all. In the chapter that follows, I list dozens of restaurants that offer entrees for $20 or less—usually considerably less. Beyond being moderately priced or cheap, these places are often chic, friendly, inventive, and sometimes all of the above. There's not a clunker on the list, I promise!

Beyond that, here are my tips for eating for less in what is becoming an increasingly pricey city:

Want to splurge? Do it at lunch: Okay, so your best buddy at home had a lovely meal at Mon Ami Gabi and has ordered you to do the same. Go instead for lunch and you'll find that entrees are a third less expensive. That's just one example. In fact, many restaurants use the same menus as they do at dinner . . . and simply shave 25% to 50% off the cost of the items. It's a great way to figure out which of the "big boys" is really worth shelling out for, should you decide to do a blowout night on the town. *One note:* If you read other guidebooks, they'll tell you to make an early dinner out of late lunch seatings at buffets and restaurants around town. This is a tip whose time has passed, unfortunately, as the powers-that-be have gotten wise to this strategy and are now moving the start of dinner earlier and earlier (at the Paris's Le Village buffet it now starts at 3:30 in the afternoon!).

Have a Strip picnic: Yes, the temperatures can get downright hellish come summer and it can get pretty chilly in December and January, but the rest of the year, the weather's, well, a picnic. So don't feel like you have to have a sit-down meal, or even a stand-up-and-graze buffet for every meal. Instead, grab some food on the run, a sandwich perhaps from 'wichcraft (p. 69) or Capriotti's (p. 89), or a sausage from Jody Maroni's (p. 70), and stroll with it down the Strip. Or if you need to sit, plop down in a keno lounge. The play's slow enough that you could sit there for about an hour for just a buck or two's worth of play.

If you're gambling, make sure someone knows it: If you lose enough of your money or time, you may just qualify for a free trip to the buffet. So do sign up for the players and slots clubs at the casinos you plan on frequenting, and let the pit bosses know how happy you are to be losing your money to them. You're most likely to get fed off the Strip, though it's been known to happen even in such posh casinos as Caesars Palace, The Venetian, or Wynn Las Vegas. A lot depends on your stamina, how busy the casino is, how generous the pit boss is feeling, and sometimes the cycles of the moon . . . you just never know. And if you're going to be gambling anyway, you may as well try to gamble for grub.

Follow Mom's advice and eat a big breakfast: In terms of bang for your buck, there are few better investments than breakfast in Vegas. Breakfast will usually cost half of what lunch does, and a third of what you'll pay for dinner, and the portions in Vegas are massive (see p. 72 for more on that). So eat up, skip lunch, and use what you've saved for a splurge dinner.

Shhhhhh . . . Half-Price Meals, On the Strip and Off

Here's the latest in restaurant discounting: cut-price meals, at some of the city's top eateries, being sold at the same booths that peddle theater tickets, **Tix 4 Tonight.** Either stop by the booth, or call ☎ 800/269-8499, request a reservation from their list of partner restaurants, and when you get your bill at the end of the evening, you'll have saved either 50% or 33% off the cost of entrees or 35% off the entire bill, including drinks (the type of discount varies by restaurant). If you make your reservation by phone, you still have to go to the booth to pick up a coupon that you then present to your waiter when you order. Occasionally, it's difficult to get the reservation time you want, but usually the process is hassle-free. Booths can be found at the following locations:

* In the Fashion Show Mall (across from the Wynn)
* In the Hawaiian Marketplace (near Harmon St.)
* Just South of the Riviera Hotel (across from Circus Circus)
* In Bill's Casino (at the corner of Flamingo Blvd.)
* In the Showcase Mall (at the base of the giant Coca-Cola bottle)
* In The Four Queens Casino (downtown, on Fremont St.)

If you prefer hooting with the owls, have dinner at 1am: While "graveyard specials" are not as prevalent as they used to be on the Strip, some of the downtown and off-Strip eateries slash prices dramatically in the wee hours of the morning. Go to the Riviera's coffee shop and you can score steak, ham, and eggs for just $6. At the Triple Seven in Main Street Station, the cost of one of their famed microbrews drops to just $1. And at the Hard Rock, $7.75 will net you a steak, three pieces of shrimp, a baked potato, and veggies if you know to ask for it (it isn't on the menu).

Go "ethnic": Every major casino on the Strip has a Mexican restaurant, and its menu is about half as pricey as the restaurants that surround it. The same can be said for the Asian noodle places that have wiggled into many of the Strip casinos. Off Las Vegas Boulevard, most of the better restaurants are owned and run by immigrants, who bring all of their skills, exotic spices, and outsized ambitions to make it in America. So you're not only getting a great meal, you're helping someone's "American Dream" come true. (Sounds hokey, I know, but it's true.)

Clip coupons: You know all those free magazines that you'll find in your hotel room? Take a quick look through 'em. Don't read the reviews—they'll be uniformly glowing, as the restaurant has paid for them to appear. Instead, troll for discount coupons. And you know those sad looking folks handing out coupons on the street—no, not the "card clickers" who will send a girl up to your hotel room; check out the *other* bored looking people. They often have some valuable coupons—$2 off this buffet, or a free dessert helping, half-price shows . . . you just never know. Collect them and use them, as they all add up.

And about those magazines (and newspapers): They often alert you to where the meal deals are. Particularly handy are the Friday papers and *Las Vegas Magazine* for word of discounted eats. Also, keep an eye out as you're strolling or driving through town for the marquees outside of casinos and restaurants advertising cheap meals. They're still out there, though you may have to hunt 'em down.

Abandon the Strip, all ye who dine there: Seriously, one of the best ways to eat more and spend less (hmm . . . that's a mighty familiar sounding phrase) is to take your meals off Las Vegas Boulevard . . . or at least off the section that begins at the Stratosphere and ends at Mandalay Bay. And believe you me, you don't suffer by doing this. If you look through this chapter, you'll find that most of the restaurants to which I've awarded three stars are not feeding tourists on the Strip. They're held accountable by the local audiences they serve, and keep up their high standards because they must rely on repeat business (unlike the Strip, where most of the traffic is transient). So when you dine at Lotus of Siam (p. 100), or Lindo Michoacan (p. 100), you're eating in a much-loved place, one that requires advance reservations (or a wait for dinner) because it is to these eateries—and others—that residents go to celebrate wedding anniversaries, birthdays, and all of those other important life events. I think you'll feel special, too, when you're dining at these places, having discovered a side of Las Vegas that very few visitors take the time to seek out. Did I mention they're also a good 30% cheaper on average? 'Nuf said.

Our pricing symbols for meals:

$: $8 and under
$$: $9–$14
$$$: $15–$19
$$$$: $20 and up

SOUTH STRIP RESTAURANTS

From lunch-only joints to some of the snootiest and most outrageously overpriced meals in Vegas, dining on the South Strip offers a wide range of options for the hungry vacationer.

$–$$ One of the best places to grab a quick lunch in this area is **'wichcraft** ★★ (at the MGM Grand; ☎ 877/880-0880; www.mgmgrand.com; Sun–Thurs 10am–6pm, Fri–Sat 10am–8pm; AE, DISC, MC, V), an upscale sandwich shop from celebrity chef Tom Colicchio, where that knotty problem of how to keep food between wedges of bread from tasting dry has happily been solved. Colicchio does it by using artisan, solid, sometimes nutty bread, and layering sandwiches with such soft, moist spreads as goat cheese, soft-cooked eggs, and pesto. In the middle are a range of meats and vegetables, from corned beef and meatloaf to marinated white anchovies or black trumpet mushrooms and white truffle fondue. My favorite is the falling-apart-tender slow-roasted pork smothered in red cabbage with jalapeño and mustard ($9), but all of the 'wiches are good, especially considering that a meal here will only cost between $6 and $9 tops. Note to carb-phobes: If you ask, they'll take the sandwich ingredients and sprinkle them over mixed greens at no extra cost. There's pleasant seating, though no table service, so you may just want to take your 'wich and head out to the fab pools out back—if you have a room key to pass the guards (or a convincing enough story on why you're lacking a key).

$ Cheap, quickie meals are available across Las Vegas Boulevard in the New York–New York food court (set along the Disneyfied back alleys of "Greenwich Village"). Along with mediocre deli food, ribs, and Chinese are two better-than-decent fast-food joints: **Jody Maroni's Sausage Kingdom** ✪✪ (in New York–New York; ☎ 702/740-6969; www.jodymaroni.com; Sun–Thurs 11am–8pm, Fri–Sat 11am–10pm; AE, DC, MC, V) and **Fulton Fish Fry** (in New York–New York; ☎ 702/740-6969; Sun–Thurs 11am–8pm, Fri–Sat 11am–10pm; AE, DC, MC, V). Maroni's is part of a growing chain of "haute dog" stands, founded on Venice Beach in Los Angeles, which can now be found in stadiums, department stores, and convention centers across the U.S. Learning the trade from his dad, Max the Butcher, Maroni took the family recipe and hippied it up (hey, he was selling 'em on Venice Beach) by keeping the chunks of meat large—no "mystery meat" here—and pairing them with such unusual ingredients as cilantro, tangerine, figs, corn, and apples. Diners can now try six sausages on an average day, which will range from the traditional (hot dogs for $3; Italian sausage, polish sausage, bratwurst, and the like for $4.90) to audacious combinations such as tequila chicken; orange-garlic-cumin, apple-maple pork; and Venetian chicken with sun-dried tomatoes and basil. One is more than enough for a meal, as it comes bedded on a soft, fresh onion roll, and can be topped with onions and peppers on request.

Fulton's fish would seem more at home in Kent, U.K., than in "New York," but never mind. Serving up fried fish and chips (french fries, for the uninitiated) for $7.50, it does a good job of keeping it all pretty light and non-greasy. It's not up to the standards of Maroni's, but still a good option for those who don't eat meat.

$ There are only two reasons to go into the Hawaiian Marketplace, a lame Aloha-themed outdoor mall that seems to specialize in plastic knickknacks from China. First is to score discounts at the Tix 4 Tonight booth (see p. 68) and the second is to score a cheap, exotic lunch at **Kapit Bahay** (in the Hawaiian Marketplace, 3745 S. Las Vegas Blvd., suite 117B; ☎ 877/KAPIT-BAHAY or 702/838-1888; daily 8am–8:30pm; AE, DC, MC, V) a West Coast Filipino fast-food franchise. Sure, it's a steam-table place, but it's clean (they post their inspection certificate to prove that), really affordable (one-dish lunches with rice are $4.95, with two dishes for $6.95), and makes for a solid introduction to this unusual cuisine. I'm partial to the *Binagoam,* pork with shrimp paste (it's a frightening shade of pink but quite tasty) and the nicely tart mackerel with vinegar and ginger sauce but it's hard to go too wrong, unless you don't like spicy food (ask about the level of heat before you order). No table service, though there are places to sit here after you get your food from the counter.

$–$$$ For visitors seeking a cheap date place, though one that's not too obviously cheap—if you take him or her to Denny's, you'll likely be leaving alone—I'd recommend **Ocean's 1** ✪ (in the Miracle Mile Shops, in Planet Hollywood Resort & Casino; ☎ 702/696-9080; www.palmgrille.com; daily 9am–11pm; AE, DISC, MC, V), formerly known as Max's Café and set in the Miracle Mile Mall. A

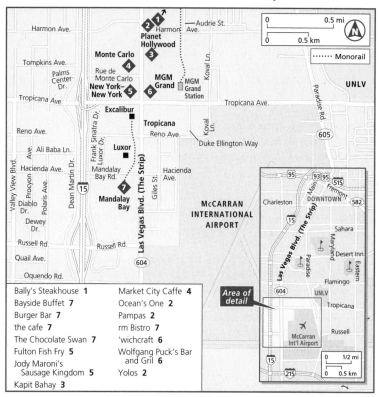

Bally's Steakhouse **1**	Market City Caffe **4**
Bayside Buffet **7**	Ocean's One **2**
Burger Bar **7**	Pampas **2**
the cafe **7**	rm Bistro **7**
The Chocolate Swan **7**	'wichcraft **6**
Fulton Fish Fry **5**	Wolfgang Puck's Bar
Jody Maroni's	and Gril **6**
Sausage Kingdom **5**	Yolos **2**
Kapit Bahay **3**	

classy-looking joint, all dark woods, white tablecloths, and chic oversized hanging lampshades, it features bargain basement pricing for darn good eats. At lunch, entrees start at just $5 and you'll have five nice ones to choose from at that price. You can get away with a $7 entree at dinner with the fancy main dishes topping out at just $20. Oversized salads are the specialty here, and they're super-fresh though not always diet friendly (the $7 goat cheese salad comes with a burger-sized chunk o' cheese). Along with the salads are appetizers, pasta dishes ($11–$13 at dinner), grilled items, and pizza. Other considerations for romance: If you run out of things to talk about, you can always turn your attention to the hourly rain "show" that takes place right outside the cafe, in full view of the patio tables.

$–$$$$ On my last visit to **the cafe** ✪✪ (at THEhotel at Mandalay Bay, 3950 S. Las Vegas Blvd.; ☎ 702/632-7777; www.mandalaybay.com; 7am–3pm Sun & Thurs, 7am–11pm Fri & Sat; AE, DC, MC, V) I brought along a group of gal pals from Los Angeles who liked it so much they deemed it "very LA." And so it is, a swank space with soaring ceilings, cushy velour upholstered chairs and booths, black parquet floors, and a higher than usual quotient of guys in suits and ties. In short, it's a much more dignified, handsome space than hotels usually reserve for their less-formal, coffee shop restaurants. Make no mistake, however, this is a coffee shop

Breakfast Bonanzas

Eggs and steam tables are a recipe for indigestion and paying $25 or more for a nip of champagne with your breakfast (as you will at many buffet brunches) is one of the greatest scams Vegas has devised . . . and that's saying a lot. Skip the buffets and go to restaurants that specialize in morning meals.

Omelet House ✸✸ (2160 W. Charleston Blvd.; ☎ 702/384-6868; daily 7am–3pm; AE, DISC, MC, V; $) has been slinging corned beef hash since 1978, and cooks here have devised 37 ways to cook eggs. They range from the standard cheese, onions, sausage, and the like, to the wacky (a "cowboy" omelet stuffed with chili; the roast beef filled "Bugsy Siegel," appropriately topped with a bloody-looking red sauce) to the sublime (artichoke, sausage, mushrooms, and hollandaise sauce). Omelets average $8.20, but request a petite, as this will shave 75¢ off the cost, and they're made with what looks like four eggs rather than a whopping seven-or-so. Eggs come sided with thickly cut, home-made potato chips (a worthy substitute for hash browns) and a huge warm slab of either banana nut bread or pumpkin bread. For those with smaller appetites, there are short pancake stacks for $4.30, and plates with two eggs and sides from $5.

Being from New York, I know that sometimes the right breakfast is a basic bagel, gussied up with a schmear of cream cheese. The closest to a New York bagel you're going to find in the middle of the desert is at **Einstein Bros. Bagels** (at the University Gardens Shopping Center, 4626 Maryland Pkwy., between Harmon and Tropicana aves.; ☎ 702/795-7800; www. einsteinbros.com; Mon–Fri 6am–6pm, Sat 6am–4pm, Sun 6:30am–4pm; MC, V; $), a national bagel chain with surprisingly decent offerings (and that's high praise for bagels from a picky New Yorker). While I always go for the classic poppy with plain cream cheese, the 18 varieties of bagels (with such uncommon choices as chocolate chip, cranberry, and jalapeño) and 11 flavored cream cheeses mean you can start your day with a burst of creative shopping. There are also eggs available, but there's a reason the place is named for its bagels, and I'd stick to them when coming here.

"Extreme breakfasts" are the lure at the California off-shoot **Hash House a Go Go** ✸✸✸ 🍳 (6800 W. Sahara Ave.; ☎ 702/804-4646; www.hash houseagogo.com; daily 7:30am–10pm; AE, DISC, MC, V; $–$$). It serves breakfasts so large they'd make a trucker faint: pancakes the circumference of large pizzas, hash and eggs served in foot-wide skillets, and platters of special Benedict eggs the length of my arm. This isn't just stunt cooking; breakfasts here are the most complex, interesting, and rich that I've had anywhere. Try the HH Original ($12) and you'll get a platter of scrumptious griddled mashed potatoes layered with red pepper cream, sweet yellow tomatoes, poached eggs, and bacon. (It looks like a small boat, served with a massive sprig of rosemary perched atop as a sail and oars of toasted angel hair pasta sticking out at either end.) The flapjacks ($5.95) are delightfully light and flavored with such naughty pleasures as Snickers, blackberry granola, butterscotch, and almonds. For your morning Joe, order up a mug of "Smores" mocha ($5.95), a blast of sweetness with the chocolaty coffee topped with a lid of flame-melted marshmallow and two graham crackers to complete the campfire illusion. Since its opening in September of 2005, it's already been covered by the likes of Martha Stewart and the *New York Times*.

Overindulgence is not on the menu at **Canyon Ranch Café** ✪✪✪ (in The Venetian; ☎ 702/414-3633; www.venetian.com; daily 7am–3pm; AE, DISC, MC, V; $$). Portions are sensibly sized, yolks are often removed from eggs, and the average breakfast here comes in at just 305 calories (and that's without resorting to their "lighter plates," which come to as little as 120 calories per serving!). The cafe abuts the famous spa, so the emphasis is on weight loss, but this is kinder, gentler diet food, so well-spiced, varied and just plain delish (see p. 84 for our lunch review) that you won't feel in the least bit deprived. Among the many lovely breakfast offerings are smoked turkey hash with eggs ($9), tropical cinnamon crumb cake with roasted pineapple ($9), and helium-light Thai-style French toast with a ginger syrup ($10). The only discomforting part of dining here is the creeping guilt you may feel as buff people in workout clothes fill up the place, glowing with that "I just trimmed 5 inches off my thighs" smugness. But, hey, eat here enough and you just may start to feel energized enough to join them.

Portion sizes are also more civilized at **Bouchon** ✪✪✪ (in The Venetian; ☎ 702/414-6200; www.bouchonbistro.com; Sun–Thurs 7am–10pm, Fri–Sat 7am–11pm; AE, DISC, MC, V; $$–$$$$). But that makes sense, as everything's civilized and ultra-refined here, from the fine flatware; to the high-gloss Parisian bistro setting (perfectly re-created down to the red leather banquettes and the tile floors); to the food, a gourmet rethink of the breakfast classics. Examples include the French toast ($12), actually a brioche bread pudding, which is layered with custard and apples; the smoky, nutty tasting oatmeal with raisins ($6.95); or the *Ouef Au Gratin* ($16), eggs with Mornay sauce, pepper-studded ham, tomatoes, and delicate, earthy mushrooms.

Also on the West Side of town, the **Cracked Egg** ✪ (7660 W. Cheyenne Ave.; ☎ 702/395-7981; Mon–Fri 6am–2pm, Sat–Sun 6am–3pm; AE, DISC, MC, V; $–$$) is the choice for diners with an insatiable sweet tooth. The lure here is a birthday cake–like wedge of buttery, light coffee cake, 10 times superior to what's served in most breakfast joints. It accompanies nearly every breakfast option on the menu (which ranges in cost from $5.25 for plain eggs with sides, up to $9.45 for four different types of eggs Benedict) and its appearance alone makes a special event out of what would otherwise just be the standard breakfast in this standard-looking midsized diner.

and its prices, remarkably, mirror the rates at the much less chichi coffee shop at the Tropicana across the Strip. But the food here is much better, in fact it's on par with the decor. A mushroom omelet ($13) for example, comes studded with rich, woodsy, exotic 'shrooms like porcini and hen of the woods. Salmon salad ($15) features a perfectly cooked hunk of fish laid across a complex jumble of edamame, tender greens, and cabbage with just the right mist of sesame dressing. Sandwiches ($13–$14) are served on warm ciabatta bread, with ingredients that seem to go that extra step in terms of quality and freshness.

$$–$$$ Another "afterthought" of a restaurant, **Yolo's** ✪ (at Planet Hollywood, 3667 S. Las Vegas Blvd.; ☎ 702/736-0122; www.arkvegas.com/restaurants_yolos. htm; Sun–Thurs 11:30am–10pm, Fri–Sat 11:30am–11pm; AE, DC, MC, V), is Planet Hollywood's Mexican joint, but is given nowhere near the publicity of that property's marquee eateries. My hunch is that call is purely pragmatic: Yolo's doesn't have a celeb chef or more famous sister restaurant behind it. Despite these factors—or perhaps because of them—it's a darn cool place to hang out; its sexy, dark wood decor highlighted—literally—by hot pink light boxes, mirroring the casino's color scheme (I love the healthy glow they give you; this would be a great place for a first date!). On the food front, you have expertly sourced takes on Mexican classics: a "street taco" ($12–$13) for example, might come braised in a sauce of *guajillo* chiles (a moderate chile more common in Mexico than here); the enchiladas ($10–$12) are often topped with *cotija* cheese, a savory, very authentic south-of-the-border dairy product much closer to Parmesan in its taste than the cheese most of us are used to in Mexican food; the taco salad ($13) is a lovely toss of mahimahi, sweet mangoes, and crisp jicama. Don't skip the taco soup ($3) a thick, rich tomato broth in which lemony chunks of avocado, shredded chicken, and taco strips bob (it may well be one of my favorite bowls of soup in Vegas).

$$–$$$$ Back to the world of buffets, where ambience truly counts (as so many of the food offerings will be the same), and the **Bayside Buffet** ✪ (in Mandalay Bay; ☎ 877/632-7800; www.mandalaybay.com; Mon–Fri 7–10:30am, 11am–2:30pm, and 5–10pm, Sat–Sun 7am–3pm and 5–10pm; breakfast $16, lunch $20, champagne brunch $24, dinner $27; AE, DISC, MC, V) has that in spades. Looking a tad like a set from a Merchant Ivory film on colonial India, the dining rooms are all teak and burnished mahogany, framed by huge, open bay windows that overlook the tropical bay. Ceiling fans lazily swish the air back and forth as you loll on your cane chair, and you half expect some chap in jodhpurs to come sauntering by smoking a stogie. So it shouldn't come as a surprise, due to the setting and casino, that this isn't one of the cheapie buffets, coming in at the high end of average pricing. I'd say the quality of the food and the shortness of the lines here more than make up for it (you could splurge at the Bellagio or Wynn buffet, but not only will you pay through the nose, you could waste up to an hour of your precious vacation just waiting to get in). You won't get as many selections here as you will at other buffets, but there's still more than you could possibly eat in one sitting, and it's tip-top, everything from sushi to bagels to snow crab legs.

Meals to Please the Entire Family

You're in Vegas, the kids are cranky because they've had to hold your hand in the casino ("Mom, I just want to try and push some of those blinking buttons, what's the big deal?"), and you've been trudging around for so many hours trying to find your car in the garage that a meltdown seems inevitable. I can't guarantee that the following restaurants will be the panacea for the smoke, noise, and visual overload that can turn even the most even-tempered of kids into Veruca Salt, but they should please the palates . . . and imaginations . . . of even the pickiest little eaters.

The Buffet at Treasure Island (p. 88): I have two words for you: cotton candy. Most kids really like the shopping aspect of buffet eating, but I think they'll really groove on Treasure Island's because it goes overboard with the sweet stuff: freshly made donuts, mounds of cookies, fresh fruits dipped in chocolate (hey, you got some fruit into 'em!), cakes, ice cream, and those pink puffs of threaded sugar I mentioned earlier.

Burger Bar (p. 76): A creative dinner, in that you get to take a basic burger and play dress-up with it, loading it with everything from cheese to three types of bacon to wacky sauces. Or you can just have the plain burger, which might be most kids' choice. But they'll enjoy helping you build yours. Did I mention that the ice cream shakes here are primo?

Cypress Street Marketplace (p. 80): A food court in Caesars Palace but with higher quality grub than the norm, and lots of the simple American stuff (pizza, burgers, hot dogs) that kids will dig. Afterwards, take them to the hourly free talking statues show (p. 118). You may wince, but they'll smile.

Pampas (p. 78): Carnivorous kids will enjoy the theatricality of this Brazilian churrascaria joint, where your dinner comes with a flourish of evil-looking knives, as meat is cut off skewers and onto your plate. A massive salad bar, included in the meals, means you can probably also persuade the tots to eat their veggies.

Peppermill Coffee Shop (p. 93): With its hot pink tubes of neon lighting, its weird fake cherry trees, and its funky booths, this may well be the oddest-looking place your children will ever dine in. They may want to spend the entire meal just staring at the surroundings, but a menu of American comfort foods will help you get them to eat.

Roxy's Diner (p. 91): Singing waiters and diner food. Need I say more?

Burger Wars

The latest trend sweeping Vegas? Gourmet hamburgers restaurants where you can pile on the fries, the beef patty, and the onion rings, but perhaps wash it all down with a fine cabernet. The following are the top combatants, to my mind:

Taking the "hold the pickles, hold the lettuce, special orders don't upset us," Burger King philosophy to the *nth* gourmet degree, the upmarket **Burger Bar** ★★ (kids) (in Mandalay Place Shopping Center; ☎ 702/632-9364; www. mandalaybay.com; Mon–Thurs 10:30am–11pm, Fri–Sat 10am–1am, Sun 10am–11pm; AE, DISC, MC, V; $–$$$) specializes in highly customizable burgers served in a dignified, pubby setting. If you're a purist you can have the top-drawer Ridgefield Farm ($9) or Angus burger ($9.50) alone, but it's a heck of a lot of fun to play chef and load up your patty with some of the 42 options available, including eight different cheeses, three types of bacon, three kinds of mushrooms, guacamole, pesto sauce, cranberry sauce, sprouts, caramelized onion, smoked salmon, and even lobster, truffles, or foie gras (you won't really taste the last three ingredients against the heft of the burger—and ordering one could up your check by $12 to $30—but this is the kind of town where people like to splurge even when it doesn't make sense to do so). The average cost of a side is between 50¢ and $2, so if you're on a budget, do the math before ordering, and consider sharing (these are big patties, and there's no sharing charge); kids burgers are cheaper, starting at $6. How good it all tastes will depend on how adept you are at mixing flavors, but I suggest skipping the pickled green tomatoes, as they come wedge-shaped and thus don't stay on the patty. Dieters, vegetarians, and contrarians can choose a veggie burger ($6), lamb burgers ($9), salmon steak, turkey burgers ($8), or a Kobe beef burger ($16 and not worth the extra dough).

BLT Burger ★ (in The Mirage; ☎ 702/792-7888; www.mirage.com; Sun and Tues–Wed 11am–2am, Mon and Thurs–Sat 11am–4am; AE, DC, MC, V; $–$$$) is a tad pricier and doesn't provide the mix-and-match fun of Burger Bar, but its patties get even more exotic. Along with the classic black ($12), it offers up a lamb tandoori burger ($13 with a mint-cilantro-cucumber sauce), a fried chicken "burger," a salmon burger, even a falafel "burger." I give it kudos for its crisp fries and the unlimited sauces—BBQ, ranch, Maytag blue cheese—that they provide customers free of charge. But the desserts and shakes aren't as solid here as Burger Bar and the atmosphere, which tends more towards soda shop than pub, is a tad too frenetic and louder, as it's off the casino floor rather than in a mall. By the way, the letters in the name have nothing to do with bacon and lettuce on your burger: They're the initials of founding chef Laurent Tourondel (the "B" stands for "bistro").

A third contender, **Strip Burger** ★★ (in the Fashion Show Mall, 3200 Las Vegas Blvd. S.; ☎ 702/737-8747; www.stripburger.com; Sun–Thurs

11:30am–1am, Fri–Sat 11:30am–2am; AE, DC, MC, V; $-$$), wins points for its fun setting, in what can only be described as a circular pod, outdoors right on the Strip. Guests sit on tall stools around brushed metal tables, the better to see the Wynn across the street. It's a hip-looking place, with a bar at the center (and fans and heat lamps to keep guests comfortable in all weather). As for the burgers ($8.95–$9.95), they're extraordinarily juicy (don't make the same mistake I did and fully take them out of the paper shell they come in; you'll need it to sop up the juices) and can come sided with luscious onion strings ($3.50, like onion rings but much thinner and crisper). There's not as much variety in the burger department as the other two, but what you have is solid (and there are both turkey and veggie burgers for those avoiding red meat). The only disappointment? The chocolate cake milkshake, which comes with an extra wide straw and is just as disgusting as it sounds. Savings tip: Go at "happy hour" (4–7pm) when mini burgers, fries, margaritas, and draft beer are all just $2!

And though it's a chain, I'd be remiss not to mention **In 'N Out Burger** ⭐ (4888 Dean Martin Dr.; ☎ 800/786-1000; Sun–Thurs 10:30am–1am, Fri–Sat 10:30am–1:30am; MC, V; $); this just-off-Strip location (you can see its trademark swoosh from the I-15) is the most popular of its kind in the nation. On my last visit, I ordered and was handed number 108; they were calling 62 at that point. No "in and out" meal for me; I got my burger ($1.80), fries ($1.30), and shake ($1.90) in about half an hour. Am I complaining? Well, maybe a little, but I'm a big fan of this anti-McDonald's, a restaurant where none of the ingredients used is ever frozen or put under a heat lamp. How do I know? They don't even have those instruments in the stores. Instead, produce is delivered every 2 days, buns baked every morning, and each and every additive-and-preservative-free burger is cooked to order. Take a peek behind the counter, and you'll see one bored-looking fellow patiently feeding Idaho potatoes into an electric mandolin, which slices them into french fry shapes, which are then poured into a vat of bubbling vegetable oil (no lard used here). For those who want something beyond the menu posted over the counter, there's a "secret" menu, with such items as the "animal style" burger (slathered with mustard, special sauce, pickles, and grilled onions) and the "Wish burger" (which may have gotten its name from people who wish they weren't vegetarians—it comes with every topping except meat). There are several websites with listings of the "secret menu," where you can find out all the variations. One is at www.rajuabju.com/literature/innoutmenu.htm. Another In 'N Out "secret" are the tiny biblical citations printed on the wrappers and cups, which subtly point diners to John 3:16 or Proverbs 3:5, some of the favorite Bible quotations of the Snyder family who still own the chain as a private corporation.

Excelling in Latin food, it serves a mean paella, excellent chiles rellenos, and the carvery/BBQ section is so generous and tasty, you'll feel like you're at a Brazilian churrascaria. The pasta is made to order, and perfectly al dente and well sauced.

$$–$$$$ I'll be blunt: I nearly cut the Paris's **Le Village Buffet** (in Paris Las Vegas; ☎ 877/796-2092 or 702/946-7000; www.harrahs.com; daily 8am–10:30pm; breakfast $15, lunch $18, dinner and Sat–Sun brunch $25; AE, DISC, MC, V) from this edition after eating there this time out. Quality has diminished and the geniuses who are setting the menu have moved away from French food. (Hello, guys? Your buffet's located in a building with a replica of the Eiffel Tower at top!) Where there once were delightful Provençal stews, meat wrapped in pastry, and other French treats, are now the usual Italian pastas (limply done), Middle Eastern spreads, and bland American soul food. There's still some French food left, but it's not as good as before. So why keep it in? First off, I still love the decor. Looking like a set from the touring production of Disney's *Beauty and the Beast,* with a faux blue-painted sky and a cute-as-kittens market square theme, Paris is such hokey fun I didn't have to ditch it. And for savvy diners, prices have gone down: Le Village is discounting through the Tix 4 Tonight booths (see p. 68 for more on that), so if you stop by one of those first, you can shave a full 35% off the cost of eating here which makes it among the more affordable options on this neck of the Strip.

$$–$$$$ I'm keeping this listing in the hope that plans to remake the **Market City Caffe** ✹ 🄺🄸🄳🅂 (in the Monte Carlo; ☎ 702/730-7966; www.marketcitycaffe.com; Sun–Thurs 11am–11pm, Fri–Sat 11am–midnight; AE, DISC, MC, V) into something chicer and pricier will be foiled by the bad economy. Right now, it's one of the most reasonable and most authentic Italian restaurants in town. Sure the setting is noisy, with the unmuffled *ka-ching ka-chings* of the casino floor overwhelming any music they might play; and yes the decor is Italian by way of Cleveland (think wicker chairs, some fake trees with white Christmas lights, and deeply yellowed walls purposely stippled to look antiqued). The food however, is the real deal, created by Sal and Chipper Cassola with the input of two Neapolitan aunts who shared their idiosyncratic recipes with the pair over the years. You'll taste the old country in the pizzas ($12–$15), which are thin crusted; topped with rich cheeses, crisp veggies, Italian sausage, or whatever you choose; and charred to perfection in a wood-burning oven. Pastas are uniformly excellent, all made with either imported or freshly made noodles, and spanning the spectrum from simple angel hair with fresh tomato and basil to a robust Italian sausage lasagna ($14). A brick oven is employed to help keep the fish dishes from over-grilling and they, too, are well cooked and flaky. And though it's not geared to families, children will enjoy the food here, and they've treated my young daughters like princesses whenever we've visited (and in case you were wondering, they didn't know I was reviewing the place). Let's hope the rumors that they'll be redoing the place turn out to be false.

$$$$ A "meat parade" is the "subtle" term used by **Pampas** ✹ 🄺🄸🄳🅂 (in the Miracle Mile Mall, 3667 S. Las Vegas Blvd.; ☎ 702/737-4748; www.pampasusa.com; Mon–Sun 11:30am–10pm; AE, DC, DISC, MC, V) restaurant to introduce potential customers to the Brazilian churrascaria. For those who've never experienced one of these carnivorous frenzies, here's what a meal entails: you first gorge on a massive salad bar (which also holds fish dishes, poultry dishes, and lots of goodies beyond traditional salad) and then turn over a card which shows that you're ready for the meat portion of this culinary orgy. Within moments, waiters carrying large skewers of meats and wicked looking knives appear. They carve off a chunk (you can request a certain doneness and they'll carve from the correct portion of the skewer) which you grab with tongs and heap on your plate. It's good, clean fun and the meat here is of quite high quality. As for the price: Though the cheapest Riodizio meal here goes for $39 a head, if you stop by Tix 4 Tonight (see p. 177) and make a reservation through it, your meal will be just $24, less at lunch.

$$$–$$$$ **The Wolfgang Puck Bar and Grill** ✪✪ (in the MGM Grand; ☎ 877/ 880-0880; www.mgmgrand.com; Sun–Thurs 11:30am–10:30pm, Fri–Sat 11:30am– 11:30pm; AE, DISC, MC, V) is no more a simple bar and grill than Kensington Palace is a one-family home. Instead, Puck luxes it up. He brings the California cuisine that was his proud invention here, marrying the French techniques he honed while working at Maxim's de Paris with the freshest of ingredients, all carted in from the state next door on a near daily basis. The food is, in a word, splendid; and Puck is such a master that he had me swooning over foods I normally avoid. (I'm not a fan of blue cheese, but here it's draped over flash-fried, still warm potato chips in the least stinky way possible. In fact, I find myself craving those chips when I'm not in Vegas.) Though some of the menu is pricey, those on a budget are pretty well served here. They can order one of Puck's famous pizzas ($13–$14), which, as at his other more pricey eateries, are coddled in a wood-burning oven and come with such signature toppings as garlic chicken, pesto shrimp, and an almost sour cream–like burrata mozzarella. The grilled chopped vegetable salad with feta cheese and sun-dried tomato vinaigrette ($14) is another Puck classic; and though it's listed as an appetizer, is big enough for an entree. For a small splurge, the calves liver in mustard sauce ($22) is superb. The truth is, I don't think you'll be disappointed in anything you order. And the setting is also nifty: a chic, glistening white eatery that seems to float in the middle of a standard looking casino, the space marked off by massive plastic light boxes onto which are projected large and color-rich photos of flowers and fields. At one end is the long bar that makes this a "bar and grill," and it's a sociable place to dine solo, or just enjoy a glass of premium wine or beer between bouts of gambling or shopping.

$$$–$$$$ The secret discounting that we discuss in the box on p. 68 is today making one of Las Vegas' beloved institutions affordable. I'm talking about **Bally's Steakhouse** ✪✪ (in Bally's, 3645 S. Las Vegas Blvd.; ☎ 888/742-9488 or 702/ 967-7999; www.ballyslasvegas.com; daily 5:30–10:30pm; AE, DC, MC, V) which now sells its massive hunks of perfectly aged beef for half off . . . to those smart enough to get the Tix 4 Tonight reservation. But though the meal is discounted, the experience shouldn't be: Bally's has the classic steakhouse shtick down pat: from the gentleman's club decor (with its framed hunting prints, brass fixtures, and its sink-into-able leather booths and couches) to the tuxedoed, joke-cracking older men who serve as waiters here (they really are a charming bunch). Even the clientele seems to come straight from central casting: When I was last there, I was one of the few women in a room filled with suited guys, lounging in the booths, arms spread in "masters of the universe" poses. This all would mean nothing, of course, if the steaks weren't prime, but they are: tender, cooked to your specifications, and available for as little as $16 (the usually $32 prime rib), $18 for filet mignon (normally $35), or $20 ($40 without the discount) for a Flintstone-sized, dry-aged, bone-in rib-eye (that's the one I recently tried valiantly to make a dent in; I ended up snacking on the leftovers for several days). Desserts ($9) are also a specialty and delicious in an old-fashioned way whether you go for the famed banana cream pie, their massive ice cream sundae, or a crème brûlée.

$$–$$$$ Those same secret discounts are making "surf" as affordable as "turf" at celebrity chef Rick Moonen's **rmBistro** ✦ (in the Mandalay Bay; ☎ 702/632-9300; www.rmseafood.com; 11am–2:30pm and 5:30–10pm; AE, DC, MC, V). Here the savings is 33%, meaning that a filet of branzino with a perfect Béarnaise sauce will come in at $20 rather than $30, a hearty gumbo that usually costs $26 drops to just $17, and Moonen's signature catfish Sloppy Joe (absolutely delish and don't just take my word for it—Oprah is also a vocal fan) comes in at $7.65 at lunch (as opposed to $11). The Bistro is the downstairs, more casual offshoot off rm, a much-lauded restaurant (the NY version was one of the few restaurants in the country to be awarded three stars by Michelin). Like its pricier sister, it uses only sustainably caught and farmed fish, so your conscience as well as your stomach will thank you for dining here.

CENTER STRIP RESTAURANTS

Home to Caesars Palace, the Bellagio, The Venetian, Palazzo, and The Mirage, this is the chicest area of the Strip, as well as the priciest, by far, for food. In general, you're going to pay a good 10% to 20% more to eat here (in every category of restaurant) than you will in most other areas of town. That said, there are a handful of places where you can have a memorable meal without feeling like you've been taken.

$–$$ At the center of the Center Strip, you'll find Caesars Palace's modern version of the Imperial Roman marketplace, the **Cypress Street Marketplace** ✦ (kids) (in Caesars Palace; ☎ 877/346-4642; www.harrahs.com; daily 11am–11pm; AE, DISC, MC, V). Unlike its ancient predecessor, you won't find unmilled grains, raw vegetables and fruits, or mice in any abundance (fun, totally random fact: mice were raised and sold as food in Caesar's day). But you will get a blessedly chain-free food court; all of the food is prepared by Caesars Palace chefs, and is of the quality . . . well mostly . . . of what's being served in the surrounding eateries. There's a bona fide south-of-the-Mason-Dixon-line BBQ shop (I'd recommend the mountainous and peppery pulled pork sandwich, $8.95); a seafood shop with a Maine-caliber lobster roll ($13); a multi-option salad stand ($9.95; you choose, they toss, and you can get as many ingredients as you like for that one price); pastries; Asian food (from noodle soups to stir-fries to potstickers); and for the kids, one stand that sells pizza, and another for burgers and hot dogs. Portions are outsized, and while you'll have to carry your own plate to your table, it'll be actual china with a cloth napkin and silverware to boot. Other civilizing touches include an attentive bus staff; the sophisticated good looks of the court itself, which mixes Roman-style statues and stone floors with oversized photos of billowing wheat and other foodstuffs; and a stand that sells wine and beer for those who want at least that taste of ancient Rome with their meals.

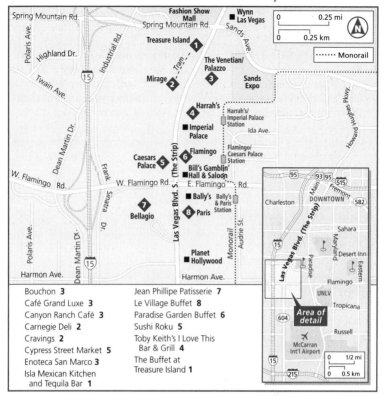

Spring Mountain Rd.
Fashion Show Mall
Wynn Las Vegas
Spring Mountain Rd.
Sands Ave.
Polaris Ave.
Highland Dr.
Industrial Rd.
Treasure Island 1
Twain Ave.
15
The Venetian/ Palazzo
Mirage 2   3
Sands Expo
Harrah's 4
Harrah's/ Imperial Palace Station
Ida Ave.
Dean Martin Dr.
Imperial Palace
Flamingo 6
Flamingo/ Caesars Palace Station
Caesars Palace 5
W. Flamingo Rd.
Frank Sinatra Dr.
Las Vegas Blvd. S. (The Strip)
W. Flamingo Rd.
Bill's Gamblin' Hall & Saloon
E. Flamingo Rd.
Bally's
Bally's & Paris Station
7   Bellagio
Paris 8
Monorail
Audrie St.
Polaris Ave.
Dean Martin Dr.
15
Harmon Ave.
Planet Hollywood
Harmon Ave.

0   0.25 mi
0   0.25 km
N
········ Monorail

Charleston
95   93 95 515
Main St.
Fremont St.
DOWNTOWN   582
15
Las Vegas Blvd. (The Strip)
Sahara
Maryland
Desert Inn
Eastern
Paradise
Flamingo
UNLV
Tropicana
604
Russell
McCarran Int'l Airport
215
Area of detail
0   1/2 mi
0   0.5 km

Bouchon **3**	Jean Phillipe Patisserie **7**
Café Grand Luxe **3**	Le Village Buffet **8**
Canyon Ranch Café **3**	Paradise Garden Buffet **6**
Carnegie Deli **2**	Sushi Roku **5**
Cravings **2**	Toby Keith's I Love This Bar & Grill **4**
Cypress Street Market **5**	The Buffet at Treasure Island **1**
Enoteca San Marco **3**	
Isla Mexican Kitchen and Tequila Bar **1**	

$$–$$$$ It's a sign of how nasty the current economic situation is when one of the chicest, most youth-oriented sushi bars on the Strip turns to that old retirement community grabber: the early-bird special. Of course, they call it by a different name, the "Red Sun Hour," but in one fell swoop, the chichi **Sushi Roku** ★★ (in the Forum Shops at Caesars; ☎ 702/733-7373; www.sushiroku.com; Sun–Thurs noon–10pm, Fri–Sat noon–11:30pm; AE, DISC, MC, V) became one of the center Strip's best bargains, at least between 4pm and 6pm. During that period, dozens of rolls, appetizers, and cocktails are going for just $3 each, meaning you could theoretically get both fed and bombed for under $15 here. And this is in a darn cushy place; in the first edition of the book, I said it embodies what most Vegas first-timers probably think the town is like after watching such slick entertainment as *Las Vegas* (the TV show) or the film *Oceans 12*. Diners here all look like they've come from central casting—the type of tan, buff-bodied, glossy-haired folk that you rarely see off the silver screen. Truthfully, everyone looks better under Roku's moody lighting, sinking into the dark soft leather banquettes and framed against the walls, a high design patchwork quilt of ornate concrete blocks, fine woods, and light boxes. This is particularly true in the back room where huge windows offer up a panoramic sweep of the Strip (it's actually a great place for a private party as it features the only private room in the middle of the Strip with

A Worthy Splurge!

$$$-$$$$ Bouchon ✪✪✪ (in the Venetian; www.bouchonbistro.com; ☎ 702/414-6200; www.venetian.com; Sun–Thurs 7am–10pm, Fri–Sat 7am–11pm; AE, DISC, MC, V) is the almost-too-perfect bistro from famed chef Thomas Keller (who founded the French Laundry in the Napa Valley, widely considered to be the finest restaurant in the United States). Set right in the heart of the casino—you actually have to ride the elevators up several floors to get here—it gives the impression of being lifted right off a street on the Left Bank in Paris. Everything is very correct, from the slightly worn but pretty tile floors to the classic zinc bar to the huge vases stuffed with giant stalks of flowers that stand bolt upright, like soldiers at a review. The ceiling is soaring, the crowd sophisticated (and slightly older), and the food is *comme il faut*. Order the classic Steak Frites ($33), and it will be tender enough to forego a steak knife; the mussels ($25) come in a saffron broth so richly perfumed you'll be tempted to dab it behind your ears (though you'll want all of it to go into your mouth, of course); and for light eaters, there's a buttery, but not too filling, Croque Madame sandwich ($16, the classic ham and cheese with a sinful Mornay sauce and fried egg) among the many other choices. Starters are just as good, from the onion soup with its silken cheese lid ($8.50) to the ever-so-tender mache lettuce and baby beet salad ($11). The only way that Bouchon strays from the Parisian formula is in the service, which isn't the brusque somewhat formal treatment you usually get in Paris. Instead, the genuinely warm waiters welcome you as if you were a long-lost cousin, cooing over small children (as they recently did with my daughter), making sure you're comfortable, and just making you feel like a special guest. Because of that, I'd pick this in a heartbeat for a classy bachelorette party (if there's such a thing) or a less formal wedding reception. To make the evening or afternoon really special, try and score one of the seats on the terrace. Bouchon is also a great place for breakfast (see p. 73).

windows that open to these sorts of views). As for the sushi, much of it is flown in daily and is expertly assembled under the watchful eye of Shima, a master sushi chef from Japan. If you come during regular hours, pieces must be ordered in sets of two and range in price from $6 to $10 (with four pieces of sashimi from $4, and rolls for $7–$14), so order carefully, as tabs do add up quickly. I'd stay away from the sushi appetizers too during the regular hours; not only are they over-priced, too many of them come doused in a very sharp, vinegary ponzu sauce, making one indistinguishable from the next. If you're on a budget and dining later, you won't be depriving yourself if you stick with the noodle dishes, which at $10 to $15 are the cheapest items on the menu and actually quite scrumptious.

$$-$$$ When you go to Chicago, you're making a mistake if you don't visit the original Pizzeria Uno. Sure, it's a chain now, but the first one still has the élan and culinary chops that its offspring often lack. The same could be said of **Café Grand Lux** ★★ 🦖 (in The Venetian and the Palazzo; ☎ 702/414-3888; www.venetian. com; daily 24 hr.; AE, DISC, MC, V), which may very well be the only chain restaurant to have actually originated in Vegas (and is the only Strip restaurant that every single one of my local foodie friends recommend). Created in 1999 by David Overton of the Cheesecake Factory, it's conceived of as the next step in upscale fast food; it's since spun off to a dozen other locations (with more in the works). Though the original was at The Venetian, I prefer dining at the dazzling branch at the Palazzo, which seems to have appropriated the color palette, style, and themes of German expressionist painter Gustav Klimt. The restaurant is a fantasy of gold leaf (fake, I'm assuming), murals, and curvaceous, *fin de siècle* lighting fixtures with hand-blown glass. In fact, it's 10 times more opulent than neighboring Strip restaurants that double its prices. As at the Cheesecake Factory, internationalism is the theme and the menu is massive, with 150 choices in all, ranging from simple burgers ($11) to addictive BBQ duck potstickers ($8.50) to a sculptural and spicy Jamaican Pork Tenderloin ($18; order it to see what I mean) or a more than serviceable plate of pasta ($12–$19). The salads are huge, with a just-wrenched-from-the-ground crispness (I particularly recommend the complex Southwestern salad with avocado, chicken, tomato, and tortilla strips, $14). In fact, you'll find a high standard of ingredients throughout, from the Angus beef used in the burgers to artisanal-tasting chocolates used in the desserts. Speaking of desserts, as at the Cheesecake mother ship, they're worth holding a bit of stomach-room. To keep costs in check, share plates and consider ordering one of the lunch specials ($8.95) or a breakfast dish; in a play for the early-bird crowd, these are held over until 2pm for breakfast dishes and 5pm on the lunch specials. There's also an appealing kids' menu.

$$-$$$$ My next pick is right in the heart of The Venetian's kitschily glamorous Piazza San Marco, where living statues and stentorian gondoliers entertain you as you dine. It's **Mario Batali's Enoteca San Marco** ★★ (in The Venetian; ☎ 702/266-9969; www.enotecasanmarco.com; daily 10:30am–11pm; AE, MC, V) and it, too, is made affordable by its participation in the Tix 4 Tonight half-off entrees promotion (see box on p. 178). With discount in hand, you can tuck into plates of gourmet pasta or thin-crust pizzas for just $8 to $10 (usually $16–$20) or perhaps splurge on a plate of crispy duck for $13 (usually $26) or plump veal and ricotta meatballs with creamy polenta ($11 discounted/$22 normally). The food arrives piping hot, the sauces are rich and perfectly seasoned, and the ambience is a heckuva a lot of fun. Though salad isn't included in the deal, I highly recommend an "aceita" or "vinegar makers salad" ($14) which comes chockablock full of crisp vegetables and can be shared by up to three people, it's that big. And as in any classic *enoteca,* there are also plates of cured meats, cheeses, and other antipasti to nibble on. My only quibble here is with the wine policy: The cheapest wines by the glass start at $8. "So what" you say, "that's standard." Well, it would be if these servings were of a standard size; instead you're given 2 ounces, or literally two gulps, of wine for that price. To get a real glass, you're going to have to pony up $16 minimum, which is a bit rich for my blood.

Desserts in the Desert

Sure you can order dessert with your meal, or grab a Krispy Kreme as you saunter down the Strip, but there are also some only-in-Vegas options that are definitely worth sinking your sweet tooth into.

My first piece of sugary advice: No matter how hot it gets, don't go for an ice cream cone. I'm not suggesting masochism, just frozen custard. Smoother, denser, and creamier in texture than ice cream (because of the use of eggs in the mixture and the low amount of air whipped in), the cones at **Luv-It Frozen Custard** ★★★ (505 E. Oakey Blvd., just off the Strip, 1 block from the Stratosphere; www.luvitfrozencustard.com; Tues–Thurs 1–10pm, Fri–Sat 1–11pm; cash only; $) beat the pants off Cold Stone, Baskin-Robbins, even Häagen-Dazs. Family-owned since 1973 (Greg Teidemann, the friendly fellow taking your order, is the grandson of the founder), the custard at this little stand is made fresh every few hours, with chocolate and vanilla always on the menu, and a rotating cast of intensely flavored specialties—two per day—as your other option. (If it's offered, try the coolingly tart lemon or the salty butter pecan.) And when you're in the mood for something a bit more extravagant than just a cone ($2.45 single scoop, $3.65 double), you can tart up your choice with a slew of sundae toppings, from gooey caramel, marshmallow, butterscotch, and hot fudge sauces; to bits of fresh fruit (including hot apple, pineapple, or half bananas); crumbled cookies; and high-quality nuts (sundaes $4.35–$5.25). And you don't have to feel all that guilty. I'm not sure if I believe it, but Teidemann claims that his custard has significantly less fat or sugar than standard ice cream.

If fine pastries and aristocratic chocolates are your indulgence of choice, drop by **The Chocolate Swan** ★★ (in the Mandalay Bay Marketplace; ☎ 702/632-9366; www.chocolateswan.com; daily 8am–10pm; AE, DISC, V, MC; $), which "flew" here about 6 years ago from a suburb outside of Milwaukee, where one of the top execs of Mandalay Bay happened to be visiting. Dazzled by the Swan's éclairs and truffles, he convinced owners Mary and Robert Basta to relocate to the new Shops at Mandalay Bay. You'll find it right next to Burger Bar on the mall level. So what makes the Swan so

$$–$$$ My final pick in The Venetian/Palazzo complex, which very few people seem to know about, is the tiny cafe tucked into the Canyon Ranch Health Spa. Called, appropriately enough, the **Canyon Ranch Café** ★★★ (in The Venetian; ☎ 702/414-3633; www.venetian.com; daily 7am–6pm; AE, DISC, MC, V), it's an oasis of healthy eating amid the gluttony that's as much the "Sin" in Sin City as anything else. I raved earlier about the breakfasts (p. 72), but the lunches are just as toothsome, surprisingly so considering their low calorie and fat count (which is listed on the menu along with the grams of fiber); the heftiest meal here is a mere 470 calories, and most fall into the 300 calorie range. Cooked with preservative-free popular? I'd have to say it's the devoted—some might say insane—care that goes into every stage of the confectionary process. First there are the ingredients, all top-flight and flown in from all corners of the globe. Next there's the care with which these ingredients are treated (if you feel the staff here seems to be "walking on eggshells," you may be right—every egg used in the pastries is first bathed in a hot bleach-water bath and then cracked into a cup. If they get a bad egg, it's tossed). You'll taste the results of these extreme efforts in the voluptuousness of the éclairs, the dense and complex carrot cake that features Viennese cream between the layers and a cream cheese frosting, and the Belgian-quality chocolates. Service is either at the counter, or at comfortable cafe tables where waitresses will go over the menu with you (for those who can't decide, they usually suggest a plate of mini pastries) and tell you about possible dessert wine pairings. It's a lovely place for an after-supper drink and sweet, with pretty good people-watching to boot.

Of course, Las Vegas is home to the world's largest chocolate fountain—well, where else would it be?—and worshiping at this shrine of indulgence at **Jean-Philippe Patisserie** ✪✪✪ (in the Bellagio; ☎ 888/ 987-3846; www.bellagio.com; Sun–Thurs 7am–11pm, Fri–Sat 7am–midnight; AE, DISC, MC, V; $) is a kick and a half. Twenty-seven feet high, with 2,100 pounds of flowing chocolate gushing through it by the minute, it has Willy Wonka–like proportions. I only wish it weren't encased in glass—I'd like to bathe in the darn thing (probably not a good idea, as it's about 120°F/49°C in liquid form). Beyond the visual stimulation, of course, is the oral stimulation, and though I can't say it's because the chocolate is churned in such a showy manner, it's top-shelf stuff. Along with a smorgasbord of chocolates, there are 26 different sorts of pastries ($5.50 each), and these are no ordinary pastries—Jean-Philippe Maury is the world pastry champion so he has a deft hand with a cream puff, let me tell you. There's also a pretty good selection of salads and sandwiches to line your stomach with so you don't get a tummy ache from all the sugar.

and additive-free food that's organic more often than not, the choices range from Asian fare to Mediterranean dishes to such all-American classics as chocolate chip cookies ($1) and Caesar salad ($9). Last time I was here, I finally gave in to temptation . . . and purchased two of the cookbooks by chef/master magician James Boyar to try and figure out how the heck they made the egg salad sandwich ($10) so appealing at just 270 calories; or the lettuce-wrapped chicken ($14), happy packets of crunchy vegetables and chicken in a hoisinlike sauce with chunks of chicken for just 365 calories. Beyond the scrumptiousness of the food, the miracle here is that they've created low-cal foods that fill you up, without your having to overorder or overspend. And in a city where quality usually comes at too high a price, they've kept their prices reasonable for this pleasant, streamlined, light-filled cafe. Now, if they would only keep the place open for dinner . . . well, I'd have no excuse for the extra 5 pounds I always seem to accumulate each time I come to town!

$$–$$$$ Most of your meals won't be healthy in Vegas . . . and would you want it any other way? So when the craving for a heart attack between two slices of rye bread hits . . . er, I mean a genuine Reuben sandwich or some other NY deli specialty, you head to The Mirage, which has its own small restaurant mirage in its re-creation of the Big Apple's **Carnegie Deli** (in The Mirage; ☎ 702/791-7111; www.mirage.com; daily 7am–2am; AE, DISC, MC, V). The original, just a hop, skip, and a jump from Carnegie Hall, has been considered one of NY's two top delis— the other is Katz's—since it opened in 1937. The black-and-white tiled floors are the same here; as are the pressed tin ceilings; and the meats, which are cured, baked, and smoked in New York and then flown in every other day. But where the walls (with all the cheesy, signed photos of B-list celebrities) should be is, well, air and a disconcerting view of the sports book. Ignore it, and tuck into the 4-inch-thick stacks of corned beef, roast beef, pastrami, salami, tongue, and the like, to which they give cute names, such as "The Mouth That Roared" and "Brisketball," ranging in price from $7.95 to $22 (there's a sharing charge of $3, but it's probably worth springing for, as no one I know can finish one of these meat Cadillacs). If you're not that fervent a carnivore, the cheese blintzes are a celebrated alternative, stuffed with cheese, strawberries, blueberries, or cherries ($12). With a good 100 or so options on the menu, from giant salads to giant knishes, burgers to gefilte fish, stuffed cabbage to matzo ball soup, there should be something on the menu to sate even the most finicky of eaters. And what about dessert? If you can eat 3 pounds or so of meat, and still be up for something sweet, you may as well put yourself under the table with the cheesecake, which is massive (of course), but oh so perfect—creamy, lightly sweet, and with a distinct taste of vanilla.

$$–$$$ Country music fans have made **Toby Keith's I Love This Bar & Grill** (in Harrah's; ☎ 702/693-6111; www.harrahs.com; Sun–Thurs 11:30am–2am, Fri-Sat 11:30am–3am; AE, DISC, MC, V) one of the most hopping eateries in town. Named for his number one hit "I Love This Bar," there is much to love about the place, including live country music every night from 9pm to 2am, with jammin' up and coming bands picked by Keith himself; one of the prettiest waitstaffs in town, outfitted in mini skirts and midriff-baring tops; and for Keith fans, a non-stop loop of music videos, and walls slathered with photos of the six-pack cowboy himself, along with dozens of pieces of memorabilia. Unfortunately, there's a lot to hate, too. Those hot servers? Well, let me put it this way: They haven't been hired for their waitressing skills—service is indifferent, sometimes rude, and glacially slow. The food is decently priced (for Vegas), though quality varies wildly from dish to dish. Interestingly, the cheap grub tends to be better than the expensive side of the menu, with absolutely fine pulled pork sandwiches ($10), nachos ($10), tangy wings ($11), and a juicy meatloaf and mayo sandwich ($10). Keith's favorite, the fried bologna sandwich ($10) on garlic toast with that most southern of toppings, Miracle Whip, is an unlikely standout. Order the catfish ($15), or the rotisserie chicken ($15), however, and you'll need to fortify yourself with lots of $6 beers—grilled to the moistness of the Sahara, you'd be run out of Kansas if you tried to serve these sorry entrees at any self-respecting roadhouse there. So what's the final assessment? Come for the music, stick with the kind of food and drink you'd order at a honky-tonk down South, and you'll saunter out with a swing in your Levis and an extra tap in those Justin boots. But don't even cross the red, white, and blue threshold if you're in a rush; like your grub on the refined side; or expect your neighbors to eat quietly (one time I was here a bunch of bombed bachelorettes turned their meal into an impromptu karaoke session). You've been warned.

$$–$$$$ Isla Mexican Kitchen and Tequila Bar ★★★ (in Treasure Island; ☎ 702/894-7111; www.treasureisland.com; Sun–Thurs 4–11pm, Fri–Sat 4pm–midnight; AE, DISC, MC, V) is an ultrasexy spot that attracts an ultrasexy crowd quaffing fine tequila and calling on the cleavage-laden "tequila goddess" to create a tree of tequila flights (actually an elaborate metal candelabra-like contraption with shot glasses on it). This lovely hostess then educates you on the vintages, which you sip carefully as tequila is a heck of a lot more potent than wine, even in "tasting" sizes. If you don't do the tasting—and it's a pricey entertainment that has the potential for putting you under the table, so you may want to skip it—you'll still find much to catch your eye and tempt your palate. Designed by Jeffrey Beers, the chic, large dining room has all the vibrant colors of a Yucatan sunrise, from the tiled bright aqua wall in the back (a stand-in for the Caribbean sea) to the deep oranges and reds of the vaguely Aztec paintings along the walls. The food is a creative retread of Mexican classics by chef Richard Sandoval, with a number of excellent entrees—tacos, enchiladas, and tamales—in the under-$15 range (a rarity for a Strip restaurant with this level of chicness). If you'd like starters pick the corn soup ($7), which tastes like summer, its sweetness balanced by a crisp ribbon of *huitlacoche* (black fungus) vinaigrette that the chef squiggles across the soup (it's so colorful it looks a bit like a late Matisse collage). Pork is also a specialty, whether you have it grilled in a taco with an excellent pineapple salsa ($10), pulled into juicy threads and stuck in a tamale with a fiery chipotle sauce ($14), or marinated with tamarind and then roasted and served with an exquisite sauce or roasted corn and pumpkin seeds ($20, a family recipe). For vegetarians, there's an impressive vegetable enchilada ($13) which absolutely bursts with flavor. Don't skip dessert, a very grown-up treat here, with not-too-sweet dulce de leche ($6) acting as an exclamation point on a terrific meal.

BUFFETS ON THE CENTER STRIP

Buffets are pricier in the "Central Zone," though sometimes that uptick isn't followed by a corresponding uptick in food quality or variety (as at the underwhelming Harrah's buffet). And there are some where the lines are so long and the prices so sky high ($36 at the Bellagio for a "gourmet dinner") that I can't in good conscience recommend them—when you're paying $30 or more for a meal, you deserve to have a maitre d' whisk you quickly to a table where you should sit back rather than having to play waiter. Long lines and jostling crowds spell airport security, not fine dining. So I'm including just three buffet choices for this area; if you're interested in trying one of the ones I'm not writing up, you'll find a chart with full pricing and hours on p. 104 for every single, darn buffet on the Strip (and some off it as well).

$$$–$$$$ The Center Strip is home to the old-school (and just plain old) Flamingo Casino, and it has a proudly retro buffet called the **Paradise Garden Buffet** ★ (in the Flamingo; ☎ 702/733-3333; daily 7am–2:30pm and 3–10:30pm; breakfast $15, lunch $17, brunch $20, dinner $22; AE, DC, MC, V), which will give you a taste, literally, of what Vegas must have been like in the '60s and '70s. The decor's been modernized; its current look has a sort of "hanging gardens of Babylon" effect—lots of fake greenery draping down from ziggurat-like setbacks—but the food's old-fashioned, and for the most part, good. Be sure to snag a seat by the floor-to-ceiling windows for calming views of the koi pond, tropical shrubbery, and coquettish pink flamingos out back. Stick with the "garden" items and you won't be disappointed; there's an abundance of sweet fruit and salads of all kinds. The cooked foods are a bit more hit and miss. At brunch, there's a good make-your-own omelet bar that offsets the rubbery pancakes. Chinese food, too, is prepared to order by an intent-looking man with a big steaming wok, and it's above average, filled with crunchy vegetables. Italian and Mexican offerings are forgettable and confusingly laid out, the toppings for the tacos nowhere near the actual tacos and meat (I almost accidentally crowned my taco with mashed potatoes one time, thinking it was sour cream!). Dinner is famous for its seafood spread, which isn't at all gourmet or unusual, but does feature huge tub-loads of steamed shrimp and Alaskan king crab legs, the latter pre-cracked for easy munching.

$$–$$$$ Designed by Adam Tihany, who also created the high-concept decor at Mandalay Bay's Aureole restaurant and didn't originally want a word as gauche as "buffet" to be used in his creation, **Cravings** ★ (in The Mirage; ☎ 702/791-7111; www.mirage.com; daily 7am–10pm; breakfast $14, lunch $18, dinner $25, Sat–Sun brunch $23; AE, DISC, MC, V) is supposed to be different from the rest because of its abundance of "live action"—chefs in their whites, carving, tossing, sautéing, and well, generally pretending that this place isn't a buffet. It is, of course, though one with a much more mod decor than most, featuring brilliantly colorful backlit glass walls, a swooping metal ceiling sculpture, and resin table tops. It all looks ultra luxe . . . until you get to the buffet itself, which is, well, sparse. Don't get me wrong, the fare is generally quite appetizing, there just aren't piles of it lying around and giving vacationers that happy Roman orgy feeling that most buffets impart. And interestingly, Cravings seems to assume that what diners are craving is really unusual fare; the Asian food, in particular, has some downright odd choices like bok choy with oyster sauce, kimchi, and *congee* (a type of pudding) when I last visited. I tried them and they were terrific, but I seemed to be one of the only people there that night with a sense of adventure. Most were sticking with the nicely tossed salads (which they do so you won't tire your arms), BBQ, pizza baked in a wood-burning oven, and standard Mexican dishes. The menu changes frequently, but there are always 11 stations to choose from. Along with the relative lack of variety, dessert is a bit of a disappointment, though they do have a lovely array of gelatos.

$$–$$$$ If you're going to the buffet really for the variety of dessert options, the one you want to hit is **The Buffet at Treasure Island** ★★ 🧒 (in Treasure Island; www.treasureisland.com; daily 7am–10:30pm; breakfast $13, weekend champagne brunch $20, lunch $16, dinner $21 except Fri–Sat when it's $26; AE,

DISC, MC, V), which takes the sweet stuff seriously. One large corner of the space is devoted to desserts, and it's the buffet's showplace, backed by a large glass wall so people in the casino can watch the three or four chefs who man the area dip fresh strawberries into rich dark chocolate, fry up mini donuts, and scoop out a rainbow assortment of ice creams (seven satisfying flavors in all). Cakes are all individually sized, a nice touch, because they stay a lot fresher than the ones that are sliced into portions and then set out at other buffets. There are also excellent crème brûlées, cookies, brownies, gooey pastry bars and glory be, puffs of cotton candy (which I take out with me; there's nothing that makes you feel quite so debauched as hitting the craps table with a cone of cotton candy in one hand and a margarita in the other. It also makes it a bit difficult to throw the dice, but that's another story . . .). Of course, man can't live on dessert alone (well, actually, this woman thinks she could), so you'll want to hit the regular part of the buffet first, which does very well with the Asian food (nice sushi and wok-sautéed fare), has a sandwich bar that's great for kids, an excellent BBQ, and a make-your-own pasta station. The disappointments here—and aren't there always some?—are in the veggie department, with the side dishes lacking oomph and the salad makers needing a bit of extra training in how to properly toss and dress (I've had salad here that was paddling around the plate, thanks to all the vinaigrette that was glopped onto it). Though it's not as swank looking as its next-door-sister, Cravings at The Mirage, the seating area—done up in dark browns with touches of orange—is attractive and modern, with a somewhat Brazilian feel to it.

NORTH STRIP RESTAURANTS

With the exception of Wynn Las Vegas, Encore, and the Fashion Show Mall, the North Strip represents the last vestiges of the "classic" Strip ambience, which is a nice way of saying dowdy, old-fashioned, and far more of a meat-and-potatoes aesthetic when it comes to cuisine. The upside: You'll find the cheapest eats on the Strip here, and in some cases the choices are just as tasty as their higher-priced counterparts to the South.

$ Consider, for instance, **Capriotti's** ★★★ (near the Sahara Casino at 322 W. Sahara Ave., and at the Red Rock Casino, among other locations; ☎ 702/474-0229; www.capriottis.com; daily 10am–5pm; AE, DISC, MC, V), an ever-expanding chain of sub shops started in Delaware, which now has 21 shops in the Las Vegas valley. I know it sounds pretentious to refer to a submarine sandwich as "gourmet," but these truly are: oozing with flavor (and sometimes dripping dressings) and top-of-the-line ingredients, they redefine the genre. Were Quiznos or Subway executives ever to visit, they'd have to commit hara-kiri right on the spot in penance for their product! Here, the turkey and roast beef are roasted on a daily basis, the smallest subs on 9-inch rolls (costing $5–$7) are big enough for a meal and a half (leave the leftovers in your fridge for your next day's breakfast), and the "larges" could feed the proverbial family of four. Most famous on the menu is the Bobbie ($6.50), basically Thanksgiving dinner—turkey, cranberry stuffing, and mayo—on a roll, and it's delish, though I sometimes prefer the Capastrami ($7), a hot sandwich of pastrami, coleslaw, melted Swiss, and thick Russian dressing. Meatballs, cheesesteak, capacolla, roast beef, eggplant parmigiana, and Genoa salami (great with sweet peppers and oil and mustard) and various combinations

North Strip Restaurants

Capriotti's **7**

Cafe Ba Ba Reeba **10**

Circus Buffet **8**

Dona Maria Tamales **1**

Florida Café **2**

Indian Oven **6**

Luv-It Frozen Custard **3**

Naga **5**

Peppermill Coffee Shop **9**

Red 8 **11**

Roxy's Diner **5**

Tiffany's **4**

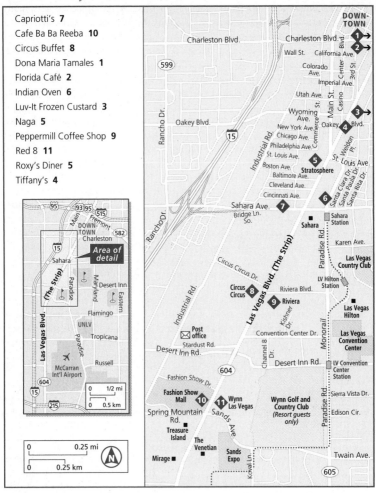

of all the above, round out the menu. For vegetarians, there's a wide selection of faux meats—turkey, baloney, salami, and hamburger—cunningly created from soy, and pretty darn good. Be thinking of where to eat your sub before you buy, as there's rarely a free table in this crowded shop.

$–$$ Just beyond the Stratosphere (which is usually considered the end of the Strip, but hey, it's walkable, so I'm stretching it here), **Dona Maria Tamales** ★ kids (910 Las Vegas Blvd. S.; ☎ 702/382-6538; www.donamariatamales.com; Sun–Thurs 8am–10pm, Fri–Sat 8am–11pm; AE, DISC, MC, V) has outlasted many a casino (it was founded in 1980) by keeping everyone who comes here extremely happy. And I mean everyone. Sports fans crowd the front, glued to the TV screens that blare out the latest exploits of the Mexican soccer teams. Locals use this as an unofficial clubhouse, the place jammed at lunch with cops and office workers, many of whom go from table to table, chatting in Spanish. Families are welcomed by the friendly waiters, and the well-priced kids' menu (all of the items are $6.85) offers both Mexican specialties, and for the unadventurous tot, chicken fingers and french fries. The occasional tourist who wanders in knows that he's in for an authentic Mexican experience as he gazes at the diner's walls covered with murals of life in the Mexican countryside and the ceilings strung with colorful *papel picado* (looping banners created from intricately cut pieces of paper). The food is also a crowd pleaser, not as fiery as in some restaurants, but accompanied by an assortment of hot sauces for those who like a touch more heat. You gotta order the tamales ($3.85 each), but don't overdo it: One or two of these fluffy, crumbly, comforting cornmeal cakes will fill you up, especially if you've dug into the warm-from-the-oven chips and salsa they'll bring you before the meal. Among the four choices—chicken, pork, cheese, or sweet (with raisins and pineapple)—the pork is the hands-down winner, a clean tasting hunk of starch and meat with a tangy, mild red sauce. You can have the tamales on combo platters with tacos, burritos, chiles rellenos, or enchiladas ($12–$13 at dinner, about $3 less at lunch), and it's all flavorsome but mighty filling, so consider sharing a platter (as they all come with rice and beans).

$–$$ For G-rated fun, that is "g" as in proudly "geeky," head directly to **Roxy's Diner** ★ (kids) (in the Stratosphere; ☎ 800/99-TOWER or 702/380-7777; www. stratospherehotel.com; Sun–Tues 11am–10pm, Fri–Sat 11am–11pm; AE, DISC, MC, V), a strangely glitzy, utterly synthetic re-creation of a 1950s diner: *Happy Days* as re-imagined by Charo, all red neon and high gloss chrome. The fun isn't the setting, though—this is just one of many Rat Pack–era diners in town—but in the fact that the charming young staff, in bowling shirts and poodle skirts, not only wait tables but sing like "Teen Angels," applying that American Idol glissando to all the dippiest hits of the '50s. Though obviously a corporate ploy by the mucky mucks at the Stratosphere to bring in business, these kids are so talented and enthusiastic that watching their little show is a joy. And the food's swell too; nothing fancy of course, but served in shareable portions and reasonably priced. Get into the spirit of it all with a straw-clogging thick shake ($5), a monumental open-faced tuna melt with a small mountain of onion rings ($5), or a steaming bowl of chili ($4). A kids' menu for the 9-and-under crowd has miniature versions of all the standard diner comfort foods plus a drink and a dessert for $5.50 (one of the cheapest kids' menus in town, by the way). The only "no no" here: Don't be conscientious and order a salad instead of fries. Are salads ever good in a diner? And be sure to brush up on your '50s-era trivia before you arrive: Several times during the day, a quiz becomes part of the show, and whoever knows the most silly stuff gets a free ice cream sundae.

$–$$$ Or you could ditch the Stratosphere altogether and head to one of the most unlikely places I've ever found for fine cuisine: HoJos. It's in this chain motel that the seriously authentic, seriously tasty **Florida Café** ★★ (kids) (1401 Las Vegas Blvd S., at the Howard Johnson; ☎ 702/385-3013; www.floridacafecuban.com; daily 7am–10pm; AE, DISC, MC, V) is bringing the comforting, garlicky flavors of Havana to Vegas. A labor of love for Cuban émigré Sergio Perez, who founded the place in 1997, it's family-run, with Sergio himself doing much of the cooking using recipes passed down from his mother and grandmother. Dishes include

Bistec de Palomilla, a lime infused thin-pounded steak ($14); *pierna de puerco asada,* a leg of pork ($14) marinated in a mojo of OJ, lime, lemon, garlic, and spices; and perfectly roasted chicken with a coat of romance-destroying (but exquisite) garlic sauce ($13). All the main dishes come with rice and beans. People with lighter appetites are catered to as well with 10 sandwich choices (the high-light: a Cuban for $7.95); and *tostones,* thick pieces of fried plantain topped with ground or shredded beef ($5.95) or shrimp ($6.95). For families, there's an American-style kids' menu, with such choices as cheeseburgers and chicken ten-ders for between $4.25 and $5.95. My only criticisms here, and the reasons this place gets two stars rather than three, are the service (don't ever come here if you're in a rush, the waitstaff is on "island time") and the decor. They're certainly trying with the latter—covering the walls with Caribbean art, putting palm frond print pillows on the chairs—but ultimately it looks like, well, like a gussied up Hojos. The Café is just a bit north of the Stratosphere.

$–$$$ Despite the hokey name, **Café Ba Ba Reeba** ★★ (in the Fashion Show Mall, 3200 Las Vegas Blvd. S.; ☎ 702/258-1211; Sun–Thurs 11:30am–11pm, Fri–Sat 11:30 am–midnight; AE, DC, MC, V) is the real deal: an authentic Spanish tapas joint from a chef of both Basque and Galician heritage. Along with the small plates are darn good paellas (a small starts at $19, but it can serve three people) and a burger-heavy kids' menu, but if you're on a budget—and you probably are if you're reading this guide—you'll want to stick with the tapas. That's primarily because they drop to just $3 during happy hour . . . and this restaurant may well have the longest happy hours in Nevada (Sun 4–10pm, Mon–Thurs 4–7pm and 9–11pm, Fri 4–7pm and 9–midnight, Sat 4pm–midnight). So you can make an early or late meal of succulent dates wrapped in bacon, potatoes *bravas* (spicy paprika-laced potatoes with tomato aioli), and perhaps some mushroom empanadas, cap it off with a glass of sangria (also $3) and pay just $12 for the entire feast. Come at the start of happy hour, though; you'll want to grab one of the outdoor patio tables with their primo Strip views, and you'll be battling locals for your seat. Las Vegas resi-dents generally avoid the Strip, but they make an exception for the affordable food and cool setting of Ba Ba Reeba—it's extremely popular.

$$ Good, affordable buffets are scarce at this end of the Strip, so I only have one to recommend: **Circus Buffet** (in Circus Circus; ☎ 877/434-9175; www.circus circus.com; daily 7am–2:30pm and 4:30–10pm; breakfast $10, lunch $12, dinner $13; AE, DISC, MC, V). Long famous as the cheapest buffet on the Strip, it's now lost that title (and the huge crowds who used to come here for that $3 meal), but may have gained a bit of ground in quality control in its stead. In looks, it's about equivalent to a college cafeteria (perhaps for the Ringling Brothers Clown School, thanks to all the circus murals lining the walls). The food is also a tad institu-tional, though the last time I visited the salad bar offered an abundance of crisp greens, the soups were top-notch, and there were some creative choices on the line, such as boiled crawfish and spicy seafood pasta. Pecan squares, NY-style cheesecake, and soft cookies up the ante in the dessert department; and service was swift and cordial. All in all, not a bad choice.

$$–$$$ If you're hankering for something a bit more unique in the realm of buffets—one that serves goat perhaps? (as this one does)—make a beeline for

India Oven ✦✦ (2218 Paradise Rd., at Sahara Ave.; ☎ 702/366-0222; www.india ovenlasvegas.com; daily 11:30am–2:30pm and 5:30–10:30pm; AE, DISC, MC, V). And don't be put off by the address: It's just one sari's throw from the Strip. Punjabi food, specifically from the area in and around Delhi, is the thing here, and at the daily lunch buffet ($11) you'll taste all the greatest hits from that region, from morsels of tandoori chicken (marinated in yogurt and a heady spice mixture called *garamasala* to lock in moistness) to vegetable curries thick with gravy to a perfectly balanced lamb *korma* that's both creamy and nutty. The fare is even more exciting at dinner, when diners can try the less famous foods of that region, a rewarding side-trip. I particularly groove on the Began Bharta ($13), which is eggplant roasted in the tandoor oven and then pulverized, mixed with tomatoes and onions to create a smoky, piquant stew. *Malai kofta* ($13), a veg version of meatballs, with a creamy sauce redolent of cumin, is another top choice. Though it's not a looker, just a simple dignified strip mall restaurant made somewhat exotic by hanging embroideries and Indian sculptures, it's quite popular and after eating here, you'll understand why.

$$$–$$$$ Half coffee shop, half swinging party den, the **Peppermill Coffee Shop** ✦✦✦ 🄺🄸🄳🄢 (2985 Las Vegas Blvd. S., near the Riviera; ☎ 702/735-4177; www.peppermilllasvegas.com/restaurant; daily 24 hr.; AE, DISC, MC, V) is one of the Strip's last vestiges of groovy '70s Vegas. Lit throughout with bands of pink neon lights and populated by leatherette booths canopied with fake cherry trees, this is where Tom Jones and Austin Powers would powwow . . . if one weren't a fictional character and the other a British secret agent (or vice versa). Even the ceiling's mirrored. If you have any appreciation for kitsch—and if you don't, what are you doing in Vegas?—you're going to love this place. Just ordering a drink is a kick; a special waitress in a Julie Christie–inspired halter-top evening gown emerges from the Fireside Lounge area to take your order (the waiters don't handle liquor, mysteriously enough). Speaking of the lounge, that's the height of fabulosity as well and you can read about it in our nightlife chapter on p. 211. So what's there to eat? Well, despite the swinging decor, it's pretty standard coffee shop fare, with a couple of curve balls thrown in, like the heat-packing Portuguese meatball soup ($5.75) I had when I was last here; and the oversized salads (a winning choice). All the servings are huge, actually, whether you settle on a burger ($9.95) or perhaps an omelet at four in the morning ($8). By the way, kids will adore this place. After all, how often do you get to eat in a spot all done in the pinks, purples, and electric blues of Barbie's dream house?

$ Looking like something Edward Hopper would have painted, **Tiffany's (**1700 Las Vegas Blvd. S at E. Oakey Blvd; ☎ 702/444-4459; daily 24 hours; cash only) is one of the last of an endangered species: a lunch counter set inside a drug store. It's so authentic looking it has served as the setting for "down and out" scenes in several movies. But don't let that stop you from eating here: the cooks care and though the food couldn't be described as anything but simple—grilled cheese sandwiches, burgers, pancakes, you know the drill—it's well made and at $4–$8 per meal, a lot less expensive than anything south of here on the Strip. The neighborhood it's in is a bit grungy—hey, the bar next door has a Drunk of the Month contest—so you may want to keep your wits about you if you come later at night.

DOWNTOWN RESTAURANTS

Honky-tonk and old-fashioned, yes, but Downtown is a mecca for high-quality, relatively low-cost eats. Take the famed $2 shrimp cocktail ($1 for slot card members) served by the Golden Gate Casino since 1959. You get a good 25 firm shrimp for that price, not to mention some just-spicy-enough cocktail sauce. Was ever a better dish invented for 2am dining? I think not. If you'd like something more substantial you have half a dozen choices, all within walking distance of each other.

$ There's **Aloha Specialties** ⚔ (in the California Hotel, 12 E. Ogden Ave; ☎ 702/382-0383; www.thecal.com; Mon–Thurs 9am–9pm, Fri–Sat 9am–10pm; cash only), a major gathering place for the many Hawaiian visitors who make Downtown their Vegas hang. Here, the food tastes just like it does in the islands, meaning that you're going to eat big, cheap, and starchy. Particularly recommended are the Saimin Noodles ($3.95), a Hawaiian specialty somewhat like Japanese ramen (though this version is made with egg, which makes the noodles more crinkly). Served in hot *dashi* (a savory bonito broth) and garnished with green onions and *kamaboko* (steamed fish cake), the small portion is a meal-sized soup; don't make the mistake of ordering the large version, which has the dimensions of a bowling ball. Also good and surprisingly fresh tasting is the *Ahi poke* with lime and a heaping helping of sticky rice ($4.75); and the gooey sweet teriyaki plate ($7.50). And if you have a sudden craving for Spam—hey, it happens—this is the place to come, as it's a staple of the menu here.

$ A different type of starchy treat, this time hailing from Idaho rather than Hawaii, is on offer at **Potato Valley** ⚔ (801 S. Las Vegas Blvd. at Gass; ☎ 702/363-7821; www.potatolasvegas.com; Mon–Fri 10am–6pm; AE, DC, MC, V) which takes the common baked potato and tops it with everything from full salads to chicken curry to Cuban fried chicken to chili. This being Vegas, the portions are super-sized—the potato hides under huge mounds of other food—but that doesn't necessarily mean meals here are unhealthy. Many of the offerings like the "South of the Valley" (a colorful collage of beans, mango, corn, and peppers) come with either low-fat dressing or a dollop of low-fat cottage cheese (which adds just the right velvety texture—you won't miss sour cream, I promise). I was very surprised how right items like lettuce and bell peppers taste on top of potato. Dishes start at $3.85 for a simple spud with just butter and sour cream, generally costing in the $6 to $7 range for a more elaborate option. Salads and sandwiches are also doable (same price range), but really, they're not the things to get here. Service is at a counter but quick and friendly, and there are plenty of tables to grab. Potato Valley was named "Best Cheap Eats" in Vegas by the *Review Journal* in 2008.

$ With its loop of Bollywood playing on the corner TV, and its paintings and wall hangings from India brightening up an otherwise prosaic storefront, **Kabob Korner** (507 E. Fremont St.; ☎ 702/384-7722; www.kabobkornerlv.com; Mon–Sat 8am–9pm; cash only) would look at home in most big American cities. In Vegas, its lack of glitz, corporate tagging, and the fact that it's not in a strip mall, make it downright exotic. That doesn't keep the locals away, they file in steadily throughout the day for simple, well-made grilled foods (everything from burgers to yes, kabobs) for a low price. That burger I mentioned is just $2.50, and pita

Fremont Street Experience

Bonanza Rd.

Reed Whipple Cultural Center

Bell

Harris

Maryland Pkwy.

Mesquite

Bonanza Rd.

Grand Central Pkwy.

Main St.

Stewart

SQUIRES PARK

Mesquite Ave.

Ogden Ave.

Fremont St.

Area of detail

■ Bus Depot

Carson Ave.

Lewis Ave.

Clark Ave.

Bonneville Ave.

Garces Ave.

Las Vegas Blvd.

Gass Ave.

Hoover Ave.

Charleston Blvd.

Casino Center Blvd.

1st St.

3rd St.

4th St.

6th St.

7th St.

8th St.

Bridger Ave.

7th St.

8th St.

9th St.

10th St.

11th St.

Charleston

DOWNTOWN

Las Vegas Blvd. (The Strip)

Paradise

Maryland

Sahara

Desert Inn

Eastern

Flamingo

UNLV

Tropicana

Russell

McCarran Int'l Airport

Aloha Specialties **2**
Chicago Joes **6**
Garden Court Buffet **4**
Golden Nugget Buffet **4**
Kebab Korner **5**
Makino **6**
Potato Valley **1**
Triple George **8**
Triple Seven Brewery **1**

sandwiches with either chicken or beef which retains a nice char from the grill, cost $5. It's quick, tasty, and just 1 block from the Fremont Street Experience.

$–$$ Closer to the Strip and within walking distance of the Marriage License Bureau, **Chicago Joes** (820 S. 4th St.; ☎ 702/382-JOES; www.chicagojoes restaurant.com; Tues–Fri 11am–10pm, Sat 5–10pm; AE, DISC, MC, V) would be a good place for an inexpensive wedding reception if your last name was Soprano, and your favorite food was anything "Parmagianed." A red sauce and garlic-bread joint set in a cozy, little brick house with white lace curtains, red and white checked oilcloth covered tables, and red Christmas lights strung along the ceiling, it's unabashedly Italian-American. No *bucatini* or *bacala* here, just the Italian fare that's grown so standard it's as American nowadays as a Big Mac. That being said, the simple food they serve—spaghetti with meat sauce ($6.50 lunch, $9.95 dinner), eggplant parmigiana ($8.50 lunch, $15 dinner), and lasagna ($8.50 lunch, $15 dinner), is well prepared; and the setting is so unpretentious and homey (this is another of the few restaurants in Vegas that isn't in either a casino or a strip mall), it feels radical for Vegas. Especially when the jokey, friendly waiters let you linger over your cannoli ($3.95) and coffee, filling up your cup over and over with nary a glance at their watches.

$$–$$$$ In the heart of downtown, just a block off Fremont Street, the **Triple George** ★★ (201 N. 3rd St.; ☎ 702/384-2761; www.triplegeorgegrill.com; Mon–Thurs 11am–10pm, Fri 11am–11pm, Sat 3–11pm, Sun 3–10pm; AE, DISC, MC, V) is where the Rat Pack would have gathered . . . if Triple George had existed back then. Purposefully designed to look much older than it is—the owner's inspiration was the Tedechi Grill (opened in 1849) in San Francisco—it's a clubby place, a haunt of the city's political elite, who favor the private dark-wood booths over the massive brass-railed bar/lunch counter (seating 36). You'll be transported back about 50 years both by the setting and the selection of steaks, chops . . . and seafood dishes named "casino" or "Louis." Most old-fashioned, both in price and selection, is the "George's Favorites" section of the menu, with its servings of pot roast ($9.95), corned beef hash ($8.95), Ham Steak and Eggs ($8.95), and beef Stroganoff ($11), among others. Best of all are the flaky, deep-dish chicken potpie ($14) and a bacon-wrapped meatloaf ($9.95) that proves my theory that wrapping bacon around just about anything is an automatic culinary home run. If you were wondering about the odd name, it's a tribute to the *menschen* or good people who helped found the restaurant (as "George" by their definition means "a person who is free in giving and sharing"). Plastered across the walls are old black and white photos of everyone the owners consider to be a George, and they'll beam benignly down on you as you tuck into your martini, saw through your hamburger steak, or buy everyone a round (another "George" quality—it makes your own drink taste better).

$–$$ **Garden Court Buffet** ★★★ 🧒 (in Main Street Station, 200 Main St.; ☎ 800/713-8933 or 702/387-1896; daily 7:30am–10pm; Mon–Fri breakfast $7, lunch $8, Mon, Wed, Sat, Sun dinner and brunch $11, Sat and Sun brunch $10, Tues and Thurs dinner $14, Fri dinner $16, children under 3 eat free; AE, DISC, MC, V), is Downtown's prettiest and most extensive buffet—and a darn good deal at half what the Strip casino's are charging for meals. Reminiscent of a Victorian train station, its ceilings are grandly arched, covered with white tile and small pinpoint lights, which glow daintily at dinnertime. At lunch, sunshine pours through the lovely stained glass windows, one of the few in-casino eateries that allow sunlight to enter (blame Vegas' large vampire clientele, I guess). It may also be the most spacious buffet in town, with tables that are shouting distance apart and comfortable chairs. The buffet itself is a massive, highly staffed affair with nine live-action stations, each attended by a friendly chef popping pizzas into a brick oven, wokking up Chinese food, or grilling to order a tender, large T-bone steak for those who stop by on Tuesday nights. Soul food, pasta, Mexican, Pacific Rim and American classics, and desserts are served at the other stations. Friday the emphasis is on seafood, and Thursday features scampi and filet. All told, I counted up a whopping 55 entrees and side dishes and 30 different desserts when I last visited, and though they weren't as exotic as what you'd find at many a Strip casino, Southern staples such as collard greens and ham hocks, black-eyed peas, mashed sweet potatoes, and finger-sucking-good BBQ compare well to what you'd get at a fine Memphis BBQ pit (and I mean that as a high compliment). Desserts are also a cut above the usual, even the sugarless ones.

$–$$ Two more buffets round out Downtown's recommended dining scene: The **Golden Nugget Buffet** (in the Golden Nugget Hotel and Casino, 129 Fremont

What You Need to Know Before
You Ever Pick Up a Menu

Would it really surprise you to learn that dining out is a little bit, well, different in Sin City? Here are some items to keep in mind:

Reservations: Always make them, no matter how humble the restaurant seems on the surface. Remember, at certain times of the year, when the big conventions hit town, dozens of people will be vying for the same spot in that restaurant you thought you'd breeze into to grab a bite. So get your act together and call in advance, particularly in the more famous places. You don't want to waste your precious vacation waiting for a table, or giving up and dining at the food court (which can also sometimes be a time waster, with astonishing lines popping up in a matter of minutes).

Tipping: Yes, you can give chips in lieu of money, but you've got to leave something—even at the buffets, and especially if it's one of those buffets where the waiters scurry around filling drink orders. A tip of 15% of the total cost of the meal is standard. An easy way to figure out what that is, is to simply double the tax that will be tacked onto your bill (in Nevada it's 7.75%). If you're happy with the meal, or the sight of your server in her Playboy Bunny–like outfit, leave more. If you get the feeling they've spat in your coffee, give less, but give something. Servers make the majority of their money from tips, so when you stiff them, you're literally ripping that spoon of baby food out of their children's mouths. (Okay, that might be a bit dramatic, but you get the point—don't be a jerk when it comes to tipping.)

Smoking: Puff away. Unlike most areas of the U.S. nowadays, smoking is still allowed in many Vegas restaurants. Smokers are placed in their own section, of course, but with the constant gusting of casino air conditioners, I often feel like my food is being flavored by nicotine. If you're like me and don't like the stink of cigarettes when you eat, take a quick look around before you accept a table and try to get as far away from the smokers as you can. It's pretty much impossible at some restaurants, but in others they separate the two groups by placing a bar or even a wall in between sections.

St.; ☎ 800/846-5336; www.goldennugget.com; Mon–Sat 7am–10pm, Sun 8am–10pm; Mon–Fri breakfast $10, lunch $11, Sat–Sun brunch $18, Mon–Thurs and Sat–Sun dinner $18, Fri dinner $21; AE, DC, MC, V) and Makino (p. 98). Located in the hotel of the same name, the Golden Nugget is a worthy choice if you don't want to leave the craps table too long. While not nearly as good as Main Street Station's Garden Court Buffet (p. 96), it's a pleasant place to eat, still carrying the thumbprint of Steve Wynn, who once ran the place. You'll see the golden lighting, ruffled awnings, cluster chandeliers, and etched glass here that he later used at the Bellagio and Wynn's Las Vegas, albeit on a much smaller scale. Small is the key word here as the buffet is quite limited, with mostly American food on offer, and the booth seating can be a bit cramped, especially if you're with a large party. But what you do get is tasty food: intensely clammy (in a good way) clam chowders, flavorful rice and beans with chunks of pork, fresh salads, crisply fried cod, and the like. Desserts are a bit of a disappointment—the Golden Nugget has no ice cream machine (gasp!) and the "famous" bread pudding must be famous as some sort of industrial glue (because no one would want to try this sticky, bland mush more than once). Friday is seafood buffet day, but you'll do better a few blocks over at Main Street Station's abundant shellfish feast.

$$ Perhaps it's a gambling superstition, but things tend to come in threes downtown. Hence the **Triple Seven Brewery** (in Main Street Station, 200 Main St.; ☎ 800/713-8933 or 702/387-1896; www.mainstreetcasino.com; daily 11am–7am; AE, DISC, MC, V), which not only has a triple title, it's one of three eateries within the Main Street Station. An actual brewery with the massive copper-brewing tanks to prove it, it's set in a soaring, high-ceilinged room that's appropriately manly, with lots of brass, dark wood, and multiple TV screens tuned to the hot game of the moment. Award-winning beers are the draw here, whether you're quaffing one of their chocolatey porters (made from five different malts), a Viennese-style lager, or their most popular: a High Roller gold wheat beer. Rotating beer specials from Blueberry Wheat Ales to Cranberry Stouts keep the locals returning time and again. The food's not up to the quality of the beer—it's just typical pub grub—but after a couple of brewskies it'll taste downright gourmet (meals tend to run in the $8–$15 range). Breakfast is served starting at midnight. They also do sushi here, alarmingly enough, but I wouldn't recommend it. Happy hour is Monday through Friday from 3pm to 6pm and there's a graveyard special from midnight to 7am, when 16-ounce microbrews go for just $1.

$$–$$$$ The perfect pit stop on a day of intense shopping, **Makino** ✮✮ (in the Premium Outlet Mall, 775 S. Grand Central Pkwy.; ☎ 702/382-8848; www.makinolasvegas.com; daily 11:30am–3pm and 5:30–9:30pm; lunch $16, dinner $24, $1 more on Sat and Sun; AE, DISC, MC, V) was named for the visionary brothers who founded the Todai chain of sushi buffets (they're now in nine states across the U.S.). The brothers sold the chain several years back to a group of investors who started franchising like mad and then, I suppose, some of the franchisees had second thoughts. This branch and its sister restaurant fairly close to the Strip (at 3965 S. Decatur Blvd., at Flamingo; ☎ 702/382-8848) are privately owned, maintaining the concept—one price for all the sushi you can eat, in plain, large dining halls—but restoring the quality that I've found lacking lately at the Todai outposts. Here you'll find 50 varieties of sushi set along a 160-foot-long buffet in a dazzling and tempting array of colors, prettier than any sweater display at nearby Tommy Hilfiger. The fish is so fresh you want to slap it, and comes in dozens of incarnations, from simple nigiri sushi, a piece of fish fitted onto a mound of vinegar rice (I counted 14 different varieties when I last visited), to elaborate multi-ingredient rolls, from which you can choose just one slice—perhaps the best sushi innovation ever! For those who can't stomach raw fish, there's also an assortment of cooked foods and salads, from do-it-yourself noodle soups (you choose the ingredients and mix it together) to tempura, baked prawns, snow crab legs, fried rice, noodle dishes, barbecued pork, and much more. But let's be real; you come here because you're in a town where two miniscule pieces of sushi can cost you $8 and a whole meal up to $100, and at Makino you can down an entire aquarium without financial concern.

RESTAURANTS EAST OF THE STRIP

This is where the budget gourmets go. Chockablock with smaller, local haunts, sometimes run by the local superstar chefs (who are rightly wary of getting into bed with the all-controlling casinos), east of the Strip is where you can eat for a third less than what you'd pay on the Strip, eat just as well (or better), and park a minute's walk from your table (though to be fair, that half-mile trek from parking garage to casino-based restaurant can sure help you work up an appetite).

$ And did I mention that deals in this part of town can be extraordinary? Take the $6.95 steak dinner at the **Ellis Island Casino and Brewery** ✦ (4178 Koval Lane; ☎ 702/733-8901; www.ellisislandcasino.com; daily 24 hr.; AE, DISC, MC, V). No, you won't be dining on horsemeat, in a room that resembles Mickey D's. This is the real thing, aged for about a minute and a half, granted, but on my last visit my 10-ounce hunk of meat was nicely charred, not at all stringy, tender, and cooked to my specifications. A baked potato with a tiny carton of sour cream and some limp veggies came with it, but for less than $7? Hey, it was money well spent. Anthony Curtis, gambling expert par extraordinaire, is a regular and once brought six out-of-town buddies here for a meal. "They came out and we all ate steak and prime rib and drank beer," he told me. "And when the check came they all jumped up and started slapping high fives. They were stunned; it was like $50 for six of us for prime rib and beer. Getting the bill was literally more exciting than eating the food." The steak dinner is not on the menu, but it's an open secret, so simply order it when you arrive, or take your choice of prime rib, pastas, burgers, you name it—this unpretentious, coffee shop has most of the standards. You'll want to arrive early, as locals keep this place crowded day and night (I had to wait about 20 min. to get in for my after-show meal at 11pm one night).

$ Like its namesake, Ellis Island also serves as a gateway to New York, culinary NYC, in this case, in the form of the finest Big Apple–style pizzas in town. Thin-crusted, with the smoky taste of a real brick oven, and a sauce made from vine-ripened tomatoes, the pies at **Metro Pizza** ✦✦ (in the Ellis Island Casino, 4178 Koval Lane; ☎ 702/312-5888; www.metropizza.com; daily noon–3am; AE, DISC, MC, V) are the genuine article. As well they should be: Founders and cousins John Arena and Sam Facchini come from a long line of *pizzaiolo* (pizza makers). When their grandparents emigrated to New York in the early–20th century, they lived just 50 yards from Lombardis, the first pizzeria in the U.S., and learned their trade there. Recipes were passed down from relative to relative over the years until 1980, when the cousins lugged two ovens to Vegas in a borrowed car and set up shop. Now a mini-chain with three shops around town (the other two are at 1395 E. Tropicana Ave. and 4001 S. Decatur Blvd.), the Ellis Island branch is the nearest to the Strip and the most bare bones, with no seating—just a glass case of freshly made pies. Still, it's a prime choice for a late-night snack; and if you're sick of bland, overpriced casino room service, you can order up a plain pie from just $6.25 (individual) to

$13 (large) until the wee hours of the morning (fixings add about $1 each). Go to one of their stores directly and you can order by the slice ($2.50).

$–$$ For many people, of course, Las Vegas itself is the new Ellis Island, a hot spot for immigration from all corners of the globe, with 8,000 new residents coming here each month. In their wake has come a flowering of ethnic restaurants, and **Lindo Michoacan** ★★★ (kids) (2655 E. Desert Inn Rd., between Eastern Ave. and Pecos Rd.; ☎ 702/735-6828; Mon–Wed 11am–10pm, Thurs–Fri 11am–11pm, Sat–Sun 9:30am–11pm; AE, DISC, MC, V) is one of the city's most extravagant blossoms. Las Vegas boasts a large Mexican community, and when those Latinos have a special occasion to celebrate, this is where they come. Founded by Javiar Barajas, who named it after his beautiful *(lindo)* native state in Mexico, the food here is heavenly . . . possibly because Barajas learned to cook from the Mother Superior at the seminary he attended as a boy. And that good lady knew all sorts of recipes that Taco Bell never heard of, making this a great place for adventurous eaters. They'll salivate over such exotica as beef tongue tacos ($13) or goat meat simmered with chiles in beer ($13, it's actually pretty amazing how well the combo works). Michoacan, the state, is famous for its *carnitas* ($16)—braised pork, marinated with oranges and spice—and this may be the one dish on the menu that's a must-order, though it gets a real run for the money from the mole poblano ($15), which had the deepest, richest mole sauce I've ever tried. Upon entering, take a peek at the ladies in the center room making the corn tortillas by hand. Lunch specials go for just $5.95 to $7.95, including a beverage. Children's plates are available for $5.95 and come with a Shirley Temple, which my kids really liked. Thanks to the mariachi music and the Crayola-colored setting, with its mottled yellow walls, mural-painted chairs, *papel picado* (cut paper banners) strung from the ceiling, and Mexican folk art pieces everywhere, it really does feel like a party from the moment you arrive. The only thing my kids didn't like—and I wasn't too pleased about it either—were the long waits first to get a table, then to get a menu, then to have our order taken . . . well, you get the picture. So pack your patience, as it will be rewarded, but allocate at least 2 hours for a meal here. By the way, if you're into celebrity spotting, you can sometimes get a glimpse of Steffi Graf and husband Andre Agassi, who are regulars; they like this place so much it's where they had their informal post-wedding meal 4 days before Graf gave birth to their first child.

$–$$ The grand poohbah of the city's ethnic restaurants, named the "Single Best Thai Restaurant in North America" by no less an authority than *Gourmet,* and my own personal pick for best restaurant in Vegas, is the venerable **Lotus of Siam** ★★★ (953 E. Sahara Ave.; ☎ 702/735-3033; www.saipinchutima.com; Mon–Thurs 11:30am–2:30pm and 5:30–9:30pm, Fri 11:30am–2:30pm and 5:30–10pm, Sat–Sun 5:30–10pm; AE, DISC, MC, V). It gets all these plaudits without all the extras that tend to dazzle diners at other restaurants. Its location is terrible, in a dingy strip mall (with a notorious swingers club several doors down); its decor ho hum, most notable for the dozens of photos of beaming, full-looking celebrities; and if you come late at lunchtime you'll likely be upset that the buffet is one of diminishing returns, as it doesn't get refilled when the food runs out. But this is not a buffet-type place anyway, nor should you just expect upgrades of your same-old, same-old Pad Thai. To really get why foodies drive down from L.A. regularly just to dine here (and I know a couple who do), you have to put yourself

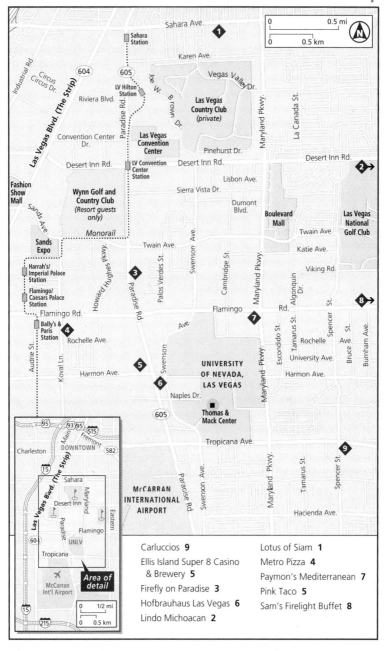

Carluccios **9**

Ellis Island Super 8 Casino
& Brewery **5**

Firefly on Paradise **3**

Hofbrauhaus Las Vegas **6**

Lindo Michoacan **2**

Lotus of Siam **1**

Metro Pizza **4**

Paymon's Mediterranean **7**

Pink Taco **5**

Sam's Firelight Buffet **8**

in Bill's hands. Bill is the husband of chef Saipin Chutina, and he makes the reverse trip to L.A. once a week to buy fresh ingredients, jetting off to Thailand about once a month to get spices blended to his wife's specifications. Bill will know what's best that day (and if Bill's not there, ask for Tony) and he'll steer you towards the Saipin (Northern) Thai specialties that really make this place unique. As an example: The Red Chili Dip, a tomatoey mix of ground pork with spices served with crudités that put chips and dip to shame. Or the *Nam Kao Tod* ($7.95), a wonderfully tart sausage, dry in texture, nutty, minty, and sided by crispy deep-fried rice. Or the jackfruit curry with smoked fish ($9.95), or a crispy mussel omelet served with a spicy red sauce that makes this dish so much more special than just eggs ($8.95). I list all of these just to give you an idea of what your meal could be like, but really, ignore what I'm writing here, and go with what Bill recommends, as he knows best. Just be sure to tell him how much spice you can take and don't overestimate your tolerance; the kitchen will sear your tongue off, if you ask for it hot. An unusually fine wine list, with lots of great Rieslings, is another unusual touch (it was compiled with the help of the celebrity Strip chefs who dine here).

$–$$ Of course, you don't have to go to a culinary powerhouse like Lotus of Siam to have a fun meal. In this, the capital of kitsch and ultratacky decor, those historic elements are reason enough to pick a restaurant, and when they are the criterion, you go straight to **Carluccios** ✰ (1775 E. Tropicana Ave., at Spencer St.; ☎ 702/795-3236; Tues–Sun 4:30–10pm; AE, DISC, MC, V). What's the story here? Well, it was owned by a certain extremely famous Sin City–based performer. The decor of the place may just clue you in to who that was. Let's see, the front of the building is shaped to look like a huge sheet of music. And in the back room the bar is painted to look like a piano, the ceilings and walls are mirrored, the chairs are a groovy '60s see-through plastic, and the piano in the middle of the room is covered with Swarovski crystals. Ooh, you're right—this was once Liberace's joint! The current owners had the good sense to keep the "music room" looking just as it did when the man with the rhinestone thumb was in charge, though unfortunately they've remodeled the rest to look like 1,200 other Italian restaurants (so request a table in the rear). Stories abound about bottles of wine flying through the air here, and racks of liquor mysteriously falling over on Liberace's birthday—a botched, other-worldly attempt to redecorate? The maestro couldn't have been complaining about the food, which, while not gourmet, is pleasant, in an Italian-by-way-of-Toledo manner. But the rolls arrive warm, the minestrone soup ($2.25) contains a garden's worth of veggies, and the red sauce is robust—though I wish it didn't arrive slathered over every conceivable entree and appetizer (pastas tend to run $9–$10, with meat, fish, and chicken dishes $12–$15). Tops on the menu are the thick, Sicilian pizzas ($12 medium, $14 large), which have a raft of choices for toppings.

$–$$ Food also seems a bit beside the point at the hipper-than-thou **Pink Taco** ✰ (in the Hard Rock Hotel, at 4455 Paradise Rd.; ☎ 800/HRD-ROCK or 702/693-5544; www.hardrockhotel.com; Sun–Thurs 11am–10pm, Fri–Sat 11am–11pm; AE, DISC, MC, V), which has a bodacious waitstaff, and a cantina-on-steroids interior, with benches so rough-hewn I worried I'd get splinters, adobe walls with endless displays of colorful Mexican folk art, and twinkling metal star-shaped lighting fixtures. A huge wooden bar with a rowdy crowd dominates the center of the room.

Oom Pah Pah Eats

Fabulous fakery—whether it's boobs or Egyptian pyramids—is a high art in Vegas, but the most convincing "tribute eatery" actually lies west of the Strip, and is worth a trip.

Hofbräuhaus Las Vegas ★★★ (4510 Paradise Rd., across from the Hard Rock Hotel; ☎ 702/853-2337; www.hofbrauhauslasvegas. com; Sun–Thurs 11am–11pm, Fri–Sat 11am–midnight; AE, DISC, MC, V; $$–$$$$), is a $7-million copy of the Munich original, and those who've visited both would be hard pressed to tell the difference between the two. It's shingled with 50,000 beavertail roof tiles imported from Germany; the famed pretzels are mixed in the Fatherland, the dough then shipped over here to be baked; and artists took extensive photos of the ornamental ceiling, walls, and beams of the original, projected them onto the plaster here, and then painted by numbers, so to speak. So all of the quaint, bucolic designs and signs are faithfully reproduced, from the portrait of King Ludwig protecting the entrance, to radishes and pretzels dancing along the beams, to the words "It's worse to be thirsty than homesick" over the stage area. Diners sit at the same long wood tables and benches that they have had in Germany for the past 400 years, ever since Duke Wilhelm V commissioned the original in 1589.

But this would all be beside the point if the beer weren't so splendid that . . . well, after a couple of steins it seems absolutely normal to link arms with the strangers around the table and sway back and forth to the insistent beats of the live German band on stage (different acts are rotated in from Germany every 4 weeks). The brew or *brau* you're drinking is also the original, shipped in from Munich, and made in accordance with the purity laws of 1516. What makes it taste so great? Glaciers. The water in these lagers, wheat beers, and dark beers is drawn from a well that is 500 feet deep, whose waters, scientists tell us, are left over from the glaciers that covered Munich during the so-called Tertiary period (bye bye dinosaurs, hello ice age).

Will you enjoy yourself if you don't like beer? Absolutely. The food, while heavy, is terrifically flavorsome, often smothered in beer gravy (cooked 48 hr. before it hits the plate) and accompanied by tangy red cabbage and sauerkraut. I'm particularly fond of the *weisswurste* (white veal and pork sausages, $14) and the roasted chicken stuffed with onions and beer butter ($17), but in truth it's all pretty delightful. There's also an inside/outside beer garden (you'll see what I mean when you get there) for folks who want to escape the nonstop party of the main hall.

Buffet-arama

Next to "place your bets," "all you can eat" may well be the most commonly used phrase in Vegas. Buffets are everywhere. I've tried to limit my coverage to those buffets that give the very best value for the money, but the truth is, you can usually scrounge up something appetizing and filling at every single buffet in town. So, in the hope of being useful, here's the M.O. of all of the major casino buffets in town.

Please note that both the adult and child prices are listed in the following chart, and the listing gives the casino's name first.

Buffet-arama

Buffets by Casino	Breakfast	Brunch	Lunch	Dinner
Bellagio	$14.95	$19.95		
Boulder Station	$6.99	$8.99	$12.99	Sun–Thurs $11.99, Fri $18.99, Sat $14.99
Caesars Palace	$17.95	$24.95	$28.95	Sun Brunch $34.95, Fri–Sat $35.95
Circus Circus	$10.49	$12.49	N/A	$13.49
Excalibur	$11.99	$14.99	N/A	$17.99
Flamingo	$14.99	$16.99	$19.99	$21.99
Fremont	$6.99	$7.49	$10.99	Mon, Wed, Thurs, Sat $12.99; Tues and Sun $15.99
Gold Coast	$6.95	$8.45	$12.95	Sat–Thurs $12.95, Fri $17.95
Golden Nugget	$9.99	$10.99	$17.99	Mon–Thurs $17.99, Fri–Sun $20.99
Harrah's	$14.99	$15.99	$20.99	$21.99
Imperial Palace	N/A	N/A	$12.99	$18.99
Las Vegas Hilton	$12.99	$17.99	$13.99	$17.99
Luxor	$12.99	$14.99	$18.99	$19.99
Main Street Station	$6.99	$7.99	$10.99	Sun, Mon, Wed $10.99, Tues and Thurs $13.99, Fri–Sat $15.99
Mandalay Bay	$15.99	$19.99	$23.99	$26.99
MGM Grand	$14.50	$17.50	$25.99	$25.99
Mirage	$13.95	$17.95	$22.95	$24.95
Monte Carlo	$11.95	$13.95	$18.95	$18.95

Buffet name	Breakfast	Brunch	Lunch	Dinner
Orleans	$7.99	$9.99	$14.99	Mon, Tues, Thurs, Sat $13.99, Sun $14.99, Wed $15.99, Fri $18.99
Palace Station	$6.99	$7.99	$9.99	$9.99
Palms	$7.99	$9.99	$16.99	$16.99
Paris	$14.99	$17.99	$24.99	$24.99
Planet Hollywood	$14.99	$18.99	$17.99	$27.99
Plaza	$7.99	N/A	$7.77	$7.77
Red Rock Resort	$7.99	$10.99	$18.99	$18.99
Riviera	$10.99	$12.99	$14.99	N/A
Sahara	N/A	N/A	$14.99	$14.99
Sam's Town	$6.49	$8.49	$10.49	Mon–Tues and Sun $10.99, Thurs $11.99, Wed and Sat $13.99, Fri $17.99
South Point	$6.95	$8.95	$12.95	Tues–Thurs and Sat–Sun $13.95, Mon $14.95, Fri $17.95
Stratosphere	N/A	N/A	Brunch daily 7am–1pm, $11.99	$16.99, Fri $20.99
Terrible's	$4.99	$6.99	$9.99	Mon–Tues and Fri–Sat $9.99, Sun and Wed $11.99, Thurs $15.99
Treasure Island	$13	$20	$16	$21
Tropicana	$10.99	$11.99	$15.99	$15.99
Wynns	$18.95	$22.95	$36.95	$34.95

Outside there's a patio overlooking the Hard Rock pool for prime hottie-viewing opportunities. Now, I know I said food is somewhat beside the point (and it is, especially during the two-for-one margarita happy hour), which makes it a cheery surprise that it's actually okay—not as good as Lindo Michoacan (p. 100), of course, but five steps above your average fast-food burrito joint. Its signature dish, the Pink Taco ($9.75) is a lovely mix of pickled onions, chunks of chicken, guacamole, and *salsa rioja* for color (if not spice) in a freshly baked tortilla. Corn tamales ($7) have such a strong taste of sweet summer corn they could almost be served as a dessert (that's a compliment), and the *carne asada* (whether on its own or in a taco) is marinated until tender and then cooked to just the right shade of pink ($17 or $12). The menu even includes some fairly unusual choices such as baby ribs in a watermelon BBQ sauce ($18); and chile relleno ($12), a roasted poblano pepper filled with beans and cheese and doused in a tomatoey red sauce. For those watching their figures—maybe they want to work here?—there are over-sized salads. Dieters, however, may find themselves slipping when confronting the "chocolate taco" ($5.50), a South of the Border ice cream sandwich, beautiful to look at, messy to eat, but oh so worth it. Oh, and if you think the name of the place is rather vulgar, well, I'd have to agree—but don't let that keep you away.

$–$$ One prime buffet choice out on the Boulder Highway (a loose slot mecca, so you could potentially gamble here long enough to score a free buffet meal) **Sam's Firelight Buffet** ✫✫ 🄺 (in Sam's Town Hotel and Gambling Hall, 5111 Boulder Hwy.; ☎_ 800/897-8696 or 702/456-7777; www.samstown.com; breakfast (7–11am Mon–Fri) $6, lunch (11am–3pm Mon–Thu; 11am–2pm Fri) $8, dinner (4–9pm Sun–Thur; 3–9pm Fri) starts at $11 but goes up to $12 Thurs for Pacific Rim night, $14 Wed and Sat for steak and prime rib night, and $18 Fri for seafood night; children pay $2 less at breakfast, $3 less every other meal; AE, DISC, MC, V) gives its customers something no other buffet can offer: dinner and a show. It's a silly show, to be sure, but kids will like watching the animatronic animals in the center of the hotel go through their shtick as an impressive rainstorm rages, and in the evening, lasers flash. To see the show, be sure to request one of the seats that faces away from the buffet and into the atrium. It's the best view anyway, now that the big wall of fire behind the buffet line (it gave it its "Firelight" name) has been permanently extinguished because of safety concerns. You'll still get a small glimpse of flame at the excellent rotisserie section, a nice innovation that makes you wonder why more buffets don't have rotisseries. Other choices include a wide array of Chinese food, chili, three types of al dente pasta (usually), pizza, a taco bar, and a superior salad bar with such nice touches as warm spinach dressing. Pies, pies, and more pies, along with cheesecakes, cobblers, and bread puddings make up the all-American dessert choices. All in all, it's a classy meal; the "nouveau Western" look of the place with its soaring ceiling, twig sculptures, and amber lighting fixtures is downright elegant. The only reminder of how little you're paying (compared to Strip buffets) is the fact that you have to go get your own beverage—no great hardship.

$–$$$ Sophisticated and urban, but decidedly friendly, the tapas bar **Firefly on Paradise** ✫✫✫ (3900 Paradise Rd.; ☎ 702/369-3871; www.fireflylv.com; Mon–Thurs 11:30am–2am, Fri 11:30am–3am, Sat 5pm–3am, Sun 5pm–2am; AE, DISC, MC, V) has a vibe that's utterly unlike anyplace else in town. By which I mean, you'll feel like you're in New York or San Francisco . . . not in a restaurant that's imitating a restaurant in one of those cities. And if you're like me you'll start looking around and wondering where these people with the blunt haircuts, the geek-cool glasses, and the intense conversations came from. I mean, I actually overheard someone discussing national politics here—and in a serious manner, too. Not to say that this is some student coffee shop–type place, this is a swinging, fun tapas bar with a killer cocktail list and overflowing pitchers of fruit-filled sangria. Tapas, after all, is a group sport that invites conviviality; diners who don't know how to play nice and share, won't be asked back. But with so much to share—62 different types of tapas—even the greediest Guses won't have any problems. The real difficulty here is picking because so much of it is so good. You could woo your date with stuffed dates ($4), which are over-the-top sinful, swathed in bacon, bathed in a red wine reduction, and filled with almonds and blue cheese. Then, for a contrast, get a plate of mouth-puckering pickled *boquerones* ($5), white anchovies with roasted red and yellow peppers. The ham and cheese croquettes ($5) are as crisp outside and molten inside as any I've ever had in Barcelona, and the chorizo sausage with clams ($9.50) plate is an inspired variation on surf-and-turf. Request to be seated on the serene porch if it's warm enough; the inside with its ochre art-covered walls and crowded bar is buzzing with energy, but can get a tad cramped.

RESTAURANTS WEST OF THE STRIP

With two exceptions, my choices west of the Strip require a car. Most of the good restaurants on this side of town are simply too far to cab to, especially if you're on a budget. That's not to say these picks aren't worth the drive—they absolutely are—it's just that the expense of getting there should be factored into the cost of the meal.

$–$$ Luckily, at **Pho Vietnam** ✪✪✪ (4215 Spring Mountain Rd.; ☎ 702/227-8618; daily 10am–10pm; AE, DC, MC, V) the meal won't be expensive and boy, is this place great. After eating here the last time, my first thought was "I wish I had more than three stars to award." I don't want to give extra points for looks—Pho Vietnam is pretty unremarkable in that department (it looks like your typical strip mall Asian food joint), but here the food reaches another level. The *pho* ($6–$9), a classic beef broth and noodle soup that comes in several varieties, has a depth of flavor that's "Top Chef" worthy. And you can play chef, too: Each bowl comes sided by a plate of extra goodies—limes to squeeze, cilantro to sprinkle, and so on—so you can customize your soup to your tastes. Or your tastes and your dining companions as the bowls are massive and definitely shareable (there's no charge, just ask for a ladle and an additional empty bowl). Or you can make a meal for a mere $3. That buys a crunchy *bahn,* literally a grilled pork sandwich on French bread topped by crisp pickled carrots, daikon, and cilantro with a mayo-mustard dressing—yum, yum! Final recommendation: the fried spring rolls ($5), which give a slight "crack" when you cut them, they're that grease free. Don't confuse this branch with Pho Vietnamese at Treasure Island at The Mirage which is more "fusion Vietnamese" food, and frankly, not as good as this place.

$–$$ In the same complex is **Sam Woo BBQ** ✪ (4215 Spring Mountain Rd.; ☎ 702/368-7628; Sun–Thurs 10am–11pm, Fri–Sat 10am–midnight; AE, DC, MC, V). Part of a small chain (also in California and Canada), you'd know that this was a BBQ joint even if you didn't know the name, thanks to the many animal carcasses (a full pig!) skewered and cooking in the front window. The dish to get here is the BBQ duck ($9 with rice) which has a skin as crisp (and addictive) as a potato chip and an interior that's superbly moist. The BBQ pork is also worthwhile.

$–$$ I think with the reputation it has as a celebrity magnet, many visitors will be surprised to find that the Palms is actually off the Strip, though not too far west of it. If you decide to head out and try and catch a glimpse of K-Fed or Carmen Electra and the hunt makes you hungry, pop in to the **Bistro Buffet** ✪ (in the Palms Casino Resort, 4321 W. Flamingo Rd.; ☎ 866/725-6773; www. palms.com; daily 8am–10pm; breakfast $8, lunch $10, dinner $17; AE, DISC, MC, V), a favorite of the locals for its reasonable prices and superior food. The Middle Eastern fare—hummus, stuffed grape leaves, *tzatziki, labneh,* tabbouleh, baba ghanouj, and phyllo pastries—is a particular treat, though I have also been impressed by the smoked pork loin, the tomato soup, large pasta selection, and the beef

Restaurants West of the Strip

Fantasy Market Buffet 8
Feast Buffet 1
Hash House a Go Go 3
In 'N Out Burger 11
Memphis Championship BBQ 2
Nora's Cuisine 7
Omelet House 12
Pho Vietnam 9
Raku 6
R.U.B 9
Rosemary's Restaurant 5
Sushi Fever 4
Tom Loo BBQ 9

A Gift to the Gals

Many food writers consider **Rosemary's Restaurant** ★ (8125 W. Sahara; ☎ 702/869-2251; www.rosemarysrestaurant.com; Mon–Fri 11:30am–2:30pm and 5:30–10:30pm, Fri–Sat 5:30-10:30pm; AE, DC, MC, V) to be the finest off-Strip restaurant in Vegas and one of the top 10 gourmet experiences in town. I'm not among them. While I find the food here, which is American with some Creole influences, hearty and usually tasty, it's never blown my socks off. That being said, I am blown away by the consideration they show to members of my gender: Every Wednesday, women can eat and drink at Rosemary's for 50% off. And there are no limits, beyond what their stomachs will hold. So give it a try and see whether I or my foodie companions are right in their assessment of the place. (With the discount, you can expect to pay between $12 and $20 per entree.)

taquitos. In the last 2 years, they've also upgraded the look of the buffet to bring it into line with the chic decor of the rest of the Palms. Children under 4 eat free, and those 5 to 9 are half price.

$–$$$ The splashiest thing to happen to Red Rock Canyon since glaciers sliced and diced its features some millions of years ago was the opening of the $930-million Red Rock Resort in the summer of 2006. And while many environmentalists are bemoaning the fact that this casino and the Summerlin community have been creeping ever closer to this once-pristine wilderness area, there is unfortunately no going back now. Which is a long way of saying that there's never been a more stylish answer to GORP than a pre- or post-hike pit stop at the **Red Rock's Feast Buffet** (in the Red Rock Resort, 11011 W. Charleston Blvd.; ☎ 702/797-7976; daily 8am–10pm; $8 breakfast, $11 lunch, $19 brunch and dinner, 50% off for children under 12; AE, DISC, MC, V). Smack dab in the middle of the buffet gang price-wise, it's working hard to prove its originality. So in the midst of each station—International Food, Sushi, Asian, BBQ, you know the drill—there's one "oh really moment" when the chefs pull out something you're not likely to see at any other buffet. Gefilte fish at the salad bar, mascarpone instead of cottage cheese, soy "chicken" among the wok fry-ups . . . it changes day to day, but there's always some little surprise. Other touches I like: They have sushi at lunch (often it's just a dinner item), and a chef mans the dessert station, cutting each piece of cake as needed to help keep staleness at bay. This buffet's a looker, too, taking its inspiration from Red Rock Canyon itself, with chicly rough hewn sandstone walls and other faux-rustic touches.

$–$$$$ "This is the best Japanese food I've had outside Japan itself," Jet Tila, a new Executive Chef at Wynn's Encore, told me, when I happened to run into him at **Raku** ★★★ (5030 Spring Mountain Rd.; ☎ 702/367-3511; Mon–Sat 6pm–3am; AE, DC, MC, V). As his PR minder, who was taking him out to dinner, looked on disapprovingly (guess he was supposed to be touting the food at Encore!) he gushed on "No, it's truly, truly amazing food. It makes your mouth

Battle of the BBQ Giants

In a smackdown that rivals any of the heavyweight boxing matches hosted on the Strip, the last 2 years have seen the rematch of BBQ greats Mike "The Legend" Mills and Paul Kirk, aka the "Kansas City Baron of Barbecue." Both have won that "superbowl of BBQing," the International Memphis in May cook-off several times and both now own restaurants in Vegas, for which they import truckloads of applewood to feed their custom-built slow cookers. Mike Mill's pits operate at the freestanding **Memphis Championship BBQ** ✸✸✸ (1401 S. Rainbow Blvd., between Charleston Blvd. and Sahara Ave.; ☎ 702/254-0520; Sun–Thurs 11am–10pm, Fri–Sat 11am–10:30pm; AE, DISC, MC, V) whereas Kirk's **Righteous Urban Barbecue** aka **R.U.B.** (in the Rio All Suites Hotel and Casino, 3700 W. Flamingo Rd.; ☎ 866/746-7671; www.riolasvegas.com; Mon–Tues 4pm–11pm, Wed–Sun 11am–2am; AE, DC, MC, V) is part of the Rio. At both, wood fires provide the low and slow heat (I'm talking 12–18 hr. for many dishes), the scented smoke, that gives the meat its distinctive pink hue and full-bodied flavor. So which is better? Truthfully, they both have their high points. At Memphis, I've found the meat to be a hair more tender and am a big fan of the deep-fried sour pickles ($3.95, they're like crack cocaine, once you start munching on them you just don't want to stop). But RUB wins in the sauce department (to my mind) and I love their burn end selection ($17). And for some, their casino location will be a big plus. At each you can get BBQ sandwiches for between $9 and $14 or go whole hog—literally—with massive plates piled with meats for about $15 to $25 or so. Memphis Championship has two additional outlets at 225 E. Warm Springs Rd., at Eastern (☎ 702/260-7909), and 4379 Las Vegas Blvd. N., in North Las Vegas (☎ 702/664-0000).

feel alive!" He then spent 10 minutes giving me and my dining companion a rundown of what we should order. Of course, we followed this expert's advice and had one of the best meals I've ever had, for a fraction of what we would have spent at a Wynn property. Amazingly, the prices at this small-plates restaurant start at just $1.50 a dish, with most in the $2.50 to $3.50 range, so you can literally get a gourmet feast for under $10 per person, if you order carefully. Let me get one thing out of the way first: There's no sushi on the menu here. Instead the food is cooked in a *robata* grill, fueled by charcoal that's created from cork and imported from Japan. According to our server, this method of cooking cooks the food from the inside out, which seems a bit unbelievable to me, but however it's done the results are sublime. Among the many dishes that seem like culinary magic tricks are horizontal slices of corn, with creamy mashed potatoes where the cob would normally be; meltingly tender grilled pork cheek; tofu made fresh that hour, with a delicate flavorfulness unlike any tofu I'd ever had before; and smoky teriyaki beef with a delicate line of wasabi giving it a subtle punch. Raku can be a bit hard to find as it's set in a nondescript shopping mall and the decor of the place, while dignified, is not at all glitzy, but make the effort to come here—it truly is one of the city's most exciting new restaurants.

$$–$$$$ Originality isn't usually a strong suit in Vegas, but I have to say that **Sushi Fever** ✰✰✰ (7985 W. Sahara Ave., at S. Buffalo Dr.; ☎ 702/838-2927; Mon–Sat 11am–11pm, Sun 4–10pm; AE, DISC, MC, V) may well be one of the most unusual, unique sushi joints I've ever been to. You wouldn't know it from the interior decoration because . . . well, there ain't much. Just a few shoji screens here and there, TV screens tuned into sports, griddle-centered teppanyaki tables, and a large rectangular sushi bar with chefs in the center. But the sushi itself is so outrageous, so untraditional, so, well, odd that it really can't be called sushi. Yes, it's centered on raw fish and wrapped with vinegar rice, but that's where the similarity ends. Because it may well be deep fried, slathered in a bright pink sauce, or served as a "shooter" in a wine glass meant to be downed like a shot of tequila. Traditionalists may find these treatments, and the frat bar names they're given— "screaming orgasm," "sex on the beach," "rock and roll"—unsettling, but I think it's great fun. Each dish is an adventure; you never quite know what flavor's going to hit your tongue next (though most of it is quite yummy). You'll get hot sushi, as with the "Mountain Roll" ($13), an inside out crab and avocado roll, swathed in salmon and a mayonnaisey sauce and then cooked to the consistency of clams casino; or tuna swathed in enough garlic sauce to stun a vampire ($6). It also comes piled high, as with the "Japanese Lasagna" ($8), which consists of layers of fish, avocado, and cream cheese with a ponzu-like sauce. The aptly named candy roll ($9) features a sweet sauce so potent that it transforms this eel, cucumber, crab, and avocado roll into a confection as satisfying as fine chocolate (order it towards the end of the meal instead of dessert). Along with the oddball rolls, there is more standard sushi and sashimi and grilled-to-order teppanyaki meals, but there's no reason to drive this far from the Strip to try those. Instead, be bold, order imaginatively, and go home with some new ideas for your neighborhood Japanese place.

$$$–$$$$ You may feel like you've driven to another city by the time you arrive at **Bistro Bacchus** ✰✰✰ (2660 Regatta Dr., near Mariner Dr., ☎ 702/804-8008; Mon–Sat 10:30am–4pm and 5–10pm, Sun 10am–3pm and 5–10pm; AE, DISC, MC, V), as it's a looooonng 30- to 40-minute trek from the center of the Strip. Once you get here, however, the calm and charm of this ultra-romantic restaurant, set in one of Las Vegas's upscale communities, will erase any of the stresses of navigating the city's sometimes confusing grid. Its setting is sublime, with tables perched on the edge of a pretty manmade lake and lit primarily by torches and twinkling votive candles. On cold or sultry nights, there's indoor seating with A/C (or heat, whichever you may need) overlooking the patio and lake. You'll start your meal by wandering into the impressive wine store at the front and consulting with the affable and terrifically knowledgeable French owner about which bottle to choose. Put yourself in his hands and he'll come up with a winner, and one that you can afford (I've never seen him push ultra-expensive wines). In fact, you'll get a superb vintage for much less than you'd pay on the Strip, even with the $10 corkage fee. Then you order in reverse, matching your meal to the wine you've selected, an easy task, as the menu was designed to enhance the vino. To that end, Bacchus offers plates of fine cheeses ($11 at lunch, $12 at dinner; it comes with a delightful grape chutney) or cured meats ($12, pates, salamis, prosciutto, and a red onion confit), which are hearty enough for a light meal and bring out the best in wine. Though the menu ranges across the food groups, I like their seafood dishes the most—the *Moules Frites* ($21) steamed in wine, are sided with delightful parmesan-crusted french fries, and the trout is painted with an unusually subtle dijonnaise sauce ($28). Truffled crab cakes, an appetizer large enough for an entrée, are pretty nifty, too ($12). Midday, Bacchus's menu is simpler: quiches, sandwiches, salads, and brunch fare on Sundays (omelets and lovely Benedicts, $10–$16). On Sunday and Wednesday evenings, live jazz music plays while you dine (now that's classy).

Remarkable Sights & Attractions

Let's rank the ones you definitely must see

TRUTH BE TOLD, MANY VACATIONERS COME TO VEGAS AND HAVE A perfectly fine vacation gambling, shopping, eating in restaurants, going to shows . . . without ever leaving their hotels. If they see the light of day, it's at the rooftop pool, and if they decide to wander out, it's to the casino right next door for a change of scenery. Are they missing out? Absolutely. Are they having the time of their lives, anyway? Probably.

Which brings us to the paradox of Vegas: In all other cities, you leave your hotel to go out and see the attractions. In Vegas, the hotels are the major attractions . . . so why go out at all?

Here's my pitch for going outside. Within the last decade, Las Vegas has moved beyond its single-minded emphasis on casinos to develop other sights and attractions. Love cars? You can spend days gawking at classic rides in showroom/museums, or hit the racetrack in a new Corvette or Hummer. Interested in seeing the great wonders of the world? Welcome to the city where the landscape is an architectural Cliff Notes. The pyramids of Egypt, the canals of Venice, the Eiffel Tower? On the Strip, you'll see all these structures and more, shamelessly cribbed from the originals. Roller coasters, history museums, top-notch aquariums, and spectacles galore are all here for the taking.

This chapter is geared towards the more active vacationer. Those who want to go out and see all that Sin City has to offer, from the absurd to the sublime. If you've come here just to gamble, then I wish you the best of luck, you can skip this chapter, and study card counting instead. But if you're here to do it all, read this chapter carefully. I've divided it into several sections. First is a brief guide to Las Vegas' top attraction, the Strip itself. Then I list the eight other top sights and attractions, followed by the attractions that should appeal to vacationers of varied interests. Be sure to check out the "Other" Las Vegas in chapter 7, as well, which promotes the types of experiences that will allow you to meet locals and get a real behind-the-scenes peek at the magic and madness of Vegas—from backstage tours, to breakfasts with the Mayor, to cooking classes with top Vegas chefs.

MAKING THE MOST OF YOUR TIME

IF YOU HAVE JUST 1 DAY IN LAS VEGAS That's more than enough to stroll its main attraction: the Las Vegas Strip. Start at New York–New York and make your way north for as long as your stamina holds up, shopping, gambling, and sightseeing along the way (and if you want to hop aboard a roller coaster or dash inside a casino museum, more power to you). Head off the Strip for dinner to the superb

Lotus of Siam (p. 100), and then rush back to take in a show (for options, see chapter 8). Afterwards hike the center of the Strip again—it looks totally different and even more dazzling at night—and be sure to pause at the Bellagio fountains.

IF YOU HAVE 2 DAYS   On your first day, use the 1-day itinerary above; for your second day, get out of town. Nothing in Vegas tops the majesty of the desert scenery surrounding it. In the morning head to Red Rock Canyon for a driving tour or hike; the intense heat won't have set in yet if you're there in summer (it's just a 20-min. drive from the Strip). In the afternoon, stop at one of Vegas' more interesting museums, either the superb Atomic Testing Museum (p. 125), the Springs Preserve (p. 126), or that kingdom of kitsch, the Liberace Museum (p. 129).

IF YOU HAVE 3 DAYS   You can divide up your time along the Strip more sensibly. Spend your first day simply exploring the area from the Luxor to the Bellagio, perhaps taking in the *Titanic* exhibit (p. 136), or the Bellagio Gallery of Fine Art (p. 123). Cap off the day with a special dinner, a show, and a stroll along the Strip. Day 2 can be spent exploring the central and northern reaches of the Strip; head to the Madame Tussaud's (p. 123) in The Venetian; wander Wynn Las Vegas, Treasure Island, and The Mirage; try the Sahara for some $3 blackjack; or go to the Stratosphere for the tallest thrill rides in the world. Have a nice, long dinner and then head to a dueling piano bar or music lounge, perhaps ending your night at one of Las Vegas' famous dance clubs (see chapter 9 for information on which option will best suit your tastes). Then make Day 3 your day to do the desert and the off-Strip museums we recommend above. For evening activities, you could see another show or simply try a new bar or club.

IF YOU HAVE 4 DAYS OR MORE   Follow the 3-day itinerary above and add a day at Hoover Dam, Lake Mead, and/or Valley of Fire. You may also want to throw in a backstage tour at *Jubilee!* (p. 187), or try indoor sky diving (p. 146). Or you could just gamble some more . . . it's Vegas, baby, and nobody's judging.

LAS VEGAS' ICONIC ATTRACTION: THE STRIP

Gaudy, glamorous, goofy—whatever your take on the Las Vegas Strip is, there's no denying that it's one of a kind. You could travel the four corners of the globe and up to Mars and back and still find no other place like it. Sin City's signature attraction is actually 4½ miles long, running from Las Vegas' own "Space Needle," the Stratosphere Hotel, all the way south to the glittering, bronze glass box that is the Mandalay Bay Resort & Casino. Someday soon, I have no doubt, it will extend even further in both directions, when the three massive corporations that control most of it get tired of bartering limited $20-million-per-acre lots back and forth. But with the economic slowdown, that ain't happening anytime soon, so, that's how it stands for now, and seven of the world's 10 largest hotels sit on its flanks, each one more stupendous—or silly (it depends on your point of view)—than the next, offering a "greatest hits" whirlwind tour of the world's architecture. When traffic is light—which is a rare early dawn occurrence nowadays—it's possible to traverse the entire length of the Strip in a car or bus in about 30 minutes. By foot, it's a more daunting trek, especially in the heat of summer, and could take an entire day, longer if you head inside the casinos and tour each of these monolithic,

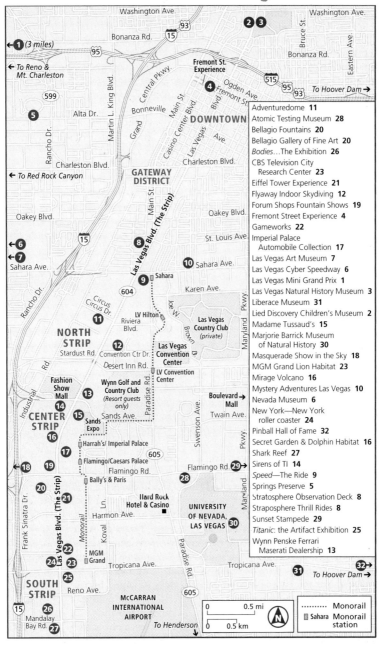

Adventuredome **11**
Atomic Testing Museum **28**
Bellagio Fountains **20**
Bellagio Gallery of Fine Art **20**
Bodies...The Exhibition **26**
CBS Television City
 Research Center **23**
Eiffel Tower Experience **21**
Flyaway Indoor Skydiving **12**
Forum Shops Fountain Shows **19**
Fremont Street Experience **4**
Gameworks **22**
Imperial Palace
 Automobile Collection **17**
Las Vegas Art Museum **7**
Las Vegas Cyber Speedway **6**
Las Vegas Mini Grand Prix **1**
Las Vegas Natural History Museum **3**
Liberace Museum **31**
Lied Discovery Children's Museum **2**
Madame Tussaud's **15**
Marjorie Barrick Museum
 of Natural History **30**
Masquerade Show in the Sky **18**
MGM Grand Lion Habitat **23**
Mirage Volcano **16**
Mystery Adventures Las Vegas **10**
Nevada Museum **6**
New York—New York
 roller coaster **24**
Pinball Hall of Fame **32**
Secret Garden & Dolphin Habitat **16**
Shark Reef **27**
Sirens of TI **14**
Speed—The Ride **9**
Springs Preserve **5**
Stratosphere Observation Deck **8**
Stratosphere Thrill Rides **8**
Sunset Stampede **29**
Titanic: the Artifact Exhibition **25**
Wynn Penske Ferrari
 Maserati Dealership **13**

115

spectacle-laden pleasure palaces (Kublai Khan decreed nothing that could top what's here).

Because you should go inside, here are my picks for the top attractions along the Strip, in the most logical order possible. Please note that the following itinerary could take several days to accomplish, particularly if you're susceptible to the lures of shopping, slot machines, living statues, or animatronic displays.

I used to start this tour with the Luxor, that gargantuan glass pyramid that's desperately trying not to be Egyptian anymore. Because of the casino execs' foolish decision to "de-theme" it, I no longer suggest you visit its now bland interior (except to go to the exhibits inside; see p. 136 and 139). But do, if you have the time, gaze at it from the outside; it's one of those rare structures that changes its face depending on the time of day. In the morning, the reflection of the sun turns its facade into a blazing golden slab, at night, like magic, the entire building disappears into the desert sky, except for a powerful river of light that streams from the top. A 40-billion-candlepower spotlight is set in the point of the pyramid that's apparently visible from space, though I've heard that the light is rarely run at its full power (even rich casinos have to worry about high electricity bills nowadays).

To my mind you can skip the tired Excalibur (its Disney castle exterior is much more interesting than anything inside) and head instead to **New York–New York** ✩, though you may want to make a detour first to two adrenaline-charged museum exhibits (yes, there is such a thing in Vegas): ***Bodies . . . The Exhibition*** (p. 139) and ***Titanic:* The Exhibit** (p. 136), which are housed in the Luxor. The front of New York–New York is a heady, three-dimensional collage of the Big Apple's most famous buildings, constructed to one-third the size of the originals. Tallest is the Empire State building, of course, standing 529 feet; the second tallest, far to its right, is a replica of the scallop-topped Chrysler building. In between and a bit to the front, a strangely smirking Statue of Liberty (she looks like she may have just won big at the craps table) raises her lamp over the Strip. You can wander across the 300-foot replica of the Brooklyn Bridge, while gazing up at the taxi-themed roller coaster (okay, that doesn't exactly replicate any structure in New York City, but it does replicate the driving of some Big Apple cabbies). The interior is not as successful to my mind, but I may be alone in that. The New York Stock Exchange actually sued the casino when it was first opened for including a simulacrum of its neoclassical facade, claiming trademark infringement (they lost). Wander through a leafy "Central Park" to a garish food court set among the cobbled streets of "Greenwich Village."

Though not nearly as fun since it ditched the Wizard of Oz theming, the **MGM Grand** ✩ is still worth a quick visit mostly for its grand size—it was once the largest hotel in the world, now it's number three—and the splendor of its restaurants and shops. If you're like me you'll find yourself hooting out loud when you read the prices on these menus. Most visitors pay their respects to the MGM Lions (p. 141) at the front, a free exhibit.

Head next to the **Monte Carlo** for the handsome Renaissance sculptures, fountain, and colonnade that adorn the exterior. Unless you have a yen to see a magic show (the fab Lance Burton performs here), you don't need to go inside.

Ah, Paree . . . well, really, ah, **Paris Las Vegas** ✩✩. It should be your next stop (unless you enjoy mall trolling; then detour to the many shops of the Miracle Mile

Mall, timing it to arrive on the hour so you can see the "rainstorm" that takes place for no good reason over a small pond) With a vaulting *trompe l'oeil* ceiling/sky depicting a perfect drizzly Paris day—in this it's accurate, as Paris gets as much rain as London—the Paris does a better job than New York–New York at simulating the looks of its parent city. Be sure to wander the Marais-like winding street of shops and eateries in the back. Every once in a while, fellows with berets and black-and-white striped shirts burst into song on the casino floor, just like in, um, Paris Disneyland? The food court here is a particularly good place to get an affordable snack if you're feeling peckish. As for the Eiffel Tower experience, I have mixed feelings (read my comments on p. 142). Be sure to get a peek at the facade, with its nifty re-creations of the Louvre, Paris Opera, and Arc de Triomphe (out back, where the taxis pull in). The fountain out front is a near perfect replica of La Fontaine de Mers (it's missing a couple of mermaids) from the Place de la Concorde in Paris.

When the **Bellagio** ✪✪ opened in 1998, it was the most expensive building ever constructed at a whopping $1.7 billion. Unabashedly high-end in its focus, it crammed its 6 million square feet of interior space (another record . . . back then) with Armani and Gucci boutiques, inlaid marble floors and walls, and a small museum where the art was actually real (a radical paradigm shift). If you ignore the track-suited, fanny-pack-wearing tourists and concentrate on the decor, it will still look quite glam, from its canopied gambling tables and grand chandeliers to the Dale Chihuly installation that graces the ceiling of the reception area. Five tons of steel hold up the 2,164 individual glass flowers on that ceiling, making it the largest glass sculpture in the world. (If you're like me, you're going to look up and think that the darn thing looks too crowded, its colors muddied. Don't blame Chihuly for that, though. The property's original owner, Steve Wynn, personally oversaw the installation of the piece, periodically climbing up on a ladder to peer at it as he suffers from macular degeneration and couldn't see it well from the ground. From that close-up angle, it apparently didn't look "grand" enough, so Wynn ordered the

> "Las Vegas exists because it is a perfect reflection of America . . . It represents all the things people in every city in America like. Here they can get it in one gulp."
>
> —Steve Wynn, *Time* magazine

artist to add more and more and more flowers, until the number of buds had more than doubled and the price tag skyrocketed to $10 million.) The real flowers of the conservatory gardens are better eye candy, I think; when the casino first opened, Wynn hired Martha Stewart to design the first Christmas conservatory. Today, the casino spends $8 million a year to create the seasonally changing displays of luxuriant flowers, shrubs, and trees that add a riot of color to the heart of the casino. In addition, the Bellagio has a massive mall (p. 263), a number of fine dining options, and the famous fountains out front (p. 118).

For a more intimate casino experience, head to the jewel box that is now known as **Bill's Gamblin' Hall and Saloon** ✪. Its ground floor is crammed with $2 million worth of Victorian bric-a-brac, from cathedral-quality stained glass windows to polished brass fixtures to chandeliers dripping with baubles. There are no attractions here, per se, but it's just so darn purty and so different from what surrounds it that it's a good palate cleanser (and has a headliner in its lounge called

Free Spectacles

Oh, this is going to sound so cynical, but with few exceptions, I think you get what you pay for with Las Vegas' free shows. (And if you calculate the cost of airfare and your hotel room into your own personal hourly rate, you'll see that, in reality, these shows ain't so free after all.)

Best of the bunch are the **Bellagio Fountains** ✪✪✪, which explode into a sound and spray show every half-hour from 3pm to 8pm on weekdays (noon–8pm weekends) and every 15 minutes after that until midnight. Set in the middle of a good-sized lake, the fountains consist of 1,200 custom jets, powered by compressed air. These powerful little water guns are able to shoot 75-gallon streams of water up to 250 feet into the air (that's nearly as tall as the hotel itself!). You may notice that these sprays don't really splash, instead the water spirals forth in axisymmetric laminar flows (no, I'm not making this up) that produce a remarkably consistent stream, kind of like a laser light. It's super cool. Each show is choreographed to a different piece of music, and, at night, lighting effects, too. Because of all the water droplets in the air, the temperature will drop a bit right around the fountains, a fun perk, especially in the summer months. Simply the best free attraction in Vegas. I could stand for days watching these darn fountains do their dance.

The next most famous shows on the Strip are the **Volcano at The Mirage** ✪ (which was recently redesigned at the cost of $25 million) and the *Sirens of TI* show at Treasure Island. The volcano was still under construction during my last visit but plans for its new show sound pretty goose-bump making. According to the Mirage folks, the top of the volcano will now include 120 "firemakers" which will shoot fireballs into the sky. Water will now spout 120 feet, steam will envelope the hill, and simulated magma will ooze forth for about 4½ minutes every hour on the hour. All of this will occur to the sounds of a percussion soundtrack created by Mickey Hart (of the Grateful Dead) and Indian music superstar Zakir Hussain. (One of the best views of the volcano is from the balcony of The Venetian across the street.) As for the pirate show: I don't think it's worth the time equity you have to put in to see it. Getting close enough often requires an hour-long wait for a 15-minute display of T&A mixed with a bit of swashbuckling. The storyline involves a bunch of seamen tangling with sexy sirens and yes, the tall-masted ship does float on that little lagoon, but that's about as exciting as it gets. I really don't think this one is worth the wait, though if you must, the shows are at 6pm, 8pm, and 10pm (but you'll have to get there at least 45 min. in advance to snag a spot).

Animatronic statues are the bizarro lure at **The Forum Shops at Caesars** and in the atrium of **Sam's Town.** Of the two, the Sam's Town show is the better one, a laser and water show called the *Sunset Stampede,* set in a mini-National Park that's right off the casino. Kids will like this one, if only for the roaring bear. Winning the prize for most peculiar is the *Fall of Atlantis* spectacle performed at Caesars by barely moving, life-sized Barbies and Kens (dressed in ancient garb, of course) who speak with garbled voices, telling a myth apparently made up by the marketing department (as if there weren't enough compelling, dramatic Greek and Roman myths to retell!). Most mysterious is why anyone watches the darn thing, which is utterly incomprehensible and visually turgid to boot. The Sam's Town spectacle takes place 2pm, 6pm, 8pm, and 10pm (evening shows have better light quality). If you must see the *Fall of Atlantis,* the shows are every hour on the hour from 10am until closing.

The **Parade in the Sky** ✪ is the half-hourly Mardi Gras parade performed at the Rio Hotel and Casino that combines a small stage show of dancers, with about five large floating floats (they hang from a track in the ceiling) filled with showgirls and the tourists who pay to stand next to them—both of whom throw beaded necklaces at the crowd below. They recently reworked the show to make if much more, well, salacious (I preferred the old one which was more dance and less simulated sex, but I may be in the minority on that). If you really want to see a showgirl (and perhaps get a photo with one), this is certainly the least expensive way to accomplish that. Thursday through Sunday hourly from 7pm to midnight.

A tank of tropical fish, visited every 16 minutes by waving mermaids, is the lure at the off-Strip **Silverton Casino** ✪ (see p. 64) and it's so darn Vegas that it actually brings a smile to the face. Even more interesting though are the afternoon feedings (1:30, 4:30, and 7:30pm) when scuba divers enter the tank to pass out food for the bottom feeders who would starve if the food was simply sprinkled from above. A staff member stands outside the tank to answer questions about the fish, which range from three species of small sharks to stingrays (there are over 2,000 fish in the massive tank).

Gardens in the desert are such an unusual concept that Steve Wynn used it three times. His first hotel, the Mirage, has an "oasis" of jungle greenery at its heart that's calming to walk through. But the plants really got extravagant with his **Conservatory Gardens** at both the Bellagio and Wynn. An up-and-comer named Martha Stewart chose the flowers for the first year at the Bellagio; now the concept has gone one more step over the top at the Wynn where the garden area is roofed in glass, allowing sunlight to stream down on the petals. At both the Bellagio and Wynn, flower displays change seasonally and sometimes can get mighty exotic, as with the bamboo plantings and sculptural additions for Chinese New Year.

Two other notable freebies include the **Fremont Experience** ✪ (p. 130) and the superb circus acts at, you guessed it—**Circus Circus** ✪✪ (p. 131).

"Big Elvis" who performs afternoon sets. His girth is too unwieldy to do Elvis's trademark hip swivels but he's an auditory twin of the King).

You may have noticed that **Caesars Palace** ✮✮✮ has no apostrophe in its name. A purposeful omission, it's meant to convey that all of us plebeians are actually "Caesars," and this is our palace. Whatever. I like the place despite the silly grammar. It's just so darn Vegas, and "new" Vegas at that—a shotgun wedding of kitsch and class. And it's been that way since the beginning. Caesars was the first of the "overtly" themed resorts in Vegas, not only picking an evocative name (as at the Flamingo) but deliberately designing every detail to enhance the illusion that you'd entered some sort of alternate reality. Jay Sarno, its original creator, evoked the decadence of ancient Rome with such over-the-top gestures as lining the stately 135-foot-long driveway with Cyprus trees imported from Italy; insisting that cocktail waitresses hand-peel grapes for guests; and installing hundreds of thousands of dollars worth of marble statuary brought over from Florence in every nook and corner.

The original is long gone, but today's version has the same touches on an even grander scale. Just walking around and ticking off the reproductions of the famous sculptures here is a kick. It begins as you enter and salute Emperor Augustus, first of the Caesars, here represented by a perfect copy of the famed statue in the Vatican Museum. (For those who care about art history, experts think the cupid at Augustus's feet is meant to show he was related to the Goddess Venus, and the dolphin he rides is in honor of his naval victories.) In the center of the little lake fronting the hotel is a copy of a Louvre Museum treasure: the 300 B.C. headless *Samothrace of Nike* (another appropriate touch, as she was the Goddess of Victory; try to conjure her help at the slot machines). In front of the main door, the racy *Rape of the Sabine Women*, the original by Giambologna of Florence, and inside the mall, another Florentine treasure: a beautiful re-creation of Michelangelo's *David*. Also keep an eye out inside for the *Venus de Milo* (and save yourself the cost of a trip to the Louvre in Paris). As before, the staff is dressed like sexy extras from Spartacus, the men in full gladiator and centurion regalia, the women in mini-togas. Armani, Versace, Bernini, Cavalli, and more of their high-fashion Italian brethren (plus fashionistas of other nationalities) inhabit the pricey mall; and some of the biggest names in the culinary world helm the restaurants. Magnificent aquariums, silly animatronic displays (p. 118), and more and more and more. I'd say Caesars is a "don't miss."

As is the **Flamingo** ✮, but not its cramped and old-fashioned casino area. Pass through that as rapidly as possible and make your way to the lush garden at the back, still one of the prettiest outdoor spaces in the city. Fifteen acres in total, it ambles past swimming pools (that pretty much anyone can swim in; they don't check keys) and aviaries where the hotel's signature pink flamingos strut along with Australian black swans, helmeted guinea fowls, and other rare birds.

From here, you may want to wander through **The Mirage,** the first of the neon-free Super Casinos built on the Strip, famed for the massive aquarium behind its reception desk, and mini "rainforest" at its core. The Mirage paved the way for today's big name Strip properties, but if you're running short on time, I think you can skip it (it's been overshadowed by its descendants) and head instead for its sumptuous neighbor, **The Venetian** ✮✮✮. Full disclosure: This is my absolute fave of the Strip enviro-tainments, maybe because I'm a sucker for the original as well. It's another $1.6-billion wonder, and you'll see where all the money went as

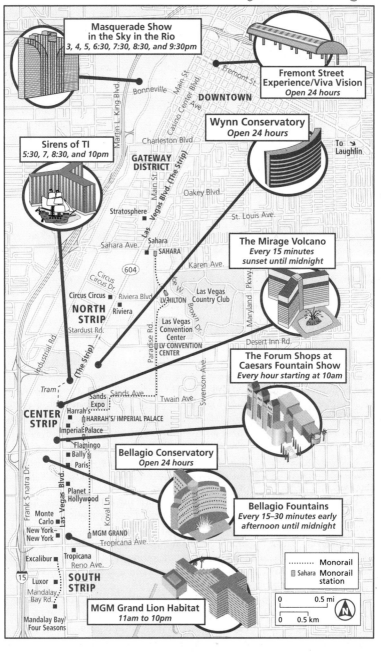

Masquerade Show in the Sky in the Rio
3, 4, 5, 6:30, 7:30, 8:30, and 9:30pm

Fremont Street Experience/Viva Vision
Open 24 hours

Fremont St.

Bonneville

Main St.

Casino Center Blvd.

DOWNTOWN

Charleston Blvd.

Wynn Conservatory
Open 24 hours

To
Laughlin

Sirens of TI
5:30, 7, 8:30, and 10pm

GATEWAY DISTRICT

Oakey Blvd.

Main St.

Las Vegas Blvd. (The Strip)

Stratosphere

St. Louis Ave.

The Mirage Volcano
Every 15 minutes sunset until midnight

Sahara Ave.

Sahara

SAHARA

Karen Ave.

604

Circus
Circus Dr.

Maryland Pkwy.

Circus Circus

Riviera Blvd.

Las Vegas
Country Club

Desert Inn Rd.

Ave. W.

LV HILTON

Brown Dr.

NORTH STRIP

Riviera

Stardust Rd.

Paradise Rd.

Las Vegas
Convention
Center

LV CONVENTION
CENTER

The Forum Shops at Caesars Fountain Show
Every hour starting at 10am

(The Strip)

Industrial Rd.

Tram

Sands Ave.

Sands
Expo

Twain Ave.

Swenson Ave.

CENTER STRIP

Harrah's

HARRAH'S/ IMPERIAL PALACE

Imperial Palace

Flamingo

Bellagio Conservatory
Open 24 hours

Bally's

Paris

Planet
Hollywood

Frank Sinatra Dr.

Las Vegas Blvd.

Koval Ln.

Bellagio Fountains
Every 15–30 minutes early afternoon until midnight

Monte
Carlo

New York–
New York

MGM GRAND

Tropicana Ave.

Excalibur

Tropicana

Reno Ave.

15

Luxor

SOUTH STRIP

Mandalay
Bay Rd.

Mandalay Bay/
Four Seasons

.... Monorail

Sahara Monorail
station

0   0.5 mi

0   0.5 km

MGM Grand Lion Habitat
11am to 10pm

you wander through. The exterior features a superb facsimile of the Doges Palace, all slender columns topped by individually carved pediments (look for Roman gods, animals, flowers) with the distinctive pink-and-white-marble diamond checkerboard pattern of the original speckling the wall above. Venice's famed campanile (clock tower) stands to the left. Inside, you'll find grand halls with marble columns the width of redwood trees, intricately inlaid marble floors, and masterful reproductions of frescoes by Titian, Tintoretto, and Veronese. Over 250 artists and art historians labored to get all the details right, from the architectural elements, to the paintings, to the gold-leaf frames that enclose them.

As in many casino-hotels, the gambling is on the first floor, with entertainment above (yup, they always want you to walk through the casino), and because entertainment here means gondola rides, the casino also represents a tremendous feat of engineering: The second floor had to be buttressed to carry a half a million gallons of water (that's about 2,000 tons). The canals run through a series of streets, under the "Bridge of Sighs" and up to a reproduction of St. Mark's Square. Above it all is, of course, the requisite *trompe l'oeil* sky. In the squares, and wandering the cobblestone streets beside the canals, are jugglers, living statues, and other street entertainers dressed in Renaissance garb. **Madame Tussaud's** (p. 123), nightclubs, theaters, and a raft of terrific restaurants round out the attractions here. Venetian's off-shoot, Palazzo, has nowhere near the level of imagination invested in it, and can be skipped I think (it's just another marble-clad box for overpriced restaurants and boutiques).

While other casinos use the great cities of the world for inspiration (Venice, Paris, Luxor, and so forth), **Wynn Las Vegas** has taken a different—and I think, deeply flawed, tactic—and simply copied another casino, a little ole place to the south called the Bellagio. It's a weird strategy (what, they think people won't remember they've seen these canopied gaming tables; lavish marble halls; water-themed, Cirque-like, rip-off show; and other elements elsewhere?). Steve Wynn, the founder here, was of course, also behind the Bellagio and the poor man is nearly blind now. One can only imagine that he went with what he knew, though the colors here are more deeply saturated colors than at the Bellagio. Fancy shops—really museums filled with outrageously priced luxury goods—are the most interesting sights, though just like at the Bellagio, there's a lush garden area, and lots of chichi restaurants. The most notable thing about the Wynn? Probably its $2.7-billion price tag, which I, personally, don't think makes it worth seeing, despite all the hype. Unfortunately, Wynn's new sibling **Encore** hadn't opened as we went to press so I can't comment on its charms.

Fans of Hunter S. Thompson who want to see the surreal side of Vegas won't want to skip **Circus Circus** ✭ While not quite as frenetic a scene as it was in his day, you'll still get a taste of the just plain weird Vegas of the '70s (and before). After all, what's weirder than circus clowns (and they're all over the place here)? Genuinely terrific circus acts, staged in a stadium floating above the casino floor, plus the world's largest indoor amusement park, will keep the young and young at heart amused.

The nearby **Sahara** ✭ is a somewhat statelier time machine, which has recently updated its '60s style with new versions of old-fashioned-looking chandeliers, rugs, and "Arabian Nights"-style architectural elements. Oddly enough, a third of the ground floor is now devoted to NASCAR, with the Strip's fastest coaster, a NASCAR simulator ride, and a NASCAR-themed bar/cafe.

If you want to get high, you go to the **Stratosphere,** which is the tallest tower in the West. The view from the top and the thrill rides up here are pretty much the only reason to venture this far down the Strip.

TOP EIGHT INDIVIDUAL ATTRACTIONS

Beyond the wandering you'll do up and down the Strip, there are eight other attractions—some on the Strip, some not—that offer as many pleasures, both visceral and/or intellectual, as the spectacle of the Strip itself.

ON THE STRIP
ART NOT KITSCH

First up is the last outpost of high culture on the Strip itself, the **Bellagio Gallery of Fine Art** ✪✪ (in the Bellagio; ☎ 877/957-9777 or 702/693-7871; www.bellagiolasvegas.com/amenities/gallery-of-fine-art.aspx; $15 adults, $12 students and seniors; daily 9am–9:30pm; AE, DC, MC, V). Once part of a triumvirate of serious art museums (along with the sadly missed Guggenheim and Wynn gallery) it's the only one left standing. Created originally by the Bellagio's founder Steve Wynn to hold his private collection of art (now gracing the walls of the Wynn gallery in Macau), today it's a partnership between the Bellagio and PaperBall, a division of New York's PaceWildenstein Gallery, which curates the museum and runs the gift shop. It's a symbiotic (parasitic?) relationship—the museum becoming a showplace for the gallery's celebrated artists, who range from Rothko, Jim Dine, and Robert Rauschenberg to Picasso and Calder. The gallery then gets the right to sell their knickknacks next door, while continuing to burnish these artists' reputations. To their credit, PaperBall has also forged relationships with major museums and collections around the country to bring in superb works of art by artists they don't rep (such as a celebrated 2008 show of such American Impressionists as Georgia O'Keefe and Max Weber that came from the Museum of Fine Arts in Boston). Whether or not it's worth the hefty price tag will depend on the exhibition of the moment, but they've had a run of star-studded retrospectives from a show of Ansel Adams photographs to one that explored Impressionist landscapes from Corot to Van Gogh. An audio tour (usually a dull one, unfortunately) is included in the price of admission. Because the museum is comprised of just a handful of galleries, you should be able to tour exhibits here in less than an hour. *Note:* The Bellagio gallery bans strollers, luggage, large bags . . . you name it. Come unencumbered, as they don't provide a place to check these objects.

As an additional plug for this fine art experience: I find it acts as a cleansing Alka-Seltzer to the greasy, overwrought kitsch of the rest of Vegas. They may help settle your stomach (or conscience, if you find that you want mind-expanding experiences when you vacation and not just mindless escapism).

CELEBRATING CELEBRITIES

The celebration of the unreal continues at **Madame Tussaud's** ✪✪ 🧒 (in The Venetian; ☎ 702/862-7800; www.madametussauds.com/LasVegas; $25 adults, $18 students and seniors, $15 children 7–12, under 6 free; Sun–Thurs 10am–9pm, Fri–Sat 10am–10pm; AE, DC, MC, V), the Vegas branch of the famous wax museum chain, where the statues are no longer the dummies they used to be. A number now interact with guests. What do I mean? Well, if you get into bed with the Hugh Hefner look-alike, who's lounging in his pajamas (appropriately enough), he'll murmur sweet nothings in your ear. If you're bold enough to touch Jennifer Lopez's derriere take a quick look up at her cheeks—no, the ones on her face— and you'll see that her blush has deepened to a dark, embarrassed red. And if

> **"** Las Vegas is an intense locus of financial activity in the middle of one of the world's most severe deserts. Like its predecessors, ranging from ancient Babylon to Luxor . . . it is able to capitalize on that fact by allowing people to imagine and then erect castles on the sand and into the air. **"**
>
> —William L. Fox,
> *In the Desert of Desire*

you're one of those coming to Vegas not to get married, you can shock all your friends with photos of you tying the knot with some famous celeb (hunky George Clooney was the groom when I was there, and yes, I do have a picture). In the chapel-like room visitors are loaned Velcro-backed wedding gowns and veils. Brave souls can sing in the American Idol area, eliciting snarky comments from Simon Cowell; or head into the genuinely creepy haunted house portion of the museum (I won't give away what happens in there, but I will warn you that some of the ghouls are alive). Madame Tussaud got into the biz by making death masks of the luminaries beheaded during the French Revolution. I have to wonder if she ever could have imagined that her small business would someday be a massive chain, or that the statues would someday cost $125,000 each to build (five are added per year; their bodies made from fiberglass—only heads and hands are of wax now).

While I've steered visitors away from Tussaud's in the *Pauline Frommer's London* and *Pauline Frommer's New York* books, here a visit seems more apropos, in keeping with the studied surrealism of the rest of the city. Plus the Vegas museum has some nifty additions, such as the all-NASCAR room (complete with racing screens and dress up clothes); an interactive celebrity poker room where you play against Ben Affleck; a teenybopper-pleasing *High School Musical* display; a Vegas legends room (featuring a Wayne Newton who looks more real here than he does in person); and a finale called "The Spirit of America" that spotlights that great American . . . Princess Diana. Seems that a poll was taken of who visitors wanted in this red, white, and blue tribute room and Shy Di won. And if that doesn't just sum up the Alice in Wonderland logic of Sin City, I don't know what does. Kids will love this place, and if you've enjoyed the rest of the spectacle of Vegas, you will too.

A word on costs: Nobody pays full price to go to Madame Tussaud's (well, maybe the geniuses who thought Princess Diana was American did). Simply take a gander at any rack of tourist literature and you're sure to see a coupon offering $5 off admission. Better still, stop by any Tix 4 Tonight booth (p. 177), and you should be able to snag tickets for $14.

SHARKS IN THE DESERT

Fish are fun. Really. Or at least the ones at **Shark Reef** ✭✭✭ 🧒 (in Mandalay Bay; ☎ 702/632-4555; www.sharkreef.com; $17 adults, $11 children 5–12, 4 and younger free; daily 10am–10pm; AE, DC, MC, V) are, as this neato aquarium concentrates on only the most Vegas-like fish-killers. Every inhabitant here is a predator of some sort, the mafia of the aquatic world, and their bloody modus operandi are explained in breathless detail when you take the audio tour (recommended). You'll see the only Thai golden crocodiles in the U.S., 20 feet long and

Coming Soon: City Center

At the very heart of the Strip, as I write this, is America's largest construction project. An amalgam of several hotels, a new Cirque theater, a casino (of course), and a mall (of course, again) it will reshape the look of Vegas once it's done. And that's not just typical Vegas hyperbole, City Center is based on a unique strategy for this town: Its operators are trying to do something genuinely creative. Instead of rehashing some other bit of great world architecture (a pyramid, perhaps or the Eiffel Tower), they've hired visionary architects and artists, most notably Daniel Liebeskind, Claes Oldenburg, and Maya Lin (of the Vietnam Memorial) to work on the project, given them the mandate to be as green as possible in their engineering and then left them to it. Liebeskind's mountainous looking mall (from the model I saw), is particularly cool. If the project's finished by the time your read this book, I have no doubt it will be drawing gawkers, and you might want to be among them.

blessed with the ability to hold their breath for up to 2 hours; fish that jump out of the water to snatch small birds from the sky; lionfish with deadly spines; and piranha with teeth engineered to sheer off huge chunks of flesh. The stars are the sharks of course, and these come in all varieties, menacing the tanks they stalk. Feeding time, which is a show in itself, is at 3pm; try and time your visit to coincide.

Allot about an hour to see the exhibit, another half-hour to stand in line (go early if you can), and a good 20 minutes for the endless walk through the casino to get to the exhibit. It's worth it: This is a genuinely entertaining and educational aquarium, the only wildlife exhibit in Nevada to win accreditation from the respected American Zoo and Aquarium Association.

A warning for parents: You exit, of course, into a gift shop (so what else is new?), and it's a difficult one to get out of quickly (hint: If you have to ward off a tantrum with a purchase, the key chains aren't too pricey).

OFF THE STRIP
THE BIG BOOM

No thrill ride on the Strip will scare the wits out of you as effectively as the **Atomic Testing Museum** ✪✪✪ (755 E. Flamingo Rd.; ☎ 702/794-5161; www.atomic testingmuseum.org; $12 adults, $9 seniors, children 7–17, and military with ID, free under 7; Mon–Sat 9am–5pm, Sun 1–5pm; AE, DC, MC, V). That's not its purpose, of course. This is a science and history museum (an affiliate museum of the mighty Smithsonian Institution) covering the 50 years of atomic testing, from 1951 to 1992 (928 nuclear tests in all), that occurred in the desert outside Vegas. But there comes a moment in the exhibit when your heart will race, your stomach will drop down to your knees, and all at once the reality of the power of the nuclear bomb will hit you with the force of a nightmare. I was a teenager in the '80s at the height of the anti-nuclear movement, so I spent my youth worried about nuclear proliferation and attending protests. But it wasn't until I visited here that I ever felt, viscerally, to my very bones, the gut-wrenching evil and majesty of a nuclear explosion. The moment comes early in the exhibit. After an effective and dramatic retelling of the history that led up to the invention of the bomb, you'll be ushered into a small room resembling a concrete bunker for a video about the testing, with shots of actual explosions. As the mushroom cloud rises in front of you, the lights flash a blinding white, subwoofers send vibrations to the center of your sternum, your bench shakes, and air cannons blast you with wind. It's intense.

After that wrenching start the rest of the exhibit helps visitors put into context what they've seen. You'll learn about the physics behind the bomb; the myriad of innovations, from high-speed photography to bigger drills, that emerged from the scientific work going on at the testing site; and the cultural "fallout," if you will, of the Cold War, from advertisements glamorizing the bomb to panic-provoking bomb shelters. Iconic items from the test site—a decoupler, a massive drill bit, a farm silo—are interspersed with news clips and state-of-the-art, truly whiz-bang, interactive exhibits. Pull your attention from these, however, if a docent happens by. Many of these volunteers are former employees of the Testing Site; no they don't glow, but get one talking and they'll regale you with insider's tales of what it was like to wrestle with the bomb, live in its shadow, and work for the government.

A number of people protested the opening of the museum, convinced that it would be a jingoistic, one-sided endorsement of the testing that was done in Nevada. Lawsuits have been brought, after all, by the so-called down-winders— people who lived near the site and later developed all sorts of horrific cancers. They and their descendants claim that the government put them in harm's way with these tests, never fully informing the public of their risks. It's a debate that still rages today in Nevada. The fact that the efforts to create the museum were spearheaded by former test site employees, and supported by big donors such as Lockheed Martin and Bechtel Nevada (corporations still involved in the Nevada testing site), only added fuel to the fire. So did the content of the exhibits, which emphasize the positive aspects of the testing from deterrence against the Soviets to scientific breakthroughs at the site. So the pro-testing part of the equation is well represented, but there's very little about the down-winders and the terrible consequences they've suffered. According to museum officials, that will be added. But it hasn't happened yet, a serious flaw. Despite all this, the museum has much to teach, and should be visited. It is, without a doubt, the most thought-provoking, important sight in Vegas proper.

One warning: The museum's signage is not very prominent, making it a bit difficult to find if you're driving yourself. Use the address to locate it; if you look for the name of the place, you may pass it (as I did, twice, the first time I visited!).

WATER WORLD, VEGAS STYLE

News flash: Vegas' raison d'être was not, despite all appearances to the contrary, gambling. The city became a city because it had at its heart a spring that could support life and, eventually, the railroads that needed a stopping off point in their trek through the desert. **Springs Preserve** ✪✪✪ 🅺🅸🅳🆂 (333 S. Valley View Blvd.; ☎ 702/822-7700; www.springspreserve.org; $19 adult, $17 seniors and students, $11 children 5–17, under 5 free, gardens only $6; daily 10am–6pm; AE, DC, MC, V) is the museum and nature part that now stands on the very spot where this important spring was, and celebrates its story.

But this is no snoozy history museum. While the stories surrounding Vegas' founding are told over the course of several galleries, the museum's strength is the way it explores the topic of water and other scarce resources. Here it pulls out all the stops, creating playable video games around the topic of conservation; planting exquisite desert gardens (at the heart of which is a shed where a local gardening celeb—he's on NPR here—will answer the gardening questions of anyone who shows up); and creating imaginative and often interactive exhibits around a whole host of green themes. My personal favorite was the building which introduced energy-conscious and recyclable home goods, such as insulation made from old blue jeans, rugs created from soda bottles, and old cork turned into fabric. The building housing it was insulated with straw, which is five times more efficient than current more standard methods. A powerful film called *Miracle in the Mojave* is the first thing most visitors will encounter and shouldn't be missed.

And boy oh boy do kids love this museum! They get to experience (safely) a flash flood, meet desert animals, play in a fabulous outdoor play area, or hike with their parents along the trails that encompass the museum. Best of all is a "nature exchange" for kids. Children bring in something they've found in nature—a leaf, say or a bit of bark—and can exchange it for something else in this "store" (a fossil perhaps or an animal skeleton). If the child does some research on his object and presents it to the curators, he gets points towards an even niftier object. It's a fabulous program, so be sure to load up your kids with stuff before they arrive so that they can trade too.

Along with the permanent exhibitions are a weekly farmer's market, cooking classes, concerts, lectures, and all sorts of other public programs so be sure to check the museum's website before scheduling your visit.

PRE-COLUMBIAN TREASURES

The Marjorie Barrick Museum of Natural History ✪✪ (on the campus of UNLV, at 4505 Maryland Pkwy.; ☎ 702/895-3381; http://hrcweb.nevada.edu/museum; free admission; Mon–Fri 8am–4:45pm, Sat 10am–2pm) is another surprisingly serious delight. Hidden on the University of Las Vegas campus—even the security guards I asked for directions didn't know where it was—it houses no less than one of the most important collections of pre-Columbian art and artifacts in the United States. Beautiful baskets, painted bowls, turquoise jewelry, 13th-century Mexican dog sculptures, intricate blankets, multi-colored bead necklaces—some of the treasures here (which come from nearly every culture of pre-Columbian Latin America, from Mexico through the extensive region dominated by the Mayans) will have you rolling your tongue back in your mouth, they're that jaw-droppingly lovely. As is the space itself, a massive gallery with high ceilings, shiny wooden floors, and huge glass cases that's as silent as the moon. In the hour and a half I spent admiring the works here, I was the only person in the entire gallery. I can only guess that this museum has been ignored because of its lack of advertising and, to be blunt, its poor wall text which, instead of helping visitors understand the significance of what they are seeing, is riddled with professor-ese—quadrisyllabic words and such meaningless phrases as "Distinctive socio-politico-religious and economic features then developed." Along with its pre-Columbian collection,

What's Where on the Strip

Casino	Arcade	Museum/Exhibit	Free Spectacular	Other
Mandalay Bay	No	Shark Reef (p. 124)	No	
Luxor	Yes	*Bodies . . . The Exhibition* (p. 116) *Titanic* (p. 136)	No	
Excalibur	Yes	No	No	
Tropicana	Yes	No	No	
MGM Grand	Yes	Lion Habitat (p. 141)	No	CBS Television City
New York–New York	Yes	No	No	
Monte Carlo	No	No	No	
Planet Hollywood	No	No	Circus-type performances in the mall	Large shopping mall (p. 263)
Paris	No	No	No	Roving show-tune singers sometimes in the casino
Bellagio	No	Bellagio Gallery of Fine Art (p. 123)	Bellagio Fountains (p. 118)	The Garden Conservatory (p. 117)
Harrah's	No	No	Free performances in Carnival Court	Top flare bartenders in the Carnival Court
Imperial Palace	No	Imperial Palace Auto Collection (p. 132)	No	"Dealertainment:" Celebrity impersonator dealers
Venetian	No	Madame Tussaud's (p. 123)	Mimes and living statues in mall (p. 122)	Gondola rides (p. 122)
Mirage	No	Dolphin Habitat and Secret Garden (p. 141)	Exploding volcano (p. 118)	
Treasure Island	No	No	Sirens Show (p. 118)	
Wynn Las Vegas	No		Lake Show	Conservatory Gardens
Sahara	Yes	No	Speed: The Ride and Cyber Speedway (p. 133)	Free, top-quality lounge acts
Riviera	No	No	No	
Circus Circus	Yes	No	Circus acts in both casino area and Adventure-dome (p. 131)	Indoor amusement park (p. 131)
Stratosphere	Yes	No	No	Rooftop amusement park (p. 131)

Please note that there are some free spectacles, most notably the "Parade in the Sky" (p. 119) at the Rio, the Mermaids at the Silverton (p. 64), and the sound and light show at Sam's Town (p. 118), beyond those on the Strip.

the Barrick hosts well-chosen touring shows, and has extensive holdings of Native American art and artifacts from throughout the Southwest, including Navajo and Hopi weavings, jewelry, pottery, and basketry; and Southern Paiute archaeological finds. Outside is a pleasant desert garden.

RHINESTONE-ARAMA

"A kitsch pianist with a scullery maid's idea of a regal wardrobe"—that was the snarky way *Time* eulogized Liberace in its 1997 obituary. Well, Mr. Showmanship is having the last laugh. Two years ago, Elvis-A-Rama, the museum devoted to that Vegas icon, unceremoniously closed its doors, but the **Liberace Museum** ★★★ (1775 E. Tropicana, at Spencer Rd.; ☎ 702/798-5595; www.liberace.org; $15 adults, $10 seniors, free 10 and under; if you take a bus or taxi save the receipt and the museum will refund you $2; Tues–Sat 10am–5pm, Sun noon–4pm; AE, DISC, MC, V) continues to chug along, drawing thousands of visitors each year. They come here to ooh and aah over his flamboyant costumes, those mirrored pianos, his fleet of Rolls-Royces and they leave . . . well, with an appreciation for the sweet-tempered, mother-loving, flamboyant dude himself. Beyond all of the froufrou and the pounds of rhinestones, what makes this museum so charming, is the genuine affection it inspires for this "kitsch pianist." In that way, it reminded me of the Louis Armstrong Museum in Queens, New York, where it was pretty obvious that the staff and guides felt that Satchmo was one of the finest fellows to have ever walked this "wonderful world." All proceeds from the museum go to support the Liberace Foundation, which sponsors dozens of college scholarships each year for students in the performing and creative arts.

Beyond the love fest you'll get from the guides and volunteers, there's a lot that's genuinely interesting to see here. Building One is for the big stuff—cars, pianos, and the story of Liberace's life. Start your tour here, wandering among 18 of the 39 pianos Liberace owned in the course of his lifetime, historic beauts from Chopin's own French Pleyel, to a Chickering baby grand that belonged to George Gershwin to a 1788 Broadwood piano, one of the oldest in existence (it predates an identical one that's displayed in New York's Metropolitan Museum). His wacky car collection is next, featuring a star-spangled Rolls-Royce and a rare Phantom V Landau Rolls-Royce (one of only seven manufactured; the British Royal Family owned another, though I doubt they covered theirs with etched mirrored tiles as he did). His personal ride was just as outré: a 1957 English taxicab that he liked to tool around in, picking up buddies.

Building Two ups the glitz factor even higher, as this is where Liberace's costumes and historic furniture are displayed. Because of their weight, costumes rotate in and out of the exhibit, but you'll possibly see a 1975 stunner covered with hundreds of black Swarovski crystals; their purchase and the cost of sewing them all on cost the pianist $750,000. It glittered so intensely the seamstresses who worked on it wore sunglasses. It may be near his 24-karat gold costume, or his famous hot pants. Each outfit has a story, so if you don't take a tour, enlist the aid of one of the docents to fill you in on their backgrounds. Among the historic furniture and flatware on display, the highlights are a desk once owned by Czar Nicholas II, where, legend has it the Russo-Franco Peace Treaty was signed; and a set of dishes that are the double of those used at Windsor Castle by the royal family (this is the only other one in circulation).

Transportation note: Tuesdays through Sundays, the museum provides a free shuttle from the Strip to the museum and back. Paris, Flamingo, Riviera, Fashion Show Mall, and Tropicana are all on the route; for specific pick-up and drop-off times, call ☎ 702/798-559 or go to the museum's website (see above).

TV TIMES 10

If expense and technological savoir-faire were enough to make a top attraction, the **Fremont Street Experience** ★★ (Fremont St., between Las Vegas Blvd. and Main St.; www.vegasexperience.com; free admission; nightly shows every hour after sunset until about midnight, times vary based on time of year) would win the prize as greatest spectacle in Vegas. A gargantuan light canopy 90 feet high and several blocks long, it carried a $70-million price tag when it was first constructed and still claims the title of biggest screen on the planet. In 2004, all of the lights were replaced with even more potent LED lamps at an additional cost of $70 million. Eight computers power the screen, the lights, smoke, and lasers that create the hourly nighttime shows here, which along with periodic concerts, monster truck exhibits, and other street fair–like events make up what is called in aggregate the "Fremont Street Experience." It certainly has livened up what had been a dying stretch of Downtown, and now streets are jammed with buskers, vendors, and partiers hopping from casino to casino most nights of the week. On weeknights, a host roams through the crowd interviewing people on the street and allowing them to see their faces the size of a house on the screen above.

So why only two stars? Because the light shows themselves are witless affairs, with little artistry and waaay too much commercial content. I'll grant that it's an impressive spectacle for the first few minutes (and the street scene on the ground is fun and very different from the Strip), but after that, well, let me put it this way: Even my bright-light-loving 5-year-old was bored (and I was, too). There are a dozen or so sound and light shows on as many themes, so some are livelier than others, but the ones I've seen haven't come close, I felt, to utilizing the full potential of all this amazing technology.

THRILL RIDES

If the threat of losing your life savings isn't enough of an adrenaline pumper for you, Vegas has enough high-speed coasters and other thrill rides to leave you more thoroughly shaken than a pair of maracas. Here's the rundown on these herky-jerky delights.

On the South Strip, there's only one thrill ride of note, and that's the prominent coaster that careens past the skyscrapers at **New York–New York Crazy Taxi Roller Coaster** ★ (in New York–New York; $14 first ride, $7 each additional, $25 all-day pass; Sun–Thurs 11am–11pm, Fri–Sat 10:30am–midnight; you must be over 54 in. tall to ride; AE, DISC, MC, V). While it ain't the fastest or most jolting coaster in town, it has the . . . er . . . benefit of height to keep it pretty scary, and I like the witty touch of having the cars painted to look like New York City taxis. Hey, I'd even say this coaster is slightly scarier than zigzagging in one of those on Fifth Avenue in the Big Apple. And if you can keep your eyes open long enough, between screams, the view from the top of the coaster is spectacular, particularly at night. Stats: The speed hits 67 mph at its fastest, and it features a 100-foot drop at a sharp 50-degree angle. Two inversions, including an unusual "heartline" twist, keep it interesting. Time on the ride is 2 minutes, 45 seconds.

The northern end of the Strip is nausea central, thanks to rides at three casinos at this end (there are no major thrill rides on the Center Strip). First up is **Speed** ✪✪✪ (in the Sahara; $10 per ride, $22 all-day pass; Sun–Thurs 10am–midnight, Fri–Sat 10am–1am Apr–Oct, closed winter; you must be over 54 in. to ride; AE, DISC, MC, V). True to its name, it's the speediest coaster in town at a heart-stopping 70 mph. That's backwards and forwards because once it hits its peak hill at 224 feet, it does the whole thing in reverse. Prime thrills of the ride are its indoor to outdoor route and the swiftness with which it reaches top velocity—a head-spinning 2 seconds from 35 mph up to 70 mph. Stats: The entire ride takes just 45 seconds. Its peak is that 224-foot climb. ***Note:*** Please turn to p. 133 for information on the Sahara's race-car simulation ride.

Adventuredome ✪✪✪ (in Circus Circus; $7 for "premium" rides, $4 for all others, all-day adult pass $25, all-day kids' pass $15; Mon–Thurs 11am–6pm, Fri–Sat 10am–midnight, Sun 10am–9pm; AE, DISC, MC, V), at 5½ acres, is the largest indoor amusement park in the United States. While none of its rides can be touted as the most scary on the Strip, the grouping of so many in one place, rideable on a pass that's no more expensive than the single-ride, full-day passes at other properties, makes it tops for value. Families will also enjoy their visits here because along with the thrill rides are tamer options for the little ones and circus shows (see p. 134, our review for the kids section). Among the offerings is the Canyon Blaster, a roller coaster that hits speeds of 55 mph and is notable for its double loop and double corkscrew (time on ride is 1¾ min.; riders must be 48 in. tall); Chaos, which is one of those madly tilting Ferris wheels that has the additional scare factor of having the roller coaster zoom by within inches of riders (time on ride is 2 min.; height minimum 48 in.); the Rim Runner, which is a soak-you-to-the-bone flume ride, featuring a 60-foot drop (2-min. ride; 48-in. height restriction); and the Sling Shot, which is just what it sounds like—a ride that launches riders up 100 feet with 4 Gs of force (that's 1 G more than a rocket blast), and down so fast you'll feel like an astronaut floating in space. This last one lasts just 1 minute (height restriction 48 in.). Of the four, the only one I can't recommend is the Rim Runner because the level of air-conditioning within the dome makes it pretty uncomfortable once you're wet. For kids too small or scared for the rides, there's a first-class circus show on the hour that my kids absolutely loved.

If height equals fright, then nothing compares with the thrill rides at the **Stratosphere** ✪✪ (☎ 702/380-7777; www.stratospherehotel.com; Sun–Thurs 10am–midnight, Fri–Sat 10am–1am; ride prices below, admission to tower $9.95; AE, DISC, MC, V). Set at the top of the tallest structure in the West, these rides hold the record as the highest thrill rides on the planet. Best of the lot is the Big Shot, which is basically the same ride as the Sling Shot at Circus Circus (see above) but has the added benefit of awesome views of the Vegas Strip (if you can open your eyes and stop screaming long enough to look). You'll get the same G-forces and the same feeling of your body floating up while your stomach crashes down. It's $13 a pop. The two other rides up here, the X-Scream and Insanity: the Ride, zoom you over the edge or whip you around over it. Because both of them have broken down in the past few years, leaving passengers stranded for quite some time dangling over the void, I decided not to try them. I plead the Katie Couric defense on that one: I have small children, and there are only so many risks I'll take in the name of journalism (not that I'm saying they're dangerous, but they sure felt like they might be). If you're braver than I am, know that you'll pay $12 a ride on each, though you can ride all three for $28, including admission to the tower. If you're really gung-ho, $34 nets you unlimited rides and the elevator ride up to the tower. *Note:* Hotel guests get a discount; ask.

ARCADE-IA

Founded by Steven Spielberg's DreamWorks SKG company, and now owned by video game giant Sega, **Gameworks** ★ 🎮 (3785 Las Vegas Blvd. S.; ☎ 702/432-GAME; www.gameworks.com; Sun–Thurs 10am–midnight, Fri–Sat 10am–1am; free admission; AE, MC, V) is the only arcade on the Strip not attached to a casino, which makes it perfect for families, and anyone who wants to trade the endless dinging of slot machines for the, well, rat-a-tat-tat, whoosh, and jangle of various types of video and pinball games. High-tech, highly interactive games are the big lure here; the popular Jurassic Park ride puts you into a small theater, in moving seats, and places a weapon in your mitt so you can hunt dinosaurs. But there are other enticements, such as the clifflike rock climbing wall at the front; an entire section of those vintage video games that boomers always gravitate to (Centipede, Moon Patrol, Galaga, and so forth); actual pinball machines; 45 driving rides, including a bunch of brand-spanking-new Sega ones; and even an old-fashioned pool table in the bar and snack area. There are various pay schemes to choose from, with hard-core fans usually going for unlimited gaming for $20 an hour. If you just want to breeze in and out, go for the $1 per game tickets.

MUSEUMS & ATTRACTIONS FOR VISITORS WITH SPECIAL INTERESTS

AUTOMOBILES

Over 300 vintage cars are parked at the 125,000-square-foot **Imperial Palace Automobile Collection** ★ (in the Imperial Palace Hotel & Casino; ☎ 702/794-3174; www.imperialpalace.com; $8 adults, $4 seniors and children 5–12; 10am–6pm daily; AE, DISC, MC, V), but because all but two are for sale, you never quite know what you'll see when you'll visit. About one a day is sold, with muscle cars and hot rods the most popular buys right now. But what makes a lot of these cars special is the roles they've played in history and popular culture. You might see "Eleanor," one of the 67 Mustangs that were built to be driven and destroyed in the Nicolas Cage movie *Gone in Sixty Seconds;* or a rare Rolls-Royce Phantom; or an actual Model T; or the Duesenberg custom-built for Howard Hughes. Not for sale and always on display are the 1942 armored Lincoln that once carried presidents Roosevelt and Truman; and Johnny Carson's first car (a video on loop shows Johnny talking about his ride). Almost all the cars have plaques attached telling their history, but the big appeal here seems to be simply gazing around and sniffing up that old-car smell. "You get a good dose of nostalgia here," says General Manager Rob Williams. "You might see the car that you dreamed about as a teenager." And if you're looking to buy, you'll be pleased to know that, yes, the car dealership does accept Imperial Palace Casino chips in payment. Folks here claim that this is the largest vintage, historic, and specialty car showroom in the world.

A note on admission: Free passes are widely available for this attraction. You'll often find them being given out in front of the hotel or on the Imperial Palace website. If you don't find them in either of those places (unlikely), look through any of the tourist magazines for a pass.

Or you can pimp your vacation . . . I mean ride, at the **Wynn Penske Ferrari Maserati Dealership** (in Wynn Las Vegas; ☎ 702/770-2000; www.penskewynn. com; admission $15; daily 10am–10pm; AE, DISC, MC, V), which is about a quarter the size of the Imperial Palace showroom, at nearly double the price. No history here either; all you'll see are insanely overpriced (think a quarter mil for a car), new Ferraris and Maseratis. I include this for informational reasons alone; if you really want to see it, you can peer in from the front and see about half the showroom without paying a cent.

You get to zip around a racetrack at the **Las Vegas Mini Grand Prix** ★ (kids) (1401 N. Rainbow Rd., just off U.S. 95 N; ☎ 702/259-7000; www.lvmgp.com; ride tickets $6.50 each, $30 for 5; Sun–Thurs 10am–10pm, Fri–Sat 10am–11pm; AE, DISC, MC, V), and that goes for speed-freaks age 32 or 13. A car-themed amusement park, it has a Chuck E. Cheese–like arcade and food-service court indoors, and five outdoor go-kart tracks that anyone 42 inches or taller can ride, plus one timed racetrack just for those with actual driver's licenses. For kids with NASCAR fantasies, this is the best place for them to safely get behind the wheel and go for it—one of the racetracks here is the longest in Vegas. There are also three country fair–type thrill rides, for those young 'uns who have no interest in cars. If you're planning on visiting midweek, be sure to call first as all tracks and rides are not always in operation. *One word of warning:* You'll need your own set of wheels to use the ones here; the Grand Prix is a *looong* drive from the Strip and would be an expensive taxi ride.

Nothing actually moves forward at the **Las Vegas Cyber Speedway** (in the Sahara; ☎ 702/737-2111; www.nascarcafelasvegas.com/cyberspeedway.php; $10 per ride, $20 for an all-day pass that also includes the Speed roller coaster; must be 54 in. tall to ride; Sun–Thurs 11am–midnight, Fri–Sat 10am–1am; AE, DISC, MC, V) but this virtual reality ride, re-creating a NASCAR race, sure makes you feel like you're hurtling through space. When you mess up and hit a wall or another car, it gives a lurch strong enough to let you feel the impact. You'll feel the curves; you'll feel the bumps; in fact, if you're like me, you'll feel pretty nauseous and sick by the time you climb out. I had to get off early, but the other "racers" I was competing against were high-fiving each other, triumphantly waving the computer print-outs that showed average speeds, number of laps around the track, and the winner of the race. A good early-in-the-day bachelor party frolic, it could be a fun, competitive warm-up for what's to come later.

CONTEMPORARY ART

Time was when the **Las Vegas Art Museum** ★★ (9600 W. Sahara Ave.; ☎ 702/ 360-8000; www.lasvegasartmuseum.org; $6 adults, $5 seniors, $3 students; Tues–Sat 11am–5pm, Sun 1–5pm; AE, DISC, MC, V) filled its halls with paintings done by the mayor's mother (no joke) and other local power players. That may be what helped secure the funding for the museum's 30,000 feet worth of space in the impressive, sky-lighted space (part of a new local library) it now inhabits, but it didn't do much for the reputation of the place. Then, in 2005, the board got smart

Keeping the Kiddies Amused . . .

. . . is sometimes not all that easy in Sin City, where so much of the "sin-ning" takes place in public that your children may have to deal with more supervision than they're used to at home. To keep the peace, try one of the following kid-friendly gems for a morning, or the day, or for as long as it takes to keep the little dears from whining they want to go home.

First choice, especially if your brood is under 7 years old, is the **Lied Discovery Children's Museum** ✮✮✮ 🆒 (833 N. Las Vegas Blvd.; ☎ 702/382-3445; www.ldcm.org; $8 adults, $7 children, but ask about AAA and other discounts; Mon–Sat 10am–5pm, Sun noon–5pm; AE, DISC, MC, V), which does what all smart kids' museums do—it puts the little ones to work. If your kids are anything like mine, they'll love pretending they're toiling away in a grocery store, a bank, or flying a plane. Imaginative exhibits let the children try on all of these different "career paths" in the course of several hours. Exhibits change regularly, but among the 50 or so options there'll likely be something on American history, and another interactive area explaining various scientific concepts. Also be sure to check what art projects are going on in the first floor activities room. We spent parts of 3 days here on my family's last trip into town, and the kids always ended up making friends, trying something new, and wearing them-selves out so thoroughly they sat quietly through the restaurant dinners that followed. It doesn't get better than that. Highly recommended.

More ambitious parents should head for the hills, really the canyons and valleys that surround Vegas. A day spent hiking in **Red Rock Canyon** ✮✮✮ (p. 284) or the **Valley of Fire** ✮✮✮ (p. 286) will be the highlight of your trip. Teens will enjoy learning about the engineering marvel that is **Hoover Dam** ✮✮✮ (p. 275).

Circus Circus's Adventuredome ✮✮✮ (p. 131) and **Midway** are the salvation of those who must stick to the Strip itself. Nearly nonstop (and darn good) circus performances, scary enough thrill rides, and an over-abundance of video and carnival games will please children of all ages. We're still living with the stuffed animals my daughters won here, and, for them, these furry trophies conjure up some of the happiest memories of the time they spent in this very adult town.

Other top stops for kids:

- **Springs Preserve** ✮✮✮ (p. 126)
- **Shark Reef** ✮✮ (p. 124)
- **Gameworks** ✮ (p. 132)
- **Las Vegas Mini Grand Prix** ✮ (p. 133)
- **Madame Tussaud's** ✮✮ (p. 123)
- **Natural History Museum** ✮ (p. 140)

and hired Libby Lumpkin, formerly of Harvard and the Bellagio Gallery of Art, as the new Executive Director. She has utterly transformed it from a provincial "showcase" museum, to one on the forefront of the contemporary arts movement. Lumpkin, a savvy curator, has achieved this by pairing exhibits of the most talked about up-and-coming new artists (Cindy Wright, Uta Barth, Ivan Djeneef) with such established names as Frank Gehry, Jean-Michel Basquiat, and Judy Chicago. As a curator, Lumpkin favors beauty over all, picking works that trade less in high concepts and more in craft, sublime color, and rich textures. She also has instituted an innovative guard program, hiring local artists and art enthusiasts to patrol the space, who then double as guides. If one approaches you and offers a tour, take them up on it; on my last visit my guide/guard took me on an erudite stroll-around, explaining how the sculptures were made, optical illusions in the pieces (she knew just where to stand), and even the history of the California minimalist movement (the topic of that particular show). Docent tours are held weekends at 2pm, but I can't imagine they're any more illuminating than the ones the guards give on an informal basis. Exhibitions change every 2 months; allot 1 hour to tour the entire museum. *A transportation note:* Unfortunately, the museum is a good 20-minute drive west of the Strip, inconvenient for vacationers without rental cars.

Now that Lumpkin is in charge, you're unlikely to see any Vegas-based artists at the Las Vegas Art Museum (it tends to trade in internationally recognized artists only). Local art, however, is playing an increasingly large role in Downtown Las Vegas, which now recognizes one former warehouse area as its very own **Arts District** ★ (see map on p. 137). It's a homegrown affair to be sure, consisting of just about a dozen-or-so galleries, two or three murals, and a monthly arts street-fair that's the pride of Las Vegas.

But its heart is in the right place, and unlike most large cities, this is one art scene that still has artists, rather than businesspeople, at its core; which makes it a messy affair, to be sure. Most of the galleries are owned by the artists themselves, meaning that the business hours posted on the doors of each are more of a wish list than a promise to actually be there. Oftentimes you'll head out to gallery-hop, and half the galleries will be shuttered, their artist-owners off "following their muses" . . . or dropping acid, or who the heck knows where they are. But for every one that's "gone fishing for inspiration" another will have its doors wide open, the gallery owner eager to chat and sometimes show you the latest work they're toiling over (at the easel in the corner). Those with wall space to fill should note that art bought here is one of Vegas' true bargains; I've seen pieces go for as little as $25 (though the majority will go for several hundred up to several thousand dollars). Top galleries (all have free admission) you'll want to hit include:

* **Dust Gallery** (at Soho Lofts, 900 S. Las Vegas Blvd.; 1221 S. Main St.; ☎ 702/880-3878; www.dustgallery.com; Tues–Sat 11am–6pm) and **G-C Arts** (1217 S. Main St.; ☎ 702/453-2200; www.gcarts-lv.com; hours vary). The two heavy-hitters on the scene, these are NOT artist-run galleries. Instead, the professional curators here bring in midcareer and established artists from all over the country, but primarily Vegas, Los Angeles, and New York. Both carry the distinction of having sold art to the "big get" in contemporary art—the Museum of Modern Art in New York City.
* **The Arts Factory** (101–109 E. Charleston Blvd.; ☎ 702/676-1111; www.the artsfactory.com; generally open Mon, Tues, Thurs, and Fri noon–5pm, and up

until 9pm on the first Fri of each month). Once a crematorium, later a paper factory (keep an eye out for the giant pencil still on the building), the Arts Factory is a literal beehive of tiny galleries set in two adjoining buildings. Ascend the paint-splattered steps here, and you'll find a warren of rooms, some of which contain commercial art concerns and about 14 dedicated to fine arts. It can be difficult to figure out if the galleries are open or not, so don't be shy about knocking. Sometimes the artists are there, but so involved in their creations they forget to sell. The focus of the artists here seems to be on abstract art, with a smattering of brightly colored representational works as well.

How good is the art on view? Ah well, that's in the eye of the beholder and the beholders haven't come to a uniform consensus. Local artist M. Griesgraber griped to me that "people could care less about the arts in this town. It's all very unsophisticated, as is the art." But just 15 minutes later, his neighboring gallery owner Alan Tager boasted "We're seeing the best in contemporary art from around the world. The city's goal is to make itself the largest art and cultural center in the U.S., and that's my goal, too." Which one is right? I'd say the reality lies somewhere in the middle.

HISTORY

Near, far, wherever you are . . . if you can't get enough of the *Titanic,* you're not alone. In the last decade or so, the tragic iceberg sinking of this ocean liner has inspired a Broadway musical, the largest grossing film of all time, and countless specials on the Discovery Network. It also has given rise to a traveling show of *Titanic* artifacts that is now docked at the Luxor. Called **Titanic: The Exhibit** ★★ (in the Luxor; ☎ 800/557-7428 or 702/262-4400; www.luxor.com/attractions/attractions_titanic.aspx; $33 with the audio tour, $27 without; reduced admission for seniors and locals; daily 10am–11pm; AE, DISC, MC, V), it showcases 300 artifacts robbed from the watery graves . . . uh, I mean rescued from the wreck 12,500 feet beneath the surface of the ocean. To be fair, the RMS *Titanic,* Inc., which holds salvage rights to the ship and retrieved many of the objects seen here (others are loaned from private collections), has left the hull and all its contents intact and has only brought to the surface those things scattered on the ocean floor. They're more than enough to keep your interest, from glass and china with the White Star logo, to jewelry, photos, lamps, and more. Along with these objects, the exhibit re-creates some areas of the ship, gives viewers an audio tour with music that goes from ragtime to gloom and doom, and offers other "experiential" touches that I won't give away here, meant to convince viewers they're actually on the ship. Some will find it touching, others ludicrous, but I'll give it this: It's difficult to get through the exhibit without feeling some small prickle of tears at the back of your eyes.

It's telling, I think, that the history of a doomed ocean liner is center stage on the Strip, but a history museum that actually details the story of Sin City itself is relegated to the side of the highway, about 10 miles southeast of the center. (This is a city after all with a penchant for bulldozing over its history and for imploding anything that gets in the way of bigger profits.) Which is a shame because the **Clark County Heritage Museum** ★★ (1830 S. Boulder Hwy., in Henderson; ☎ 702/455-7955; $1.50 adults, $1 seniors and children 3–15; daily 9am–4:30pm; no credit cards) is a real gem, chockablock with richly evocative artifacts and

The Arts Factory **3**	Dust Gallery **5**
Art @ The Funk House **6**	Gainsburg Studio **1**
Commerce Street Studios **8**	G-C Arts **4**
Dray's Place Fine Art Gallery **7**	S2 Art Center **2**

interactive exhibits detailing the story of the area, from Native Americans through gangsters through the pack of corporate thieves who control the Strip today. And for a museum set this far off the Strip, and so cheap to visit, it's startlingly high tech: Sensors turn on narration, sound effects, and even visual effects whenever a visitor enters a gallery, and many of the exhibits are interactive. Highlights (for me, at least) are half a dozen actual houses that you wander through, hearing about the lives of the real people who lived in them at different times in the area's history, from a Paiute twig hut village to a house lived in by men involved in the construction of the Hoover dam, to a gold miner's house and a 1960s abode from the Atomic Testing Site. As you enter, you'll hear period music as a narrator picks out the specific artifacts you should look at closely. The houses are fantastic, as is the 1932 Boulder Train Depot that's also displayed here. Back outside is a garden with native plants, all well marked along winding trails. Even though the museum is close to the highway and the area is fast becoming one long stretch of boxy developments, you can still get the sense of being way out in the middle of nowhere. Severe mountains loom in all directions beyond the barren desert plain. I found the whole thing pretty thrilling. The downside: Because it is a good, long drive from the Strip, you'll need a rental car to get here. A taxi really isn't practical.

My least favorite of the city's history museums, **The Nevada Museum** (700 Twin Lakes Dr.; ☎ 702/486-4202; $4 adult, $3 seniors, free for children; daily 9am–5pm), is currently a dusty collection of stuffed animals, dried cacti, and historic postcards interspersed with wall text and photos about the mob, magnesium, and the state's history. There's also an odd set of rooms which are meant to re-create the look of a typical casino (as if the viewer couldn't simply drive 10 minutes and get to a real one!). I don't want to beat up on it too harshly as a brand spanking new space for the collection is being built next to the Springs Preserves and can only improve upon what's here. If that's open, give it a chance but there's not much point in going to this location (which is also well off the Strip, by the by).

MYSTERIES

Let's first discuss what the **Mystery Adventures Las Vegas** ✰✰ (1100 E. Sahara, Ste. 105-A; ☎ 877/893-6449 or 702/893-6500; www.mysteryadventureslasvegas. com; $40 adults, $25 ages 6–17; Mon–Fri 7pm, Sat–Sun 1pm and 7pm; AE, DC, MC, V) isn't. First off, it's more of a role-playing game than an actual tour. And it has nothing to do with Las Vegas really, its history or its culture. It is instead, a darn engrossing romp through the violent world of murder mysteries. Participants are deputized as "assistant detectives" and then are taken to several purpose-built sites (in strip malls, of course) where they must figure out how to break into computers, crack locks, open secret doors, and the like. In addition, small talismans are hidden that have nothing to do with the crime being investigated but have a point value: Collect enough and you get a t-shirt *(woo hoo!)*. These are aimed more at the children brought on the tour, though to be frank with its gory imagery (blood spatters, bullet-pocked walls, fake human remains) this could be a nightmare-creator for more delicate little minds. I'd say the tour is only appropriate for kids who don't scare too easily. Adults who enjoy murder mysteries, though, are going to lap this all up. The experience usually takes between 2 and 3 hours (the time difference depends on how quick your group is at solving clues). Important: Coupons are everywhere (online and in those hotel brochure kiosks) for discounts on this tour, so snag one before signing up for savings of $5 to $10.

NEON SIGNS

The grandly titled **Neon Museum** (www.neonmuseum.org), is, in actuality, 11 classic Vegas signs, fully restored to their original luminescence and scattered in and around the Fremont Street Experience area. This puts them into well-trod areas of Downtown, but unfortunately sets them up in an unwinnable competition with the massive LED light canopy that overhangs many of them. You simply can't see their true colors against such a huge light source. If you're in the area, and have nostalgia for the Vegas of the gangster days, seek them out as you walk Downtown. You'll see one for "wedding information," a Genie's lamp from the old Aladdin, a vintage liquor store sign, and so forth (each has a plaque explaining its provenance). I don't think that this "museum" is worth a special trip. Much more evocative and interesting are the tours of the **Neon Boneyard,** where many more of these signs are stored (see p. 173 for more on that).

PINBALL

If you've been playing the silver ball ever since you were a young child and still have the supple wrists to show for it, make the pilgrimage out to the **Pinball Hall of Fame** (3330 E. Tropicana Ave., at Pecos Rd.; www.pinballmuseum.org; free admission, games cost 25¢; Mon–Fri 11am–11pm, Sat–Sun 11am–midnight). Set in an obscure strip mall about a 20-minute drive from the Strip, this nonprofit "museum" is simply a huge arcade crammed with 158 pinball games. The oldest is a 1948 Rondeevoo; the rarest is an unproduced prototype called Black Gold, and each machine has a story that the owner of the museum has scrawled on index cards and taped to them. If you're a child of the '80s like me, you'll enjoy playing the classic video games that are here. From Paper Boy (a personal fave that I credit with dropping my GPA down a point in college) to Asteroids, the place holds an additional 48 of these types of video game machines as well. "This place is one of a kind," Walter Day, author of the *Official Video Game and Pinball Book of World Records,* told me. He just happened to be refereeing a world championship Galaga match when I dropped by.

SEX, YES, SEX

I've been to a number of sex museums now (hey, it's my job . . . somebody's got to do it!) but the **Erotic Heritage Museum** ★★ (3275 Industrial Way; ☎ 702/369-6442; http://eroticheritagemuseum.com; $20 adults, $15 seniors, free military and retired military; Tues–Sun noon–midnight) is the first I've seen that is unapologetically focused more on porn than on its subject. And yes, there is a difference. Here, the first exhibit visitors come to is a serious one (some might say a serious buzz kill) on the censorship and First Amendment battles of the last 70 years. This is followed by massive blow-ups of porn stars with wall text about their artistic achievements (no joking), very realistic-feeling plastic molds of their private parts (and I'll remind you again that it's my job to touch these things), and theaters where you'll see clips of some of the most infamous porn films of all time. Much of this is eye-opening, like the "penetration machines" created by tech-inspired fetishists; and the ancient erotic sculptures (there's even a centuries old Japanese stone deflowering tool that looks mighty painful). If you're not prudish, you should find this quite a fun and, um, educational night out (a date night perhaps?). And along with permanent and changing exhibits, the museum sponsors a number of lectures, performances, and workshops, including the always popular "Bondage for beginners" and nude drawing classes. This large, bi-level museum even has an erotic wedding chapel. The museum is located along a row of strip clubs and has a well-stocked gift shop should you be inspired by any of the displays.

SCIENCE & WILDLIFE

Possibly the most controversial exhibit to tour the United States since Andres Serrano's *Piss Christ* was making the rounds, ***Bodies . . . The Exhibition*** ★★ (in the Luxor Hotel and Casino; ☎ 800/557-7428 or 702/262-4400; www.luxor.com; $31 adult, $29 seniors and students, $23 kids 4–14; daily 10am–10pm; AE, MC, V) does something much more subversive than submerging a statue of Christ in urine: It robs graves (according to some). Splashed across the front pages of many newspapers, this is the notorious show that displays actual corpses, and yes, there have been serious issues raised about the provenance of the cadavers. They were legally obtained, but because these are "unclaimed bodies" from the People's Republic of China many believe they may have been executed prisoners of the State. As well, none of the people in this exhibit gave permission for their bodies to be used in this way.

If these issues concern you, skip this one. But I have to say that despite these ethical issues, the intent of the exhibition is noble. It's meant to teach, not titillate; to help average Americans better understand their own bodies, and in doing so, take better care of them. Along with the healthy cadavers (if there's such a thing) are displayed body parts that tell distressing stories: The misshapen and blackened lung of a smoker; the mottled brain of a stroke victim; a liver slashed with scars from cirrhosis; an obese body, the corpulence as much a disease as anything else here.

In the course of the exhibit, visitors journey across the landscape of the human body from the skeleton, to the musculature, to the circulatory system, nerves, and reproductive organs. One room apiece illustrates each of these topics (and others) and the cadavers are posed in various ways—shooting a basketball, or sitting in the same position as Rodin's *Thinker*—with different parts exposed to illuminate different aspects of the body. One's cut in 2-inch sections like those you'd see in an MRI while another's muscles are filleted out like a rose, so that the viewer can easily view the intricate layering of muscles throughout the body. The corpses, in case you were wondering, have been preserved through a process called "plasticination," with polymers replacing the water in the body, stopping the cadavers from decaying and allowing them to retain their natural colors. All in all, it's likely to be one of the most intellectually satiating hours you'll spend in Vegas and worth the high cost of admission (head to the Tix 4 Tonight booth for $22 tickets; or download a coupon from BroadwayBox.com before you come to town).

Science isn't nearly as glitzy off the Strip, but the local **Natural History Museum** ✿ (kids) (900 N. Las Vegas Blvd., at Washington Ave.; ☎ 702/384-3466; $8 adults, $7 seniors and students, $4 children 3–11; two-for-one discounts on website; daily 9am–4pm; no credit cards), dusty though it may be, still tickles the brain with its ever-expanding mix of interactive exhibits, video presentations, live fish, and lots and lots of taxidermy. It's grown kind of as things in nature do, based on the resources it's been able to suction up, starting as a repository of mounted animals donated by a collector named Bruno Shear. These still hold pride of place at the front of the museum, but what lies behind these grimacing, glassy-eyed, sometimes mangy stuffies, is far more compelling. Skip the first two rooms and head straight back to the dinosaurs, which were built with the help of a fairly recent endowment and are Jurassic Park–quality monsters, 35 feet long and able to growl and move (when you push the appropriate buttons). Deductive text next to the exhibits teaches children (and adults) about their habits and the theories surrounding their extinction. Along with the dinos are rooms with live reptiles and fish (including a neat bamboo shark hatchery and nursery, where you'll see the tiny killers wiggling in their translucent egg sacks); a room of interactive physics and chemistry experiments; and for a dash of controversy, a detailed, realistic-looking group of sculptures representing human evolution, from ape on up, based on the latest findings in the field. It's actually quite well done. "We are stewards of the world," Marilyn Gillespie, the Executive Director told me. "We are becoming so urbanized, we're out of touch with nature. Our purpose is to instill an appreciation for wildlife and the environment in all who come here." Not a modest goal, but one that I think is being modestly accomplished here. Bring the kids when they, and you, have gotten tired of the brain-freezing thrills of the Strip and you need to thaw out.

In 2003, during the 5,749th performance of Siegfried & Roy's legendary magic show, the white tiger Montecore refused a command to lie down. When Roy Horn pulled on his leash (or stumbled, accounts vary) Montecore attacked Horn, grabbing Horn's forearm with his mighty fangs, eventually dragging him by the neck across stage until a stagehand was able to rescue the wounded magician. Horn was rushed to the hospital and survived the attack, though the show was permanently closed. Horn is still recovering from the muscular and neurological damage inflicted that day. Montecore, in the meantime, was put into quarantine for 10 days as required by law, and when no odd behaviors were noted he was returned to his home: **The Secret Garden & Dolphin Habitat** (at The Mirage; ☎ 702/791-7111; www.mirage.com; $15 adults, $10 for ages 4–12; Mon–Fri 11am–6pm, Sat–Sun 10am–6pm; AE, DISC, MC, V). He's now been removed from the exhibit, but you will see 10 other large cats that once disappeared on cue, pacing restlessly in the junglelike enclosures of the garden to this day. Perhaps because of that history, or perhaps because the animals look so sad and bored, I'm not a big fan of the place. Or the processes used to create these tigers (they do not exist in the wild), for that matter. The white tigers are actually Bengal tigers; the white coloration is a genetic abnormality that results from inbreeding and is often accompanied by a host of other genetic defects such as clubfeet, abnormal kidneys, crooked backbones, and cataracts. Purposefully creating these beasts is a cruel practice as is keeping these natural roamers in confined spaces. Though the tigers do return to their larger home at Siegfried and Roy's ranch at night, the hours spent at this garden look like a prison sentence, to this outsider.

Somewhat better is the attached **Dolphin Habitat,** which consists of two oversized pools inhabited by 10 bottlenose dolphins, many of whom were born in this facility (all of these dolphins were born in captivity, with none taken from the wild). There are no shows here, but the dolphins are put through a series of exercises on a daily basis, which keep all the mammals, those in the water and those watching them, entertained. Research studies on a number of topics are being conducted with these expressive, highly animated beings making this exhibit feel less exploitive than its sister one. The Dolphin Habitat has a "Trainer for a Day" program which I profile on p. 168.

Big cats are on display at the **Lion Habitat** (at MGM Grand; ☎ 800/929-1111 or 702/891-7777; www.mgmgrand.com; free admission; lions on display daily 11am–10pm), which places lethargic lions in a glassed-in and large terrarium-like compound right off the casino. Again, they look depressed to me, so I'm not a big fan of the exhibit (though when one is lying on the glassed-in tunnel in the middle of the space it is fascinating to walk under and get a close up view of lion belly). Inside is a photo op for $25 allowing visitors to hold a lion cub and smile for the camera (when I was last there, all the cats were too old for this money-maker).

TELEVISION

If you've ever felt jealous of those Nielsen families, here's the chance to make your opinions heard. At three different focus group centers—in the **Miracle Mile Mall** (p. 263), **MGM Grand** (p. 34), and **Mandalay Place** (p. 260)—visitors act as guinea pigs for the new pilots the major networks are considering adding to their line-up. These might include CBS, NBC, and ABC as well as MTV, VH-1, Nickelodeon, UPN, King World, Paramount Television, Showtime, TNN, and CMT. There are sessions for adults only as well as for families (usually, the child-friendly programming is screened earlier in the day). You'll see uniformed employees handing out tickets to the screenings right in front of the three Research Centers and sometimes elsewhere in the casinos or mall. As you watch, you jiggle a little knob up and down indicating how much you like or dislike what's happening on the screen. I've reviewed a new network this way (one that would have no words played, only music and images) and an execrable sitcom that never made it to air, giving it "2s" for most of the half-hour; because I enjoy prank-ing, I upped my rating to a "10" every time the dog entered the room. (Hee, hee, hee.) I have to say, even though the show was the pits, I enjoyed the experience and the weird feeling of power it gave me . . . but that may just be me. I write guide-books, so I probably have some sort of strange gene in my system that compels me to review things. ***One note:*** Because participants are so valuable, many of these booths have now taken to rewarding those who give their time with either cash (an average of $25 is common) or free entry to nearby attractions or nightclubs.

VIEWS

The lights swirl and the crowds develop intriguing patterns when you take in the Strip from an angle usually reserved for eagles. Taking in the view is a top activity in Vegas, whether you do it from the balcony of a hot dance club (p. 199) or through the window of a high up, Strip-facing hotel room. But if you're not into clubbing or get a room that faces the hills, what do you do? Possibly, you might pay the steep fees it takes to get to the top of the **Eiffel Tower Experience** (in Paris Las Vegas; ☎ 888/266-5687 or 702/946-7000; $12 adults, $10 seniors and chil-dren 6–12; daily 7:30am–midnight; AE, DISC, MC, V) on the Center Strip; or up to the observation deck of the tallest building in the Southwest, the **Stratosphere Observation Deck** (in the Stratosphere; ☎ 800/99-TOWER or 702/380-7777; $14 adults, $10 seniors and children 4–12; Sun–Thurs 10am–1am, Fri–Sat 10am–2am; MC, V). The first is a slavish re-creation of the actual Eiffel Tower, but at a third of the size (540 ft. tall), its observation deck gets pretty crowded. I also have a friend who found the height and the speed of the elevator up so discombobulating that she spent the rest of the day fighting wooziness. Still, it's a lovely view, especially if you time it to be up there during the Bellagio Fountain show (it's just across the street). At the Stratosphere you're higher (857 ft. at the top observation deck), there are explanations of what you're seeing marked at the bottom of the viewing window (you can also go up to the amusement park area for an outdoor view), and the entire space is much, much larger and rarely feels overcrowded. But you're at a less visually potent end of the Strip, so the view is, arguably, less dramatic. Is either worth it? On a view to value ratio, I'd say the experience doesn't tip partic-ularly in either direction. It's pleasant but not something I'd go out of my way to do again.

Note: When it gets too windy, the Eiffel Tower does close, so call and check before trekking over there if it's a blustery day.

SPORTS & RECREATION

Want to watch sports? You can do so in any casino on the Strip, and most of the off-Strip ones as well, in the Sports Book area. But the teams that are being bet on will never be hometown teams . . . because they simply don't exist. Beyond the UNLV Division I college teams, this large city has no major league teams (yeah, there's the Wranglers, who play hockey, but are you really in Las Vegas to watch minor league ice hockey?).

So if you want to see sports live, you'll have to confine yourself to the non-team sports. Vegas is a major boxing town, with the big Strip hotels serving as the setting for some of the most intense knock-down, drag 'em out brawls in recent history (it was at the MGM Grand that boxer Mike Tyson got his first taste of ear, biting down on Evander Holyfield's left one in 1997). For information on how to obtain tickets to these events go to p. 196, but I'll repeat here the advice we give in that chapter—don't bother. Concerts and matches cost more in Vegas than in any other part of the country, and it's near impossible to get a discount. You'll see the action better on pay-per-view than you will in the cheap seats you can afford.

Car races are also major events in Vegas, held at the impressive $100-million complex known as the **Las Vegas Motor Speedway** ✖ (799 Las Vegas Blvd. N., across from Nellis Air Force Base; ☎ 702/644-4443; www.lvms.com; tickets $11–$261). Here you'll find a 2½-mile FIA-approved road course, a 1½-mile super speedway, paved and dirt short-track bull rings, a 4,000-foot drag strip, and more NASCAR action than your mammalian brain can incorporate (I'm talking painted chests, screaming tykes, and air scented with *eau de beer*). The famed Nextel Cup is held here, giving the speedway the nickname of the "Blue Oval" thanks to the domination of Ford drivers in that event. The Speedway is accessible via public transportation (go to the website for schedules and maps).

The **PGA Tour's Las Vegas Senior Classic** (held in Apr; www.pga.com) and the **National Finals Rodeo** (in Dec at the Thomas & Mack Center; see p. 197) are two annual events that add to the town's sports roster; you'll also find the occasional bull-riding championship, super-cross matches, and NBA games on offer.

RECREATION

Set on one of the most beautiful stretches of the Mojave Desert, Vegas offers all types of wonderfully relaxing, challenging recreation activities, with hiking, biking, and rafting opportunities galore (which you can read about in Chapter 12). You don't need to go too far beyond the city limits, however, to pep up those endorphins or work up a sweat.

GOLF

Weather, water, and wishful thinking: Those are the three elements that make Las Vegas the most expensive place in the United States to play golf. Let me explain. Drought conditions—this is a desert after all—mean that the courses must be seeded several times a year to keep everything green (and that costs money). Brutal summer temperatures and chilly winter mornings drastically cut into the number of days most visitors are willing to play (even more cash lost for the courses). And because many people who vacation in Vegas treat their greenbacks like Monopoly money, golf-course owners have steadily increased fees, getting nary a whisper of protest, even when 18 holes of play prices out at an outrageous $500 (as it does at the Mandalay Bay's private course).

Because this is a budget guide, I won't be profiling any of these costly courses. It's hard for me to imagine that several hours of swatting a ball around could ever be worth that kind of money. Instead, here are my picks for the top value golf courses in Vegas (and a website for last-minute deals, should you have the yen to play one of the pricey ones):

There are all types of golfers out there, but most will find something they like at **Black Mountain** (500 Greenway Rd., Henderson; ☎ 702/565-7933; www.golf blackmountain.com; $95 Labor Day to Memorial Day, $50–$70 in the summer months, $75 if you play after 12:30pm; AE, DISC, MC, V), which is really three courses in one, each with its own personality. The "Founders" course has the feel of a Midwestern country club with large trees, bordering homes, and green grass. A lack of neighboring fairways almost guarantees privacy as you play; it's very unusual to run into other golfers on this one, even on crowded days. The "Horizon" course is "go for it" golf, featuring a number of wide open shots where you can hit long—it's great for beginners. And the "Desert 9" is the most contemporary of the courses, with undulating greens and desert patches, meaning you must leapfrog from one hole to the next, playing real "target golf." The 9th hole on this course was listed in the book *1001 Golf Holes You Must Play Before You Die,* and each shot is a challenge on this one. A relaxed club (jeans are fine here), this 48-year-old course is a favorite of both locals and visitors. Book at least 5 days in advance to get the tee-time you want.

Last-minute bookings are no problem at the **Desert Rose Golf Course** (5483 Clubhouse Dr.; ☎ 702/431-4653; http://desertrose.americangolf.com; weekdays $69, $49 twilight play, weekends $89 and $49; AE, DISC, MC, V). So long as you have three or fewer players with you, they'll likely be able to work your party in. And this is a fun course to play. Designed by Bert Stance, it offers the longest drive in Las Vegas and just a few out-of-bounds conditions. There are also two washes that run through the course. A more traditional course than many in town, with mature trees, many consider it the best value in the county. The one major negative here—a fairly perfunctory and small clubhouse.

Once the golf club with the highest elevation in Nevada, **Highland Falls** (10201 Sun City Blvd., Summerlin; ☎ 702/254-7010; www.golfsummerlin.com; prices $90–$120, depending on season; AE, DISC, MC, V) ceded that title to a handful of new courses in the last decade. But for budget players, this is still the highest-altitude affordable golf course in the state, at an elevation of 3,053 feet, offering its players exquisite views as they traverse the course. It also has a good level of difficulty, as this is not a typical flat course; players must contend with a number of challenging elevation changes, making proper club selection key. Because of increasingly high prices for water, they removed 25 acres of turf from their driving range, giving it a prototypical desert look. It doesn't offer twilight rates in peak season, but its primetime rates remain lower than many other courses' twilight rates, so that may be a moot point. The course has a par of 72 and is 6,512 yards.

Built in 1959, the **Wild Horse** (2100 Warm Springs Rd., Henderson; ☎ 702/434-9000; www.golfwildhorse.com; $85 weekdays, $108 weekends, $58 twilight; MC, V) was once owned by Howard Hughes. Older golf fans will recognize the name as it hosted the PGA in the '60s and '70s. Now a municipally owned golf course, it gets a crowd that's 80% locals. But that doesn't mean you shouldn't join them. It got a darn nice redesign in 2004, turning it into a par-70 course. It's an easy one to get around, so if you only have a limited amount of time for your 18 holes, you can probably do this one in about 4 hours or less if you maintain a brisk pace. ***Note:*** Seniors are eligible for discounts of as much as 50%; ask.

BOWLING

From tiny balls to big ones (insert your own double entendre here), bowling is quite popular at the off-Strip casinos. Fifty to 80 state-of-the-art lanes are the norm at these places, as are video scoring screens with cute graphics, extensive arcades, bars, cafes, pro shops, and more. Average rates are $3 per game, plus $2.50 for shoe rental. In alphabetical order, the places you'll most enjoy slamming down pins are:

- **Gold Coast Hotel** (4000 W. Flamingo Rd., at Valley View; ☎ 702/367-7111; www.goldcoastcasino.com; daily 24 hr.; AE, DISC, MC, V)
- **Orleans** (4500 W. Tropicana Ave.; ☎ 702/365-7111; www.orleanscasino.com; daily 24 hr.; AE, DISC, MC, V)
- **Sam's Town** (5111 Boulder Hwy.; ☎ 702/456-7777; www.samstown.com; daily 24 hr.; AE, DISC, MC, V)
- **Santa Fe Station** (4949 N. Rancho Rd.; ☎ 702/658-4900; www.stationcasinos.com; Fri–Sat 24 hr., Sun–Thurs 9am–1am; AE, DISC, MC, V)
- **Suncoast** (9090 Alta Dr., in Summerlin; ☎ 702/636-7111; www.suncoastcasino.com; daily 24 hr.; AE, DISC, MC, V)

HORSEBACK RIDING

The new **equestrian center** at the South Point Casino (p. 64) is bringing the cowboys back to Vegas, filling the arena there with world-class horse shows and rodeos nearly every weekend of the year. If you'd like to get back in the saddle yourself, however, your best options are to head east rather than south, towards Red Rock Canyon (p. 284). **Bonnie Springs Ranch** ★★ kids (☎ 702/875-4191; www.bonniesprings.com; $35 per hour; daily 10am–6pm; AE, DISC, MC, V; for more go to p. 286) has complete stables, offering trail rides daily starting at $20 per person. Its competitor, **Cowboy Trail** ★★ kids (☎ 702/948-7061; www.cowboytrailrides.com; shortest trail ride is $69 for 11/2 hr.; AE, DISC, MC, V) is a family-owned operation that offers campfire cookouts along with its rides. Both allow children over the age of 6, can customize their itineraries to suit beginners or more advanced riders, and neither enforces a weight limit (though if you're an adult, you do have to be able to get on and off your mount with minimal assistance). Which is better? Cowboy Trail Rides is pricier but offers a wider range of hikes, and (some assert) better mounts. But if you're a beginner, either one should do fine; really it's all about being a cowboy for the day, in the midst of some of the most glorious scenery in the U.S.

INDOOR SKY DIVING

In the 1960s, the military constructed the first vertical indoor wind tunnel to develop the skills of its sky-diving troops. The object was for these soldiers to fall from the sky and land on target with a James Bond–like accuracy. "Controlled bodyflight," the technique created from these training sessions, is still in use by the military. I guess the word got out from all those soldiers whooping it up on gusts of air, and a bit over a decade ago the first tunnels were opened to civilians and a new extreme sport was born.

I'm not a skateboarder, I've never tried surfing, but I have to say that if a wind tunnel opened up in my hometown of New York City, I might well become a tunnel rat. The sport is that exhilarating, an out of body body-centric thrill that's a rush like no other. While exiting from an airline feels like a fall, here you grab as much air as possible so that you can be lifted up, Peter Pan without the pixie dust. It's expensive, but so frigging fun I'd say it's worth it. This is one of those extraordinary experiences you come to a city like Vegas to try.

You have the ability to try this new sport at **Flyaway Indoor Skydiving** ✪✪✪ (200 Convention Center Dr., just off the Strip; ☎ 702/545-8093 or 702/731-4768; www.flyawayindoorskydiving.com; $75 for flights and instruction, various packages for more than one session or groups of five or more, visit the website first or pick up a coupon for $5–$15 discounts; daily 10am–8pm; AE, DISC, MC, V), Las Vegas' only tunnel. After watching a training video; signing a terrifying waiver; and suiting up with goggles and a floppy, wind-catching jump suit; you'll be taken to the tunnel where one by one you'll lie down on the steel cable mesh. Below it sits a 1,000 horsepower DC-3 airplane propeller. An instructor holds your hands guiding you towards the center of the stream, helping you control your trajectory and, when you're done flying, fall easily into the padded walls of the tunnel. Though you'll only get to try this three times for the initial payment, it feels much longer; this is one of those activities where time slows to a crawl.

No experience with sky diving is necessary, but only those with healthy body mass indexes are allowed to fly. It actually has nothing to do with how much you weigh, but with how the weight is distributed. Men over 6 feet tall can weigh 220 pounds max, under 6 feet and 200 pounds. For women, it's 180 pounds over 6 feet, 160 pounds for those between 5 feet, 6 inches and 6 feet, and 140 pounds for those who are shorter. Is it safe? It seems to be for beginners, as the flying you do is quite limited, with an instructor keeping hold of your hands most of the time; those more advanced, who start practicing flips and the like, are at greater risk, but even with those folks no one has ever died at this facility (and apparently only one person has died in the 2 decades people have been engaging in this sport). With 30,000 people coming through the facility yearly, they get about three injuries per year.

6 Say "I Do" to Vegas

It's the quickest, cheapest, but often weirdest way to get wed in all the land

$28,584.

Contemplate that number, all ye brides-to-be—and weep. Because that's the average cost—the average!—of a wedding in the United States today, according to a study conducted by the Wedding Report Inc. (a trade group). Instead of investing in the down payment on a home, or putting away money for the college education of future offspring, couples are frittering away that huge sum on flowers, embossed napkins, and chicken Cordon Bleu for 100.

It doesn't have to be that way, as couples who go the Vegas route know. Every day, budget-conscious twosomes are getting hitched in no fuss, no muss ceremonies for as little as $100 (including the cost of the marriage license). That's for a quickie "drive-through" wedding ("do you take this woman to be your lawfully wedded wife, and would you like a side of fries?"), but even those who arrive with bridesmaids, guests, and mothers-in-law in tow, can pull off fun nuptials, with a ceremony, reception, and photos for between $500 and $15,000 (depending on the size of the wedding party and the venue). In Sin City, holy matrimony is one of the biggest industries going, and local chapels know how to do the deed efficiently, cost-effectively, and, usually, breezily.

Which may be why those mojito-fueled, Britney "oops" weddings seem to be on the way out (though they still happen), and 70% of Vegas weddings are now planned well in advance. In the chapter that follows I'll examine all the steps involved in planning a wedding from afar, in addition to giving you price ranges for the wide variety of locations you'll have at your disposal.

And if you're reading this book drunk in a casino somewhere—drunk on love, or booze, I'm not judging—and decide that you want to marry the exquisite person who may be reading this over your shoulder, this chapter will work for you, too. Flowers, tuxes, wedding dresses, licenses, Elvis impersonators: These can all be rustled up within 2 hours or so, making last-minute weddings easier to arrange here than any other place in the world. Unless it's Halloween, New Year's Eve, or Valentine's Day (the most popular days of the year for weddings), you'll always find room at the chapel. One caution: Saturday nights do get booked far in advance, meaning you may have a bit of a wait if you try for a last-minute ceremony then (consider holding the reception before the ceremony!).

Whatever kind of wedding you're contemplating—plan ahead or "let's just do this"—know that when you do it in Vegas, it's likely to be a good cocktail party story ever after. And for the rest of your life together, you'll certainly get some kind of reaction—from a "wow" to an "ugh"—when you tell folks you got hitched in "Pair-O-Dice."

Beyond the convenience and low cost of weddings in Vegas, it's that reaction that's the lure. Getting married here injects a hint of rebellion, of nose-thumbing, of raw unadulterated sexiness into what can be a stodgy old ritual. "After 25 years of happily living together with my girlfriend we decided to get married," wrote a California man on the PBS website about Las Vegas. "We had always felt our love never needed the approval of church or state, so we went to Las Vegas, where neither church nor state seem obviously apparent . . . Reverend Betty, who officiated, was at least 70 years old, with a voice like Lauren Bacall and a face as dry and craggy as the desert itself. When we put our rings on the middle finger, she told us 'that's the wrong finger.' But in our unconventional way, we had decided that was what we wanted to do, so my new bride simply said, 'No, it's not.' Betty shrugged and said, 'It's Vegas. Do what you want.'"

PLANNING THE BIG DAY

It's stupefying how easy it is to plan a wedding in Vegas, even a big one, and even if you have to do it over the phone. That's because, unlike your neighborhood church or temple, wedding chapels here are in business only to perform marriages. They each are, in effect, mini-Walmarts of wedding services; once you choose your chapel, you'll use it to plan all of the other elements in the wedding. Actually, you'll have no choice: The chapels are highly proprietary about couples using services from outside vendors; don't try it, or you could get booted from your own wedding!

The following services are standard at all of the chapels we'll be discussing:

Photography & Videography: Unless you buy pictures and videos from the chapels, you won't have them. Personal cameras are always banned (with one exception that I know of, see p. 154), so this may be the one case where it's the better part of wisdom to spring for the more expensive package (you want something to show your grandkids, right?). Costs for these services will vary widely from chapel to chapel and are actually a bit hard to figure out, as they're usually mixed in with bouquets, boutonnieres, and commemorative poker chips (you get the drill); but from surfing through the catalogs, I'd say the least you're going to spend is $50 extra, which will buy you 9 to 12 prints. While that sounds high, there's the age-old question: How often do you get married (don't answer that one if your name is Larry King)? More elaborate packages, for three-camera video shoots, numerous prints, framed photos, and so forth, will be pricier.

Most chapels will also stream video of the ceremony on the Internet, either live or within 24 hours, for friends and family who weren't able to make it . . . but also for any schmo who likes to watch weddings of strangers (so there is some argument for turning down this service).

Bouquets & Boutonnieres: Every chapel can get you something to carry in your hands or pin in your lapel, with a number of chapels featuring on-site florists. If you're happy with a standard dozen roses, those can usually be picked out on the spot (average cost: $50), but more elaborate hand-tied bouquets almost always must be ordered in advance; how far in advance will vary by chapel—it can be a day to a week—so be sure to ask. Some chapels will even throw in a rose for the bride to carry in their most basic ceremonies, but the costs for flowers usually vary so widely that there's no point in printing ranges here.

Commitment & Renewal Ceremonies

Gay marriage is not yet legal in Nevada. However, a growing number of couples are coming to Vegas for commitment ceremonies, during which brides and brides or grooms and grooms pledge their love to one another in a non-legally binding ceremony.

You'd think in such an "anything goes" type of town that these ceremonies would be widely performed, but the truth is that prejudice exists even here and not all chapels will accommodate same-sex couples. Of the off-Strip chapels, the only one that does it (that I know of) is the gay-owned **Viva Las Vegas Wedding Chapel** (and they throw a *fabulous* ceremony, see p. 152). Of the hotel chapels, you have a choice of the Paris, Caesars, the Imperial Palace, and the Riviera.

Renewal ceremonies, where an already-married straight couple reaffirms their commitment to one another, are easier to arrange. In fact, every chapel in the city will take your business. Simply show up, no license necessary, and book a spot. Elvis can officiate if you wish, or you can do it seriously with a minister. Do I need to mention once again, how easy it is to express "straight" love in Nevada? Sad that it's the state with the highest divorce rate in the nation.

Costs for both types of ceremonies are equivalent to what you'd pay for a wedding.

Wedding Clothes: If you don't bring your own, gowns and tuxes can be rented on-site—I'll note the chapels where that can be arranged—or at nearby stores that the wedding coordinators will help you contact. Pricing on this makes no sense either, ranging from $50 up to several hundred for a more elaborate gown, so leave room in your pocketbook. Or skip the poofy white dress altogether. It's your wedding and you can show up in jeans and flip-flops without anyone blinking an eye. Weddings in Vegas are as formal, casual, or downright sloppy as you want to make them (no birthday suits though . . . sorry).

Transportation: In front of each chapel you'll see two or three limos that are for guest rental. These are available as part of different packages and are often touted as being a "free" service. That's an outright lie, as the cost is factored into the package you're buying and an additional tip to the driver is mandatory.

The Minister: In order for the marriage to be legal, the minister must be licensed in the state of Nevada, which is a big bugaboo, because getting licensed is a lengthy process. You probably won't be able to bring your hometown minister with you to do the service. If you want to make the effort, contact the Marriage License Bureau (p. 150) for complete information.

There are ministers aplenty in Las Vegas itself, of course, and every chapel has at least one on hand, and sometimes more. You won't get to choose your minister, however, and it's unlikely you'll have more than 5 minutes to chat, so don't expect to be able to "customize" your ceremony. In fact, asking for extras, such as a poem being read or a first dance performed, will often cost you more, as any time above the 15 minutes most couples get in the chapel for the service and photos, is money out of the chapel's coffers. So if you really must hear "The Song of Solomon" on that solemn day, inform the chapel first and see if it's doable. If they turn you down . . . try another chapel. You've got over 60 to choose from.

Bear in mind that the minister's fee is never included in the cost of a wedding, so you will be expected to "tip" the person who performs the service. The standard tip is between $50 and $75 for a chapel wedding, and $25 for a drive-through window or gazebo ceremony.

A Word on Service: I strongly advise you not to book online. Why? Well, you won't be able to judge what the service is like at the chapel that way. Weddings are high-stress events, so you don't want a snippy receptionist working your nerves. Have a short chat over the phone with chapel officials, just to find out how responsive they are to questions and how they treat potential brides and grooms. They should be able to answer whatever question you've posed to them and do so in a friendly, considerate way. After you've spoken with two or three you'll realize that there can be huge differences in basic manners from one to the next. It's a life-changing day, so why not do it in a chapel that treats it as such?

GETTING THE MARRIAGE LICENSE

Again, it's easy, easy, easy. Simply make your way to the **Clark County Marriage License Bureau** (200 S. 3rd St., at Bridger Ave.; ☎ 702/455-4415; www.co.clark.nv.us/clerk/marriage_information.htm; daily 8am–midnight). You won't need a blood test, there's no waiting period, and you don't even have to prove that you're single. All you'll need with you is:

◆ Proof that you're who you say you are and over the age of 18 (a driver's license, birth certificate, or passport will suffice)
◆ $55 in cash (no credit cards or checks accepted)
◆ A Social Security number (for Americans only)
◆ Your intended in tow. The last item is important. You can't get a marriage license when both of you aren't present, so scotch any plans for springing a surprise wedding on your beloved.

Wait times can vary greatly, depending on the time of year, day, and how loose the slots have been in the previous hours—you never know. You could be standing there for just 15 minutes or an hour and a half. If possible, pick up your

Rice: Not Nice!

The only thing that's verboten in Vegas: rice. No one wants to clean it up, and it has the unhappy side effect of making the stomachs of the birds that eat it explode . . . and I can think of few less romantic sights than an exploding fowl.

Charging Your Love

Yes, you can use your credit card to pay for a wedding at all of the chapels listed in this chapter. Just pull out your Amex, Visa, MasterCard, or Discover Card, find the right person to marry, and you should be all set.

license a day or two before the ceremony (the marriage license is good for a year from the date of issuance).

After the ceremony, the chapel will mail all of the necessary legal documents back to the Marriage License Bureau for you. If you want to have a copy of the marriage certificate, you'll need to write to the marriage bureau to request one; the cost is $10. All this information is available on the Clark County website (see above).

CHOOSING THE CHAPEL

Your most important task. You want to find a setting that will be meaningful to you and will fit into your budget. I've divided the following list by type of chapel—that is, casino-based or free-standing—but know that the free-standing chapels are almost always less expensive than those run by the casinos. In a plug for these independent businesses, they also usually have more interesting histories as well, with long lists of celebrities who married in them (some more than once). Please note that this list is not meant to be encyclopedic. These are recommendations for the places I think are special in some way; you'll see many others when trolling the Strip (and in surrounding areas).

One more caveat: You don't need to get married in a chapel at all. If you're more interested in saying your vows in a hot air balloon, at the lip of the Grand Canyon, or while chugging down Las Vegas Boulevard in a white stretch limo, those adventurous weddings can be arranged as well. See the box on p. 156 for many of the available options.

OFF-STRIP CHAPELS

Below, I'll be listing the price for a basic ceremony at each chapel to give readers a general look at price differentials. But let's be real: Very few people ever take the "basic" because it's flowerless and photoless. So be sure to add up all the numbers when booking a chapel; sometimes, one that's among the cheapest on its basic ceremony may be among the more expensive for packages.

I happen to think that the **A Special Memory Wedding Chapel** ★★★ (800 S. 4th St.; ☎ 800/962-7798; www.aspecialmemory.com; basic drive-up package $25, basic chapel $49; Sun–Thurs 8am–10pm, Fri–Sat 8am–midnight) is the prettiest of the off-Strip chapels by a hair, but then I have a thing for classic, clean-lined New England churches, and A Special Memory was built from scratch in 1996 to evoke that "Cape Cod" look. Handmade stained glass windows, solid oak pews, and soaring, gabled ceilings put a button on the ambience. Do your best to book the "Special Memory" chapel even if you have a small party (it can hold up to 110 people), as it's a much more attractive space than the tiny, Wild West–themed

Royal Chapel. And in the larger chapel, the bride makes her grand entrance down a pretty circular staircase from a private dressing room—you can't beat that! Out back is a sweet gazebo where couples can incorporate dove and butterfly releases into their ceremonies. This being Vegas, it can't all be "Kennedy-esque," of course, so those couples who enjoy a good laugh can choose to drive through the marriage "takeout" window at back. A menu above it spells out your options, the "appetizer" ceremony being the cheapest, with those buying "breakfast" getting a rose, a photo, and the wedding march (lunch and dinner guests get even more amenities). During the 2008 Las Vegas marathon, 50 couples held "jog through" ceremonies here in the middle of the race.

A Special Memory's major competitor in the looks department is the **Little Church of the West** ★★★ (4617 Las Vegas Blvd. S; ☎ 800/821-2452 or 702/739-7971; www.littlechurchlv.com; basic ceremony $75 weekdays, $100 weekends; Mon–Thurs 8am–11pm, Fri–Sat 8am–midnight), a comely, smaller chapel that's on the National Register of Historic Places for its "California Mining Town" design. If you can ignore the highway just outside, you'll feel like you've been transported back to *Little House on the Prairie* days, the gleaming California redwood interior, lit by four antique Victorian lamps (probably taken from old railway cars), being the perfect setting for a traditional ceremony. In fact, this may be the only chapel in town that doesn't have Elvis on speed dial; while they won't ban "the King" from appearing at your ceremony, they don't book impersonators (a sign of how unusually classy this place is). Originally part of the Last Frontier Hotel, it debuted in 1942, moving to its current site south of the Strip in 1996, and has seen more celebrity weddings than just about any chapel in Vegas (see box on p. 155.

Lollapalooza, theatrical, imaginative, outrageously fun weddings are the forte of the **Viva Las Vegas Wedding Chapel** ★★★ (1205 Las Vegas Blvd. S.; ☎ 800/574-4450 or 702/384-0771; www.vivalasvegas.com; basic ceremony $150; daily 9am–10pm), so if you're hoping for a ceremony your family will talk about for years, you come here. "I look at weddings as a production," says Ron de Car, the owner and former lead singer at the Tropicana's *Folies Bergere*. "And who better to pull it off than someone in showbiz?" To that end, there's a complete costume shop on-site, for the bride looking for the perfect wedding gown, or better yet, a poodle skirt, Marilyn Monroe's famous white dress and blonde wig, or a gold Cleopatra number, among dozens of other looks (there are equivalent outfits for the grooms). The lighting's theatrical and sharp, and the sleek, high-ceilinged Southwestern-style chapel is rigged with trapezelike gear for those who want to float 20 feet in the air, in a "Cirque"-style wedding. Once you have your guests in place—the chapel can seat 100, though many bring fewer (a reception hall on-site seats only 60)—they're treated to a little show with you as the star . . . sometimes backed up by a small army of dancers and singers. Elvis weddings are, of course, most popular, and they come in a number of variations from Blue Hawaii to Pink Caddy (where you drive the convertible right through the large doors of the church), but you can also have a "James Bond Wedding" officiated by 007, backed up by Bond girls; a fog-and-candelabra *Phantom of the Opera* ceremony; a pirate wedding; a hippie wedding; a cowboy wedding . . . if you can dream it up, they can make it happen. Beyond Elvis, what gets the most requests? Gothic weddings, believe it or not, where the couple dress as ghouls; the minister rises up from a coffin; and the Grim Reaper appears to speak the words "'Til death do you part."

If you've had that picture in your mind of a nervous couple knocking on a minister's door at 3am for a living room ceremony . . . well, that sort of thing doesn't exist anymore in Vegas. The closest you'll come to it is **Wee Kirk of the Heather** ★★ (231 Las Vegas Blvd. S.; ☎ 800/843-5266 or 702/382-9830; www.weekirk.com; $65 for a basic ceremony; daily 9am–9pm), which has the honor of being the oldest continuously operating wedding chapel in Vegas and started life as a minister's home (and, yes, that minister did conduct ceremonies in the living room, now a wedding chapel). If you look beyond the steeple and the gaudy neon sign out front, it still looks like the small, residential house it once was. Besides the name, and the fact that occasionally the grooms will wear kilts, there's not much that's Scottish about it. Wee Kirk has the same pew-and-flower urn, and the somewhat Victorian, somewhat kitschy decor of so many others, though it's spiffier and less tacky than some, having been recently refurbished. But the service is genuinely "old school," warm and caring, which may be why (along with the history of the place) so many people send their children and grandchildren to be married here, and renew their vows at Wee Kirk when their own 25th anniversaries roll around. If you want to get a glimpse of what it looks like, rent the films *Fools Rush In, Mars Attacks,* or *Vegas Vacation*—Wee Kirk had cameos in all three.

Graceland Wedding Chapel ★★ (619 Las Vegas Blvd. S.; ☎ 800/824-5732 or 702/382-0091; www.gracelandchapel.com; basic ceremony $65; daily 9am–11pm) was never owned by Elvis—the former owner did ask the King for permission to use the name—but it has real rock-and-roll cred nonetheless, having served as the nuptial spot for the likes of Jon Bon Jovi (and his vow renewal ceremony); Billy Ray Cyrus; and members of the Thompson Twins, Def Leppard, Deep Purple, KISS, and the countless other musicians who favor the place (you'll see their framed photos in the front). One of the oldest chapels in town, housed in a freestanding 1922 church complete with a little steeple, it's a simple-looking place of wooden pews (seating up to 34), wood walls, and a dove-themed stained glass window. It may be most famous for its "Elvis, Elvis, Elvis" ceremonies where not one, but three "Elvi" marry you: young Elvis, middle-aged Elvis, and fat addicted Elvis. In fact, Graceland claims to be the first chapel in town to have hosted an Elvis ceremony, though that's difficult to prove. Fresh or silk flowers for the bride to carry are provided free of charge.

Convenience is king . . . or perhaps "the bride" . . . at **Vegas Weddings** ★ (555 South 3rd St.; ☎ 800/823-4095 or 702/WED-DING; www.702wedding.com; basic ceremony $45; daily 8am–midnight) which sits kitty-cornered from the courthouse. Theoretically, you could get your license and be joking about "the old ball and chain" 10 minutes later. But this isn't just a place for quickie nuptials; purpose built and opened in 2008, much thought has gone into trying to make the place as romantic and flexible as possible. Custom-made stained glass gleams throughout, the main chapel is on the second floor (unusual for Vegas and giving it a nice feel of privacy), there's an infinity waterfall as a photo backdrop and an outdoor terrace for those who want to release things (balloons, doves) as they lock themselves into matrimony. Bottom line: It's a dignified place to get married (and I say that despite the fact that Nicky Hilton chose the older incarnation of this chapel to start her own 2-month stint as a wife). Like many of the others, it also offers drive-through services, webcast ceremonies, and all the help you'll need to throw together an affair to remember in under half a day.

Christian couples seeking a more religious experience generally head to **The Stained Glass Chapel** ✦✦ (901 E. Ogden Ave.; ☎ 866/384-4340 or 702/384-4340; www.stainedglasschapel.com; basic wedding $40; Mon–Tues and Thurs–Sun 9am–midnight, Wed by advance appointment only) which is one of the few chapels that's also a full-blown church. So instead of the usual secular symbols of rings or roses, its stained glass depicts Jesus and scenes from the New Testament; and in its second chapel is an ornate and quite beautiful pulpit taken from a 17th-century church (though the minister I spoke with couldn't say that the pulpit itself was from that era). Along with the usual ceremony, it's not unusual for scriptural passages to be included in the service. Don't get me wrong: This is still a fun place to get married—along with the two chapels, folks can get married outside overlooking a pool and a statue of Elvis, in mid-gyration. But if you want a bit more, well, God in your ceremony and you're Christian, this is where to come (the church is non-denominational and set in a lovely historic home, once the residence of Las Vegas' first marshal). Two big perks here: Unlike every other chapel I know, this one allows folks to take their own pictures at the ceremony; and by getting married here, you'll be helping pay the bills for a growing, inner-city congregation. And one big negative: The neighborhood the church is in is a bit dodgy, so while you're doing a good deed supporting the parishioners here with your wedding choice, you might want to book it for a daytime or early evening wedding.

A Little White Wedding Chapel ✦ (1301 Las Vegas Blvd. S.; ☎ 702/382-4983; www.littlewhitechapel.com; basic ceremony $55 chapel, $40 drive-through; daily 7am–midnight) is perhaps the most famous—or notorious—wedding chapel in town, as this was where Britney Spears consecrated her first marriage, pictures of the bombed-looking bride sweeping the news media. They haven't yet gotten around to memorializing that auspicious event; instead, their large Las Vegas Boulevard sign touts the fact that Michael Jordan and Joan Collins married here (I did a double-take at that one . . . until I realized that they didn't marry one

---

Sinatra Was My Best Man

Everybody knows about Elvis weddings, but fellows in white pantsuits and pompadours are only one breed of faux guest. Most wedding chapels will also be able to arrange the following impersonators (and others) to either officiate or perform:

Austin Powers	Rodney Dangerfield	Marilyn Monroe
Tom Jones	The Blues Brothers	Liberace
Elvira	Cher	Grandpa Munster
Garth Brooks	Tina Turner	Frank Sinatra
Madonna	Elton John	Dean Martin
Neil Diamond	Jerry Garcia	Johnny Cash

Who Got Married Where

Little White Wedding Chapel: Judy Garland, Mickey Rooney and Ava Gardner, Frank Sinatra and Mia Farrow, Patty Duke, Michael Jordan, Bruce Willis and Demi Moore, Joan Collins, Britney Spears, Natalie Maines

Little Church of the West: Betty Grable, Mickey Rooney, Judy Garland (yup, both of them got married here too!), Dudley Moore, Richard Gere and Cindy Crawford, Angelina Jolie and Billy Bob Thornton, Deanna Durbin, David Cassidy, Redd Foxx, Telly Savalas, Mel Torme, Dinah Washington, Margaret Whiting, Robert Goulet, Jodie Sweetin

Graceland Wedding Chapel: Jon Bon Jovi; Billy Ray Cyrus; members of the Thompson Twins, Def Leppard, and Deep Purple

Las Vegas Wedding Chapel: Nicky Hilton

Little Chapel of the Flowers: Carmen Electra and Dennis Rodman

The Bellagio: Leah Remini and Angelo Pagan

Mirage Hotel: Pamela Anderson and Rick Salomon

The Old Aladdin Hotel: Elvis Presley and Priscilla Beaulieu

The Flamingo: Joan Crawford, Wayne Newton

The Riviera Hotel: Ann-Margret

Caesars Palace: Xavier Cugat and Charo

Sahara Hotel: Kirk Douglas

another). "We do Elvis, Johnny Cash—you know, the traditional Vegas weddings here," Rosanne, the chatty receptionist told me. Definitely a wedding mill—for all the good and bad that implies—Little White is tops for one-stop shopping. Along with four kitschy, frilly on-site chapels (some featuring velvet love seats instead of pews), it has a huge tux and bridal gown rental store, an on-site florist, and every wedding souvenir you could ever want, right at the counter. This is also the chapel that gave the world the first "drive-through" weddings; today couples motor through a "tunnel of love," its ceiling painted with clouds and cupids. (Rosanne warns against driving through in a taxi, though. "It's terrible," she says. "The grooms usually spend the ceremony watching the meter.") While service here can be a bit brusque—they've got a lot of couples to usher in and out, 24 hours a day on weekends—and the lack of a real waiting area is annoying, if you're looking for that over-the-top, gaudy Vegas wedding, this place is one you should consider. *A word of warning:* Don't book the gazebo. It's right off Las Vegas Boulevard, and you won't be able to smell the flowers for the exhaust fumes or hear the minister over the sound of cars rushing past.

A Proposal You (Hopefully) Can't Refuse

Though there are no stats, I would guess that as many people get engaged in Vegas as get married here. Of course, there's no right or wrong way to do it—well actually, having your proposal tattooed across the bare fannies of the gals in the *Crazy Girls* show might be the wrong way—but here are some spots where the scenery may help sway your beloved in the "yes" direction.

Up high: Propose on the observation deck of the Eiffel Tower (p. 142), at the chic rooftop Mix Lounge at THEhotel at Mandalay Bay (p. 204), or the Stratosphere (p. 143)—that way, if she says "no" you can throw her over . . . literally. Just joking. The top of Vegas' Eiffel Tower is fenced in as is the Mix, and the Stratosphere also has a safety guard. Of the three, you'll get more of a close-up view of the Strip from the Eiffel Tower, as it's right in the center of it and significantly lower than the Stratosphere or Mix. Problem is, you'll also get a close up view of that guy in the Bermuda shorts next to you, as the observation area is pretty cozy. If you want a bit more privacy, head to the spacious Stratosphere or the Mix at sunset, before it turns into a loud dance club. And if she says "yes" at the top of the Strat you can celebrate with a stomach-churning ride on the Big Shot, the highest amusement park ride in the world.

Take her to the waters: There's something almost biblical about seeing huge sprays of water out in the middle of the desert. So maybe sights such as the Fountains at the Bellagio (p. 118), the canals at the Venetian (p. 120), or Lake Las Vegas will convince your intended to take seriously that injunction from Ecclesiastes, "Two are better than one." If you decide to go with the fountains, snag a spot on one of the Bellagio's balconies (much less crowded than the sidewalk right in front of the fountains). Shows take place on the half-hour between 3pm and 8pm on weekdays, noon to 8pm on weekends, and every 15 minutes thereon until midnight.

Carmen Electra and Dennis Rodman, and their short-lived marriage, gave the **Chapel of the Flowers** ✦ (1717 Las Vegas Blvd. S.; ☎ 800/843-2410 or 702/735-4331; www.littlechapel.com; basic wedding $75 weekday, $150 weekend; Mon–Thurs 9am–9pm, Fri–Sat 9am–10pm) a notoriety it doesn't deserve. Yup, they tied the knot here, and yup, they both now claim that they were out-of-their-minds drunk . . . but really, I promise, you're not going to run into blasted NBA stars and *Baywatch* babes on your special day. Instead, you'll be ministered to by a gracious staff of 45, from the on-site florists and staff photographers, to a cadre of bright, attractive young women who serve as wedding planners (all great bridesmaid material, should yours get waylaid by slot machines). So the service is top-notch (they'll even allow you to customize the ceremony by faxing short readings

The Venetian gondola route is pricier, but if you want to propose in a splashy manner (sorry!) here, you can do it in front of all the people who line the canals, as your gondolier croons "That's Amore." This is not the option if you're shy. For that, go the quieter gondolier route on Lake Las Vegas about a half-hour's drive south of the Strip. Though the lake's a fake, it's still lovely and you can ask that important question in peace and quiet, either in a boat or simply standing atop the PonteVecchio bridge.

Head into the desert: The twinkling lights of the Strip can be pretty, but they pale next to the majesty of Red Rock Canyon (p. 284) or the Valley of Fire (p. 286). Grab a bottle of wine, 2 gallons of water (always recommended when going out into the desert), and head out of the city. Red Rock Canyon is about a 30-minute drive from the Strip (depending on traffic); at the end of the "Icebox" trail is a lovely little waterfall. If you have shoes with good treads, you could probably get down on one knee in front of it without sliding into the water. Or do the deed at one of the many scenic overlooks facing those famous red rocks (the best ones are actually closest to the visitor center as you enter the park). At the Valley of Fire (about an hour's drive from the Strip), I'd recommend a hike along the Mouse's Tank trail, which leads into a canyon festooned with ancient petroglyphs; perhaps one of them means "would you be my wife?"

Garden of love: Fabulous photo ops at the Bellagio Conservatory Gardens, the Wynn Gardens, or the tropical gardens behind the Flamingo Hotel make them another top proposal spot. After she consents, you can whip out your camera phone and send off a photo to all your waiting family and friends. Go early or late in the day if you want to avoid crowds, though quite honestly these are popular spots, and it's unlikely you'll be alone in the first two—even at 2am.

in advance, a rare amenity). But because this small complex of chapels has so many people on the payroll, its prices are a tad higher than you'll find at most of the other free-standing chapels. It also has the bad habit of levying extra charges for items you don't need or get free elsewhere (for example, they'll charge you a special fee to arrange for the bride and groom not to run into one another before the wedding; they also offer to accompany you to the marriage license bureau for $75, another utterly unnecessary expense). Still, the chapels are bright and shiny, and suitably romantic in that synthetic Vegas manner (one's "Italian," another "Victorian," the third pale yellow one meant to evoke the "Old South," as well as a street-facing gazebo) and as I said before, you'll be well taken care of. Chapels here can hold between 20 and 70 guests, and there's a small outdoor space with a

Not Going to the Chapel, Still Going to Get Married

This is Vegas, baby, you can think outside the chapel if you wish, for locations in which to exchange your vows:

- In a helicopter while swooping over the Strip, Hoover Dam, or the Grand Canyon
- Perched on a chopper in the Harley-Davidson Café
- Backed by lascivious-looking nude statues at the Erotic Heritage Museum (p. 139)
- Floating in a gondola at The Venetian or in a boat on Lake Meade
- On the observation deck at the top of the "Eiffel Tower"
- Hiking Red Rock Canyon, the Valley of Fire, or on a local golf course
- While indoor sky diving

For the gondola or Eiffel Tower wedding, contact The Venetian and Paris Las Vegas, respectively, to inquire. For a biker wedding, contact the Harley-Davidson Café (3725 South Las Vegas Blvd.; ☎ 702-740-4555; www.harley-davidsoncafe.com). Any of the others can be arranged through the free-standing chapels recommended earlier in this chapter. Shop around and go with the one that gets you the best value.

waterfall and glass blown flowers *a la* Dale Chihuly that's appropriate for small champagne receptions.

CASINO CHAPELS

Personality ain't a strong suit of the casino chapels. Oh, yes, there are some exceptions (such as getting married in the gardens of the Tropicana or Flamingo, or doing a medieval bash at Excalibur), but in general these chapels are not as, well, gloriously tacky, or wacky, or just plain festive as what you'll find off the Strip. I'm not saying there aren't advantages to getting married in the same place that you'll be sleeping—the honeymoon can start a good 15 to 20 minutes sooner, obviously. You'll also have half-a-dozen restaurants and banquet halls to walk to right from the ceremony, an on-site beauty parlor, and the chance to parade through a smoky casino in your wedding dress (don't smirk, I know some gals who find that exciting). But you'll pay a lot more for what may turn out to be a fairly homogenized experience (casino chapels are much less amenable to special requests) . . . and you run the risk of losing the best man to the craps table on the way to the service.

There are exceptions, however, and the **Riviera Royale Wedding Chapel** ✪ (in the Riviera Hotel & Casino; ☎ 800/242-7322 or 702/794-9494; www.rivierahotelchapel.com; basic wedding $199; daily 9am–7pm) is one of them. Not only is it reasonably priced (its cheapest package includes champagne, photos, music, and flowers for a third what the off-Strip chapels charge), it also has a groovy '70s Vegas sensibility that's perfect for the couple looking to giggle their way into wedded life. I'm talking a sparkly antacid pink and white room, complete with a gleaming white grand player piano programmed with arpeggio-heavy, romantic pop tunes, which play the guests in before the ceremony. (The chapel holds a maximum of 20.) Kudos go to the staff here, an extremely experienced and peppy bunch.

Lushly tropical, flower-filled, and watery . . . no, I'm not suggesting you jet off to Hawaii. If you can't afford a trip to the islands, your next best option is **The Garden Chapel** ✫✫✫ (in Flamingo Las Vegas; ☎ 800/933-7993 or 702/733-3232; www.harrahs.com; basic package $425; Sun–Fri 9am–7pm, Sat 9am–8pm). Really, I mean it. These 15 acres of meandering streams, strutting flamingos, and extensive greenery are among the classiest setting for vow-taking on the Strip, a surprise to anyone who has only visited the casino itself, which is the usual low-ceilinged, older property. Among the five options for couples are a pretty vine-covered white gazebo (in an area that can hold up to 110) and a mini-Niagara Falls, where the bride makes a dramatic entrance, totally dry, from inside the waterfall (now there's a photo op). An indoor chapel is available for the rare rainy day, but otherwise it should be skipped—you choose this location for its spectacular gardens.

The thatched-roof church that is the **Island Wedding Chapel** ✫✫ (in the Tropicana Resort & Casino; ☎ 800/280-1187 or 702/739-2451; www.tropicanalv.com; basic ceremony $399; Sun–Thurs 10am–6pm, Fri–Sat 10am–8pm), with its bamboo walls and rough-hewn beams, is another Tiki-tinged fantasy and a surprisingly elegant one at that, considering the casino that surrounds it. Set in a superbly landscaped garden, filled with flowers, pools, and palm trees, there's also a little wedding gazebo. But the hut, which can seat up to 50 and is a replica of an actual South Pacific church, is the truly special option here.

Try and ignore the fact that Guinevere cheated on King Arthur, ran off with Lancelot, and basically destroyed the idyllic kingdom of Camelot by trampling on her wedding vows. Otherwise, you'll shy away from dressing up like that medieval pair on your own wedding day at the **Canterbury Wedding Chapel** ✫ (in the Excalibur Hotel; ☎ 800/811-4320 or 702/597-7278; www.excalibur.com; basic chapel-only wedding $175; with flowers, photos, and champagne $395; weddings by appointment only), which is the big fun in getting married here. It's the only casino chapel I know that has a costume shop on-site for theatrical couples. Of course, you don't have to put on a sword or laced-up peasant blouse to marry here; many couples simply like the Gothic chic of these chapels, with their tall stained glass windows, fluted columns, and carved wood altars. (The largest can seat 72 and stand 10–15 more.) I've found the service here to be a bit snippy, though I know a couple who felt they were treated like . . . well, a king and queen on their own wedding day . . . so reserve judgment until you talk with the staff yourself.

The pretty Art Deco trappings, live piano music, and black-and-white photos of Golden Era Hollywood stars do a lot to differentiate the **Forever Grand Wedding Chapel** (in the MGM Grand Hotel and Resort; ☎ 877/750-5464 or 702/587-7777; www.mgmgrand.com; most basic package $699; Sun–Thurs 11am–5pm, Fri–Sat 11am–8pm) from other casino chapels. It's also a good option for those with large families; while its biggest chapel only accommodates 60, they can arrange very private poolside or banquet hall weddings for up to 400 (and all your guests would also be able to be housed on-site, as this is the largest casino-hotel on the Strip).

7 The Other Las Vegas

CARE TO KNOW HOW THE RESIDENTS OF LAS VEGAS LIVE? HOW THEY learn their trades, hone their skills, pursue their ambitions, and kick back? In a city as weird as this one, those subjects can be more interesting than you'd think.

In this chapter, I'm going to take you into the showgirl's dressing room, to the schools where dealers learn to take your money, into the tanks where trainers teach dolphins their tricks, and more. And I won't simply be describing these local activities; I'll tell you how to share in them, how actually to experience the work, play, and learning that goes on in Vegas each and every day. I can guarantee this will be as much fun as anything that happens at the craps table.

HOW VEGAS RESIDENTS LEARN

In Vegas, the American Dream is built on tips—gratuities. Thousands come here every month because they know that the lack of a college degree won't hold them back as it will in other parts of the United States; that a high school graduate, or someone who never even made it that far, can earn between $45,000 and $70,000 a year just parking cars. Skilled jobs offer potentially bigger rewards. To help newcomers acquire those skills a number of schools and classes have sprung up around town.

DEALER SCHOOLS

Most common are the "dealer schools," where anybody who's reasonably math-savvy and coordinated can learn how to rook all of us vacationers . . . er, I mean deal cards. Some are fly-by-night operations, to be sure, but there's one with such an impeccable reputation and track record that it's considered the Harvard of gaming schools.

That standout, the **Casino Gaming School** (900 E. Karen Ave., Suites 216, 218, 220; ☎ 702/893-1788; www.learntodeal.com), is run from a large second-floor suite at the back of the Commercial Center strip mall. Admittedly, it has no ivied walls or campus. But despite its faceless, somewhat grubby appearance, this is a dedicated center of learning, as intense in its own way as an Ivy League university. And that's largely due to the efforts of owner Nick Kallos, a slight fellow with bristly salt-and-pepper hair and a goatee, who has the looks and manner of a more-groomed Ratso Rizzo, but the enthusiasm, energy, and love of teaching of a Mr. Chips. Nick and his staff of veteran dealers (every teacher here has at least 5 years' experience working in a major casino) patiently teach novices the rules and rituals of each game. Because the school is always looking for new students, they allow outsiders to come in and audit classes for free. You can stay for an entire morning or afternoon session, or come and go as you please. You don't even have to pretend to reside in the city. The no-nonsense but ultimately friendly Kallos, whose school has appeared in numerous Travel Channel specials, is rightly proud of his operation and welcoming of visitors.

Watching a session has varied pleasures. You'll definitely come away with some strategies for your own gambling. If you're like me you'll also leave with an appreciation for the complexity of the dealer's work. I spent about 10 minutes on my last visit just watching students practicing the mechanics of the job: One fellow pitched cards endlessly on a blackjack table ("You want Ray Charles to be able to read that from across the room," the teacher next to him exhorted) as another worked on picking up the chips without spraying them all over the table (harder than it looks; it's all in the pinkie), while still a third would-be craps "stickman" arched his stick in the air over and over, working to cleanly pull the die aside in a movement that seemed to have as much to do with fencing as gambling. "It's not brain surgery," says Kallos, "but it does take time and practice." Just as intriguing to peek in on are the sessions discussing various strategies for blackjack, poker, and the like. Anyone who enjoys gambling will get a kick out of hearing an insider's point of view on these topics.

COOKING VEGAS STYLE

Haute cuisine is hot in Vegas, with more star chefs arriving each day than Elvis impersonators (well, almost). As Catherine Margles of the Creative Cooking School puts it: "Las Vegas has gone from buffet to gourmet. Every major celebrity chef in the U.S.—Wolfgang Puck, Charlie Palmer, Alain Ducasse, Hubert Keller—now has restaurants here." For those entering the industry, there's a feeling—perhaps justified, perhaps not—that a cooking career in Vegas puts one on the fast track in the culinary world.

It's no accident therefore that so many of the restaurants in town have also been able to create a profitable sideline in teaching their recipes. Such is the foodie excitement here that the idea of getting a behind the scenes peek at one of the kitchens is a big draw. Here are just some of the restaurants where the chefs moonlight as teachers several times a month:

- ◆ **Café Ba Ba Reeba (p. 93):** On the last Saturday of the month at noon, this Fashion Show Mall restaurant teaches paella making. The $35 price tag covers the class, plus glasses of sangria and tapas to nibble on as you learn.
- ◆ **Giorgio Ristorante (in Mandalay Place; ☎ 702/336-0259):** Demonstration classes focusing on such Italian treats as *osso buco,* tiramisu, and wild mushroom risotto. There's no discernible schedule to the classes (which are taught by the Executive Chef), and they're pricey at between $85 and $110, but you'll get a complete meal, the chef's bio and photo (woo hoo!), and recipes to take home. Call for info.
- ◆ **Valentino (in The Venetian; ☎ 702/336-0259):** Italian again, but here you have the choice of learning to make your own pastas and salads ($100); pastries and other desserts ($50); or wine tasting ($65). Various members of the staff teach, call to learn when upcoming classes are scheduled.

◆ **Sushi Samba (in the Palazzo; ☎ 702/607-0700):** Every Wednesday from 7pm to 9pm diners will learn to roll their own sushi and what sakes to pair with it at this $85 class. Students will take away a glossary of terms, a booklet of recipes, and a full stomach.

Because it's the luck of the draw whether you'll be in town on one of the dates when these restaurants are offering classes, the next best option is an impressive operation called **The Creative Cooking School** (7385 W. Sahara Ave.; ☎ 702/562-3900; www.creativecookingschool.com; $99 for 3-hr. class; Tues–Fri 6–9pm, Sat 10am–2pm). Offering a mix of recreational classes and certification courses for would-be pros, it's intimately connected with the Sin City sautéing scene, drawing much of its faculty from the kitchens of the big Strip restaurants. When you take a class here, you'll likely be taught a recipe currently being used at one of Wolfgang Puck's branches, or Roy's, or an Emeril Lagasse venture. Each student leaves with a thick sheath of recipes tucked under her arm, a much better Vegas souvenir than fuzzy dice.

She also may leave with a raft of new friends, as this is not only a learning experience but a highly social one as well. Classes are hands-on affairs, so you'll be cooking in a group of no more than four students, with a maximum of 16 students grouped at four marble-topped cooking islands, as glossy and high-tech a facility as any you'll see on the Food Network. Two TV monitors broadcast the view from cooking cams aimed right into the mixing bowl or frying pan the instructor is using, ensuring that everyone gets a good view of the instructor's technique. Class topics change by week, but you might find yourself baking (as I did in my last class), or learning how to roll sushi, or creating a gourmet meal in 30 minutes, or making appetizers to go with margaritas (yup, you get to drink 'em). And you not only cook and chat with your fellow students but feast on what you've made at the end, and will probably be given a doggy bag to take home the extras. "It's like a dinner party and a college-level class all in one," says Catherine Margles, founder of the school—and she's right.

The food was scrumptious on the day I last visited, and though I consider myself a good cook, I learned a number of new techniques, including how to best hand-whip cream (a figure eight with the wrist works best), where to order ingredients, and how to create the right-sized "well" when incorporating liquids into flour. My teacher was Anthony Sinsay, a roly-poly charmer who has toiled in the kitchens of both Wolfgang Puck and Nobu and is now a personal chef and instructor full time. A mini-Emeril, with the same verve, spirit, and remarkable eye for detail as that famous chef, Sinsay cracks jokes while cracking eggs, giving the class its marching orders with such exhortations as: "If you haven't tried a Florentine bar, you haven't lived yet! So let's melt that chocolate!" He's a heck of a lot of fun, as are the other instructors, who include such Vegas notables as the "Dancing Gourmet," cookbook author and former prima ballerina Linda Hymes; and Stephen Gillanders, who appeared on the *Today* show's "next Celebrity Chef" competition and has won a number of other national cooking competitions.

STRIPPING 101

Yup, this is a class that teaches you how to strip. Don't snicker. The art of the strip tease is alive and well in Las Vegas and is supporting numerous families. Some say Vegas has the finest strip clubs in the country. I'm not enough of a connoisseur to weigh in on the matter, but there's no underestimating these clubs' popularity or the fascination among the clothed about this type of career.

So a blonde, leggy, warm-hearted dancer named Trixie, who worked as an ecdysiast for 13 years, has started classes for women interested in learning the "how to's." Called **Stripping 101** (in the Miracle Mile Mall; ☎ 702/260-7200; www.stripper101.com; $40 for the class and a drink, $60 with a 5×7 photo and T-shirt; Mon–Wed 5pm, Thurs and Sun 3:30 and 5pm, Fri–Sat 3:30, 5, and 6:30pm; AE, DISC, MC, V), the class gets the basics across in a non-exploitative, terrifically enjoyable, empowering manner.

First things first: These classes are for women only. Men are not allowed to participate, or even watch. In case you were wondering—and I can't imagine that you wouldn't be—there's no nudity. And you're not going to be trying your moves among hardened pros. Trixie does ask at the start of the class if anyone attending is a stripper or is hoping to become one, but it seems like the women who show up are doing so out of simple curiosity. Students range in age from 20s to 60s and come from all walks of life (librarians, nurses, stay-at-home moms, you name it). Don't worry about wearing work-out clothes; the dancing you'll do is not all that strenuous, and Trixie is able to modify the moves she teaches for anyone with an injury.

So what do you learn during the hour-long class? A heck of a lot, actually, from the stripper's saunter—step, hip, drag—to such stripper tricks as playing with your hands and running them along the body to keep the focus where you want it to be, helpful if you're stumbling on your stilettos ("Where your hands go, his eyes will follow," announces Trix). To make this all palatable to average Janes, Trixie encourages participants to imagine their "significant other" being the audience, and to use the class as practice for the private dancing you might want to do for him (or her). Whether you're practicing lap dances or floor moves, it's all based on the "tease" part of the striptease—a pattern of come-hither and go-away that should work as well for date nights as it does for stripping.

The highlight? The pole work, of course. Who knew that those poles come in two varieties: those that swivel ("this is like driving an automatic") and those that don't ("like driving a five-speed"). Trixie teaches the class to slide on their backs down the pole; to twirl around it with legs extended (much harder on the stationary one); and in the case of advanced students, to do the darn thing inverted. By this point, the classmates have become buddies, cheering each other on, high-fiving, and making suggestions. It's a perfect bachelorette party activity, but pretty darn fun even if you come alone.

PLATO IN THE CASINO

Beyond the practical learning that goes on in the schools above, there are two experiences that one can have in Las Vegas that move into the realm of learning for learning's own sake. Deep thinking just for the fun of it. Intellectual stimulation as its own reward. Wait, don't recheck the cover of this book, you're still reading about Vegas.

Every Tuesday evening at 7pm, at the Mandalay Bay Hotel & Casino, just outside The Reading Room bookstore, with the dinging of slot machines in the background and scantily clad cocktail waitresses in view, a group of strangers meet to discuss the meaning of life. No, really; and it's not a cult, I promise. The group was inspired by a book called *Socrates Café* by Chris Phillips, which encourages everyday folks to get together and discuss the important issues in life: What is justice? What is truth? What does it mean to live a good life? This ever-changing assemblage—anyone is welcome to attend, and you don't have to have any knowledge of philosophy to do so—has been tackling these big questions since the spring of 2004.

Here's how it works. A moderator opens up the discussion by describing what we are there to do. On the night I last attended, there were a lot of first-timers— some students from UNLV, a tourist, a casino worker, and myself—so he laid out the basics. "We're here to reclaim our right to think and speak for ourselves," he said, quietly looking around at the group sitting in a circle of chairs. "This is not about furthering any political agenda or religious dogma or selling timeshares. We're here to have a good time and practice the art of conversation." We then voted on a topic to discuss, ultimately choosing the question "Does politics corrupt those who engage in it?" and we were off. For the following, too-short hour and a half, every one of the 16 people there spoke, sometimes heatedly, but always civilly, batting big ideas back and forth, agreeing, disagreeing, laughing at one point so loudly that gamblers nearby stared at us all puzzled, trying to figure out what the heck was going on.

It was, without a doubt, the most exhilarating time I spent in the 7 weeks I was in Vegas researching this book, and when I am next there on a Tuesday, I plan to return to the circle. Some participants find it so addictive that they rearrange their lives to attend. A retired teacher told me, "I have to have something intellectual in my life. I quit a singles club just so I can be here every Tuesday."

VAN GOGH IN THE DESERT

The second "learning just for the joy of it" experience is a most unusual tour . . . in which you don't move for 4 hours. Instead, you go out to some of the most beautiful areas outside of Las Vegas—**Red Rock Canyon** (p. 284), **Mount Charleston** (p. 288), the **Valley of Fire** (p. 286)—draw up a stool and an easel, and try to re-create what you see before you on canvas. Geared to novice painters, **Scenic Pleasure Painting Tours, Inc.** (☎ 888/302-8882 or 702/256-8882; $200; tours every Thurs and Sat; AE, DISC, MC, V) is the brainchild of artist Loretta Reinick, who began these tours in 2005 and attracts a steady stream of vacationers and locals who simply want to try painting. Reinick, who leads every tour, has an unusual talent for helping totally inept painters—which is how I'd classify myself—to quickly understand the fundamentals of the art, create a darn good painting, and have a great time doing it.

She does this by outlining some very concrete steps towards the goal. The first thing our group did was gather stones from our immediate area that mirrored the colors of the landscape. Loretta then squeezed just the primary colors and shades onto our palette—red, blue, yellow, white, and black—and had us mix colors until we had several piles of paint that came close to matching the tones of the rocks, and thus our landscape. After simply mixing colors for a good hour (a very Zen, relaxing experience, I might add), she demonstrated how to sketch the landscape on our canvas, concentrating on painting the distance first and then moving forward. After an hour of base painting, we broke for a picnic lunch with wine—and that sure helped the art-making!—and then returned to dabbing and molding and streaking. Reinick walked from painter to painter as we worked, offering pointers and advice. Several times, if someone looked nervous about what was on their canvas, she repeated, "It's just about playing with the paint. If you approach it that way, you'll have better results."

At the end of the 4 hours, we looked up from our own easels, startled that the time had rocketed by, and startled, too, by how different each painting looked. This is no paint-by-numbers class; Reinick was able to help bring out each participant's personal style. I have to say, I was so happy with my painting that it's now framed and hanging in my bathroom. Another highly recommended experience.

A word about the cost: The tour, as you'll note above, is a full $200, which puts it on the pricier side of the options listed in this chapter. But because it includes lunch, transportation to the site, a lot of expensive materials, and at the end, a frameable painting, I think the price is justified.

BACK TO THE ATOMIC AGE

Vegas may not have Victorian mansions or neo-Gothic churches. Its architecture, beyond the fantasies on the Strip and the neon-slathered buildings of Downtown, tends to run horizontal, sitting low to the ground, its oldest buildings dating not much further back than the swinging '60s and Googie '50s. And local architectural boosters wouldn't have it any other way. Calling themselves the **Atomic Age Alliance** (www.atomicage.org), a group of Las Vegas residents are doing their darndest to promote preservation of what they call "Mid Century Modernist" buildings, signage, and sculptures and as importantly, to teach others to appreciate and therefore want to protect them. To that end, they've put together a self-guided tour booklet of the neighborhoods of Las Vegas that points visitors towards the remaining Maoi statue from the Aku Aku Tiki Bar that once graced the Stardust Hotel, an iconic Palmer and Krisel–designed tract home, the classic Googie hotels of the Boulder Highway, and more. You can order the booklet online.

Or you might be lucky enough, as I was last time I visited, to be in town when they offer an open house tour. I spent a Sunday morning driving from perfectly preserved home to home admiring the lime green and ochre walls, the dolphin fixtures in the bathroom, the mirrored dividers and sunken tubs. It was a hoot, bringing me back to my toddler-hood, a sensation enhanced by the fact that the owners of the homes were serving midcentury snacks—deviled eggs, tollhouse cookies, punch—to all those who took the free tour. See the website for info on upcoming events.

HOW VEGAS RESIDENTS WORK

Sure, there are janitors, nurses, and lawyers in Vegas, but there are also those with much more glamorous, sometimes odd-ball, jobs. If you'd like to find out what it's like to do one of these jobs, and meet the people who perform them, try the following Other Vegas Experiences.

HOPE (AND SHOWGIRLS) IS THE THING WITH FEATHERS

Male or female, gay or straight, you gotta admit that it's a thrill to meet an actual showgirl. It's the quintessential Vegas experience, akin to chatting with a geisha in Kyoto or a matador in Barcelona. And when you take the *Jubilee!* **Backstage**

Wedding Crashers

Owen Wilson and Vince Vaughn showed the world how to do it. It's even more fun in Vegas, and you don't have to pick up wedding guests, lead the conga line, or pretend you're a distant cousin. Simply go to any of the wedding chapels listed in this book, and ask the couple of the hour, politely, if they'd mind if you watched their ceremony. Most are happy to oblige. You won't have any problem finding a wedding to watch in this, the wedding capital of the world, and trust me—it's a sweetly kitschy, intriguing, usually moving way to spend the afternoon or evening. Don't feel shy about asking; I found that every couple I approached was happy and proud to have an outsider witness this important event.

The funkiest weddings will be at the **Viva Las Vegas Chapel** (1205 Las Vegas Blvd. S.; ☎ 800/574-4450 or 702/384-0771; www.vivalasvegas. com; daily 9am–10pm), which specializes in production weddings (and also has a very helpful, friendly staff who will tip you off as to when the most unusual weddings are taking place). I sat through three here and used up an entire little handy pack of Kleenex. My favorite was the French couple who giggled their way into the chapel dressed as Marilyn Monroe and Elvis (in costumes lent by the chapel), only to break down in heart-felt tears when the Elvis minister asked the groom if he'd give his bride a daily "hunka hunka burning love." (I have a feeling they might have mis-interpreted what he was asking.) I was the only witness to that wedding, but I was made to feel just as welcome at the next one, a fairly large affair with 40 guests. The bride and groom drove through the wide doors of the chapel in a pink Cadillac for a more elaborate (and expensive) Elvis cere-mony. Third was a traditional ceremony for a man who looked to be AARP-age (to put it politely) and a young woman from Brazil who couldn't have been older than 22. That was a somber, somewhat strange affair, and kept my head buzzing for days afterward with questions that wouldn't have been polite to ask. But being there in the midst of such a dramatic if dis-comfiting event made me feel like I had landed in the middle of some mys-tery movie.

Really, is there any activity more "Vegas" than a 15-minute wedding? Give it a whirl.

Tour (Jubilee Theater in Bally's; ☎ 702/946-4567; $15 without a *Jubilee!* ticket, $10 with; tour limited to those 13 and older; Mon, Wed, and Sat 11am; AE, DISC, MC, V), you not only meet one of these fabled creatures—they're the guides!—but you learn all about their lives and the over-the-top production, *Jubilee!*, that has kept showgirls in feathers for the past 28 years. When it debuted in 1981, it was the most expensive production ever mounted in Vegas, with a price tag of $10 million (at a time when a half a million was the standard cost for a production show). A full $2.5 million of that went just into the costumes; their creation sparked (gasp!) a world-wide shortage in rhinestones.

In the course of the tour, you'll climb up and down the many stairs the dancers traverse each and every show (because dressing rooms are in the basement, the performers go up and down 8,000–9,000 steps per show); descend into the bowels of the basement to view the truck-sized elevators that whisk huge set pieces into place in 30 seconds or less; and stroll the dressing rooms and workshops to visit the magnificent costumes designed by Bob Mackie and Pete Menefee. That's the photo op moment, as you'll be allowed to try on a retired headdress (though not Delilah's, as that weighs 25 lb., is 2 ft. tall, and requires more than a little training just to keep on one's head).

The big question on most visitors' minds: How realistic was that cult classic, the Elizabeth Berkley movie *Showgirls* (which was based on *Jubilee!*)? The answer: kinda close. Nobody has ever become a star as a Vegas showgirl, of course, but the backstabbing and jostling for position is common (or so our guide implied, but never said). You'll also find out what a difficult life these performers lead. They must re-audition for their roles every 6 months (competing against dancers in New York, Chicago, Los Angeles, and Orlando, as simultaneous auditions are taking place in those cities); they must maintain the exact same weight they had when they were hired; and their pay is so miserly that many work second jobs on top of the 12 shows a week here. At the end, you'll feel like you've not only met a showgirl but a real Wonder Woman of sorts. And to be blunt: The tour is much more interesting than the show itself (p. 187), so if you're looking for that Vegas showgirl experience, but on a budget, this is the way to go.

KEEPING FISH ALIVE IN THE DESERT

Remember those three goldfish you had in a tank with a little bubbler in grammar school? The Forum Shops at Caesars (in the same area as the moving statues show) has one of those, too, but because it's apparently the law in Vegas that everything must be super-sized, theirs is a 500,000-gallon tank filled with 400 fish of 150 species. It is, in effect, a mini-aquarium, and every weekday at 3:15pm sharp, the men and women who work full-time here to keep all these fish healthy offer a free tour of their fishy facility that's surprisingly scholarly.

You'll start at the aquarium itself where a keeper may well be diving into the exhibit, in a wet suit and full scuba gear, to hand feed the stingrays (because they're bottom feeders with flat, small teeth that crush rather than tear, they can't be fed in the same ways the others are). Your guide will point out the different species— puffer fish, clown fish, leopard sharks, lionfish (with venomous spikes)—explaining a bit about the fish, and sometimes, the personalities of the ones who live in this tank. As they tell it, keeping the aquarium is akin to being a sheriff in a rough old Western town; fish with "shoot 'em up" personalities brawl, biting each others' tails and trying to claim territories for themselves in the artificial reef. Those miscreants who are too much of a menace to society are thrown into jail. Well, really the isolation tanks in the basement, where you'll repair after doing a full tour around the aquarium itself.

Once in the basement of Caesars, the technical part of the tour begins, which anyone who owns an aquarium will find riveting. Here, the trainers—one of whom came to Vegas after 14 years at SeaWorld in Orlando—are experimenting with "green methods" of keeping the fish healthier longer. They'll explain their use of gravel to house bacteria that will process the nitrates in the tank, and algae for purification. If it sounds eye-glazing . . . well, it can be (though the fish aficionados on my tour seemed really into it). But the tour guides are savvy enough to move onto the tank where the outlaw fish are kept to tell their funny stories; you'll also get to ooh and aah at the nursery tank where you may see baby sharks squirming around in translucent egg sacks. We were also ushered into the "education room" where the Caesars fish folks teach school groups and where we got to touch some of the small crustaceans. In all, the tour will take about an hour.

For those who want their aquatic activities more interactive, the **Trainer for a Day program** (at The Mirage; ☎ 702/792-7889; www.miragehabitat.com; $550 per person; children over 13 are allowed to participate) is at once the priciest recommended activity in this chapter and one of the most rewarding. Yes, it involves dolphins, but unlike most other programs around the world, there's no swimming to be done. Instead, for an entire day from 9:45am until about 3:30pm in the afternoon, guests become assistant trainers, learning how to feed the dolphins, put them through their exercises, and give appropriate rewards. Despite the hefty payment and the gourmet breakfast and lunch (included in the cost), it feels like a genuine apprenticeship.

Over the course of the day, participants chuck 20 to 30 pounds of fish to the dolphins (and are entrusted with keeping each dolphin's bucket separate, as the animals have different and strict diets); and learn a complex series of hand signals that show the dolphins when they should jump, raise a fin for a handshake, or do some other sort of exercise. Physically challenging—trainers and assistant trainers spend much of the day running from one end of the pool to another with the dolphins following them—the program is not appropriate for people with mobility impairments and would be agony for anyone who's at all shy. Because there's no formal show here, the trainers, the participants, and their exercises with the animals become the show that day; you'll be learning how to deal with the dolphins in a tight-fitting wet suit in front of a crowd of people.

But that's what the trainers do, and perhaps better than any other such program in the world, this one gives participants a genuine understanding of what it takes to be an animal trainer, its rewards and its headaches. Paying about equal to what they'd pay to simply take a short dip with the dolphins, participants really get to know these mysterious creatures in a very individual way.

"Dolphins are all different from one another with different personalities," a trainer told me. "Some are thinkers and some are more acrobatic. There are some who are really cuddly and like to be petted, and the younger ones tend to be really playful and energetic." In the day I spent observing (as they only allow three to four participants per day I wasn't able to do the training myself; spaces are tight and it's necessary to reserve far, far in advance), the amount that the participants grew in their 1-day jobs was remarkable, as they became more proficient at keeping eye contact with the dolphins, mastering the timing required to "command" a dolphin, and playing with them when it was time for a reward. The trainers here believe the program also benefits the dolphins. "They really enjoy working with new people, it keeps them interested," one told me. "And there's one who likes to give the new trainers a bit of a hard time. He's a devil, so he gets a kick out of it toying with the participants."

Is it worth the money? Only you can decide, but one participant I spoke with at the end of the day gushed, "After my wedding day, this was the best day of my entire life!"

MARTINIS WITH THE MAYOR

Oscar Goodman, mayor of Las Vegas, is everything you'd think a mayor of this over-the-top city would be: a brash, controversial, humorous character who makes a point of going to most public ceremonies flanked by a showgirl on one side and an Elvis impersonator on the other. He made national headlines in 2005 for telling a local fourth-grade class that if he were marooned on a desert island the one item he'd bring would be a bottle of gin—and that one of his favorite hobbies was drinking. Before becoming mayor, Goodman was most famous as a mob lawyer, having represented some of the city's most famous accused criminals over the years including Meyer Lansky, Nicky Scarfo, and "Tony the Ant" Spilotro.

That's all part of the public record. But what most people don't know is how accessible Goodman makes himself to his constituents. At least once a month he holds a "meet and greet," where he goes to either a local diner or restaurant and invites whoever wants to show up, to have either "Martinis with the Mayor" or "Breakfast with the Mayor." You can find out where and when he'll be doing his thing by surfing to **www.lasvegasnevada.gov;** the website will list the date and place, and then, you just go (there's no admission charge).

Do I have to make the point that this is a fellow who's a heck of a lot of fun to hang out with? At the breakfast I showed up for, I asked him what his favorite martini bar was and he had me in stitches with a long drinking story that ended with his admitting "After two of them, it doesn't really matter where I'm drinking." It might not sound funny on paper, but he said it with such good humor and such a twinkle in his eye that the whole place cracked up.

Beyond meeting Goodman himself, it's pretty compelling to watch the wheels of local government turn. As I sat there, a parade of locals came up to make some sort of case, much in the way townspeople probably approached their feudal lords back in medieval Europe. One gray-haired gal complained about noise from her noisy neighbors; a man wanted the mayor's help in starting an art gallery that would somehow fund stem cell research; still another had a lot to say on traffic problems at a certain intersection. Goodman listened politely to each, turning to the staff members who accompanied him with questions or requests to follow up. Everybody who came up got some sort of response and seemed to leave satisfied . . . which may be the reason this former mob lawyer and all-around-rascal will probably breeze into his next term as mayor.

Tip: If you're not going to be in town during one of Goodman's official pow-wows, drop by the bar at Triple George (p. 96) on a weekday between 5pm and 7pm. Goodman's often there nursing a martini; just ask the bartender when you get in and go on over to say "Hi." Goodman's third and final term in office ends in 2010.

IN THE CHOCOLATE FACTORY

No Oompa Loompas toil here; still, **Ethel M Chocolates** (2 Cactus Garden Dr., just off Mountain Vista Rd. and Sunset Way in the Green Valley Business Park; ☎ 888/627-0990 or 702/433-2500; www.ethelm.com; free admission; daily 8:30am–6pm) is a moderately interesting side trip, especially for chocoholics. If you hit it right, you'll see chef-capped and hard-hatted workers actually toiling at gleaming copper kettles, massive steel machines, and conveyor belts creating this exquisite chocolate.

Informative wall text under the large glass windows will explain the processes you're watching. On the opposite wall is a fairly interesting history of chocolate (fun fact: The Mayan word *cocoa* meant "food of the gods," and they used chocolate as money). Problem is, because this fine candy is made without preservatives and thus can last only 2 weeks on the shelves, it's only manufactured when orders arrive. So you could show up to view an empty factory—there's no way to know whether or not they'll be in production the day you visit (it's best to show up mid-morning, as the work day often ends at 2:30pm, even when orders have come in). But even if you do show up when there's nothing much happening, the workers here do their best to sweeten the experience with unlimited amounts of free chocolates, and I mean unlimited: I left with a smile on my face and a whopping tummy ache. (Not bad considering the self-guided tour itself doesn't cost a penny.)

Ethel M chocolates were a labor of love by the Mars Chocolates founder, Forrest Mars, who came out of retirement to create this gourmet chocolate alternative to the family's stock-in-trade: M&M's (he named the company for his mother Ethel). His second love was botany, so outside the factory is an impressive 4-acre cactus garden. Wander through before you leave; approximately half of the plants you'll see here are from the American Southwest, the rest from Australia and South America. The little water they get is provided by a "green" water recycling plant which uses algae, bacteria, fish, snails, and plants to remove pollutants from the gray water that emerges from the factory. You can tour that as well by walking to the very back of the garden.

HOW VEGAS RESIDENTS PLAY

There's a myth in Las Vegas that residents live and work here, but don't really gamble all that much. T'ain't so, and the so-called "local's casinos"—basically, any place off the Strip—can be great places to mingle with the locals, learn what Las Vegas is really like, and enjoy lower table minimums. Just don't try the poker tables at these places; sharks don't only live in the ocean, they enjoy desert life, too.

For non-gaming ways to party with the locals (it's fun, trust me), try the following:

ART IN THE STREETS

On the first Friday of each month, the sometimes gloomy, sometimes cool Downtown area known as the "Arts District" erupts into a boisterous, zany, chaotic street fair, one that's totally homegrown and utterly unexpected in a town this corporate. Called—you guessed it—**First Friday** (www.firstfriday-lasvegas.com; $2 admission), it's an out and out celebration of art and community that begins promptly at 6pm and wends its way on into the evening. Every artist's studio in the area is open, often debuting new shows on that night, and most visitors spend part of the evening simply walking from gallery to gallery with a glass of wine in hand, chatting with locals and the artists themselves, who usually make it a point to show up for this event. Out in the streets, people are making their own art. Street performers breathe fire; when it's cold enough sculptors carve ice statues; local bands play; and squads of children, armed with chalk, transform the streets into multicolored murals. Don't worry about the event taking place during the dinner hour—there are a number of street vendors around selling perfectly palatable grub.

First Friday tends to be centered around the area where Charleston Boulevard and Main Street connect, but there are free shuttle buses that will take you around to all of the various galleries. If you're driving to the event, park near the El Cortez Casino to catch the shuttle bus there. Those taking a taxi and a bus should also head for Government Center, the easiest hopping off place for the party, as many of the streets are closed to traffic.

CELEBRITY & MAGIC KARAOKE

What do performers do on their nights off and after their shows? A lot of them like to keep on performing, and they do that primarily at three locals' bars. If you attend you can, if you're brave, pit your talent against the pros, or simply sit back and watch a Strip-caliber show for free.

If you're around on a Monday night, head to the **Bootlegger Bistro** (7700 Las Vegas Blvd. S.; ☎ 702/736-4939; www.bootleggerlasvegas.com; daily 24 hr., shows Mon 9pm; AE, DISC, MC, V), which is owned by former lounge singer and lieutenant governor Loraine Hunt. Its "Celebrity Karaoke" sessions are really that, regularly drawing some of the most prominent performers in the city, including Clint Holmes, the Amazing Jonathan (yes, he croons, too), Cook E. Jarr, and countless other local acts. Singer/comedian Kelly Clinton emcees and while she'll let anybody up, you can tell immediately how worthy she thinks you are by whether or not she lets you sing more than one song.

Needless to say, this ain't the place to try karaoke for the first time, but a lot of talented performers do come here hoping to be discovered (can't say whether that works). If you want to sing, get here early—there can be up to an hour-long wait to hit the stage (go up to the front to choose your song and get on the list). Also be ready for a crowded bar scene, as the place gets packed; if you want to sit in comfort, make a reservation, but get ready to order some food, too, as the tables are reserved for diners.

Vegas may also be the only place in the U.S. where karaoke isn't confined to crooning. On Wednesday nights beginning at 10pm, magicians take over **Boomers Bar** (3200 N. Sirius Ave.; ☎ 702/368-1863; daily 24 hr.; AE, DISC, MC, V). More of an unofficial seminar than a performance, magicians come from all over to exchange trade secrets, practice tricks on one another, and impress any muggles who might wander in. Lance Burton and Siegfried and Roy have been known to drop by and mingle with the other talented and lesser-known lovers of trickery. On Sunday nights, the open mic is taken over by aspiring comedians.

MACHINE GUN FUN

It's still the "Wild West" in Nevada, as far as guns are concerned. Las Vegas law doesn't require that gun owners get a "carry permit" for their weapons, as so many other areas do. Gun clubs are popular, as are shooting ranges, and there are shooting competitions somewhere in the greater Vegas area most every weekend. To get a taste of this trigger-happy life, you can do what many locals (and tourists) do, and spend an afternoon with an AK-47 in your mitt. Hard to believe, but there are several ranges in town where just about anyone can walk in, choose a machine gun, pick a target (and they have all kinds, from simple bulls-eyes to life-sized portraits of Saddam Hussein, Osama Bin Laden, and other baddies) and—bam, bam, bam, bam, bam—blow it to pieces.

I have to admit it's a huge rush. And I'm a person who'd never touched a gun before I went to Vegas and wish that gun control laws were stronger. But there's something about shooting a machine gun that feels at once Zeus-like and like holding a raging tiger in your arms. It's a very powerful and absolutely terrifying feeling, kinda like that sensation you get when you're at the edge of a tall building or cliff and you start to imagine, half-wistfully, what it would be like to just jump off (oh, don't close the book—we've all had those weird, heart-pounding fantasies, right?). As Chris Irwin, an owner of one of the ranges in town put it, "People can't believe they're allowed to do something they've only seen before in the movies. It's like Disneyland to them."

Of all the ranges in town, I like the **Gun Store** (2900 E. Tropicana Ave.; ☎ 702/454-1110; www.thegunstorelasvegas.com; daily 9am–6:30pm; AE, DC, MC, V) most, because it uses frangible ammunition, which has less of a chance of ricocheting back on you (it breaks up on contact) and is better for the environment, as it contains no lead. There are 15 lanes here, each of which allows the shooter 15 yards to the target. To shoot a machine gun costs $25 to $45 for 50 shots (depending on the ammo and gun you choose; larger bullets are more expensive). For a regular handgun, you'll pay about $36 for 50 shots. The store will also provide you with a teacher, protection for the eyes and ears, and a target, at no extra cost. And if you seem drunk, happily, they're going to turn you away, so if you're thinking of this activity for a bachelor party, go earlier rather than later. And go on weekdays if you can, as sometimes there can be a wait of up to 30 minutes to shoot on weekends.

Tip: Visit the website and print out one of their $5 discount coupons before arriving. The Gun Store also has frequent promotions such as "Ladies Free on Tuesdays," so check the site for those as well.

TWO UNUSUAL TOURS

Though it seems like everything that's not nailed down gets imploded here, the past is not dead in Vegas. In some ways it's just as compelling as anything on the Strip or off. The following insider's tours explore the area's colorful, controversial, sometimes extremely dark, history.

In the 1950s, the mushroom cloud blossoming just beyond the city's skyline was as much an iconic Vegas image as that of the Rat Pack or a showgirl in heels. The source of those explosions, the Nevada Testing Site, then known as the Nevada Proving Ground, became instantly famous, with Huntley and Brinkley doing live broadcasts from the site, clouds thrusting up behind them. From the mid-'60s to the '90s, it was a magnet for protesters worried about nuclear proliferation, who camped heroically for days on end in the blazing heat just outside the gates of the site.

For most of that time, the site was a world unto itself, a closed-off place open only to the workers cleared to serve here and some in the political world. Though the ground shook in Vegas and piercing white lights struck the sky, no outsiders were allowed to tour until the late '70s, when finally the gates were opened . . . a small crack.

But if you can make your way into that crack and catch one of these once-monthly **tours** (☎ 702/295-0944; www.nv.doe.gov/nts/tours.htm; tours are free), you're in for an exhausting but brain-expanding day, when you'll meet a number of workers who were at the site during its heyday; see with your own eyes the shocking power of nuclear energy; and join the small club of people who have ever gotten onto the grounds of this Rhode Island–sized patch of desert that is arguably one of the most important scientific landmarks in the country. Reservations are *essential* for the tour; reserve at least six weeks in advance, or even further ahead if you can (as of February 2009, the tours were fully booked through June). Reserve online at the website above.

After a short introduction at the Atomic Museum, you'll be bused a little over an hour to the site and undergo fairly elaborate security procedures. Then for the rest of the day you'll drive around the site, debarking occasionally to stare down the lip of a crater created by a bomb or at a steel bridge meant to mimic an urban overhead light rail system that was warped into an ugly U by the force of the shock waves that hit it at 500 miles per hour. You'll also drive past derelict test houses once filled with dummies, and through the famous Frenchman Flats.

As the guides are former workers, you'll learn a lot about what it was like to live and work here in this remote, removed spot which at its peak housed 10,000 workers (all of whom were single, as families weren't allowed). About 4,000 still work here today, monitoring the ground water and animals at the site, and aiding in Homeland Security training sessions. There's an actual airplane on-site, dealing with the radiological side of a terrorist attack (other areas are set up for training with chemicals and other hazardous materials).

Note: If you decide to visit the test site for these once-monthly tours, know that it will eat up an entire day. You leave before 8am and may not return to Vegas until sometime after 4pm. Visitors are advised to bring lunch with them, wear sturdy shoes, and wear sunscreen.

Celebrating a happier history, the **Neon Boneyard** (☎ 702/387-NEON; www.neonmuseum.org; $15 per person; tours by appointments only, call in advance; no credit cards.) is where old neon signs go not to die, but to wait in a kind of purgatory until a museum can be created to house them. Visiting is an otherworldly experience, like stepping into the carnival scene from Disney's *Pinocchio* when all of the flashing lights had been extinguished, and the boys turned to donkeys. It has the same kind of glamorous junkyard look, the same artful chaos.

Over 100 signs from the 1940s through today are dumped in this outdoor lot, unceremoniously surrounded by a chain-link fence. Many were iconic symbols in their day. There's the giant slipper covered with hundreds of bulbs that once shone so brightly it kept Howard Hughes awake at night. To shut it off, he bought the Silver Slipper hotel it crowned, as well as the Desert Inn where he was staying, setting off a buying spree that would reshape Vegas. Nearby is an original Caesars Palace sign, the regal "Coin King" from the Coin Palace casino that once sat on Fremont street, and a large Aladdin's Lamp (from the '70s). Along with these famous signs are some prosaic ones as well, as interesting in their own way. There's a Kentucky Fried Chicken bucket in its original design, McDonald's Golden Arches, and a fabulously rococo sign for a Chinese restaurant. Each has its own artistry, hand welded, hand cut, and hand painted. "This collection represents a lot of the artistic history as well as the history of Vegas," our guide told us. "Vegas was known as an oasis of light in the middle of the desert, and it's these very lights that did that." Today, most of the signage is from LED screens featuring more natural-looking, muted colors, but I for one prefer the blatant primary colors of the old neon. You'll see the difference when you visit (or when you tour the Neon Museum on Fremont Street; see p. 138).

Because there's very little funding for the upkeep of the signs, and even less for security, I can't tell you where this "boneyard" is, but when you call for a tour, you'll get the address.

8 It's Showtime

More than a hundred stages compete with gaming tables for your time and dollars

LAS VEGAS IS AS MUCH ABOUT SHOWS AS IT IS ABOUT GAMBLING. EVER since the days when Frank Sinatra and the Rat Pack boozed their way through legendary performances at the Sands (even rolling a bar cart onto the stage to mix drinks in between songs), casinos have featured heavily promoted entertainers alongside their roulette wheels and craps tables.

The emphasis was once entirely on individual stars. Vegas, according to the spin, was where all the big names came to cut loose in the desert, performing as they would for close friends around the piano at home. If you wanted to see Elvis or Dean Martin at their best, you made your way to Nevada.

Today things are a bit different. Very few shows simply feature a famous voice, a bunch of horns, and a handful of comely showgirls. Over-the-top is the key word, with million-dollar sets populated by battalions of acrobats, dancers, jugglers, and genetically perfect (or enhanced) women.

But the raison d'être hasn't changed all that much. On Vegas stages all is comedy, good times, bare breasts and butts, and stars who seem to be performing for the sheer fun of it (shhh . . . don't tell the audiences about those multi-million-dollar paychecks Cher and Barry are taking home).

A MASSIVE ATTRACTION, A PRICEY CHALLENGE   It's a formula that works well. City promoters call Vegas the "Entertainment Capital of the World," and the numbers support their boast. There are currently over 80 permanent productions on the boards, plus dozens of other 1- and 2-night concerts and touring events, making Vegas one of the biggest theater towns in the U.S. So, yes, if you're in the mood to see a show, Las Vegas is a heck of a good place to visit.

And thanks to the weakening economy, average show prices are holding steady and haven't significantly increased from last year. Sure, about a quarter of the shows have top ticket prices that break a Benjamin, but the average price of a ticket is now $70 (the same as it was in 2007), and very few theatergoers are paying even that. Read on.

THE TRUTH ABOUT TICKET PRICING   Quite simply: Discounting has gone into overdrive. Sure, you'll probably have to pay full price for a show as popular as Cirque du Soleil's *O* or Cher, particularly when Vegas is busy. But even the hits have slow nights (see the discussion below) and quite frankly, in the current economic climate, those "off" nights are getting to be more common than the "on" ones.

Below I'll lay out all of the methods for obtaining a discount on shows, from day-of-performance discounts to advance purchases to other ways in which you may be able to weasel yourself into a better seat. I'll also offer my reviews of all of the long-running shows in town, opining which to see and which to skip. And below that you'll find information on the major venues that host touring shows and concerts.

If you just want to be entertained, and you don't have a real preference about what you want to see, you should have no difficulty finding a good deal, even when the city is roiling with conventioneers. There are always discounts to be had, somewhere, sometime. It's all in how you play it.

GETTING DISCOUNTED TICKETS

Booking tickets before you arrive is the most time-effective strategy: You're able to plan ahead, get dinner reservations in a restaurant convenient to the theater, and avoid wasting any of your precious Vegas vacation tussling with box offices. The problem is you won't find the range of choices that you will at the booths that sell tickets the day of a performance. The few sites that post advance discounts simply don't have that great a reach; I guess producers aren't too keen on giving their shows a bargain basement reputation.

But if convenience is more important to you than which show you get, try one of the following four websites:

* **Goldstar Events (www.goldstarevents.com),** a site that offers discounted bookings for an average of 25 shows at a pop. Goldstar isn't the gold standard, so you're never going to find anything produced by Cirque du Soleil there, but you will find a number of showgirl reviews, magic shows, and Broadway-style productions. Discounts can range from 55% (usually on daytime shows) to a little over 30%, and compare well with the competition. Note that Goldstar Events adds a $6 booking fee to all sales.

* **Broadway Box (www.broadwaybox.com)** is a bit more hit-and-miss. On the face of it, it looks like it has a number of big name offers for headliners such as Donny and Marie, Cirque shows, and other hard-to-snag tickets. Surf further and some of these offers turn out to be come-ons for full priced tickets either bundled into stays at the sponsoring casino; or with such gimmees as a Carrot Top DVD. Among all the dross there is a tiny sparkle of gold, such as "twofer" tickets to impersonator shows, or 20% off T&A extravaganzas. Bottom line: It can't hurt to look (I once found a 25% discount for Celine Dion's show here), but be prepared to be disappointed.

* **Las Vegas Leisure Guide (www.lasvegas-nv.com):** Coupons, coupons, coupons! For everything from wedding chapels (free "designer" garters!) to helicopter tours, with 10-or-so discounts for shows. Unlike other sites that simply copy down discount codes and reprint them (as Broadway Box seems to do), this site has its own coupons, each vetted and with clear expiration dates (always be wary of coupons without expiration dates, as they may be counterfeit). Two-for-one discounts are most common, meaning that a quick glance here may yield a 50% discount for a couple. The only disappointment, and it's a big one, is that almost all of the coupons must be used in person, at the box office, so you'll have to wait until you get to Vegas to buy.

Still, you could buy your tickets on-site several days in advance. You also don't have to contend with a booking fee for this option.

◆ **Show Tickets for Locals (www.showticketsforlocals.com):** The oddest, but potentially most valuable of the lot, this site gives away free tickets. Why? It's called "papering the house." If a show is new and needs an audience there to create buzz (or to fill seats on a night critics are coming), it'll give away seats. For some shows, the producers figure the drinks sold before, during, and after the show will be enough of a profit-source to make these freebies profitable. There are dozens of reasons why producers "paper" and in Vegas, they do it through this site. Here's how it works (and why it might be rough for tourists to participate): You sign up at the site for free, providing your e-mail address but no other personal information (despite the name, they don't check to see whether or not you're actually local). Then when shows become available, they send out an e-mail giving a phone number for tickets. Once all the tickets are gone, another e-mail is sent out to that effect. Problem is: Most tourists won't be sitting around waiting for the e-mail, they'll be out on the town. However, if your phone is of the sort that can get e-mails, this could possibly work for you.

TICKET BOOTH DEALS

For variety, good prices, and a chance at scoring some of the top tickets in town for less, Vegas' half-price ticket booths can't be beat. Two companies now compete: **Tix 4 Tonight** (www.tix4tonight.com; daily noon–9pm) and **All Access Entertainment** (www.showtkts.com; daily 10am–6pm, 8pm at the Circus Circus locale) offer the same discounts off the same shows (or so it seems). They get these from the theaters themselves, as well as from other ticket brokers who buy up popular show tickets well in advance and then sometimes find themselves unable to unload them (which may be why you'll occasionally see shows that can't be purchased from the box office for full price selling here at a small discount). As with the online discounters, there's a range of price cuts, from 55% to as little as 10% off—all will depend on the date and time (though to be fair, the majority of shows on the boards are reduced by half). "We've had every show on the Strip, every single one, up for sale at our booths," says Kim Simon of Tix 4 Tonight "You just have to hit it at the right time." She's right. I was astounded by the range of shows I saw listed at the booth during the month I spent in Vegas, which ranged from low profile impersonator and magic shows to the real Bette Midler and Cirque du Soleil.

And the odd thing is: Every once in a while, the discounted price for a show will be the same as the lowest price being sold by the box office. So why patronize the discounters? Because the ticket booths and websites that mark down tickets are often able to get better seats at those lower prices than you'll get direct at the box office. Sad and annoying but true.

There are some differences between the two companies. Tix 4 Tonight has recently branched out into discounted golf and discounted restaurant meals (see p. 68), making it an excellent place to plan an entire evening (or an entire day for that matter). Though it opens later, its booths also stay open later, so this is the better option for procrastinators. All Access is the early bird's fave as its booths open at 10am; and because it's a new organization it doesn't get nearly the crowds

Ticket Booth Locations

Tix 4 Tonight Booths:

* **Fashion Show Mall** (in front of Neiman Marcus)
* **The Hawaiian Marketplace** (at the Polo Towers, South Strip)
* **On the North Strip,** just up from the Riviera
* **On Fremont Street** in The Four Queens Hotel
* **In the Showplace Mall on the Strip** (in front of the giant Coca-Cola bottle)
* **Inside Bill's Gambling Hall** on the Strip

All Access Entertainment Desks:

* **Circus Circus Hotel and Casino**
* **Fashion Show Mall** (in the food court)
* **Tuscany Suites and Casino**
* **Tahiti Village**
* **South Point Hotel, Casino and Spa**

that Tix 4 Tonight does, meaning it's unlikely you'll have to spend any time in line (at Tix 4 Tonight you could wait up to 30 minutes to buy your seats). See the box for locations of the booths.

A word on timing: Many buyers assume that the best seats and tickets will be gone if they don't get to the booths early, and therefore show up just as the booths are opening. In reality, tickets are released throughout the day, so getting there early won't necessarily work in your favor. I've seen Cirque du Soleil's *Mystère* go up at 4pm; those who dropped by earlier had to make do with *Bite* (and that really bites, believe me). Come by when it's convenient for you to do so; if the line's too long— and early in the day, the wait can be up to a half-hour—simply come back later.

One final tip: If you're planning on going to Tix 4 Tonight and you have a certain show in mind, call ☎ 877/849-4868. That's actually the number for people wanting to make restaurant reservations, but the folks sitting there can see the listings of shows and will usually, if you ask nicely, tell you what's up and what's not that day. You'll also see about eight "sneak previews" listed on the Tix 4 Tonight website.

SOME GENERAL RULES ON DISCOUNT TICKETS

Obviously, you're going to pay a lot less to see a show on Fremont Street than you will Elton John on the Strip. But that's not really a strategy, that's more a sad fact of life. To save on the shows you want to see:

* **See the early show.** If there are two shows in one evening, the earlier one will sometimes be cheaper.
* **Pick up coupons wherever you see them.** Don't walk blindly by the folks handing out discount coupons on the Strip—they're sometimes for good

shows! You'll likely find these glad-handers in front of Harrah's and the Flamingo. You can also find valuable coupons in the free tourist magazines you may find in your room or at the rental-car counter, so take the time to flip through them.

* **Gamble . . . strategically.** It's no secret that Big Rollers get lots of freebies (though one could argue they're paid for in losses). If you're planning on hitting the tables or slots anyway, and there's a particular show you're just dying to see, make the casino that houses it your home away from home. Let the pit boss or slot host know you're there, be upfront about your goals, and you just might find yourself front and center at *Mystère*. Be realistic, though: For a top show, this strategy could take several days and will likely work better midweek and in the off season. But get to know the hosts, be friendly, dress nicely, and see what happens. At worst, this tactic will gain you access to the VIP line to enter the theater. You may still have to pay, but you'll spend less time in line, and for those showrooms that don't assign seats, you'll probably bag a better view of the stage. Every so often, guests are offered free tickets just for signing up for a casino's slot club (Harrah's has been known to give away freebies to Mac King, and the former editor of this book got a twofer at the Trop for the *Folies Bergere*).

CHOOSING WHICH SHOWS TO SEE

In his stand-up routine, Louis Anderson quips that seeing a show is a great way to save $100. Yeah, you might pay that much to see the show, but at least you won't have tithed it to the roulette wheel. Choose the right show, though, and you'll get more than just an hour-and-a-half-long break from losing; you'll likely come away with a handful of great jokes to tell your friends at home, or a vision of remarkable beauty (if you go the Cirque route or to one of the showgirl and guy shows around town—hey it's all a matter of taste), or a renewed appreciation of such classic Vegas performers as Wayne Newton or George Wallace, who consistently blow the roof off their showrooms. Seeing a show can be one of the greatest delights of a Vegas vacation.

That's not to say that there aren't some dogs among the pack of long-running shows. There are, and this section will help you cull the winners from the losers (wish I could do the same for slot machines!).

In addition, I'll give you the real costs for many of the shows—not only the "official" price, but the prices that the half-price ticket booths have been charging

Pricing in This Chapter

I've listed the normal regular prices for each show, along with the prices I've seen them sold for at the discount ticket booths (these are marked as discounted). Because I think they're a rip-off, I haven't listed the prices for VIP packages, but if you want to have someone else make dinner reservations for you and sweep you to the front of the line, the websites for each show will give you full pricing info for these packages. As I said, I don't think they're worth it, but it's your party.

> " *Las Vegas without Wayne Newton is like Disneyland without Mickey Mouse.* "
>
> —Merv Griffin

of late. I can't guarantee that you'll be able to snag these exact discounts from the booth, as I wasn't able to get them from an official source (that would have violated these brokers' contracts with the producers), but these were the prices being charged at the half-price booths when I last checked—several times, actually—and thus should serve as a good general guideline as to which shows you can get for less (and how much less).

And now, the shows themselves, grouped as to theme or content.

DIVA LAS VEGAS

Among the most coveted shows are those of the Vegas headliners, the folks whose likenesses loom 20 feet high over the Strip, who grin at you from the sides of buses, and welcome your arrival at the airport's luggage carousel with a never-ending video loop of their performances. After this constant barrage, you may feel like you've already seen their shows, but for the most part, these performers live up to the hype.

Of the really big names in Vegas, there are few who can compete on the level of sheer, unadulterated showmanship with Mr. Las Vegas himself, **Wayne Newton** ★★★ (will likely be playing at MGM Grand, though he moves around from theater to theater; check www.waynenewton.com for his schedule; ticket prices usually cost $65). He sings, he dances, he plays the banjo, he plays the drums, he plays the fiddle, he kisses EVERYONE . . . and it's an utter delight. Even though Newton's voice is no longer the honey-toned instrument it once was (it now has the rasp of Carol Channing), he has the uncanny ability to make even the mustiest of standards sound brand new and touchingly meaningful. I was not a Wayne Newton fan until I saw him in the course of researching this book, but like he's done for so many thousands of others he won me over (I even purchased a CD). There's a reason he's a legend, so go see him now because he won't be around forever.

Another surprise, at least for me, is how utterly charming, self-deprecating, and fun **Manilow: Music and Passion** ★★ (in the Las Vegas Hilton; ☎ 800/222-5361; www.musicandpassion.com; $95–$198, $78 discounted; Wed–Fri 9pm, Sat 7:30 and 10pm) is. On my first encounter with him, I expected a snoozy nostalgia-fest, but Barry Manilow has not lost his zest for performing or for redefining himself: A full third of the concert was taken up with songs from his latest hit album, and he very obviously relishes performing them. Of course, he also does "Mandy," "Looks Like We Made It," "Can't Smile Without You," and a number of his other hits, sounding as silken as he always has, and backed by a quartet of multitalented singer/dancers. And I'll admit it, when the confetti started falling and a walkway suddenly jutted out over the audience for "Copacabana," I went as wild as the rest of the crowd . . . and I never particularly liked that song.

Perhaps the greatest compliment I can pay to **Bette Midler: The Showgirl Must Go On** ★★★ (the Colosseum at Caesars Palace; ☎ 702/731-7208; $86–$227; Tues–Wed and Fri–Sun 7:30pm) is to say that she's on the same plane as

Wayne, but of course, raunchier and with a refreshingly progressive and *au courant* edge to her patter (I saw her during the election and her Sarah Palin jokes were killer; two of the jokemeisters for the Oscars writer her material and keep it fresh week to week). And boy, does she know how to put on a show! A huge orchestra, dozens of showgirls, spiffy choreography, dazzling costumes, heartfelt singing, and a rapport with the audience that's impressive, especially considering how large the Caesars theater is. It's clichéd but: Run don't walk to get tickets to this show. It truly is one of the top five on the Strip right now.

When Bette's out of town, **Cher** ✪ (the Colosseum at Caesars Palace; ☎ 702/731-7208; $86–$227; Tues–Wed and Fri–Sun 7:30pm) assumes the mantle of head-liner at Caesars Palace. I wish I could say she wears it comfortably. But rumor has it that she's been suffering from what's called in these parts "desert throat," a problem with the dryness of the air here, which can wreak havoc on the vocal chords. When I saw the show, she seemed to be not only vocally having problems but her energy was lacking, too. That may be partly the fault of the show, which has nothing like the clever writing and staging that goes into Midler's extravaganza. Cher fans will probably come away satisfied (if only because of the montages of Cher's past work that remind us why she's such a star); others may want to pass.

And speaking of '70s variety shows, why do the Scintas when you can see **Donny and Marie** (at the Flamingo; ☎ 888/902-9929; $85–$115, $65 discounted; Tues–Sat 7:30pm) re-creating theirs? Here's another walloping dose of sibling rivalry schtick, along with dance numbers, comedy bits, and even, Lord help us, opera (Marie confesses midshow that it's her fondest wish to someday sing opera at the Met in NYC; she then whips off an Andrew Lloyd Webber aria that reveals she won't be doing duets with Placido Domingo anytime soon). This is another case where, if you're a fan, you'll probably be delighted with this show. And if you're not . . . well, it ain't going to change your mind.

COMIC HEADLINERS

As I write this, there are six comedians with their own permanent shows on the Strip. The deliciously witty **Rita Rudner** ✪✪✪ (at Harrah's; ☎ 702/369-5222; www.harrahs.com; $54, $39 discounted; Mon–Sat 8pm) wins a favorite performer award from one local organization or another each year and after you see her show, you'll understand why. Sophisticated but never smutty, she makes you rethink parts of your life even as you're doubled over laughing. Highly recommended.

I also loved **Wayne Brady's** *Making @#! Up* ✪✪ (at The Venetian; ☎ 866/641-7469 or 702/414-9000; Thurs–Mon 9pm) . . . . the first two-thirds of it. You see, Wayne's got a real Achilles' heel as a performer (and I guess as a human being). He's been endowed with an almost superhuman power to improvise hilarious material on pretty much every subject under the sun (you may remember him doing that on *Whose Line Is It*

> ❝For the grand debut of Monte Carlo as a resort in 1879 the architect Charles Garnier designed an opera house for the Place du Casino; and Sarah Bernhardt read a symbolic poem. For the debut of Las Vegas as a resort in 1946 Bugsy Siegel hired Abbott and Costello, and there, in a way, you have it all.❞
>
> —Tom Wolfe

Comedy Clubs

Beyond the headliners, the following clubs host up-and-coming stand-ups every night of the year. Because the comics are different each week, there's no way to say which one is "best." I'd suggest checking the line-up on each club's website before showing up.

One of the most inexpensive entertainment deals in town, **The Comedy Stop** (in the Tropicana; ☎ 888/826-TROP or 702/739-2714; www.comedy stop.com; $20, includes drink but coupons cut that price in half; nightly 8pm and 10:30pm) switches up its headliners three times a week, keeping the show fresh. In ambience, it's akin to a sports bar, with long covered tables that have candles actually screwed into them (a not-so-subtle commentary on the demographic), and card-style chairs tightly packed next to one another.

Part of a chain that was founded in New York in 1963, **The Improv** (in Harrah's; ☎ 800/392-9002; www.harrahs.com; tickets $29, with discount; Tues–Sun 8:30 and 10:30pm) features three comedians nightly, with new talent brought in each week. In spite of the name, the acts don't always involve improv.

LA Comedy Club (in the Miracle Mile Mall; ☎ 702/275-3877 $26, $18 discounted; Fri–Sun 7:30–9:30pm) was named Best Comedy Club in Vegas in 2008 by the *Las Vegas Review Journal* and it's no mystery why: It's got the spiffiest setting by far, set in Trader Vic's restaurant and with a glass wall offering views of the Bellagio Fountain (you can glance over there when the comics are tanking). Weekends only, though.

The Riviera Comedy Club (in the Riviera; ☎ 800/634-3420 or 702/794-9433; www.rivierahotel.com; tickets $25; nightly 8:30pm and 10:30pm) has been around since the late '80s, and looks like an understated comedy basement. In addition to revolving comedians, the Riv also brings in ventriloquists and hypnotists. The lineup changes weekly.

Anyway?). But it turns out that what Brady really wants to do is croon, and while he has a pleasant voice, the musical part of the show is nowhere near as entertaining as his improv. Do me a favor: Write Brady, and ask him to stick with the comedy. The world has enough Mariah Carey wannabes and so very, very few truly funny people.

If you like edgy, political humor and lean a bit to the left, I highly recommend **George Wallace** ✪✪ (at the Flamingo; ☎ 702/733-7333; www.caesars.com/flamingo; $75, $50 discounted; Tues–Sat 10pm) for his wry commentary on the state of nation. His set pieces on people who "should be beaten" will delight anyone who's ever had an unpleasant boss, dealt with an officious cop, or had a clingy girlfriend or boyfriend (and that may be most of us).

Louie Anderson ✪✪ (at Excalibur; ☎ 702/597-7600; www.louieanderson.com; $30; Sun–Thurs 7pm), of the Emmy Award–winning *Life with Louie* and

Family Feud, has a mild, Midwestern manner that masks a sharp intelligence. His show is the most G-rated of the bunch, but it's deftly amusing, and by the end of his hour-long set, you'll feel like you just left the most delightful of cocktail parties (as Anderson often engages the audience in a friendly, nonthreatening way).

If you've ever seen **Carrot Top** ✪✪✪ (at Luxor; ☎ 800/963-9634 or 702/262-4400; www.carrottop.com; $50–$65, $39 discounted; Wed–Fri and Sun–Mon 8pm, Sat 9pm) on Letterman or Leno, you know what he's all about: hilarious props, inventions really, that he pulls out of four large trunks in the course of the show. There are toilet seat cover plates for bulimics, face-covering pacifiers for "very ugly babies," a "Dick Cheney shotgun" (with a boomerang curve), and literally a hundred other amusing sight gags. But the biggest visual surprise of all may well be Carrot Top himself, who's bulked up to Schwarzenegger proportions and uses his new pecs as part of the act.

The newest Strip comic, **Vinnie Favorito** ✪ (at the Flamingo; ☎ 703/733-3333; $47 at box office, $30 discounted; nightly 8pm) is best known as a

Family-Friendly Shows

If you're looking for a fun show for the kids, without the threat of a "Janet Jackson" moment, here are six that you can book worry free:

Lance Burton (p. 189): Las Vegas' top magician will mesmerize even the youngest theatergoers (my 3-year-old sat like a stone throughout his entire show). Plus he brings kids up to the stage as assistants and if that doesn't excite 'em, I don't know what will.

Mac King (p. 195): An afternoon comedy-magic show that will delight both kids and adults, it's another cheapie. Big bonus here: Mac meets everyone and signs autographs after the show.

Tournament of Kings (p. 185): Horses, knights in shining armor, and permission to eat with their hands! Kids will love this cornball dinner show (and you may find yourself grinning as well).

Blue Man Group (p. 190): Yes, it's performance art and slightly surreal, but most kids groove on the fact that you've got three grown-ups throwing food, making a mess, and playing music really loud. My 7-year-old went nuts for this show.

Mystère (p. 184): With the exception of *Zumanity,* you can take your kids to any Cirque show and they'll be re-enacting it for months to come. But *Mystère,* which follows the adventures of two oversized babies, is the funniest and cheapest of the lot—a winning combination.

Popovitch Comedy Pet Theater (p. 196): Unless they're allergic to cats—and the tricks they can do—the under-10 set will find this old-fashioned circus delightful.

"celebrity roaster." You may have caught his act on Comedy Central turning the screws on such luminaries as Larry King, Tom Arnold, and Jerry Springer. He does the same routine here, with the audience substituting for the celebs, and Favorito impressively riffing about the lives of a dozen audience members after just a few sentences of conversation with them. Some of the humor relies on cultural stereotyping, but as he plays up his own "goombah" persona, it's rarely offensive and usually quite funny. For a show this cheap—there are always twofers being handed out outside—it's one heck of a good time.

THE SIX CIRQUE DU SOLEIL SHOWS

"A band of stilt-walking street performers gives Vegas a makeover." If you saw that headline in a newspaper you'd think it was a joke, but that's exactly what happened when Cirque du Soleil—the famed Canadian circus that began its existence performing on the streets of Montreal—came to town in 1993. Within less than a decade it utterly transformed the face of Vegas theater, creating critically acclaimed permanent shows on the Strip (and inspiring dozens of imitators). Pity the poor executive at Caesars Palace who decided that Cirque's offerings were too "far out" to play well in Vegas and put the kibosh on plans for Caesars to become the first Cirque venue. Instead, that honor went to Treasure Island, and ever since audiences have thrilled to these whimsical, surreal, highly sophisticated productions, which are part circus (no animals, but lots of awe-inspiring acrobatics and circus tricks), part commedia dell'arte, part mime, part modern dance, and part, well, part intense acid trip . . . without the horrific hangover the next day.

The least expensive of the five, simply because it's been playing the longest, is **Mystère** ★★★ 🧒 (in Treasure Island; ☎ 800/963-9634 or 702/796-9999; www. cirquedusoleil.com; $60, $75, and $90 at box office, $70 discounted; Wed–Sat 7:30 and 10:20pm, Sun 4:30 and 7:30pm). I'd say it's also the most child-friendly, as it's the funniest Cirque show by far, centering on the antics of two clown "babies" who crawl, cry, and adopt an audience member as a surrogate parent for most of the show (if you don't like audience participation, don't sit in the front row). Around these two young 'uns swirl dancers and acrobats, performing feats of strength and agility that would make an Olympic gymnast blanch . . . and Mary Lou Retton never had to tumble or do triple flips on a trampoline while wearing a mask and dressed like a creature out of Doctor Seuss. There's no plot to speak of, but the show is, in its own way, quite moving—a metaphor for the cycle of life, with its babies and elderly clowns, and all of the mysterious creatures that blossom in between.

If you read the program notes, you'll find that Franco Dragone, the director, gave Cirque's next smash hit its one-letter name because it's a symbol for infinity; moreover, "O" is the phonetic pronunciation of *eau,* the French word for water. Go to see **O** ★★★ 🧒 (in the Bellagio; ☎ 877/922-9228 or 702/531-3855; www.cirquedusoleil.com; $94–$150; Wed–Sun 7:30 and 10:30pm), and turn your attention from the stage for a moment and you'll find another reason for this odd title: the saucer eyes and open mouths of the audience. This is simply the most astounding, profound, exhilarating, eye-poppingly beautiful show in Vegas. I know that's a long chain of superlatives but if I had more space, I'd probably add a couple more (I had a friend tell me that she just sat and cried through the entire show, she found it so movingly lovely).

The Dinner Shows of Vegas

Their pluses? You don't have to look for parking twice, and you know where your next meal's coming from. The minuses? Let me put it this way—the cast knows that you're eating while you watch them. This may not sound like a big matter, but I think it leads to performances that are a tad more, well, casual than most, lacking that spark of excitement that accompanies live theater.

But not always. *Hitzville* (at the Harmon Theater at Krave; ☎ 702/617-0672; www.hitzvilletheshow.com; $55, $28 discounted; Wed–Sun 6:30pm) is a high-powered Motown revue that gives the Platters and Coasters show (see p. 193) a run for its money. Here, the music is performed by a team of six, three men and three women, one of whom, Jin Jin Reeves, has the wattage of Tina Turner and the pipes to match. She electrifies the proceedings (though the mellow harmonies of the men are pretty swell, too). Perhaps the key here is that the food—a decent soul food buffet—is served BEFORE the show, so there's no slurping during the performance.

Tony and Tina's Wedding ✸ (in Planet Hollywood, 3667 Las Vegas Blvd S.; ☎ 702/785-9030; www.tonyandtinavegas.com; $90; Mon–Sat 7pm) and *Tournament of Kings* ✸ kids (in Excalibur; ☎ 702/597-7600; www.excalibur.com; $55; Mon–Wed and Fri–Sat 6pm and 8:30pm), are the two other major dinner shows in town, and they're fun, in a goofy, totally cheesy way. *Tournament of Kings* is a jousting tourney between *GQ* cover guys, er . . . I mean the many kings of Europe, hosted by the legendary King Arthur. Each section of the audience is assigned a king to cheer for (ask at the box office for the Russian king's section—in a throwback to the Cold War days, he's the bad boy of the lot) and this they do, pounding the tables, clinking their tankards of soda (sorry, no mead though you can order wine or cocktails), and waving guinea hen legs in the air. No silverware is supplied, so you'll be eating with your hands just like they did back when there were . . . mechanical dragons? Well, anyway, kids will like it, as will adults with pliable imaginations (or bellyfuls of margaritas).

Tony and Tina's is another pageant, this time of the marital bliss sort, and the audience members are wedding guests who become an integral part of the show. You'll do the conga, you'll probably have to dance with the soused bridesmaid, and you'll eat typical banquet food as you watch the cast run through every wedding cliché there is in a humorous, genial manner. There are also about 20 subplots in the show, which I won't give away.

A final dinner show which I'll mention just as a warning to skip it, is *Marriage Can Be Murder* (in The Four Queens Casino, 202 Fremont St.; ☎ 702/616-3322; www.marriagecanbemurder.com; $60, $41 discounted) which plays Downtown. The food is mediocre, the performances even more so, and the plot less mystery than utter befuddlement. It's a mess; even if you get a huge discount, it ain't worth it.

The show is centered around a 1.5-million-gallon pool, which is an engineering marvel: In seconds flat it transforms from pool to a shallow African watering hole, to a dry platform filled with dancers and acrobats, to a plateau with dancing fountains, or to a shimmering lake studded with islands and clown-steered houseboats. Synchronized swimmers plunge into its depths, staying submerged for what seems like 10 minutes while above-the-water divers twist and knife in, as brilliantly costumed parades traverse the edges of the water. It's a spectacle like no other and does the impossible: It tops all of the other brilliant Cirque shows. Yes, it's expensive, but you'll understand why when you see the show (there's no worthier splurge in town).

Most controversial among Cirque's offerings, **Zumanity** ★ (in New York–New York; ☎ 800/963-9634 or 702/796-9999; www.cirquedusoleil.com; $69–$129; Fri–Tues 7:30 and 10:30pm) is an erotic circus that celebrates sexuality in all its myriad incarnations: men with women, women with women, men with men, senior citizens with other seniors or with young folks, little people with Amazon-sized women, group sex, masturbation, you name it. Which means that when the two strong men are lifting one another in the classic "watch our veins pop out as we imitate Atlas" act, it's clear that there's a lot more than just lifting going on between these two. And when the aerialist hanging from the long silk ribbon is flinging herself around the stage, it's all about S&M and autoerotic asphyxiation. Those who are open-minded will find the Cirque magic here, as much of it is visually arresting, thought-provoking, and sexy. When I was last there, however, a number of people did walk out, so think honestly about what makes you squeamish before you book.

All of the Cirque shows have rich, evocative musical scores, but in **LOVE** ★ (in The Mirage; ☎ 800/963-9634 or 702/792-7777; www.cirquedusoleil.com; $93–$150, $73 discounted; Thurs–Mon 7pm and 10pm), the music itself is the focal point. Using master tapes from the Abbey Road studios in London, Sir George Martin (the Beatles' first producer) and his son Giles Martin created a brand new score of Beatles music as the basis for the show, mixing classic tunes with some unreleased recordings. Blasted through speakers at the back of each seat, the effect is like being with Ringo, John, Paul, and George in a live concert—it's brilliant. As for the show itself, it's a bit of a muddle. Some sections are stunning—a parade of fantastical instruments, a "Back in the USSR" where hippies and cops fly through the air via trampoline, a riff on crossing Abbey Road—but at other points, the show feels like more of a rough draft, the stage pictures diffuse and unfocused. All in all, it's a good experience, but perhaps not quite of the caliber of *O* or *Mystère*.

Despite its elaborate and expensive bells and whistles—computer-generated video projections, shooting fireballs, giant puppets, a 50-foot onstage cliff, and sets that wrap around the front of the theater, projecting into the audience—**KÀ** (in the MGM Grand; ☎ 866/774-7117 or 702/531-2000; www.cirquedusoleil.com; $69–$150; Tues–Sat 6:30 and 9:30pm) is not as satisfying as *Love, O, Mystère,* or even *Zumanity.* Which is disheartening, because this show was supposed to represent the next step for Cirque; unlike the others, it actually has a plot. Problem is, the telling of this tale takes time, and as no Vegas show can ever be more than an hour and a half (heaven forbid! I think there must be a law somewhere on the books), that's less time for the imagery and acrobatics that make Cirque unique.

And the story itself is no great shakes, concerning a pair of imperial twins who someone attacks—you never figure out who or why—who must then regain the throne, find one another, and find love along the way. Or something like that. It has one intensely cool scene in which the actors are supposed to be underwater, and as they drift down (they're suspended above the stage on wires) infrared sensors are triggered by their movements, sending up perfectly synched projections of air bubbles. It's an incredible effect.

Last in the canon, is **Criss Angel: Believe** (at the Luxor; ☎ 800/557-7429 or 702/262-4400; $59–$150; Fri–Tues 7pm and 10pm) the show that definitively proves that we're all human and sometimes make big mistakes, even the Cirque folks. Every one of the other Cirque shows boasts moments of pure poetry, and thus reasons to buy a ticket. *Believe* on the other hand is flat, and to be frank, pretty distasteful from the get-go. I'm talking close-ups of Angel getting his "face burned off" in an electrical fire, followed by giant rabbits ripping apart his corpse and devouring it. This description is actually making it sound more interesting than it is, but the problem is you can see the effort (and sometimes the wires) that allow these illusions to take place and the unrelentingly morbid and gory tone of the show is finally just depressing. Even if your teen begs you to go, having seen Angel perform death-defying stunts on TV, resist her entreaties. She'll be disappointed and so will you.

Finally, there's **Le Rêve** (at Wynn Las Vegas; ☎ 888/320-7110 or 702/770-9966; www.wynns.com; $99–$179, but I've seen tickets being given away free right before the show, so give it a try if you happen to be in the vicinity; ages 12 and older only; Thurs–Mon 7:30 and 10:30pm), which is actually not a Cirque show, though many lump it in with them because it was directed by former Cirque mastermind Franco Dragone and revolves around a giant pool of water and the antics of a lot of elaborately costumed actors, who dive and flip and clown about (hmmm . . . where have I seen that before?). A blatant rip-off of his much better work in *O*, *Le Rêve* is not worth the high price of admission and was about two-thirds empty when I attended.

GLITZ, GLAMOUR & EYELASH GLUE: THE PRODUCTION SHOWS

Once upon a time, there were a dozen Vegas shows built around the simple act of draping sequins and feathers on gorgeous showgirls. Only one survivor of this genre exist today, as tittie shows have gone from this relatively innocent playbill format to raunchier *Penthouse* magazine–type entertainments (p. 194). But if you'd like a topless show that you could (possibly) take your mother-in-law to, you have one one choice: **Jubilee!** ✮ (in Bally's; ☎ 800/237-SHOW; www.harrahs.com; $50–$90, look out for twofers to cut these prices in half; Sat–Thurs 7:30 and 10:30pm), which features statuesque, real-looking women (breast enhancements are frowned upon); dazzling headdresses and costumes; full orchestras; and scores of dancers.

Jubilee! was the first of the multi-million-dollar extravaganzas in Vegas when it opened in 1981. Its cast numbers 100, 50 stagehands are required to move the colossal sets, and the costumes designed by Bob Mackie (Cher's favorite designer) and Peter Menefee are so bespangled that their creation sparked a worldwide rhinestone shortage (no joke). And it was such a hit that the show was frozen for all time; what you see today is almost exactly the same show—with different performers of course—that you would have seen then (the only changes: Two short numbers were taken out).

That's both its lure and its curse, because, let's face it, the show was created in an era when *Cats* was considered high art, and Michael Jackson a sex symbol. So some of the numbers are snicker-into-your-program ridiculous, such as the over-the-top restaging of the biblical Samson and Delilah story, complete with a top-less Delilah and her G-string-clad male attendants; and the "let's all cha cha cha until the ship starts to sink" *Titanic* scenes. In its defense, this all has a time warp charm to it, with jugglers, strong men, and, of course, dozens of dance numbers; and the costumes are still eye candy of the first degree. I found the backstage tour (p. 165) to be as much fun, if not more, as the show, and highly recommend doing both in tandem.

Though not a "showgirl" extravaganza, the variety show **V** ✪ (in Miracle Mile Mall; ☎ 702/932-1818; $62 adult, $33 children, $27 discounted; daily 7:30 and 9:30pm), originally created for The Venetian, belongs to the same genre. It's old-fashioned vaudeville, filled with the kind of novelty acts that were popular in the heyday of that form of entertainment, with a couple of showgirls thrown in for good measure (you'll see them in the magician's act). Though the bill is constantly changing, you might see Trenyce Cobbins, who came in fifth on *American Idol* (the year Ruben won, but Clay got the career); and grimacing, grappling Russian strong-men Iroui and Nikolai. My only peeve is the cramped theater itself, with some of the least comfortable seating in town.

Showgirls on ice (but never topless) is part of the appeal of **ICE: Direct from Russia** ✪✪ (at the Riviera Hotel; ☎ 702/794-9433; $67, $49 discounted; Sat–Thurs 8pm), the women in the show are almost supernaturally beautiful, but also talented, as are the men for that matter. And the *ICE* performers leave Tara Lipinski and Sarah Hughes in the dust (or would it be ice chips?). Not only do they flawlessly perform the same kind of leaps and spins these gals do (plus the tricks the pairs skaters do), but they also juggle on ice, do cartwheels and flip, glide on stiltlike skates, and play the trumpet and violin while they zoom around the rink. It's an unexpectedly terrific show—the creators of the show have displayed the same level of creativity and skill as the Cirque folks do, though they don't have the budget for the same types of production values.

MAGIC SHOWS

Making things disappear—usually bank accounts, sometimes marriages and careers—is a Vegas specialty. Which may be why Sin City is such a hot spot for magic shows; I'd guess that there are more magicians here, and certainly more famous magicians here, than anywhere else in the U.S. (not to mention magic supply stores at nearly every casino on the Strip—who knew the market would be that big?). But though these performers use many of the same props and wear roughly the same outfits (tuxes and waxlike hair gels seem to be the norm), they're a remarkably varied bunch.

There's magic for cynics, from cynics, at **Penn & Teller** ✪✪ (in the Rio All-Suite Hotel & Casino, 3700 W. Flamingo Rd.; ☎ 702/777-7776; www.playrio.com or www.pennandteller.com; $85 or $96, $52 discounted; Wed–Mon 9pm). **Notorious**

You're Getting Sleepy, Very Sleepy

Hypnotism is big in Las Vegas and not just the trance certain gamblers fall into in front of the slot machines. I'm talking about shows where men with soothing voices lull volunteers into doing embarrassing things while their friends giggle, then buy the show's video tape so they'll always have a useful instrument of blackmail (hint: under no circumstances volunteer at these shows!!). You'll hate yourself in the morning for it, but you'll probably love these shows, as they're at the same time horrifying, fascinating, and funny.

With the grin of Mephistopheles and the imagination of Larry Flynt **Anthony Cools** ★★★ (at Paris Las Vegas; ☎ 877/374-7469; www.paris lasvegas.com; $53 box office, $39 discounted; Thurs–Tues 9pm) is the most entertaining of the bunch. And he entices audience members to do the most obscene, humiliating acts in public that you've probably ever seen. It's intensely compelling theater, and often outrageously funny, though part of me felt bad every time I laughed at the poor suckers on stage (and I was laughing until the tears streamed down my face).

Dirty Hypnosis ★★ (Harmon Theater at Krave; ☎ 702/737-2515; $43, $27 discounted; Tues–Sun 9pm) is just what it sounds like—a show in which the participants are convinced that their vaginas are talking back to them or that they're madly in love with the hypnotist. It isn't quite as creative as Cool's show, but it is as prurient so if that's what you're looking for, you'll find it here at a lower price than Cools.

The touchy-feely hypnotism show, *Dr. Scott Lewis' Outrageous Comedy Hypnosis* (at the Riviera Hotel and Casino; www.vegashypnotist.com; $25, $18 discounted; Mon 9pm) is not nearly as obscene, but he's not as funny as the other two either. Still if you're interested in hypnotism and squeamish about the humiliation factor, this is probably the best show for you.

debunkers—they spend about half their show revealing how the tricks are done and dissing other magicians—this is the show that features that tall, motor mouthed guy who juggles sharp objects such as chainsaws (that would be Penn), and his tiny, eerily silent partner (the misnamed Teller) whom Penn tortures in various ways through the show. It's a talky show, too talky for some (especially those who've seen their act on TV, as much of that material is recycled here), but when they get down to the actual magic, their tricks can be astonishing and elegant.

To revel in the romance of magic, pick **Lance Burton** ★★★ 🅺 (in the Monte Carlo; ☎ 877/386-8224 or 702/730-7160; www.lanceburton.com; $66–$72, though periodically Burton posts $10 discounts for his 10pm shows, so check his website; Wed–Fri 7pm, Tues and Sat 7pm and 10pm), who puts on what is, in many ways, the most mind-boggling show. There are dozens of moments when your brain must struggle to catch up with your eyes as doves transform into clouds of confetti and Burton appears in places that bend the laws of physics. With the chiseled good looks and laid-back delivery of Clint Eastwood, Burton mystifies debonairly, helped along by seven cheerfully gorgeous showgirls, and one of the best back-up acts in Vegas, comedy juggler Michael Goudeau. The highlight of the show? The child volunteers who come up from the audience to assist Burton. Through their delighted responses, you'll remember how absolutely magical magic shows can be.

I like to think of **Steve Wyrick** ✪✪ (in the Miracle Mile Mall; ☎ 800/210-1745; www.stevewyrick.com; $70, discounted $33; Sat–Thurs 7pm and 10pm) as "Son of Lance Burton." He has the same relaxed charm, the same way with disappearing birds and he creates big production pieces that absolutely baffle the audience (I still am trying to figure out how he got the diamond ring of an audience member onto another audience member's finger). He also includes the kids in the audience in his tricks, so bring along the young ones—it's a highlight of the show. And because Wyrick is more likely to be deeply discounted than Burton, this may be the show you choose to take the family to—it certainly will be more affordable.

Barely a magician, **The Amazing Johnathan** (Harmon Theater at Krave; ☎ 888/LAS-VEGAS or 702/737-2515; www.amazingj.com; $65 box office, $24 with discount; Tues–Sat 9pm) has an act built around not being able to do magic well (don't under any circumstances give him a $100 bill if he asks for it!). That's the supposed humor of his act, but his banter, which is extremely blue, is more coarse than funny, and often just plain boring. There are better shows for comedy and magic.

TRANSPLANTED NEW YORK SHOWS

About a decade ago, a whole bunch of casino folks went east to New York City to poach. Their booty? Celebrity chefs and stage shows. The former has been a much more successful transplant than the latter, as *Hairspray, We Will Rock You* (from London's West End), and *Avenue Q* each failed in quick succession to find a Vegas audience.

But just because they're being marked down doesn't mean they're not worth seeing (and some are doing quite well; see below). Employing top-notch casts, top writers, and cutting-edge stage techniques, these imports have a polish and depth that their Vegas counterparts sometimes lack. **Blue Man Group** ✪✪✪ 🎈 (in The Venetian; ☎ 877/883-6243 or 702/414-1000; www.venetian.com; $72–$121; Sun–Thurs 7:30pm, Sat 7:30 and 10:30pm, Fri 8pm), to take one prominent example, may well be the first example of "performance art" that many Las Vegas theatergoers will have ever experienced. Exploring themes of alienation and the making of art, it certainly has a deeper subtext than most Vegas shows, but the three bald, stone-faced, azure-colored fellows are so darned funny these "lessons" go down easily. (The show has proved to be both portable and long-lived: The original is still running off-Broadway, and there are additional Blue Men companies in Chicago, Boston, Orlando, as well as in Berlin and Tokyo). Watching these three oddball aliens as they make an "art meal" (by blowing pellets of paint onto a canvas), create a chorale from the amplified munching of Captain Crunch, or wildly jam on PVC pipes, is good, clean, absurdist fun. Though the price of tickets will inhibit many parents from taking their kids, this was one of my 9-year-old's favorite Vegas shows.

Come on Down! You're the Next Contestant . . .

The big question, to my mind, about the live version of *The Price Is Right* ✦✦ (in Bally's; ☎ 800/237-SHOW; www.harrahs.com; $40; must be over age 21 to play; Tues–Thurs and Sat 2:30pm, Fri 7:30 and 10:30pm) is why no one in Vegas ever thought of doing this before. A chance for average Joes to gamble . . . surrounded by showgirls . . . in front of an audience . . . and possibly win a car. It's like some great God of Kitsch came down and blessed the city with this perfectly fitted entertainment.

I happened to catch the live *Price Is Right* during the first week of its run, and it was already a success, filling the showroom with wildly enthusiastic fans who seemed to know every game and even some of the "classic clips" that are played at intervals during the afternoon. In the one deviation from the TV version, contestants aren't randomly chosen. They must compete to answer trivia questions as quickly as possible to get onstage. Other than that, all the elements are in place, from the plastic looking host, Todd Newton of TV's *Instant Millionaire* ("I'm truly honored to say Bob Barker is one of the kindest, most generous and elegant man I've ever met," he solemnly intones halfway through the show) to the games the contestants play, such as "Plinko" and the yodeling mountain climber game. And the prizes are as good as on TV: A 52-inch plasma TV! An air hockey table! A 2009 Mustang!! So is it worth seeing? Heck, yeah. Uncool and retro as it may be, there's something about the chance to guess the price of a can of tuna fish or a bottle of hairspray that's deeply satisfying (I'm embarrassed to say). A long list of game show hosts have been cycling into and out of the live version, so there's a chance that you could play the game with (drumroll please): Chuck Woolery.

It's common in reviews of bad musicals to say that you left "humming the set." Of course, the tunes in the *Phantom of the Opera* (in The Venetian; ☎ 877/883-6243 or 702/414-1000; www.venetian.com; $76–$150; Sat Tues and Thurs 7pm and 10pm, Sun and Fri 7pm) could never be called not memorable. But in this drastically truncated version of the show (it's been squeezed from 3 hours to just 1½) it's the set that makes the biggest impression. The entire auditorium has been turned into a grand opera house, with a monster of a gilded chandelier and boxes around the theater, filled with elegantly dressed dummies. It's impressive. Unfortunately, the show itself registers as little more than a pageant. For those who've never seen it, it's now impossible to follow the plot and though the singing is top-notch, the performances seems a bit rote.

The producers of *Jersey Boys* ✦✦✦ (in the Palazzo; ☎ 866/641-7469 or 702/414-9000; $65–$135; Mon, Thurs, Fri, and Sun 7pm, Tues 6:30 and 9:30pm, Sat 7pm and 10pm) bucked the system and refused to shorten it (though they have instituted the most cruelly brief intermission anywhere which only allows determined sprinters to use the loo). As a result, the show is as electric as it is on

Broadway, a warts and all retelling of the history of the pop group The Four Seasons. The performances are spot on and the show itself it ultimately quite, quite moving (this may be the only Vegas show that brought me to tears). A top pick!

As we go to press the Mandalay Bay theater, previously the home to *Mamma Mia,* is being refitted to hold Disney's fantastical *Lion King* ✪✪✪ (at Mandalay Bay; pricing and schedule unavailable at press time). Though I haven't seen the Vegas version (obviously), my guess is that it should be a smooth transition from Broadway as this is a show that's always been more about the spectacle than the story. So even if they do cut down the running time, I'm betting that the magic of the show's giant puppets and visual effects won't be diminished.

I have to say, I really expected to hate *Defending the Caveman* (at the Excalibur; $40–$50 evening shows, $35–$45 matinees [including souvenir T-shirt!], $22 with discount; Sun, Tues, Thurs 3pm, Fri and Sat 3pm and 7pm) a long-running one-man show about the war between the sexes. It gets gentle yucks on such topics as sharing the TV remote control, shopping, and sports. Not earth shattering, or even very insightful stuff, but not at all the misogynistic rant I expected. A lot of its charm is due to the wonderful performance of Kevin Burke, the Las Vegas "caveman." (According to the company's website, there are approximately a dozen different "cavemen" touring the country, as well as international cavemen!) A decent date show . . . especially if there are some issues you've been wanting to bring up with your significant other.

IMPERSONATOR/TRIBUTE SHOWS (OR PERFORMERS WHO WISH THEY WERE SOMEONE ELSE)

Though he's been dead nearly 30 years, Elvis is still a headliner in Vegas, as is Frank Sinatra, Dean Martin, and a whole bunch of live celebs who aren't anywhere near Sin City. Conjured up in tribute shows all over town, this perplexing genre (full disclosure: I don't really get the appeal of it) is as popular as the magic shows, with eight thriving long-run tribute shows.

Danny Gans ✪✪ (at Encore; www.dannygans.com; Tues-Wed and Fri-Sat 7:30pm; $95–$120) is the king of the fakers, transforming himself during the course of his hour-and-a-half-long concert into some 100 or so famous personages from Jeff Foxworthy to Katharine Hepburn to Garth Brooks to Louis Armstrong. And he does have an admirable accuracy and clarity to his work, getting not just the voice (singing as well as speaking; an impressive big band backs him up) but the gait, gestures, and facial expressions of his subjects (he even plays the trumpet as Louie). You'll hear an audible grunt of recognition from the audience, followed by a happy "I guessed that!" applause from the audience at each transformation. Whether this well-honed parlor trick is worth the hefty price tag is an open question; I personally think there are more dynamic shows, but I'm giving it two stars, as I'm in the minority on that—Gans is consistently voted best entertainer in Vegas year after year.

The bargain basement Gans, **Larry G. Jones** ✪✪ (at the Royal Resort on Convention Center Dr.; ☎ 800/595-4849; www.larrygjones.com; $24; Mon–Wed 9pm) performs his show in a curtained off corner of the lobby of the Royal Hotel. He has no band, and the night I was there, the guy running his recorded music was having problems with the system, forcing Jones to vamp while it was rebooted. Despite that, Jones puts on a heartfelt, witty show in which he not only re-creates the sounds of the folks he's imitating (everyone from Bruce Springsteen to George Bush to Tina Turner), but also has some darn funny comedy pieces vamping on these celebs' reputations. Perhaps it was the "let's put on a show, kids" vibe, or the tiny theater, but I found myself being far more drawn into Jones's performance and laughing more heartily than at the other impersonator shows. At the end, he gets a well-deserved standing ovation.

Gans and Jones are unusual in that they are both one-man shows. Other impersonator shows feature one performer per celeb, and they vary in quality based entirely on the talent of the performers, the trick of their make-up, and sometimes simply the coincidence of physical appearance. At **Barbra & Frank: The Concert That Never Was** ✮ (at the Riviera Hotel and Casino; ☎ 702/794-9433; www.rivierahotel.com; $50, $32 discounted; Tues–Fri and Sun 8:30pm), both performers are dead ringers for their subjects and sing beautifully. Unfortunately, they've imagined that a concert featuring these two legends would be a contentious one, and so much of the act is taken up with bickering and unkind putdowns. When they're not at each others' throats it's actually rather enjoyable. I just wish some director had trimmed about a third off the show.

Frank makes another appearance in **The Rat Pack Is Back** (at the Plaza Hotel Downtown; ☎ 800/633-1777 or 702/952-8000; www.plazahotelcasino.com/entertainment/rat_pack.php $52 at box office, $22 discounted; Sat–Thurs 8:15pm), a show that aspires to bring back the suave camaraderie of the Rat Pack. I love its setting, in one of the grandest old showrooms in Vegas and the horn-laden band is fab. Unfortunately, this show's Frank sings flat, Sammy can't dance, and Dean has all the charm of a chimp. You can do better.

The Fab Four ✮ (in the Miracle Mile Shops, at Planet Hollywood Resort & Casino; ☎ 702/932-1818; $49 adult, $24 discounted; Fri–Wed 5:30pm) is an hour-long concert featuring the many incarnations of the Beatles, from the mop-top hair and Norfolk suit days through Sergeant Pepper and the later post-band period. For me, listening to the Beatles is always a great time, and though "Paul" has some trouble with the higher notes, for the most part the imitation is dead on.

If you want an advance peek at Jay White's impersonation of **Neil Diamond** (at the Riviera Hotel and Casino; ☎ 702/794-9433; www.rivierahotel.com; $50, $24 discounted; Sun–Thurs 7pm), rent the movie *Frost/Nixon* as he appears as the man himself there. I'll be honest, I'm at a bit of a loss reviewing this one, as I never paid much attention to Diamond's work. But the audience I was with seemed to eat it up, and White is certainly a committed performer.

American Superstars (in the Stratosphere; ☎ 800/99-TOWER; www.stratospherehotel.com; $46 adult, $18 discounted; Sun–Tues 7pm, Wed and Fri–Sat 6:30 and 8:30pm) is a variety shows that mixes together celeb tributes from a number of different eras. Justin Timberlake, Madonna, Elvis, Jay Leno, Ann-Margret, and Donna Summer were on offer in 2008, but the shows do change every 6 months or so, so I can only promise that you'll see Elvis (a permanent fixture in this city of 1,000 Elvis impersonators). *One warning:* Some of the performers do lip sync, ruining some of the illusion.

Finally, there's the **Platters, Coasters, and Drifters Show** ✮✮ (in the Sahara; 702/737-3515; $49, $36 discounted; daily 7:30pm), which is a beast of a slightly different shade of faux, because although none of the performers were actually in these groups, they're nearly the same age as the folks who were, and two of the groups have secured permission from the originals to use their name. It leads to a different audience/performer interaction, with less of an emphasis on comparing these folks to the originals (let's be real—does anyone really remember that clearly what the originals were like?) and more of a concert experience. And if you enjoy smooth harmonies and classic pop such as "Up on the Roof," "Poison Ivy," and "Stand By Me," you'll likely love this show.

But this all begs the question: Is it worth it to go see an imitation in a town where the real thing—inevitably more compelling and quirky—is also on display? I personally find Wayne Newton's or Bette Midler's shows, to name just two Vegas headliners, a far better time than any of the impersonators . . . and you can pay less for them than you will Danny Gans.

EROTICA (STRIPPERS, BOTH MALE & FEMALE)

Gander and goose both get their day in Vegas (and it's often the day just before the wedding). These casino-based erotic shows, with their jugglers and singers, are the slightly more refined brethren of the out-and-out strip clubs off the Strip. To read about the latter, go to p. 217.

I'll start with the shows that feature male strippers and are purportedly for women (though gay men will occasionally attend): *Chippendales* ✫✫ (in the Rio, 3700 W. Flamingo Rd.; ☎ 702/777-7776; www.playrio.com; $58, $36 discounted; under 18 not admitted; Sun–Tues and Thurs 8:30pm, Fri–Sat 8:30 and 10:30pm) and *Thunder from Down Under* ✫ (in Excalibur; ☎ 702/597-7600; www.excalibur. com; $44, $24 discounted; under 18 not admitted; Sun–Thurs 9pm, Fri–Sat 9pm and 11pm). *Chippendales,* as you can see from my star rating, gets my endorsement for all-around best. Here, the choreography is fluid, there's the most variety in terms of fantasies fulfilled (fireman, policeman, soldier: Whatever uniform you dig, these hunks will strip out of it), and though it seems odd to say it, the greatest level of commitment in the performances—the guys' gazes are intent, they make eye contact, they dance all out, and they willingly maul any woman who volunteers for special treatment.

Thunder from Down Under is all handsome Aussies. Their dancing is much clunkier, which oddly makes them seem a bit more, well, straight than the *Chippendales'* fellows. And let's face it, that Aussie accent notches up the sexiness quotient. The real downside here is the showroom, which is cheaply done and nowhere near as comfortable or large as the *Chippendales* theater.

If you appreciate the female form, you have seven long-running shows to pick from, each with its own gimmick. If you're going to take a date or your spouse, you'll probably want to choose *MGM Grand's Crazy Horse Paris* ✫✫ (in the MGM Grand; ☎ 877/880-0880 or 702/891-7777; www.mgmgrand.com; $59, $29 discounted; under 18 not admitted; Wed–Mon 8pm and 10:30pm), which is far and away the classiest of the group. Based on the show at the Crazy Horse in Paris, its purpose is to explore the beauty of the female form—*L'Art du Nu* (the art of the nude), as they say—in many different, sometimes slightly Dada-esque settings. So there are numbers where you'll only see the legs of different showgirls at odd angles or where the bodies will be speckled by such bizarre lighting that they won't look like flesh. The pictures they create are truly artful and visually arresting, and the

DON'T FORGET YOUR EARPLUGS (What?)

One word of warning about all three "Chicks Night Out" shows: If you're at all sensitive to noise, stay away; the booming music and endless screaming (reaching a Beatles-on-the-Ed-Sullivan-Show pitch at times) can be headache inducing. If you drink heavily—I'd say half the crowd at these shows arrive already bombed—all of this Dionysian revelry will seem quite appropriate. Otherwise, well, you've been warned . . .

performers may well be the most stunningly lovely in town (though the girls of *Fantasy,* see below, do give them a run for their money). Set in a very small showroom, there's no need to pay for VIP seating here, as every seat is close to the stage.

The second most intelligent tittie show—and only in Vegas would one even think of ranking strip shows in this way—*Fantasy* ✹ (in the Luxor; ☎ 800/557-7428 or 702/262-4400; www.luxor.com; $45, $25 discounted; under 18 not admitted; Mon, Wed, Fri, Sat, Sun 10:30pm, Tues 8pm and 10:30pm) cunningly melds its advertising campaign with the show itself, giving each of its performers a jaunty personality on the posters, which they then act out over the course of the show. Top-notch dancing, a skilled impersonator for comic relief, a comfortable theater, and drop-dead gorgeous girls, make this show an excellent value for those seeking this sort of entertainment.

A gay friend of mine finds fake breasts so fascinating that he goes to see **Crazy Girls** (in the Riviera Hotel & Casino; ☎ 702/794-9433; www.rivierahotel.com; $35, discounted $17; under 18 not admitted; Wed–Mon 9:30pm) each time he's in Vegas, as the boobage here is the most extreme on the Strip. In its own way, the show itself is also extreme, veering from truly sensuous, *Penthouse*-type strip teases to flat-out weird comedy numbers where the girls lip-synch to parody songs such as "Silicone Is a Girl's Best Friend" and "You've Got to Have Boobs." *Crazy Girls* is now in its 22nd year. Look for the brass statues of the nude chorus line out in front of the Riviera; the butts have been polished to a shine.

There's no tease in the strip at **Bite** (in the Stratosphere; ☎ 800/99-TOWER; www.stratospherehotel.com; $57, $24 discounted; under 18 not admitted; Fri–Wed 10:30pm)—the women rip off their bras as if they're on fire, whipping their long hair around in a clunky imitation of MTV video dancers. A vampire-themed show with a coven of leather-clad, toothsome chicks helping their master, a butch, cat-eyed fellow who does cheesy magic tricks, find the "perfect bride." With its pseudo-Satanic rites, flowing blood, and fake "audience participation" (wow, that sexy blonde from the front row doesn't seem to be at *all* upset that her dress is being torn from her body!), it probably embodies every fear that the Religious Right has about what goes on in Vegas.

DAYTIME SHOWS

The best daytime show, in fact one of the most exceptional shows in Vegas period, the *Mac King Show* ✹✹✹ 🧒 (in Harrah's; ☎ 702/368-5000; www.mackingshow.com; $25 box office, $11 discounted, free if you sign up for Harrah's slot club;

Tues–Sat 1pm and 3pm) is that rare breed of entertainment that's not only appropriate for all ages, it's actually a show that junior, grandma, and the hot date you met in Vegas will enjoy. A comedian with a big talent for magic—King is the only magician who was asked to appear on all five of NBC's "World's Greatest Magic Show" specials—King looks like a refugee from *The Music Man,* wearing an old-fashioned plaid suit and a goofy aw-shucks expression. His tricks are oddball illusions (featuring fellows in bear suits, a "cloak of invisibility," and disappearing heads), which he performs with a generous dose of whimsy and intelligence. If there's any justice in the world, he'll soon be headlining his own evening show. He's that good.

I should also mention that ***X-Treme Magic with Dirk Arthur*** (at the Tropicana; ☎ 800/829-9034; www.tropicanalv.com; $24 at box office, $12 discounted; Sat–Thurs 2pm and 4pm) keeps afternoon hours, but with King as his competition, he might as well pack it in. Yes, this is the only show on the Strip to now feature white tigers (ever since Siegfried and Roy's horrific incident), but the poor cats behave like they've been injected with multiple doses of valium, and so does dull Dirk.

From big cats to tiny ones, **Popovitch Comedy Pet Theater** (kids) (in the V Theater, in the Miracle Mile Shops; ☎ 702/932-1818; $49 adults, $18 discounted; Fri–Tues 4pm) is an act you may have caught if you happened to be wracked with insomnia and watching one of the late-night talk shows. You know, the fellow who's trained stray cats to do all sorts of odd and unusual tricks? He intersperses the cats with dogs, and ferrets and mice and, yes, humans, for a mishmash of juggling, silly costumes, a little dance, some acrobatics. All in all, I think anyone under the age of 10 would probably find this show delightful. For those a bit older: It all depends on your tolerance for whimsy and juggling.

CONCERTS, BOXING MATCHES & OTHER BIG-TICKET ITEMS

Las Vegas is now the most expensive stop on concert tours in the United States. Call it an unofficial sucker tax aimed at free-spending tourists.

Daren Libonati, who runs UNLV's Thomas & Mack Center, explained the price policies this way to the *Las Vegas Sun* newspaper: "They're [the band] planning 50 dates. And then they take Vegas and say, 'Let's pretend Little Rock, AR, fails miserably.' If you're a promoter or an agent and you lose money on that date, you want to be able to use Vegas as a makeup." When the Rolling Stones tour rolled through town, for example, Vegas tickets started at $200 more per person (a whopping $570) than anywhere else in the nation.

But heck, you're on vacation. If I haven't steered you away from the concert scene, here's a rundown of the venues:

◆ **The MGM Grand Garden Arena** ✯ (in the MGM Grand; ☎ 800/929-1111 or 702/891-7777; www.mgmgrand.com), a 16,000-seat stadium, brings in the biggies from Madonna to the Jonas Brothers. The arena was patterned after Madison Square Garden and is also home to boxing matches and other sporting events. The Grand Garden's most famous moment was the Mike Tyson/Evander Holyfield ear incident.

Music on the Beach

Leave your shoes on the sandy beach and let the waves lap at your legs as you dance to the poppy tunes of the Go-Gos, or other light and grooving bands, who take over the stage in the middle of this 1.6 million gallon wave pool. **The Mandalay Beach Summer Concert Series** ✯✯ (in Mandalay Bay; ☎ 877/632-7000 or 702/632-7777; May–Sept) is a swell spot to take in shows. Tickets are more affordable than most venues, usually costing less than $50. And there's no assigned seating. Grab a towel and dig in the sand or dance in the warm waters at Mandalay's 11-acre pool area. The series brings in summery bands such as Counting Crows, The Beach Boys, Pat Benatar, and Los Lonely Boys.

- **Mandalay Bay Events Center** ✯ (in Mandalay Bay; ☎ 877/632-7800 or 702/632-7580; www.mandalaybay.com) has stadium-style seating for 12,000 and often hosts boxing matches and other sporting events.
- **The Theater for Performing Arts** (in Planet Hollywood; ☎ 877/333-9474 or 702/785-5000; www.planethollywood.com) can hold up to 7,000, giving it more of a theater than a stadium feel. Along with musicians, it gets touring Broadway shows and comedians.
- **The Thomas & Mack Center** (4505 S. Maryland Pkwy.; ☎ 702/895-3900; www.thomasandmack.com), which holds 18,000, has that hot-dog-in-a-stadium atmosphere, which is appropriate considering it's home to the University of Nevada–Las Vegas sometimes-nationally-ranked Rebels basketball team. It also brings in other sporting events, car and truck shows, the rodeo, and, of course, concerts and festivals.
- **Sam Boyd Stadium** (7000 E. Russell Rd.; ☎ 702/895-3900; www.thomasandmack.com), which is affiliated with the Thomas & Mack Center, holds a whopping 40,000, making it the home to the annual Vegoose music festival, held in late October, which draws in alternative and rock bands and fans from across the country. Sam Boyd is outdoors, so it can be risky, weather-wise, and parking tends to be a nightmare.

SMALLER MUSIC VENUES

- **House of Blues** ✯✯ (in Mandalay Bay; ☎ 702/632-7600; www.mandalaybay.com) brings in the most varied lineup in town, from the largely unknown (The Sound of Animals Fighting) to classics (The Pretenders) and lately lots of comedians with tickets that are occasionally affordable at prices below $20 (though tickets to see mainstream bands are never that low). With three bars, multiple levels, and a maximum occupancy of 1,800 there's an intimacy to HOB that you won't find at the larger venues, but it's far from cozy. Because there are no seats, you can select your own spot.
- **The Joint** ✯ (in the Hard Rock Hotel; ☎ 800/HRD-ROCK or 702/474-4000; www.hardrockhotel.com) tries very hard to feel dangerous. The decor is filled with guns, hypodermic needles, and other nasty objects, and the room is

purposefully rough looking, with dark board walls curved like a whiskey vat. As for it's lineup, it's no stranger to talented niche performers such as Rufus Wainwright and Jet, though it also hosts burnt-out rockers of yesterday, such as Twisted Sister and Guns N' Roses. Prices are, unfortunately, often higher than they should be.

◆ The most affordable concert venue of its size in town, the **Orleans Arena** (in the Orleans, 4500 W. Tropicana Ave.; ☎ 888/234-2334 or 702/284-7777; www.orleansarena.com) specializes in acts that appeal to the whole family, from music to the circus to hockey games. But there's a reason for its affordability. This 8,000-seat, off-Strip midtier casino, which caters to locals as much as tourists, occasionally brings in music acts, though you're more likely to see the tour of *Dancing with the Stars* here or a live version of *High School Musical.*

9

Bars, Clubs & Other Nighttime Diversions

They're of every variety, sinful and non-sinful, chic and cheap, worth a stop and not

by Pauline Frommer and Kate Silver

DRIVE TO VEGAS AT NIGHT AND YOU CAN SEE THE CITY NEARLY AN HOUR before you get there, its glow emerging from the ink black desert. It's a helluva time to arrive, because unlike almost every other city in the world, the streets of Vegas are as alive and crowded at midnight as they are at noon (if not more so). The spotlights bathing the Strip erase any of the dusty tawdriness that's so evident during the day; and the gambling, drinking, and general carousing reaches an "end of days" intensity once the sun has set. You could keep vampire hours in this town, rising at dusk and hitting the pillow at dawn, and truly not miss a thing.

Because the shows of Vegas—the Cirque shows, the various headliners, magicians, impersonators, and more—are such a phenomena in this town, we've devoted one complete chapter to them (see p. 175). In this chapter we'll discuss all the other nightly shindigs: the city's many bars, dives, lounges, ultralounges, nighttime tours, strip clubs, dance clubs, and even the swingers' clubs that help to make Sin City so, well, sinful. There's a lot of territory to cover, so let's dive right in.

CLUBS & "ULTRALOUNGES"

Organic. That's not a word you hear often in discussions of nightlife. But the odd truth is that in other cities, nightlife does have a more organic growth, fueled by what the local population finds "cool" and "of the moment." While the after dark scene in Vegas is glitzy and vibrant, because it's fueled largely by tourists, it's driven more by savvy marketing pros than hipsters looking for the next hot thing. That's particularly true of dance clubs and ultralounges. Because there's no such thing as "local buzz" in a city this transient, the clubs that are hot are those that have appeared in the national gossip magazines and on the TV shows that follow the foibles of celebrities. And here the vicious cycle begins: publicity breeds profits which the nightclub owners then use to "rent celebrities" (yup, Paris and K-Fed and Mariah are paid to party, it's an open secret) which in turn creates more publicity.

So year after year, the same clubs get the crowds while the rest scramble for the overflow. In this section, we'll profile the biggies and then give some (hopefully) compelling arguments why the less "hot" venues may just have as high a ratio of fun.

As for what you'll pay: Prices are all over the map when it comes to clubbing, and vary by who's "hosting" the party, the night of the week and season, and

199

A Truly 24-Hour Town

In this "city that never sleeps" (eat your heart out, New York), many bars and clubs never close—or shut down way, way late in the wee hours of the morning. What's more, there's no Nevada or city law mandating a "last call" for drinks—the liquor keeps flowing 'til you put a stop to it (or the bartender puts a stop to you).

probably the phases of the moon—you just never know. In general, you'll pay between $10 and $30 to get into a club, though women often pay a third less than the guys do.

One note: We've combined ultralounges with clubs because they're really the same thing, the only difference being the lounges are smaller. But at both the prime activities are dancing, drinking, and scouting for someone to take home at the end of the night.

THE "BIG FIVE" CLUBS

Staples of reality TV, with reporters from TMZ permanently camped outside, the following clubs are probably the most difficult to gain entry to and will often be jammed more tightly than a Tokyo subway car. But if you want to party in the orbit of Britney Spears and Lindsay Lohan (knowing that you'll be a distant star to their planets, craning your neck to get a small glimpse of them in the roped-off VIP sections), here's where you want to go:

◆ **PURE** ✪✪✪ (in Caesars Palace; ☎ 877/427-7243 or 702/731-7873; www.purelv.com; Tues and Fri–Sun 10pm–4am). All white in its center room—"pure," get it?—with 36,000 feet total, Pure has long been the Godzilla of Vegas clubs. It was the biggest (until Palazzo opened its own monster in early 2009), and it tends to get the most press coverage (flash: Mariah Carey dancing in the VIP area! Double flash: Lindsay Lohan shows up in her court-ordered ankle monitoring device—now that's some kind of fashion statement!). With four different rooms and a different DJ and sound system in each (playing different types of music—house, rock, re-mix, and hip-hop), this is like one-stop shopping for clubgoers—there's something for everyone. One of the most appealing spots here is the rooftop patio, where you arrive by either glass elevator or winding staircase. "The Terrace," as it's called, hosts a bar, VIP cabanas, and a stunning panoramic view of the Las Vegas Strip. The Pussycat Dolls Lounge is also located here and it offers nightly Burlesque-style shows that are classier than most, being more "tease" than "strip" and featuring women who actually sing and dance quite well, and have the happy good luck of being drop dead gorgeous. Let me put it this way: I'm a straight woman and even I thought this T&A show was enter-taining and darn sexy. Having it as a prequel to dancing is one of the ele-ments that makes Pure such a stellar party place.

◆ **Rain** ✪✪ (in the Palms; ☎ 866/942-7777 or 702/942-6832; www.palms.com; Thurs–Sat 11pm–5am). If you didn't see Rain on the E! Network's *Wild*

On shows, you probably saw it on *Real World: Las Vegas.* And thanks to the publicity, this club is consistently flooded with people. The line outside is so massive they actually have someone taking drink orders to make the wait more palatable. As for the club itself, it's a gargantuan warehouselike space, with a large, open, main room that has none of the enclaves and nooks that more modern clubs have embraced. Though there are many roped off VIP areas, the bulk of the club is a three-story space bordered by walls of water. The dance floor is surrounded by a moat and is consistently packed. Above it hang cranelike mobile metal lights that swing up and down, flashing different colors on the revelers below, and fire regularly explodes, blasting the room with heat. That device, along with Perfecto nights, when giant robots stride around the dance floor, make this one of the more dramatic of the clubs, and we think, more fun than many (despite the horrific lines).

- **Body English** ✿✿ (in the Hard Rock Hotel; ☎ 800/HRD-ROCK or 702/693-4000; www.bodyenglish.com; Fri–Sun 10:30pm–4am). With its dark interiors, mirrored wall, and crystal chandeliers, this is the kind of club Anne Rice would enjoy, if she likes hip-hop, rock, and house music as she gets her goth on. In the depths of the Hard Rock Hotel, beneath The Joint (see p. 197), you descend a dimly lit staircase to get to this club, which might best be described as an elegant dungeon. It's one of the few spots in town in a basement (a desert isn't the best medium for underground structures), and it appeals to a particularly beautiful set of partiers. The dance floor is on the bottommost part of the club, and patrons can be voyeurs, peering down from above. There are also secret nooks and VIP rooms masked with mirrors, adding an even more mysterious allure to the club. Lines can be long but are worth the wait. While so many of the popular clubs try to be on top of the latest trends, Body English manages to do its own thing, and do it successfully. Though by the end of the evening, the decor may have you wishing you'd brought your cape.

- **Tao** ✿✿ (in The Venetian; ☎ 877/883-6423 or 702/388-8588; www.taolas vegas.com; Tues–Wed 11pm–5am, Thurs–Sat 10pm–5am). Four times the size of the original New York location, the line to get in here rivals the population

More About Cover Charges at Clubs

Getting past the velvet ropes may be a free stroll if you're cute, the club needs more women, or the doorkeeper is having a good night. Otherwise, you're likely to get hit with a cover charge which can run anywhere from $5 to $25, depending on the night of the week, the specific "party" being promoted or just the mood of the club's managers. Before paying, look around the lobby of the casino you're in to see if there are any coupons being given out for free entry. It's more common than you'd imagine. You're also less likely to be hit with a cover charge if you arrive early in the evening.

Crowd Control

Huge lines outside are a point of pride for Vegas clubs, so if you're into dancing, you may spend a good chunk of the night single file, double file, or in an enormous unwieldy cluster out front—particularly on Friday and Saturday. We're not kidding: Lines can be hours long, and once you get to the front, you'll find that there's no actual order. You're at the mercy of a power-wielding, eye-contact-avoiding "executive doorman"—bouncer—who gives attractive women priority.

To try and minimize your time in line, try the following strategies:

Call ahead. Many clubs will put you on the guest list at no cost if you merely call and request it. But be on time. Reservations are quickly cancelled if you're late.

Arrive before 11pm. The busiest period at clubs is between 12:30 and 1am, and you'll have a harder time getting in if you show up then.

Group yourself smartly: The larger the group, the longer the wait—especially a large group of mostly or all guys. So split up if you have to but always keep some women with each part of your group (it's much harder for unaccompanied men to get into the clubs).

If you're trying to tip your way in, don't make it obvious. It's a negotiation. Don't wave cash above your head (the IRS has recently been clamping down on unreported tip income, so that tactic will make you *very* unpopular). Discreetly and respectfully hand the doorman $20 and ask if he can take care of you.

DON'T buy a VIP Pass: Can you say "scam"? Many require you get there before midnight (a time when there'd normally be no line) and with others you're paying big bucks just to have someone make the call ahead that you could have made yourself. Again: *Don't* fall for this scam.

Dress to impress. For women: Antediluvian but true—showing more cleavage is a line-skipping tactic. If that's not an option, stick with a little black dress or nice jeans and a sexy or club-wear-style top. For men: Look good. Avoid baggy jeans, shorts, tennis shoes, or work boots. Nice jeans or pants and a collared shirt work well. If you can, attaching yourselves to women waiting in line is all the better.

Look confident. While cockiness never helps, assertiveness never hurts.

of a small town. But if you're bent on seeing A-list celebs, this is one of their destinations. This book's co-author Kate was dining here (there's a surprisingly decent-but-overpriced restaurant and lounge in addition to the club) when Britney Spears threw a birthday party for her then-husband, Kevin Federline, which featured little people running up and down a long table carrying his birthday cake. Charming. Once inside, the line and celeb appeal make sense. The club is stunning, and as over-the-top as themed Vegas gets. It was built to resemble an Asian temple and is strewn with statues of Buddha (271 of them in just one room), red Gothic chandeliers, and a koi pond. Scattered throughout the club are bikini-clad models, bathing in rose-petal-filled bathtubs and it seems, practicing transcendental meditation (they really don't seem to notice the crowd at all). That's about as Zen as it gets here; otherwise expect thumping music and a jam-packed dance floor. The club is now a daytime venue, too (see the box, "Pool Parties").

◆ **Tryst** (in Wynn Las Vegas; ☎ 888/320-9966 or 702/770-3375; www.wynnlas vegas.com; Thurs–Sun 10pm–4am). Interestingly, Tryst has maintained its stature by eschewing advertising and the "Rent a Star" game. Spending not a penny on marketing, it's managed to become the most profitable nightclub in Vegas (according to several sources we interviewed). The keyword here is "class." Yes, there's thumping music and a sprinkling of yahoos getting drunk—this is Vegas after all—but the friendly, respectful demeanor of the staff (all eye candy, by the way), the "library" area, the marble entryway, red-velvet walls, and, most of all, the outdoor space give Tryst a more sophisticated vibe than usual (and this despite its spotlighted stripper pole). The garden out back, with its small grottoes, trees draped with colorful lanterns, and 80-foot waterfall is key in keeping things civilized. Somehow the water sounds, even when mixed with the musical mash up, help give the place a mellower vibe. Women enter free on Thursdays and Sundays.

For the rest of the clubs, we'll try and divide them by particular appeal. We won't really be discussing what kind of crowd each gets because, frankly, that depends on what conventions are in town as much as anything else. Unlike other cities where locals set the tone in the various clubs, here you get basically the same stream of tourist being diverted into each of these "dance ponds." The one exception are "industry nights" when locals are given a discount to get in; these tend to fall during the week rather than on the weekend, so if you're interested in meeting Las Vegans, plan your clubbing for then.

A Word on "Bottle Service"

See those cozy-looking people in the booth off the dance floor, resting their tired feet and chatting it up? They're paying at least $400 for the privilege of sitting down. Well, actually they're paying $400 for that $30 bottle of vodka set in the middle of the table, but without that obscenely expensive bottle, they wouldn't be allowed to occupy that coveted booth. The new rule in Vegas and in many clubs around the country: Seating is reserved for those who order "bottle service." No ifs, ands, or buts. So don't think you're clever if you arrive early and snag a nice sofa for you and your friends. Unless you ante up for a bottle (and $250–$400 is the average going rate), you're going to be unceremoniously booted out, relegated to standing with the "common folk."

ULTRALOUNGE, ULTRA VIEW

High-rise clubs have less of a decor challenge. Nothing they could put on the walls beats the scene through floor to ceiling windows, so most rely on the swirling, glittering spectacle that is Vegas at night to create their ambience. Ones with a view to die for include:

Mix Lounge ★★★ (in THEhotel at Mandalay Bay; ☎ 877/632-7800 or 702/632-9500; www.mandalaybay.com; Sun–Tues 5pm–2am, Wed and Fri–Sat 5pm–4am), on the 64th floor, where even the bathroom stalls have huge windows (stunning views as you do your business). The lounge is attached to Alain Ducasse's swank champagne-and-caviar-style Mix restaurant and is a swell place to come up and just watch the sunset (there's no cover until 10pm). The best place to hang is on the balcony, where you're practically a part of the view. While you're up here, be sure and wander into the restaurant to see what a $500,000 blown-glass chandelier looks like.

VooDoo Lounge ★ (in the Rio; ☎ 800/PLAY-RIO or 702/777-7800; www.riovegasnights.com; nightly 5pm–3am), is technically lower than Mix, being on the 51st floor, but who's counting? The view's what matters and this slightly pulled back one (the Rio is actually west of the Strip) is still jaw-dropping. As for the rest of the ambience it's good kitschy fun with black lights casting a glow on the rudimentary voodoo-design scrawled decor, along with animal skin prints on chairs and a red glow emanating from the bar. The outdoor patio/dance floor is a highlight with an additional bar and go-go dancers who actually appear to be suspended along the skyline.

Then there's **Ghostbar, Moon,** and **The Playboy Club** ★★ (in the Palms; ☎ 702/942-7777; www.palms.com; nightly 8pm–3am). You have a trifecta of mile-high nightlife at the Palms, each with a different appeal. Silver sofas and glass walls give Ghostbar a neat *Jetsons*-vibe. More intimate than the other two, it's more of a place to hang with an overpriced cocktail than dance (though I have seen people sway back and forth or occasionally move their feet here). Ghostbar's biggest disappointment is the famed translucent area on the floor of the patio that's said to give a palm-sweating view straight down the 55 floors to the ground. In reality it's just a rectangle a little bit larger than a laptop, and too scuffed to allow for any sense of anxiety or a clear view. You'll pay one cover charge to get into both the Playboy Club and Moon and the combo of the two is appealing. At Moon you have a rather standard dance club but with a whiz-bang retractable roof that allows you to dance under the stars (which is pretty swell on warm, clear nights). The Playboy Club is ferociously retro, with a roaring fireplace at one end and loving portraits of Hugh with his pipe throughout. Yes, the ladies are squeezed into those viselike bunny outfits; they act as both dealers at the gaming tables and waitstaff. We thought it would be more male-dominated here, but the access to Moon keeps the ratio between the sexes fairly even.

CLUBS & LOUNGES WITH A FLAIR FOR THE DRAMATIC

LAVO ★★ (in the Palazzo; ☎ 702/791-1818; www.lavolv.com; Wed–Sat 11pm–3am) is an offshoot of Tao, with the same sort of movie-set-like looks, here meant to evoke a Mediterranean bathhouse (love those Middle Eastern–style decorative screens, the gently warped tiles, twinkling metal lanterns, and the grand domed ceilings). Continuing with the "let's get sexily clean" theme are bathtubs set in nooks, usually inhabited by models languorously soaping themselves up. One of the smaller dance clubs in town it nonetheless manages to convey a sort of pop-grandeur. Those who eat at the restaurant can enter the club for free and as the restaurant is fairly priced and pretty good, it's a worthwhile strategy.

rumjungle ✪ (in Mandalay Bay; ☎ 877/632-7800 or 702/632-7408; www.mandalaybay.com/dining/rumjunglelounge.aspx; Mon, Wed, and Fri–Sat 11pm–4am; Tues, Thurs, Sun 11pm–2am) is the Cirque du Soleil of nightclubs, with a 22-foot-tall wall of fire at the entryway, aerialists zooming across the room on zip lines, go-go dancers, water walls, and giant drums competing for your attention. You'll need a shot of rum from the world's largest rum bar—measuring 144 feet long and 9 feet high and serving 200 different varieties—just to calm the sensory overload. Yet, despite the symphony of distractions, it works. They all complement each other in some way, brought together by the conga players, who make you feel like you're in some kind of jungle village where rum is consumed like water and dancing is an accepted form of communication. This is not a place that attracts trendsters, so there's usually not much of a wait to get in anymore.

Jet ✪✪ (in The Mirage; ☎ 800/374-9000 or 702/792-7900; www.jetlv.com; Fri–Sat and Mon 10:30pm–4:30am) is actually all about light—psychedelic, swirling, complexly patterned light which you dance through as much as under (it's a very cool experience). Creating these special effects is a one-of-a-kind video lighting grid made of 68 panels that projects colors and images onto the main dance floor below; at $1 million, it's the most expensive club lighting system ever built. Take a look at the DJ booth: Right next to the guy choosing the beats is a fellow playing what looks like a giant keyboard. That's actually the lighting "DJ" who creates the ambience from moment to moment in accordance with what's playing. Beyond the light show, we'll give Jet an extra star for consideration: The outlying areas, both the two rooms off the main one and the areas in the main one where you can stand and watch the action, are actually fairly spacious, and there are small shelves on the walls where you can rest your drink, which is a rarity in the club world. Friday and Monday Mirage guests with room keys enter free.

Ivan Kane's Forty Deuce (in Mandalay Bay; ☎ 877/632-7800 or 702/632-9442; Thurs–Mon 10:30pm–dawn; burlesque shows are every 90 min. starting at 11:30pm) is a tiny speakeasy-styled lounge owned by actor, screenwriter, and nightclub impresario Ivan Kane. There's some dancing here, but its mostly by the dancers in this increasingly coarse burlesque show. Unfortunately, what used to be a charming and witty show has grown rather grim and heavy-handed. We're keeping it in the book in the hopes that it will improve though.

CUTTING EDGE OR COUNTRY

At **Christian Audigier** ✪ (in Treasure Island; ☎ 702/984-7580; www.audigier lv.com; Thurs–Sun 11pm–3am) your outfit can match the decor of the club! Christian Audigier, he of the tight highly decorated club t-shirt and fashionable trucker caps, is expanding his empire into the club world here, and you'll see his swirling, neo-baroque style in the wallpaper, couch coverings, and waitress uniforms. Because the brand recognition is still not quite mainstream, this club does attract more of a younger crowd of folks devoted to this fellow's fashions. Thursday is "decorate a waitress" night, with body paint artists brought in to objectify the gorgeous staff even further.

Pool Parties

Hot DJs, hot bodies . . . hot sunlight? Yes, the latest trend in Vegas nightlife is actually "daylife," parties with all the elements of a night out at the disco but set around a swimming pool. Up and down the Strip and at the chic casinos off it, partiers are lining up to dance, flirt, down $17 cocktails, and stand around in swimming pools (which are usually too crowded during these events for actual swimming).

It's become quite the scene, with revenue for these parties approaching what the dance clubs pull in (Rehab made some $35,000 an hour in 2008 according to the *LA Times*); big spenders splurge on cabanas, which often require the purchase of several bottles of alcohol. For the rest of us plebes, there are lounge chairs and room in the water. Partiers needn't be staying at the hotel in question to attend the pool party (which is a difference from these resorts' usual pool policies), however, there is an entry fee which will vary by day of the week, who's hosting the party, and who the DJ is. In general, you can expect to pay between $10 and $20 if you're a woman; and $30 to $40 for men (sorry fellows!). And sorry again, those under 21 are not admitted to any of these parties.

Here are my picks for the top parties. As you might assume, these venues are only open in the warm weather months (roughly mid-Apr through mid-Oct):

- **Rehab** (at the Hard Rock Hotel and Casino; www.lvrehab.com): The grandfather of all of the pool parties—it pioneered the concept— Rehab is still considered, well, the "sickest" of the parties. Expect crowds in the thousands, lots of alcohol flowing, floating dance floors, top-shelf DJs, and camera crews roving around (TruTV now

You gotta head off the Strip nowadays if mechanical bulls and line dancing are your thing (not to mention mud wrestling which happens every Wed). **Stoney's Rockin' Country** ✪✪✪ (9152 S. Las Vegas Blvd., #300; ☎ 702/435-2855; www.stoneysrockincountry.com; Wed–Sun 7pm–2am) is set in a re-created barn, down to the rough board walls and bales of hay scattered here and there. This is the real McCoy, and cowboy-booted crowds gather here to dance in front of a jumbo screen which plays a rousing mix of Top 40 country hits to an enthusiastic crowd. If you've never line-danced or two-stepped before, show up at 7:30pm for the nightly class. On Thursdays, women's drinks are just $1. Yee haw!

LATE-NIGHT CLUBS

The ultimate in late night, of course, is **Drai's** ✪✪✪ (in Bill's Casino and Gamblin' Hall; ☎ 702/737-0555; www.drais.net; Thurs–Sun 1am–8:30am), which has been around since the '80s and like the classic it is, refuses to change one iota. So you'll still see the zebra-patterned banquettes, the Morehead paintings, and in the films the high jinks here for its reality TV series on the party). Rehab's in session on Sunday afternoons and some Friday evenings as well.

- **Wet Republic** (at the MGM Grand; www.wetrepublic.com): This place puts the "pool" into party with a massive complex of spaces to play and dance in, some with waterfalls, and two filled with salt water (the only salty pools in town). Dancers keep, um, hydrated with Veuve Clicquot slushies and Red Bull Vodka popsicles. Daily 11am to dusk.
- **Moorea Beach Club** (at Mandalay Bay): Yup, you get sand here, 11 acres of it plus indoor, climate-controlled gaming areas right off the waters. And during these parties if you tan, it could be without tan lines as the sunbathing here is "European style" (translation: topless). And no, the topless ladies who come here aren't pros; those would be the gals at the **Sapphire Pool** (at the Rio Hotel and Casino). The Rio has apparently entered the first partnership between a strip club (The Sapphire Gentlemen's Club) and a casino. One of the strippers enticed to come and hang out here by the offer of free food and drinks told Reuters she likes to hang out at the pool so she can "network." I have no idea what to say about that, and I wouldn't dare comment on whether you should go and, er, network back. Open Thursday through Sunday 10am to 5pm.
- **Tao Beach Club** (at The Venetian): An off-shoot of the popular nightclub, it goes for a mellower vibe, with statues of Buddha and Hindu gods dotting the poolside, and a purposefully smaller area to make the experience more sophisticated, a bit less "Girls Gone Wild." Monday to Saturday 10am to sunset, Sunday 10am to 10pm.

"Library" area family photos of owner Victor Drai. When the rest of the town is fairly quiet this place is pumping. It's famous for it's 8-week battle of the DJs which attracts some of the finest talent from across the U.S. Because it's one of the only games in town for those who want to dance 'til dawn, everyone comes here from big-name celebs, to dealers getting off a late shift, to folks with an early morning flight . . . and no hotel room anymore. It's a hilarious mix and has more spirit than pretty much any other dance club in town.

Then there's **Tabú Ultra Lounge** ★ (in MGM Grand; ☎ 877/880-0880 or 702/891-7183; www.tabulv.com; Wed–Sun 10pm–5am). So we all know that after a few drinks your judgment can be off. Well, imagine if you'd had a few and you stuck your hand into a projection of light, and whatever image was there before you stuck your hand in it actually changed? Sure, go on, blink hard and try it again. It still works—and that's not the alcohol talking. It's the "Human Locator" technology, which responds to touch and motion, at work at Tabú. This was Las Vegas' first "ultralounge," and it's set itself apart from all other clubs, lounges, and bars, thanks to the design expertise of Jeffrey Beers combined with master of the surreal Roger Parent, who's a former executive producer of Cirque du Soleil.

The visual indulgence doesn't stop with the lights. There are also lighted, revolving liquor towers at the main bar and a mural that fills an entire wall with its desertscape. Only, this isn't any old mural. It's an "animated mural" that each person will see differently, depending on the lights and images that are projected upon it during the time that they're gazing at it. Plus, the club stays open a good 2 hours longer than most of the others (though not as a late as Drais) so the scene can get truly surreal.

BARS OF ALL TYPES

There are about as many different types of bars as there are cocktails in Vegas. You have themed bars on the Strip, each with their own spelled-out ambience where you'll pay $11 to $17 to drink and rub elbows with your fellow tourists. More functional, nondescript casino bars are also common (you'll generally pay less for your libation here), and if you start tapping away at the slot machine built into the bar, you'll drink for free.

Then there are the off-Strip bars. Many are located in strip malls (there are so many uses for the word "strip" in Las Vegas!) and get by on their video poker profits while also serving as a neighborhood watering hole. Chain bars, like PT's pub, have a sporty overtone and do their part in keeping suburbia intoxicated.

And there are a few stand-alone bars with style and panache, many of which are older and still emanate that Rat Pack Vegas cool. In general, you can expect that if you're gambling $10 to $20, you won't have to pay for your drinks.

One word on hours: Most off-Strip bars are open 24 hours while Strip bars tend to close around 3 or 4am, about the same time as the clubs, but open up again in the late morning or late afternoon, depending on the location.

Below are our picks for the best places on and off the Strip to knock back a few:

BARS ON THE SOUTH STRIP

Nostrovia, comrade! Though **Red Square** ★★ (in Mandalay Bay; ☎ 877/632-7800 or 702/632-7407; Sun–Thurs 5pm–2am, Fri–Sat 4pm–4am) charges inflated Strip prices, it's one of the tourist bars with such quality black humor that it actually appeals to jaded locals, too. Sitting in the shadow of a giant headless Lenin statue, this Russian-themed bar takes you back to the Bolshevik days. More than 100 kinds of vodka are served here, and you might decide to tipple in the "Vodka Locker" (a freezer off the side of the bar; it's here that you'll find the head to that Lenin statue). They no longer require that you buy a complete bottle to drink in here, but there's still more than a little irony in watching people sipping high-priced cocktails in a veritable Siberia (the freezer is kept at a steady 8°F/–13°C temp for the, er, comfort of the patrons).

An even chillier experience is in store at **Minus 5** ★★ (in Mandalay Place; ☎ 702/632-7713; www.minus5experience.com; daily 10pm–3am), North America's only year-round ice bar. And yes, it's minus 5 degrees Celsius (23 Fahrenheit) inside so before entering you're loaned a coat, mittens, hat, and boots so you'll actually enjoy the experience. Once inside, your drinks are served in glasses carved from, what else, ice served by a guy standing behind an ice bar and you sit on an ice couch surrounded by ice sculptures. Every 3 months or so all the ice is traded out to keep it clean and to change up the statues; pre-made ice is shipped in from Canada from a plant that creates ice with no impurities, so it's clear as glass. All this effort is costly, as must be their cooling bills, which is probably why the entrance fee, which includes one drink, is $30 for 30 minutes. It's high, we know, but the cold causes your metabolism to drop, meaning that one drink will get you drunker than you usually get on one drink (you can order two, but you have to down them in 30 min. for safety reasons; a timer is hung round your neck to remind you and the staff). All in all, I found it to be pricey but kinda . . . we have to say it: cool.

What kind of tippling grounds would the Strip be if it didn't offer at least one Irish bar? **Nine Fine Irishmen** (in New York–New York; ☎ 866/815-4365 or 702/ 740-6463; www.ninefineirishmen.com; cover Fri–Sat $5 men, ladies free, local men free; daily 11am–2:30am, with live music 9:15pm) is a two-story Irish pub named for nine Irish nationalists who fought for Irish independence in 1848 and lost. The British government sentenced them to death but commuted their sentence to avoid making them into political martyrs. They were exiled to Tasmania, but only six went. The other three came to America. None are in any way related to this bar, but their story inspired its name. And, no doubt, many toasts. If it looks authentic despite being stuck in the middle of a casino, that's because in a way, it is: Its dark wood decor and deep green furniture were imported from the Old Erin. Because of its tourist draw, this inner casino hideaway is pricier than most Irish pubs, but gets appropriately rowdy thanks to the soundtrack of toe-tapping jig inspiring tunes and, well, because tourists are suggestible and because they're in an "Irish" bar, they feel free to act like they're in an Irish bar. Service isn't great, but if you have enough pints and enjoy looking at the servers' exposed bellies and short kilts, while listening to the live Irish band, you'll stay entertained enough.

For extreme theme overload, there's **Coyote Ugly** (in New York–New York; ☎ 866/815-4365 or 702/740-6330; www.coyoteuglysaloon.com; cover $10 after 9pm; daily 6pm–4am), which is a bar based on a movie that was based on a New York City bar which may or may not be the original Coyote Ugly or the similarly themed Hogs & Heifers (it's a long-standing and rather esoteric debate, as bar debates go). Coyote is part of a chain of 12 bars, all of which are known for their honky-tonk, trash-talking women servers. The walls are studded with bras, license plates, and American flags—and there are no chairs or barstools so it ain't the most comfortable place to hang. But who needs comfort when there are hot barmaids stomping across the bar and screaming at the mostly male crowd? Those daring enough to get up on the stage are thanked with a shot of something brightly colored and overly sweet (like Pucker) poured directly into their mouths. It's primarily a tourist spot. When locals are looking to be abused and titillated they're more likely to head to Hogs & Heifers, located downtown.

"There's televisions everywhere," says an athletic-looking man, practically drooling like Homer Simpson as he walks into **ESPN Zone** ✮ (in New York–New York; ☎ 866/815-4365 or 702/933-3776; www.espnzone.com/lasvegas; Sun–Thurs 11am–midnight, Fri–Sat 11am–1am). With 150 TV screens surrounded by scoreboards, scrolling neon news tickers, and anything else that's distracting and related to sports, this is the ultimate sports bar. And even non-sports fans (like us)

Sing Us a Song, You're the Piano Man

Here's a dirty little secret about the town's dueling piano bars. There are only so many pianists who have the skill to trade jibes while playing duets and leading singalongs. Those with these finely honed talents are in high demand and tend to do a circuit of the bars that offer these entertainments. So while **The Bar at Times Square** (in New York–New York; ☎ 866/815-4365 or 702/740-6969; www.nynyhotelcasino.com; cover $10 after 8pm; 24 hr., with entertainment Sun–Thurs 8:15pm–2:15am, Fri–Sat 8:15pm–3:15am) has a much grittier vibe than the downright elegant cigar bar **Napoleon's** (in Paris Las Vegas; ☎ 877/796-2096 or 702/946-7000; www.parislasvegas.com; Tues–Sun 9pm–1am; a single pianist plays Mon 9pm–1am), you're still going to be hearing a lotta Billy Joel and jokes about breasts in both places, and likely from the same entertainers. The same can be said for **Piano Bar** (in Harrah's; ☎ 800/392-3002 or 702/369-5000; www.harrahs.com; dueling pianos 9pm–2am nightly) though here, two blonde keyboard-playing identical twins are often (but not always) the irresistible draw and manage to draw a crowd inside and outside of the bar, even spilling into the casino's table games area.

Wherever you end up, know that you're going to have to pay to play. If you must hear "Dancing Queen," it'll cost you a tenner (and perhaps some embarrassment as the pianists ask you to explain your choice).

can't avoid getting at least a little carried away with the theme while sitting in the restaurant at a booth with our own touch-screen television and surround-sound speakers. With all of the togetherness a vacation can bring, there's sometimes no better way to spend a meal than staring at a screen (or 150) and taking a break from conversation. Upstairs is an arcade with miniature bowling, air hockey, video games, and more.

BARS ON THE CENTER STRIP

When it comes to a dedicated fan base, Jimmy Buffet's Parrotheads have got to be right up there with the Grateful Dead's Deadheads. Only, we shudder to think of what a Deadhead-themed bar would resemble (pass the brownies, indeed). Not so with **Jimmy Buffett's Margaritaville** (in the Flamingo; ☎ 800/732-2111 or 702/733-3302; www.margaritavillelasvegas.com; daily 10pm–2am), one of seven in a chain, where Hawaiian shirts are practically camouflage in the tropical decor, and boat drinks circulate with wild abandon to the tune of piped-in Buffett songs. The restaurant and bar is three stories tall, going up, up, up to a patio that overlooks the Strip, and the first-floor bar is dwarfed by a three-story volcano that spews margarita mix into blenders every hour. Despite its salt-of-the-earth appeal, Margaritaville charges tourist-style prices, with the average drink costing about $10.

It's not just the bar and grill that Toby Keith loves at **Toby Keith's I Love This Bar & Grill** (in Harrah's; ☎ 800/392-3002 or 702/693-6111; www.harrahs.com;

Mon–Thurs 11:30am–2am, Fri–Sat 11:30am–3am, Sun 10am–2am; live music 9pm–2am). Judging from the interior decorating, he thinks pretty highly of himself, too. Framed pictures of Keith fill the walls. There he is looking pouty. Then coy. Playful. Sexy. Sexily pouty. Poutily coy. You get the picture. The bar is decorated in a kind of nouveau honky-tonk and the crowd has the expected big hair, cowboy boots, and even a rhinestone belt or two. Despite the redneck overtones, this place isn't so overly steeped in its theme that a non-country fan can visit without feeling like a fish who done gone fallen out of the crick. That is, as long as you can stomach a little bit of live country music. Keith selects the bands himself, so if you have an aversion to the electric slide, sit as far from the dance floor as possible.

The bar where patrons are most likely to spontaneously form a conga line is **Kahunaville** ★ (in Treasure Island; ☎ 800/288-7206 or 702/894-7390; www.kahunaville.com; daily 11am–2am). It's a loud and festive place where the staff won't berate you, but they may throw things. This bar and restaurant is tropical-themed in decor and relaxed in atmosphere, with flair bartenders (a la Tom Cruise in *Cocktail*), who juggle bottles, throw ice, and dance to the tune of their own mixology as they prepare popular frozen drinks that are bubbling with dry ice. Don that Hawaiian shirt if you really want to fit in.

BARS ON THE NORTH STRIP

The **Horse-A-Round Bar** ★★★ (in Circus Circus; ☎ 877/434-9175 or 702/734-0410; www.circuscircus.com; Fri–Sat 4:30–11:30pm) is a mandatory stop for lovers of the surreal. Set in the middle of the casino's Midway, where children scream for money and stuffed animals, and the looks on adults' faces hint that they might be resisting infanticide, the Horse-A-Round Bar is a revolving carousel, lined by horses and poles. The area where the actual bar is remains stationary as the chairs and booths swirl around it, and harried parents duck in for a quick shot. It's no wonder that Hunter S. Thompson couldn't resist highlighting this bar in *Fear and Loathing in Las Vegas*.

Vintage Vegas

No Las Vegas visit is complete without a stop at **Peppermill Fireside Lounge** ★★★ (2985 Las Vegas Blvd. S.; ☎ 702/735-4177; www.peppermilllasvegas.com; 24 hr.). With the bubbling fire pool, mirrored walls, circular booths, neon tubes of blue and pink, and cocktail servers dressed in elegant black gowns, this is the epitome of what Vegas once was. In a city where implosion trumps preservation, it's a wonder that the Peppermill is still around. Voted one of "America's 10 Best Make-Out Bars" by *Nerve* magazine, this is not the bar to bring someone who wants to be "just friends." It is, however, the bar to bring someone who appreciates colorful cocktails and who can hold their liquor—the signature Scorpion ($15) is an alky's dream come true, with six different kinds of liquor and ice cream, and is served in what looks like a fishbowl. It tastes great going down but by the time you get to the bottom of the 64-ouncer, the flavor will be the least of your concerns.

Teetotalers Beware

One of the reasons Las Vegas is called Sin City is that its residents and leaders don't hide their vices behind closed doors. Take Mayor Oscar Goodman, a former mob lawyer. If you couldn't tell by his red nose, you'll catch on quickly by that martini in his hand: He loves to drink, and gin is his hooch of choice. In 2002, the mayor became a spokesperson for Bombay Sapphire Gin. The $100,000 he received for the project was split between a local private school founded by his wife and the other half went to pay for services for the homeless. Goodman is a regular at Triple George, where they strive to have his Sapphire martini with a blue cheese–stuffed olive ready when he walks through the door.

BARS DOWNTOWN

Mayor Oscar Goodman has heavily focused on revitalizing Downtown in recent years, and the effort has really started to ferment. A couple of different pods of bars have popped up, catering to a crowd that's divided between tourists and locals. Though some of the spots are in areas that used to primarily draw prostitutes and drug dealers, the city's efforts are beginning to show signs of progress.

Dino's (1516 Las Vegas Blvd. S.; ☎ 702/382-3894; www.dinoslv.com; 24 hr.; karaoke with Danny G Thurs 9pm, Fri–Sat 10pm; no credit cards) bills itself "The Last Neighborhood Bar in Las Vegas," and none of its regulars would dare contest that. Once you've visited a few times, the patrons here are like family . . . in a creepy, drunken uncle kind of way. Still, if dive bars are your speed and you've got a thick skin, it's a diamond in the Las Vegas rough. Heck, you may make it into the running for the monthly "Drunk of the Month" competition (the winner gets a premier parking spot). There's a small stage that's run by Danny G, the karaoke king, who does a killer rendition of Pure Prairie League's "Amy" and anything Elton John, entertaining the drunkards 3 nights a week.

Owned by one of Mayor Oscar Goodman's favorite Elvis impersonators, **Art Bar** ★ (1511 S. Main St.; ☎ 702/437-2787; 24 hr.; cash only) is low on frills (aside from the Velvet Elvis room) and cheap on booze. This lurid-green bar is located in the heart of the burgeoning Arts District and displays the works of local artists. Though it could be said that some of the unique drinks here are works of art themselves—try a shot of Burnin' Love, which is an actual plastic shot filled with Jell-O and vodka injected into your mouth ($5, or two for $8), or sample *Agwa de Bolivia,* which involves an elaborate production of chopping up lime salt in lines a la Robert Downey, Jr., that are then sucked through a straw into your mouth and are said to activate the coca leaf within the herbal drink. Art Bar has great happy hour specials ($1 domestic beer and two-for-one well drinks), has free Wi-Fi, and draws in the angst-ridden artists.

FREMONT STREET AREA BARS

In our favorite area for bar-hopping in all of Sin City, the three bars just a block east of the canopy of the Fremont Street Experience each have a gritty, unique vibe and attract the most vibrant young crowd in town. At **Beauty Bar** ★★ (517 Fremont St.; ☎ 702/598-1965; www.beautybar.com; Sun and Tues–Thurs 9:30pm–2am, Fri–Sat 9:30pm–4am) the spirit of a salon meets a salon of spirits. It's part of a chain of six bars that originated in New York and were made popular by *Sex and the City*. Old hair dryers and beauty chairs, which were salvaged by owner Paul Devitt from the Capri Salon of Beauty in Trenton, New Jersey, line the pink sparkly walls, providing the few available seats. You'll often get arts events along with your libations here; the last time we visited, a painter was doing abstract portraits of customers out front, a band was playing in the backyard, and a manicurist was busy giving "nail demonstrations" at the front (legally she couldn't be giving a manicure in a place that serves alcohol, but there is painting of nails going on here; go figure).

Two storefronts over, **The Griffin** ★★★ (511 Fremont St.; ☎ 702/382-0577; Mon–Sat 5pm–close, Sun 9pm–close) has a Kerouac/James Dean kind of hipness to it, a moody bar with arched brick ceilings, dim lighting, two round open fireplaces in the center, and lots of nooks for groups to gather and talk intensely about poetry (okay, they might be discussing sports, but you wouldn't feel out of place spouting a sonnet here). A killer jukebox with an eclectic selection of indie hits adds to the appeal as does the crowd itself, which is sexy, young, and very chill. They have talented and friendly bartenders, too.

And just around the corner is the slickest of the bars in this particular barhopping jaunt, **Downtown Cocktail Room** ★ (111 S. Las Vegas Blvd.; ☎ 702/880-3696; daily 5pm–close), which could have been airlifted from Los Angeles. It has that SoCal cool, with a deep red and bamboo decor, scorching bartenders, and a crowd that looks like they rarely step out of their stilettos. Still, it's a reasonably sane place for a drink with music that's never too loud for conversation and the kind of dark lighting that erases all facial evidence that you partied too ferociously the night before.

BARS AT THIRD & OGDEN

When the Henry Brent Co. purchased the old Lady Luck casino in 2005 with plans to renovate, they also purchased the block across the street. Hoping to capture the barhopping, urban spirit of San Diego's Gaslamp Quarter, a series of bars have opened up. There's a long way to go before the Gaslamp comparisons are on target, but because many locals still avoid going Downtown, it's generally easy to find a seat at any of the following:

From its African teak floor to its retro pillows and white leather couches, **Sidebar** ★ (201 N. 3rd. St.; ☎ 702/384-2761; www.sidebarlv.com; Sun–Thurs 3pm–midnight, Fri–Sat 3pm–2am) located in a block-long building that also includes Hogs and Heifers, is a refreshing upscale alternative to the club and dive bar scene that rules the town. With monthly wine tastings and food prepared by the chef from Triple George, the restaurant next door, Sidebar is the perfect place to sip a sidecar and discuss the revitalization of urban Las Vegas.

If your neck's feeling a tinge red (and your mood is tolerant) keep on walking down to **Hogs & Heifers** (201 N. 3rd St.; ☎ 702/676-1457; www.hogsandheifers. com; daily 1pm–4am; no credit cards) where the beer guzzling, rowdy, female-run bar stylings are similar to Coyote Ugly. You might want to avoid mentioning that here. They're like the Hatfields and McCoys when it comes to who started this shtick first. This biker bar is run by sexy bartenders, who shout at the crowd and dance on the bar, inviting customers to do the same. The clientele is heavily male, as well it should be, considering the way the bartenders seem to ignore female patrons and go straight for the testosterone. So, if you like your domestics cold and your women mean, Hogs & Heifers won't disappoint.

OTHER FUN LOCAL BARS

The best bars in Vegas are the ones that aren't connected to chains or replicas of cool from other cities. They're the homegrown places built by locals with locals in mind. These are the places where you'll get a true taste of what people who live in this offbeat, tourism-driven town are like.

Dark, dingy, and dive-ish, **The Double Down** ★★★ (4640 Paradise Rd.; ☎ 702/791-5775; www.doubledownsaloon.com; 24 hr.; no credit cards) is a Las Vegas institution. Recently named one of the nation's top bars by *Esquire* magazine, it's splayed with trippy murals painted by local artists and has pinball machines and pool tables to break up the drinking. Tattoos mingle with suits, piercing is rarely used as an adjective, and "Ass Juice" (it's a secret recipe) and bacon martinis (complete with their own oil slick as garnish) are signature drinks. There's never a cover charge here, and they bring in local and imported bands (surf, punk, rockabilly, and more) and sell "Puke Insurance" for $20: If you buy it and you puke, they'll clean it up. Otherwise, as one of their signs says, "You puke you clean."

The Freakin' Frog ★★ (4700 Maryland Pkwy., #8; ☎ 702/597-9702; www.freakinfrog.com; daily 11am to "until the freakin' fun is done") is the beer lover's Tower of Babel. It takes a dossier of a menu to outline the more than 500 kinds of beer and 300 kinds of wine. Situated across from the University of Nevada–Las Vegas, the crowd here is a smart mix of students, professors, and beer snobs, and they serve up some mean corn dogs and fried macaroni and cheese (that is, "Crack N Cheese"). The atmosphere is brighter than most bars and fairly plain, save for a piano that musicians have been known to play in exchange for their bar tab. This is more of a place to meet and have an intellectual discussion about Lithuanian beer while watching the cult classics that play on the big screen than it is a place to whoop it up like a drunken frat boy.

Dark and ornate, **Hookah Lounge** ★ (two locations within Paymon's Mediterranean Cafe: 4147 S. Maryland Pkwy.; ☎ 702/731-6030; and 8380 W. Sahara Ave.; www.paymons.com; Sun–Thurs 5pm–1am, Fri–Sat 5pm–3am) is a romantic Middle Eastern nook where even nonsmokers indulge in the flavored tobacco water pipes. Sit down in the plush red velvet seats, and a hookah master will soon approach, offering you such tempting flavored tobacco as Turkish, apple, jasmine, cherry cola, and more. Then, take your disposable mouthpiece and puff away! (No, it's not the wacky tobaccy, and no, you can't supply your own, and yes, they've already been asked that 10 million times.) A low-key spot that's conducive to conversations, Hookah is perfect for small groups or a date. The lounge is attached to Paymon's Mediterranean Cafe. Stop in for happy hour (5–7pm) when most drinks and hookahs are half-price.

The Artisan ✦ (1501 W. Sahara Ave.; ☎ 702/214-4000; www.theartisanhotel. com; 24 hr.) is just a dab over-the-top in about everything it does, but hey, so is Vegas. From the fountain in the lobby to the paintings, dangling golden frames festooned on every inch of every wall and even every inch of the ceiling, and ornate statuary, there's simply no place else in this town, or other towns, like it. With a killer happy hour (two-for-one house wines, wells, and domestics) the lounge/bar here is the perfect place to kick back on one of their comfortable couches and make use of the free Wi-Fi, or grab a book out of one of the many bookshelves and learn a thing or two while you drink. See p. 197 for a review of the hotel.

GAY BARS

Because of Vegas' transient nature (8,000 people moving here a month, 2,000 leaving), the town lacks a sense of community in most cultures and subcultures, and the GLBT arena is no different. The conservative and Mormon overtones that heavily influence the city and its politics also don't make for the most gay-friendly city. Not that the atmosphere is openly hostile. It's just that the political climate of the town, by and large, isn't exactly progressive. But in the past few years, more gay bars have opened up in the area off Paradise Road between Flamingo Road and Tropicana Avenue, now called the "Fruit Loop." Perhaps more tellingly, a gay club has opened on the Strip itself and it's thriving (see below for more on Krave).

Sometimes otherwise "straight" venues host gay nights as well; for information on these changing venues, as well as entertainment news and listings, pick up a copy of *Q Vegas* (**www.qvegas.com**), available at LGBT nightclubs and bookstores, Borders, Tower Records, most libraries. There's also a calendar of events at **www. gaylasvegas.com**.

GAY NIGHTLIFE ON THE CENTER STRIP

Krave ✦✦ (3663 Las Vegas Blvd. S., in Planet Hollywood; ☎ 702/836-0830; 11pm–close, closed Mon) has officially (and successfully) brought "alternative" to the Strip. It's about time. Playing the roles of theater (the Harmon Theater is here), lounge, and nightclub, and catering to both tourists and locals, Krave has found multiple niches and is filling them all quite well. It's a lesbian hot spot on Saturday nights, hosts "So you think you can strip?" parties on Wednesdays, Latin night on Thursday, and something else every day of the week.

Krave sells "memberships," which may well be a ploy for them to make money, but if you're planning on visiting the club often it will, indeed, help you to save. General memberships cost $25 for 6 months and net you about $5 off the cover charge (usually $20) and allow you to take advantage of cheap drink specials.

GAY BARS IN THE "FRUIT LOOP"

The best gay club hopping is on Paradise Road; here are my picks for the best of the best here:

8½ Ultra Lounge and **Piranha Nightclub** ✦✦✦ (4633 Paradise Rd.; ☎ 702/ 791-0100; www.gipsylv.net; nightly 9pm–close) have become two of our favorite places in Las Vegas—gay, straight, or otherwise. Though both are in the same

Nighttime Tours of Las Vegas

Not all of Vegas' history has been imploded away. With these two nighttime tours, you get to experience some of the most gruesome but fascinating aspects of the city's past.

◆ **Haunted Vegas Tours** (☎ 702/737-5540; www.hauntedvegastours. com; $56, discounted $26; children under 13 not admitted; Sat–Thurs 9:30pm). If you think Vegas is spooky at night, you're not alone. Countless suicides, bloody warfare among the settlers and Native Americans, and mafia hits have filled this town with ghosts . . . or so say the experts (quacks?) who study this sort of thing. According to them, there are 21 documented haunted sites in Vegas and it was only a matter of time before someone concocted a tour to see many of them. Led by an Alistair Cooke look-alike (he's quite a funny guy with a deep knowledge of local history), this witching hour bus tour hops from the Flamingo Hotel, where you wander the gardens looking for Mafioso Bugsy Siegel; to a park in Henderson where a group of settlers were supposedly murdered by Native Americans; to the former home of Redd Foxx, now an office. I can't say whether it was the power of suggestion, but a number of us on the tour were sure we saw someone moving the blinds as we parked outside. You'll find discount coupons for the tour all over town as well as big discounts at the Tix 4 Tonight booth, so keep an eye out for them. The tour lasts 2½ hours.

◆ **Las Vegas Mob Tour** (www.vegasmobtour.com; $56, discounted TK; children under 16 not admitted; Sat–Thurs, 6pm) actually covers some of the same ground as the Haunted Vegas tour (so I wouldn't recommend doing both; you'll spend way too much time staring at strip mall parking lots and wandering through the Flamingo), but in some ways it's even more gruesome. Get ready for a lot of talk about heads being put in vices, popping eyeballs, and rivers of blood. At 2½ hours, this one feels a bit long (in fact it feels longer than the haunted tour), but those who are into the history should enjoy it. Retired FBI agent Dennis Arnoldy, former mobster Frank Culotta, and journalist Dennis Griffen were all involved in the scripting of the tour, so its filled with telling details and unusual insights into the mob culture that shaped Vegas. Along with driving to different stakeout and murder spots, a video plays so you get to see the mugs of the mugs you're discussing.

building, they offer two distinct atmospheres. 8½ Ultra Lounge (named for the Fellini film, or . . . something else?) manages somehow to feel like a swanky house party, between its decor and regular beer busts (all-you-can-drink beer for cheap), its different rooms, done in lush reds, filled with comfortable seating in discreet nooks. The bar is enormous and maintained by shirtless male bartenders who are all impressively ripped. In addition to different theme nights, such as BVD night, eye candy night, and karaoke, they offer happy hour with $2 drink specials until midnight.

Where 8½ is warm yet sophisticated, there's a stark minimalism to Piranha Nightclub—and a coolness that matches the aquariums full of actual piranha that line the entry. Both Piranha and 8-½ bring in different DJs that play different music each night, and they target different genders, depending on the date. Wednesday is Orchid Night, for women, and Thursday is Boy's Night. All are welcome, but I've found that the men tend to outnumber the women. 8-½ and Piranha are the most upscale of the gay bars along the Fruit Loop, which tend to be exceedingly casual. Enter Piranha Nightclub from 8-½ Ultra Lounge, or use the separate patio entrance.

Next door is **Gipsy** ★★ (4605 Paradise Rd.; ☎ 702/731-1919; www.gipsylv. net; Wed–Mon 9pm–close; no credit cards), which is practically an icon on the Nevada gay scene, having been around more than 2 decades. It's easy to strike up a conversation here, the staff is friendly and they're welcoming to all. The club is centered around a stage and dance floor, and like Piranha and 8-½, there are different nightly themes and entertainment, from female impersonators to DJs to go-go dancers and beer busts (these all-you-can-drink fests are popular in the Fruit Loop). Males dominate, but there's a decent number of women in here, too. Gipsy is under the same ownership as Piranha.

Aside from the once-a-week "girlbar" at Krave, Las Vegas doesn't have any lesbian bars. They're all either directed towards men or mixed. When it comes to the ratio of women to men, **Freezone** ★ (610 E. Naples Dr.; ☎ 702/794-2310; www. freezonelv.com; 24 hr.) is about as close as it gets to being predominately lesbian, though there is still a fair share of men—and the bartenders are male and topless. Freezone is a little bit of everything: dance club (complete with stripper pole), pool hall, foosball hot spot, a lesbian club (Tues), and a gay club (Thurs). It's the Goldilocks of gay bars: not too fancy, not to divish, but just right. It's also a popular dance spot for straight women who don't feel like fending off the wandering palms of strange men. They have unbeatable $1 happy hour specials daily from 4 to 8pm, and an array of beer and liquor (or, "Lick Her," as they call it) busts throughout the week.

Filled with bristly, brawny men who immediately bring the bar's name to life, **The Buffalo** (4640 Paradise Rd.; ☎ 702/735-8355; 24 hr.) is lined with ads about contests concerning leather, chest hair, and bears (large, hairy gay men). If you're a woman here, you're going to stick out, but you'll probably just be ignored. Drinks are cheap and served in plastic cups, and pool tables give these men ample opportunity to show off their stick-handling abilities.

STRIP CLUBS

Strip—"gentleman's"—clubs are to Las Vegas what the theater is to New York and sports are to Chicago, though with more cleavage and less social acceptability. They're a specialty, and considering the reputations they must maintain, they rarely disappoint.

There are different levels of strip club. The ones we've gone into in the most detail are some of the more popular topless clubs. Here, women don't quite go the

Full Monty—a skimpy thong tends to cover the most private of parts. In recent years, these clubs have taken on an upscale nightclub approach. With elegant furnishings and bottle service, this is no longer your big daddy's smoky grind joint. Though there are certainly still a number of seedy options, the larger clubs are all competing to be the biggest around with the most beautiful women and, even, oddly enough, the nicest restaurants. Per the rules of capitalism, competition has done the industry good. Nevada residents should note that many of the clubs waive the cover charge with a local ID.

Las Vegas also has a number of all-nude clubs, such as **Little Darlings** (1514 Western Ave.; ☎ 702/366-1633; www.littledarlingsnv.com; cover $25; Mon–Sat 11pm–6am, Sun 6pm–4am), where it's all flesh, all the time, but because of the nudity, these places aren't allowed to serve alcohol. The only exception is **The Palomino Club** (1848 N. Las Vegas Blvd.; ☎ 702/642-2984; www.palominolv.com; cover $20, plus 2-drink minimum; daily 4pm–5am), which opened in 1969 and was grandfathered in when the Clark County government decided that the nudity and alcohol were perhaps too complementary and shouldn't be served at the same place.

A few things to keep in mind about strip clubs is that the dancers here are for you to look at, not touch—even when said performer is grinding on your lap. In Las Vegas, there's no minimum distance requirement, meaning the dancer can come as close as she wants—and the more money you have to offer, the closer she will get. The standard for lap dances is $20, and there's the more intimate option of V.I.P. services, which mean the dancer (or entertainer—do not call these women "strippers") will generally escort you to a more private area and give you three or more dances for a set fee, usually about $100. If you're interested in watching and not being touched, you can sit around the stage where the women perform. But if you sit here, be prepared to tip.

Remember the movie *Showgirls?* **Cheetah's** ★★ (2112 Western Ave.; ☎ 702/384-0074; www.cheetahsnv.com; cover $10; 24 hr.) used to be famous for its cameo role in it (before the lead becomes a showgirl, she's shown working as an exotic dancer here). In the last several years, that's been eclipsed by the FBI's Operation G-Sting, an investigation into extensive political corruption that's even managed to shock jaded Las Vegas locals. Cheetah's was the place local politicians worked out backdoor deals and played around with "no touching" ordinances and distance requirements for dancers in exchange for cash.

It's easy to understand why this was their choice. It's lively and loud, and, unlike Club Paradise and Sapphire, where the fleshy distractions are the main attraction, Cheetah's is set up more like a regular bar, with areas where men can

For Men Only?

Many of the strip clubs will not allow women in unless they're escorted by a man—presumably to protect ogling husbands from suspicious wives. If you're looking for a ladies' night out and want to check out the topless action, be sure and call ahead to find out what each individual club will allow.

Question Your Cabbie

If there's a particular strip club that you want to visit, don't let your cab driver talk you out of it. Clubs give cab drivers kickbacks for delivering customers. So be leery of drivers who suggest one club over another. They may be making $20 for delivering you there. And don't accept a higher cover charge than we've listed here; the clubs are trying to get you to cover the kickback they just gave the cabbie.

do business and then pause when they feel like a lap dance (before getting back to business). It's loud, dim, and packed—enough so that your (or a politician's) anonymity can be maintained.

Known for its especially beautiful strippers and "ultralounge" vibe, **Club Paradise** ✪ (4416 Paradise Rd.; ☎ 702/734-7990; www.clubparadise.net; cover $20; daily 5pm–6am) is one of the few clubs in town where women aren't required to have a male escort (but they do have to pay the cover). When the dancers here aren't performing, they make their way through the crowds in elegant gowns that, with quick sleight of hand, seem to just disappear, giving way to the flesh. Breasts are everywhere.

In addition to the shows on the main stage and side stages (and by show we mean one or two dancers writhing to music), aerialists dangle from the ceiling throughout the night, and choreographed shows interrupt the stripping monotony.

The classic Vegas strip joint, **Olympic Garden** (1531 Las Vegas Blvd. S.; ☎ 702/385-9361; www.ogvegas.com; cover $20; 24 hr.) is a favorite among purists because of its no-frills appeal. Laid-back and unpretentious, yet not divey or seedy, men sit around three stages watching topless women dance. One of its downfalls is that if you're not sitting around the stage, there just aren't too many seating options. The OG may lack the glitz and marble of some of the newer spots, but the entertainers are still attractive (some are even natural). Upstairs, the **Men of Sapphire** perform for ladies on Friday and Saturday nights (p. 221).

Sapphire ✪ (3025 Industrial Rd.; ☎ 702/796-6000; www.sapphirelasvegas. com; cover $20; 24 hr.) was described by Jay Leno as the place "where Costco meets Hooters." Like the, ahem, enhancements of many dancers, the club is huge—the showroom, alone, is 10,000 square feet, and posh. It's one of the new breed of high-end gentleman's clubs, and, like Club Paradise, is similar to an "ultralounge," where the entertainment just happens to be topless. And rubbing on your lap. Sapphire Women are everywhere, and so are patrons, but tables are spread out, giving more privacy, and there's an air of sophistication. You can choose to sit at one of three bars, in VIP skyboxes, or even at a table located below the see-through stage. The stage is multiple levels, and there's no such thing as a bad view.

Spearmint Rhino ✪✪✪ (3440 S. Highland Dr.; ☎ 702/796-3600; www. spearmintrhino.com; cover $20; 24 hr.) is the big daddy of strip clubs. There's simply no comparison. While all of the clubs have dancers roaming around, Rhino is teeming with them—all 18,000 square feet of the club stay crowded. It's like a

Sex Doesn't Sell—Legally

Prostitution is not legal in Las Vegas proper, as it's part of Clark County, one of three counties in Nevada where the profession is banned. For that kind of action you'll have to drive to a brothel in Nye County, the closest of which lie in the town of Pahrump—"head over the hump to Pahrump," as residents like to say. The two most popular are **The Chicken Ranch** (www.chickenranchbrothel.com) and **Sheri's Ranch** (www.sherisranch.net). Besides being illegal in Las Vegas, the venues that seem to be advertising sex aren't always legitimate. Places known as "clip joints" take men in and tease them out of hundreds of dollars, only to turn them away last minute before any services are actually rendered. Conversely, there are massage parlors and escort services, which are known for going a bit further than they advertise. If you're having trouble falling asleep in your hotel room one night, it's interesting to breeze through the "Escort" section of the Yellow Pages. There are practically enough entries for classification as a novella. If you call them up and engage in acts of prostitution you are taking a risk. If you're caught, you will be prosecuted.

refined Cheetahs, multiplied by 10, with scads of beautiful, nearly nude women everywhere, and men, dripping in pheromones, enjoying the view.

Known for having some of the hottest entertainers in Vegas, Rhino is part of a chain, which, in Vegas, is rarely a bad thing. With its dark paneling, leather seating, and curtained VIP cabanas, this club was clearly designed by men for men, and then doused with estrogen for their viewing pleasure. Be sure and take out money before you come here—the on-site ATM charges an exorbitant $5 fee to make a withdrawal.

STRIP CLUBS FOR WOMEN

As one of only two options in town to see male strippers (where is the equality?), **Olympic Garden** (1531 Las Vegas Blvd. S.; ☎ 702/385-9361; www.ogvegas.com; cover $20; Sun and Wed–Thurs 9pm–2am, Fri–Sat 8pm–4am) is packed with squealing, giggling, flushed women. They surround the single stage where, occasionally, a man will thrust and gyrate to music. But most of the entertainment takes place on the floor, where nearly nude men (they're wearing about the equivalent of a sock with a strap) wander through the club, trying to talk the women into buying a $20 lap dance.

Watch as the women's faces change from innocently shy when the dancing begins to coy to flummoxed as a ridiculously muscular and well-endowed man practically dry humps them. If you come here expecting to just watch the dancers, you better have strong resolve and the ability to repeatedly say "no thank you." The men are here to make a living, and they know how to talk you out of $20. And if you're not buying, your friends will probably be doing it for you. It's some kind of unwritten rule (until now!) that women are more likely to buy dances for refined Cheetahs, multiplied by 10, with scads of beautiful, nearly nude women everywhere, and men, dripping in pheromones, enjoying the view.

Known for having some of the hottest entertainers in Vegas, Rhino is part of a chain, which, in Vegas, is rarely a bad thing. With its dark paneling, leather seating, and curtained VIP cabanas, this club was clearly designed by men for men, and then doused with estrogen for their viewing pleasure. Be sure and take out money before you come here—the on-site ATM charges an exorbitant $5 fee to make a withdrawal.

STRIP CLUBS FOR WOMEN

As one of only two options in town to see male strippers (where is the equality?), **Olympic Garden** (1531 Las Vegas Blvd. S.; ☎ 702/385-9361; www.ogvegas.com; cover $20; Sun and Wed–Thurs 9pm–2am, Fri–Sat 8pm–4am) is packed with squealing, giggling, flushed women. They surround the single stage where, occasionally, a man will thrust and gyrate to music. But most of the entertainment takes place on the floor, where nearly nude men (they're wearing about the equivalent of a sock with a strap) wander through the club, trying to talk the women into buying a $20 lap dance.

Bachelor Party Basics

If you're headed to Sin City for a last fling before the Big Day, I'm assuming you've got the "strip club" part of the itinerary covered, since you're looking at this section of the book. But the bachelor party can't begin and end at that (well, it can, but you'll come off the weekend stinking of smoke, with a major hangover and a serious dent in your wallet . . . even if you've put it in your back pocket). Here are some other items to consider:

1. **Daytime activities.** Sure, sleeping all day is a possibility. But isn't there always some guy in the group who wakes everyone up and tries to guilt them into "doing something"? If your group's athletic, consider a hike at Red Rock Canyon (p. 284). Pals who enjoy competing against one another? Spend the day at golf (p. 143), learning to indoor skydive (p. 146) or doing target practice with machine guns (p. 172). Into more intellectual pursuits? Head to the Atomic Testing Museum, (p.125) a Smithsonian affiliate.

2. **Food.** Since the "gentleman's clubs" are off the Strip, take the opportunity to dine off Strip, too. Prices will be lower and you're less likely to encounter waits. Some excellent off-Strip options include Raku (p. 109), Lotus of Siam (p. 100) and Lindo Michoacan (p. 100)

3. **Getting wheels.** As we said earlier, if you show up at a strip club in a taxi, you'll end up paying significantly more because you'll be covering the kickback your driver gets. Instead, rent a car or van for your group. It'll give you a wonderful sense of freedom, too. And let's face it: That may be the last taste of freedom the groom-to-be enjoys!

Watch as the women's faces change from innocently shy when the dancing begins to coy to flummoxed as a ridiculously muscular and well-endowed man practically dry humps them. If you come here expecting to just watch the dancers, you better have strong resolve and the ability to repeatedly say "no thank you." The men are here to make a living, and they know how to talk you out of $20. And if you're not buying, your friends will probably be doing it for you. It's some kind of unwritten rule (until now!) that women are more likely to buy dances for their friends than themselves. Keep your eyes on those "friends."

You might want to wear your garlic and crucifix to **The Men of Sapphire** ★ (3025 S. Industrial Rd.; ☎ 702/796-6000; www.menofsapphire.com; cover $25; Fri–Sat 10pm show). Kate was sitting quietly in the back of the "Playgirl Lounge," minding her own business while a firefighter or police officer or some such stereotypical fantasy was disrobing on stage, when Marcus from Transylvania (whose onstage character is the *Phantom of the Opera*) came over and tried to talk me into a lap dance. I politely declined and then felt something sharp and wet on my shoulder. "Come on," he said, devilishly. "I don't bite. Hard." My shoulder begs to differ.

The Men of Sapphire is a kind of Chippendales-meets–Olympic Garden. There's a choreographed show taking place on stage, and the men (who are all in incredible shape and almost questionably well endowed) are acrobatic musclemen, with routines ranging from back flips, to pushups on chairs, to yogalike balancing acts with women on top of them, all the while mouthing the words to the song that's playing. It's corny and crass, but that tends to be the norm when it comes to male strippers.

Despite an immediate desire for Purell (and a tetanus shot), I prefer Sapphire to Olympic Garden, because there's always something going on onstage, and even if it's laughable, a lot of choreography has gone into the show, and for what it is, it's well done. If you do choose to get a lap dance ($20), be aware that the men will be rubbing and wagging their body part in your face and placing your hands in places that you may or may not want them to be.

For more on venues where scantily clad men "dance," see chapter 8, "It's Showtime."

SWINGERS' CLUBS

The swinging lifestyle, one in which couples like to bounce around and get it on with other couples and singles, certainly isn't unique to Las Vegas. But like most things, we're more open about it here, or, at least, more willing to profit off of it, and there are two different establishments that cater to what's known as "The Lifestyle."

One of life's little secrets: Exhibitionists and voyeurs aren't the most attractive people. Case in point: **The Red Rooster** (5010 Steptoe St.; ☎ 702/451-6661; www.vegasredrooster.com; suggested "donations" Mon–Sat $30 couples, $10 single women; Fri–Sat $50 single men; Sun $20 couples, $30 single men, single women free; office hours Mon–Thurs 5–11pm, Fri–Sat 5–11:30pm; Red Rooster Parties Mon–Thurs 9pm–2am, Fri–Sat 8pm–3am, Sun 6–11pm; no credit cards) swingers' club, where nudity (and *amour!*) comes in all packages. It opened in the early '80s and belongs to a couple who actually live on-site.

When you enter, prepare to feel like a show cow at a 4-H competition being sized up. A close-knit community hangs out here, and they're welcoming to new blood, but also curious about what opportunities that new blood might offer. About 200 people a night will move through here Fridays and Saturdays, and fewer than 100 each night during the week. The main room downstairs is the social club of the house, where nudity isn't allowed. There's a Neil Diamond impersonator/DJ (I requested "Shiloh," and he happily crooned it) and a bouncing, sweating, grinding, sandwiching dance floor is located next to a bar, which offers soda and mixers, but you have to bring your own alcohol.

Outside is a pool that, if you're not careful, could probably impregnate you. Couples let loose and get their sex on here and in the hot tub. Chairs line the perimeter and are generally filled by a few singles, their attention focused on any nude activity and, to put it mildly, bobbing heads. Inside, off the main room, there's a group room that sees its share of action. Much of the action happens behind closed doors and in the upstairs area, which is for couples only.

The Rooster is located out of the way in a typical stucco-filled neighborhood. Patrons make their cash "donation" at the office, which advertises itself as a mini–storage facility, and receive directions to the residence. To get there, from Las Vegas Boulevard, head east on Tropicana Avenue for 7¼ miles, and turn right on Steptoe Street. The office is on the left.

For more of an amateur/curiosity-seeking adventure, **The Green Door** (in Commercial Center, 953 E. Sahara Ave.; ☎ 702/732-4656; www.greendoorlas vegas.com; prices range from $5 per single female to $65 per male or $55 per couple; Mon–Fri 1pm–5am, Sat–Sun 1pm–7am) is an introduction to swinging. Known as Las Vegas' premiere "social" club, the sign outside The Green Door seem fairly innocuous—it just says "The Green Door." But step inside and note the raunchy variation on Starbucks (just switch one of those consonants out for an "f")—you're clearly not in Kansas anymore.

Inside are dim dens with smaller rooms branching off of them. A veritable maze of vinyl beds, cubbies with computers and porn, showers, and stripper poles, it's divided into areas that are couples-only, and others that are open to everyone. Room themes, such as "The Dungeon," "The Golden Shower," "The Shadow Room," and "The Doctor's Office" vary throughout, surrounded with plastic glowing beads and bad erotic art. Oh, and there are countless boxes of tissues and bottles of cleaning fluid. Eww.

Expect to see some action here, whether it's self-serving or couples or groups. When Kate was last touring the couples' room, poking at a hanging swing, she heard movement just outside, next to what I thought was a mirror. Turns out it was a window, and in the 2 minutes or less that I was in the room, a man unzipped and went at it. Right there. For all to see.

This is the real deal—visitors certainly aren't paying those entry fees for the juice bar (if you want to drink alcohol you have to bring it yourself and the bartender will store and serve it). Whether this is your thing or not, you can count on an experience you won't forget. Or one you may not want to remember.

10 Gambling

From slots to poker and more, learn the rules and the odds before the games begin

by Kate Silver

LAS VEGAS ISN'T JUST A CITY THAT SPROUTED UP IN THE MIDDLE OF A HARSH and unforgiving desert. It's a concept, the notion that anything can happen brought to life. From the sphinxes of the Luxor to the canals of The Venetian to the dancing fountains of Bellagio, the underlying language of Las Vegas beckons to the masses in a whisper—and sometimes a scream—"Your fantasy can come true."

And what is one of the most common fantasies? (Banish those dirty thoughts!) Riches. The equal ability of anyone and everyone to pull a handle, flip a card, select a number, and suddenly have their entire life change. Gambling, or gaming, as we in Las Vegas refer to it (the latter sounds so much more civilized), has the capability of making dreams reality. And that—coupled with liquor, sex, and the mob—has made Las Vegas, "Lost Wages," as some say, what it is today.

What was once a secret vice for men, played in dark, smoky back rooms and basements, has long become a respectable pastime. In fiscal year 2008, casinos in the state of Nevada won $12.5 billion. That's actually down 1.87% from the year before, reflecting a negative nudge from the slogging economy. Nearly half of the state's gaming income—$6.7 billion—went to casinos on the Strip, which is a decrease of 1.5% from the previous year—while Downtown Las Vegas' take decreased by 0.4%.

Las Vegas isn't the gambler's only option, and casinos know it. At the time of this writing, most states have either riverboats or American Indian casinos or both. This isn't so much of a threat to Las Vegas as it is a challenge to go bigger, better, and brighter. As though the city really needed more incentive.

LUCK OF THE DRAW

Each casino is meant to be a fantasyland for its visitors. Consider the skimpy cocktail waitress outfits, the free drinks, the absence of clocks, the aromatherapy pumped into the casinos, and, of course, the floor plans that are based on countless studies to make a gambler so comfortable (or dazed) that he'll stick around longer and gamble more. Casinos are well-oiled sociology machines that know just what they're doing when they mysteriously manage to make you forget you're actually spending your hard-earned cash—and at an alarmingly fast rate.

But as everyone knows, those towering casinos filled with alluring canals, roller coasters, and an Eiffel Tower weren't built off of gamblers' winnings. Fantasy aside, the underlying law of economics applies just as much in Las Vegas, Nevada as it does in Sheboygan, Wisconsin: The more elaborate the decor and entertainment, the bigger the bottom line, the more the casino needs to earn. Which is why many seasoned gamblers prefer to play in smaller Downtown casinos, or in neighborhood casinos (which are located off the Strip and targeted toward Las Vegas residents, rather than tourists), where they don't feel as though they're playing to pay for the pirate ships and pyramids, the volcanoes and dancing fountains. Instead, they feel like they're playing to win.

These professional gamblers, these consistent winners, have studied their games with more dedication than many doctors, honing the skills necessary to beat the casino. It's not something Joe Blow can expect to do on his first pilgrimage to the gambling mecca. But he can at least read up on the games and master a strategy or two to increase his odds. A good place to start is with books published by Huntington Press, which is located in Las Vegas and run by former professional gambler Anthony Curtis (see p. 248 for suggestions on particular books). They can also read up on Curtis's *Las Vegas Advisor* (**www.lasvegasadvisor.com**), which is full of tips, deals, coupons, and behind-the-scenes knowledge of how Las Vegas works.

You won't find such elaborate strategies in this chapter. Entire books have been written on the varied approaches to each game, and to even try to fit them in here is impossible. What you will find is a guide on the basic rules of the most common games, and tips from the experts on what to play and how to get the most for your money.

You'll also notice that I've left out descriptions of each casino and its offerings. That's because, aside from a couple of categories differentiating them, casinos are by and large the same when it comes to gambling. Themes, size, location, and degrees of fancy change, but the table games and the odds are comparable; all of them have slot machines and video poker; and most of them have some kind of player's club. Depending on the caliber of the casino you'll find variations in minimum bets and payoffs, differences in the sizes and styles of poker rooms and sports books, and the fancier the casino you're in, the more you typically have to play to receive any comps. Slots tend to be "looser" (that is, pay out more money) away from the more stately casinos. You simply have to decide whether you prefer to gamble in the shadow of a theme

> *A dollar picked up in the road is more satisfaction to us than the 99 which we had to work for, and the money won at Faro or in the stock market snuggles into our hearts in the same way.*
>
> —Mark Twain

(major Strip casinos) or gamble with a higher chance of losing less (smaller Strip casinos, Downtown, and locals' casinos) and then get rolling. But before you win anything, you need to know how to play the games, and what advantage the casino has over the players with each.

SLOT CLUB CARDS

You've seen the little twirly leashlike things that seem to attach gamblers to the slot machine they're playing. This isn't just their way of claiming a death-grip on "Wheel of Fortune." That cord is attached to a slot club card, which is stuck in the slot machine or video poker machine to track how much money the player is spending. Many casinos will also give credit to the cardholder when they play table games, by recording the amount of time played and the average bet.

The House Edge

The house edge is the advantage that the casino has over the player. In the chart below, the "bet" is used in games where the variables change and the person betting has a choice. For example, in baccarat, you can bet on either the player or the banker, and the odds, or house edge, are different for each. The house advantage also changes in blackjack, according to the number of decks involved in the game.

Game	Bet	House Edge
Baccarat	Banker	1.06%
Baccarat	Player	1.24%
Blackjack	Single Deck	0%
Blackjack	Double Deck	.3%
Blackjack	Eight Decks	.6%
Caribbean Stud		5.3%
Craps	Pass/Don't Pass	1.4%
Craps	Don't Pass/Don't Come	1.4%
Keno		25%–30%
Let It Ride		3.51%
Pai Gow		2.5%
Roulette (single zero)		2.7%
Roulette (double zero)		5.26%
Slots		4.5%–9%
Video poker		–.77% to 5%

The slot club is a way of rewarding visitors for gambling on their property. The cards are based on a point system, which varies by property, that measures the amount of money you cycle through slot and video poker machines (note, it's the amount of money you gamble, not the amount of money you win or lose). Once a player has spent a certain amount of money gambling he or she starts getting comps. Lower-level comps include free buffets and coffee shop meals, and some places allow players to trade their points for cash. The more you gamble, the more comps you'll receive—free rooms, show tickets, and even airfare are common incentives. The casinos offer different deals that double, triple, or some will even go up to five times the usual number of points if you play there at a particular time (see **www.lasvegasadvisor.com/greatdeals-slotpromotions.cfm** for which slot clubs have the best promotions). That way, the casino keeps you coming back, and you receive a token of their appreciation for spending your money there. The slot clubs are what keep some of the professional gamblers going; because they use tested strategies and win more than the average gambler, the comps are sheer bonuses. But average gamblers should know that if they're spending hundreds of dollars just to win a free buffet, they need to re-examine their strategy.

Many people are wary of handing over their personal information to the casinos, which, frankly, is a healthy concern in this day and age. But the experts say giving up that info is about the best thing a gambler can do. Think of it like this: If a gambler slips a dollar in a machine in the middle of a casino and no one hears the machine accept it, did the gambler really play? You get the picture. If there are certain perks available for spending money you'd already planned on spending anyway, why wouldn't you take advantage of them? Once you sign up for the slot club (which, in many places, you can do online, or through the mail, or directly at the property) the casino will also include you on their mailing list, which means you'll get coupons and more incentives to play, including discounts on rooms and sometimes, at the cheaper casinos usually, even free rooms.

THE GAMES

There's no doubt about it—gambling can be intimidating. Particularly when you're walking up to a table of strangers and playing a game for the first time. The following game descriptions are a starting point for your preparation. It's also a good idea to take lessons provided by the casino (times and places are listed later in this chapter), or, at the very least, get your feet wet at a time when the casino's not busy, like midweek in the daytime. People come to casinos to win money—not to hold the hand of the newbie as he learns the rules of the game. Unless you're in a poker room, of course. Then you're playing against each other, rather than against the casino, and your fellow gamblers will gladly take your money as quickly as you'll lose it to them.

BACCARAT

If you see a roped-off, fancy-looking area in the casino, one where the dealers may be wearing tuxedos, that's baccarat territory. If you say it out loud, it's bah-kuh-*rah,* which is the French pronunciation for the Italian game. It translates as "zero," which is the value given to the face cards and "10." Bets in this game can be high—$150 to $15,000 or more, as the casinos are trying to attract a high-rolling crowd. Still, anyone can play, and because it's a game based primarily on luck, not skill (the dealer must follow a firm set of rules, and the only decision players make is whether to bet on the bank or the player).

But if you must know more: The baccarat table is large, with room for three dealers and 12 to 14 players. Though players all bet, only one hand is played at a time. This is a community game, so people bet on hands that are not their own, meaning they wager either on the bank, or the single player that the bank is up against. Players can also bet on a tie, but the house advantage on that bet is 14.4%, so it's not recommended.

Eight decks of cards are used at a time. Two cards are dealt to the player who has the largest wager against the bank, and two are dealt to the bank. Whoever gets a number closer to nine without going over, wins. When the number reaches the double digits, only the digit on the right side actually counts. For example, if a "9" and a "5" are dealt, the total is 14, but since only the digit on the right side counts, the total is actually four. The best a player can hope for is to get a natural nine, meaning a "9" dealt with the first two cards ("4" and "5"). As mentioned, the dealer follows detailed rules, and aside from betting, the only other role that players have is to deal the cards when the shoe is passed to them. The shoe makes its way around the table counterclockwise. If a player doesn't want to deal, he or she can pass.

the baccarat table

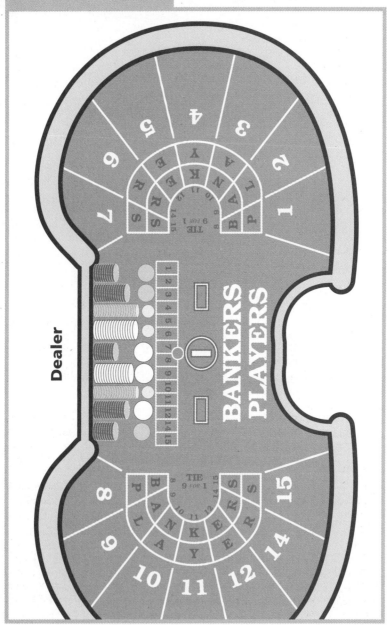

Baccarat Rules

Player's Hand

Having

0-1-2-3-4-5 Must draw a third card

6-7 Must stand

8-9 Natural. Banker cannot draw.

Banker's Hand

Having	Draws When giving player 3rd card of	Does Not Draw When giving Player 3rd card of
3	1-2-3-4-5-6-7-8-9-10	8
4	2-3-4-5-6-7	1-8-9-10
5	4-5-6-7	1-2-3-8-9-10
6	6-7	1-2-3-4-5-8-9-10
7		Must stand.
8–9		Natural. Player cannot draw.

Note: If the player takes no third card, the banker must stand on "6." No one draws against a natural "8" or "9."

Because the rules of the game dictate that the banker's hand wins more than the player's, players who win off the banker's hand must pay a 5% commission. Again, the dealer keeps track of these, so you won't have to bother doing the calculations (the commission is charged either at the start of a new game or when you leave the table).

Mini-baccarat differs only in that it's played at a smaller table; betting minimums are lower; games tend to move more quickly; the game itself has a less formal air; and players don't deal the cards, the dealer does.

BIG SIX

Big Six is basically roulette meets *Wheel of Fortune*. There's a wheel with 56 positions, 54 of which are marked $1 through $20, and the other two are jokers, which pay 40 to 1. You pick a number and if it lands on that denomination, those are the odds it pays. So if you picked $20, it pays 20 to 1. If you picked $12, it pays 12 to 1, and so on.

BINGO

The skills you learned in elementary school classrooms and parish halls can now be put to use in exchange for cold, hard cash. The basic concept is as simple today as it was when you learned it, but with the bonuses and the different types of shapes that can qualify as "bingo," this is a new world for those who have never played in a casino setting. And in Las Vegas, the game is taken very, very seriously (there's even a monthly newsletter devoted to bingo called *The Bingo Bugle*).

Buy as many bingo cards as you want to play. You'll find that most rooms have a minimum and a maximum, and you'll usually have to play between 6 and 12 cards at a time for about 12 games. Each session lasts about an hour, and newbies will be amazed at how frenzied and exhausting it can get to keep track of so many cards at once. Each card is a 5 × 5 grid containing 24 numbered spaces and one "free" space. To mark the card you'll need to either bring your own dauber, or you can purchase one on the premises. Another option is The Electronic Dauber (or T.E.D.), which is a computer-like dauber system used to track multiple bingo cards, and many of the hard-core players look upon it with distrust (simply for their old-fashioned sensibilities, not because of any charted corruption).

The game starts when the caller announces the first combination of a letter and a number, drawn at random. The object is to be the first to get the letter and number combinations laid out in such a way that they form a vertical, horizontal, or diagonal line across the board. When this happens, you yell out "bingo," a casino employee verifies it and the game is over. Bingo rooms also call games where you're trying to mark all corners, or line up your combinations in a particular shape, or "cover-all," which means you cover every combination on your card. When they do this, that shape will be shown on a screen to avoid any confusion.

Be sure that when you call bingo you actually have it. These players can be ornery and take their games incredibly seriously. To call a game at the wrong time could result in a sharp lecture from a dauber-wielding senior. Bingo games are primarily found in locals' casinos and cards cost $1 and up. Bingo hot spots include Red Rock Casino, Arizona Charlie's Decatur and Boulder locations (which are open 24 hr.) (p. 52), Terrible's (p. 53), Palace Station (p. 61), and Gold Coast (p. 61). To locate other bingo games, see **www.bingoupdate.com**.

BLACKJACK

On a cursory level, blackjack is one of the easiest games to grasp, which has helped make it one of the casinos' most popular table games. It's also the table game with the best odds for the player.

But, like most casino games, it's more complex than it appears. This was the first table game I ever played, and like many newbies, I didn't know there was much to the game outside of trying to get "21." Everyone else at the table, it seems, had some kind of strategy. It only took a few hands for the glares to begin (I think I did something as tragic as hitting a hard "18" or splitting "10"s). After long bouts of growling, the table eventually emptied out. The dealer had to explain that they left because they thought my uneducated plays were affecting their hands. I've since learned that this is absolutely not the case—the odds of my uninformed play affecting them negatively are just as good as them affecting them positively.

Of course, you should always come to any table prepared (you'll needlessly lose money otherwise), but also come with a thick skin and don't let other players affect you mentally.

Slots to Tables & Back

Your slot club card works even when you're playing at the tables. But you have to speak up. Give your card to the dealer, and the casino will track what your average bet is and multiply it by the amount of time you're playing. Be advised however, that many casinos (especially on the Strip) will not rate your play unless you consistently bet a minimum amount on each hand (often $25). If you're unsure, you can always ask the pit boss whether betting minimums apply.

The purpose of blackjack, also known as "21," is to get a hand whose value gets as close to "21" as possible, without going over aka busting. Here's how you go about getting there:

1. Place the number of chips that you want to bet on the betting space on your table. All tables will have a minimum bet. You may be able to find some $3 and $5 tables on the Strip (see p. 234), but it's more common to find $10 to $25 and up, particularly during busier times, such as Friday and Saturday nights. Watch and you'll see that as the number of players increase, more tables will open (generally with higher minimums) in response to the demand. Once all players have bet, the dealer will deal two cards to each player as well as two cards to herself. Only one of the dealer's cards, however, will be dealt face-up. The dealer will then move clockwise around the table to allow players to play out their hands.

2. Look at the first two cards the dealer starts you with. If you wish to "stand," then wave your hand over your cards, palm down (watch your fellow players), indicating that you don't wish any additional cards. If you elect to draw an additional card, you tell the dealer to "hit" you by tapping the table with a finger (watch your fellow players). Generally speaking, you should not hit a hand that totals "17" and over. Whether to hit a hand with a total value below "17" will depend on the card that the dealer is showing to the table. For proper strategy, see the "Basic Blackjack Strategy" chart on p. 232.

3. If you do hit your hand and your count goes over "21," you are "bust" and lose. Note that unless a dealer has blackjack, players always play their hands out before the dealer, so even if the dealer also goes "bust," you still lose.

4. If you make "21" in your first two cards (any face card or a "10" with an ace), you've got blackjack (also known as a natural). In most cases you will be paid 1½ times your bet (though some casinos pay out only 6 to 5 on 1- and 2-deck shoes), provided that the dealer does not have blackjack, too, in which case it's a "push," and nobody wins.

5. If you find a "pair" in your first two cards (say, two "8"s or two aces), you may "split" the pair into two hands and treat each card as the first card dealt in two separate hands. You will need to place an additional bet, equal to your original bet, on the table (so if your original bet was $10, you need to put down another $10). The dealer will then deal you a new second card to the first split card and play commences as described above. This will be done for the second split card as well. Players are advised to always split "8"s, since

Blackjack

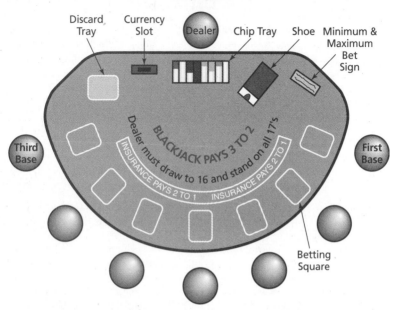

The Dealer Is Showing:		2	3	4	5	6	7	8	9	10	Ace
Your Total Is:	4-11	H	H	H	H	H	H	H	H	H	H
	12	H	H	S	S	S	H	H	H	H	H
	13	S	S	S	S	S	H	H	H	H	H
	14	S	S	S	S	S	H	H	H	H	H
	15	S	S	S	S	S	H	H	H	H	H
	16	S	S	S	S	S	H	H	H	H	H

S = Stand   H = Hit

they equal 16, which is the worst number you can get. Never split face cards or "10"s, as a "20" is likely a winning hand. ***Note:*** If you split aces, you will receive only one additional card per ace and must "stand."

6. After seeing your two starting cards, you have the option to "double down." You place an amount equal to your original bet on the table and you receive only one more card. Doubling down is a strategy to capitalize on a potentially strong hand against the dealer's weaker hand. Though most casinos will let you double down on any card (DOA), a few out there limit it to hands that total 10 or 11. Tip: You may double down for less than your original bet, but never for more.

7. Anytime the dealer deals himself or herself an ace for the "up" card, you may insure your hand against the possibility that the hole card is a "10" or face card, which would give him or her an automatic blackjack. To insure, you place an amount up to ½ of your bet on the "insurance" line. If the dealer does

Basic Strategy

The Dealer Is Showing:	2	3	4	5	6	7	8	9	10	Ace
Your Total Is: 4–11	H	H	H	H	H	H	H	H	H	H
12	H	H	S	S	S	H	H	H	H	H
13	S	S	S	S	S	H	H	H	H	H
14	S	S	S	S	S	H	H	H	H	H
15	S	S	S	S	S	H	H	H	H	H
16	S	S	S	S	S	H	H	H	H	H

S = Stand   H = Hit

Soft Hand Strategy

The Dealer Is Showing:	2	3	4	5	6	7	8	9	10	Ace
You Have: Ace, 9	S	S	S	S	S	S	S	S	S	S, H
Ace, 8	S	S	S	S	S	S	S	S	S	S
Ace, 7	S	D	D	D	D	S	S	H	H	S
Ace, 6	H	D	D	D	D	S	H	H	H	H
Ace, 5	H	H	D	D	D	H	H	H	H	H
Ace, 4	H	H	D	D	D	H	H	H	H	H
Ace, 3	H	H	H	D	D	H	H	H	H	H
Ace, 2	H	H	H	D	D	H	H	H	H	H

S = Stand   H = Hit   D = Double Down

Splitting Strategy

The Dealer Is Showing:	2	3	4	5	6	7	8	9	10	Ace
You Have: 2, 2	H	H	SP	SP	SP	SP	H	H	H	H
3, 3	H	H	SP	SP	SP	SP	H	H	H	H
4, 4	H	H	H	H	H	H	H	H	H	H
5, 5	D	D	D	D	D	D	D	D	H	H
6, 6	H	SP	SP	SP	SP	H	H	H	H	H
7, 7	SP	SP	SP	SP	SP	SP	H	H	H	H
8, 8	SP	SP	SP	SP	SP	SP	SP	SP	SP	SP
9, 9	SP	SP	SP	SP	SP	S	SP	SP	S	S
10, 10	S	S	S	S	S	S	S	S	S	S
Ace, Ace	SP	SP	SP	SP	SP	SP	SP	SP	SP	SP

S = Stand   H = Hit   SP = Split   D = Double Down

Doubling Down

The Dealer Is Showing:	2	3	4	5	6	7	8	9	10	Ace
Your Total Is: 11	D	D	D	D	D	D	D	D	D	H
10	D	D	D	D	D	D	D	D	H	H
9	H	D	D	D	D	H	H	H	H	H

H = Hit   D = Double Down

have a blackjack, you get paid 2 to 1 on the insurance money while losing your original bet: You break even. If the dealer does not have a blackjack, he or she takes your insurance money and play continues in the normal fashion. Note that if a dealer does have blackjack, it's always revealed before players play out their hands. *Tip:* Unless you know how to count cards (and you'd better not get caught doing it in a Vegas casino), insurance is a sucker bet and should be avoided.

8. If there's no chance of the dealer having blackjack, the players play out their hands, and then the dealer flips his remaining card over. Generally speaking, a dealer must hit his hand if the total is less than 17 or if he's showing a "soft 17," (meaning an ace and a "6") and must stay if he's got a "hard 17" or a total above that. Players whose cards are higher than the dealer's win an amount equal to their bet. Should the dealer bust, everyone still in the game wins.

Note that the above advice is just the tip of the iceberg. A good (and cheap!) investment is to buy one of the small laminated basic strategy cards you'll find in stores all over town. The casinos will let you consult it at the table, and it can save you from making a costly mistake. Dealers also, in my experience, can be incredibly helpful and even patient with slow (or intoxicated) players. They'll add up your cards and even make suggestions as to what you should and shouldn't do. Blackjack can often be a social game where you make new friends and have a great time.

Another note: Though some blackjack tables still play with one or two decks of cards dealt by hand, most use six or eight dealt from a shoe to make it more difficult to card count (a practice that is both extremely difficult and forbidden in Vegas casinos). Though your odds of winning are usually better the fewer decks in play, the casinos have largely watered down advantages by reducing the payouts on these short decks, or forbidding players to enter games middeck.

CHEAP(ER) BLACKJACK

Despite the exorbitant minimums at large Strip properties, $5-and-under black-jack isn't obsolete yet. You just have to know where to find it.

Single-deck blackjack for $5 and less can usually be found Downtown at El Cortez, Four Queens, and at the Western.

Double-deck blackjack can usually be found at neighborhood casinos such as Boulder Station, Palace Station, Santa Fe Station, Texas Station, and Wild West Casino.

Other spots that generally offer $5-and-under (but usually with more than two decks) include the following locations on the Strip: Bill's Gamblin' Hall & Saloon, Excalibur, O'Sheas, the Riviera (usually not during peak hours), the Sahara, Casino Royale, Circus Circus ($3), Slots-A-Fun (as low as $2 and $3), and the Tropicana.

CRAPS

That raucous screaming, the jumping up and down that's going on near the tables? Oh, they're excited because they finagled a night with Demi Moore. Crazier things have certainly happened at the craps table.

For the thrill and popularity, you'd think craps would be easier to learn, but it takes some thought and planning, and practically picking up a new language, what with the "Come," "Pass," "Yo," and more. Newbies may want to watch for a while before throwing themselves in. While women who are new to the game are considered good luck, novice males are considered bad luck. Either way, if you're clueless about how to play you'll make enemies quickly—you're all in it together, and basically betting on the luck of the guy with the dice (the Shooter), until he craps out and a new shooter takes over. Many of the casinos offer free lessons, and if craps interests you, I'd advise you to take them. It's much easier to pick up while playing—and without everyone at the table hating you for spoiling their game.

If you play it right, you can make your money last a while and have a rip-roaring time. But heed these words: Never utter "seven" at the table. That, too, is considered bad luck. And when it comes to gambling, luck is really all you've got. "Big red" and "six ace" are viable alternatives for the unlucky number.

The game begins with the shooter rolling what's called a **Come Out** roll to establish a **"point,"** that is, the number the shooter is going for. If the Come Out is a "2" or "3" (also known as "craps"), those who bet on the Pass Line lose, those who bet on the Don't Pass Line win, and the shooter continues rolling. If a "12" (also known as "box cars") turns up, Pass bettors lose and it's a push for Don't Pass bettors. Rolling a "2," "3," or "12" on the Come Out is referred to as **crapping out.**

If a "7" or "11" ("11" is also known as "yo") comes up, those who bet on the Pass Line win and those who bet on the Don't Pass Line lose. The shooter keeps rolling, but a point has still not been established on that roll.

If a "4," "5," "6," "8," "9," or "10" is rolled, the point is established and the shooter continues rolling with the goal of hitting that same number again. The roll is no longer called the Come Out.

If you bet on the Pass Line, you're betting that the point will be rolled before a "7" (which, statistically, is the number that comes up most often). The shooter continues rolling the dice until either the point or "7" comes up. If the point comes up, Pass bettors win and Don't Pass bettors lose. But if a "7" comes up first, Don't Pass bettors win, Pass bettors lose, and the shooter is done rolling the dice. The shooter's turn can generally go on for a number of rolls, or it can end with two, if the shooter first establishes a point and then immediately rolls a "7." Those are the basics of craps. Outside of Pass/Don't Pass there are many varied bets, which add to the excitement of the game. The person standing next to you could be relying on a completely different number to come up than anyone at the table. I'll go through a few of the more basic bets.

To add a more advanced dimension to the game, you can also bet on Come and Don't Come. The Come point is established directly after the Pass point. Let's say a shooter rolls a "5" for the point. The next roll is an "8," which becomes known

To vs. For

Be aware of the difference between "to" and "for" when it comes to odds.

- 5 to 1 means that if you win you receive five times your original bet, plus you get the original bet back.
- 5 for 1 means you only get five times the bet back.

The difference may seem small, but in the long run it can make quite an impact.

Gaming Vocabulary

Betting Limits: In a table game, the minimum or maximum a player can wager on one game.

Black Book: The Nevada Gaming Control Board's list of known men and women who have cheated at gambling or have been caught counting cards and are now banned from entering casinos.

Blind: An early forced bet required to begin some poker games.

Bust: When your cards total over 21 in blackjack.

Call: Poker term, meaning to match the current bet.

Card Counting: Method of mentally tracking cards in blackjack and playing according to mathematical probability. Vegas casinos ban known card counters, and their mugs can end up in the Black Book.

Chips: Round plastic tokens used in betting. Each color represents a cash denomination.

Croupier: French word meaning "dealer." Used in roulette and baccarat.

Deuce: A "2" in dice or cards.

Eye in the Sky: The surveillance cameras in a casino's ceiling.

Face Cards: King, queen, and jack.

Hard 18: In blackjack, "hard" denotes a hand without an ace (which equals 11 or 1, player's choice), so this would be two "9"s or a "10" and an "8." A "soft 18" would be an ace and a "7."

High-Roller: A player that consistently wagers large amounts of money.

Hit: Receive another card.

Hole Card: In blackjack, the face-down card of the dealer. In Texas Hold 'em, the face-down card is dealt to players.

House: The casino.

Insurance: A side bet in blackjack that the dealer has blackjack—it's largely a sucker bet and should be avoided.

as the Come point. As the shooter continues to roll, the goal is similar to Pass bets: If a "7" or "11" is thrown, Come wins, Don't Come loses. If a "2" or "3" is rolled, Come loses, Don't Come wins. If a "12" pops up Come loses and Don't Come ties. If an "8" is thrown before a "7," Come wins, and Don't Come loses.

Megabucks: A popular progressive slot machine game.

Odds: Probability of the casino winning versus the player winning.

Pot: In poker, the total amount of the players' antes, bets, and raises in a game. The pot goes to the winner.

Progressive: A game where the payout increases each time someone plays.

Push: Tie.

Rake: The amount that the casino charges for a hand of poker, usually a percentage (5%–10%) or flat fee taken from the pot.

Rated: Years ago, the term "rated" applied to a gambler's skill level. A "rated" player was recognized as a professional by the casino and taken care of. Recently, the definition has changed and the term "rated" applies to anyone with a player's card. The player's card puts your name into the casino's computer, which tracks your average bet size and frequency to determine when you'll receive comps.

Royal Flush: The best possible hand. An ace-high straight flush.

Shoe: A small box from which multiple decks of cards are stored and dealt.

Snake Eyes: Rolling two "1"s on the dice.

Soft 18: In blackjack, "soft" denotes a hand with an ace, so this would be an ace (which equals 11 points or 1 point, player's choice) plus a "7." A "hard 18" would be a "10" and an "8."

Stay: Your hand should remain as is.

Suit: One of four types of cards: hearts, diamonds, spades, or clubs.

Toke: A tip.

Wager: Any bet.

Whale: The highest of high-rollers.

The Odds Bet on a craps table is known as one of the best bets in gambling. It's so good that it's not marked on the table like the sucker bets—it's just for those in the know. For the actual odds (on which the payoff for the odds bet is based) and possible winning combinations at the table, see the Craps Odds chart below.

Progressive Bingo

Station Casinos (www.stationcasinos.com), a company that owns neighborhood casinos located away from the Strip, offers a Jumbo Progressive Bingo game at the beginning of each session. The game is linked to all seven Station properties, and the minimum prize, if won in the posted amount of numbers called, is $50,000. Other casinos have cash giveaways and other incentives, and jackpots around town can range from the hundreds to well into the thousands; each casino is different—actually, each session at each casino could be different. This is not your grandmother's simple bingo game. For details on the different payouts, go to www.insidervlv.com/bingo.html.

As you can see by the chart, there are more combinations that add up to "7" than any other number (six to be exact), and that's what will come up most often. On the other hand, "2" and "12" will be rolled with the least frequency. To place an Odds Bet, place your wager behind your Pass Line or Come bet, between the rolls of the dice. Say you bet $5 on the odds and the shooter rolls a "4." Because the odds of a "7" coming up before the "4" are 2 to 1—that is, there are six ways to make a "7" versus three ways to make a "4"—you get paid those odds, in addition to the even money for your Pass Line bet.

The payoff goes as follows:

Point	Payoff
4	2 to 1
5	3 to 2
6	6 to 5
8	6 to 5
9	3 to 2
10	2 to 1

There's also a Field Bet, which is for one roll only and pays 2 to 1 for a "2" or "12," and even money for "3," "4," "9," "10," and "11" (experienced craps players rarely take this bet). A "Big 6 and 8" bet pays even money if the "6" or "8" are rolled before the "7." This only pays even money and the house has a huge advantage (9.1%). The "Any 7" bet pays 4 to 1 if the "7" is thrown directly following the wager. The odds of actually getting this, however, are 5 to 1, so you should avoid this bet.

Betting on "Any Craps" pays 7 to 1 if a "2," "3," or "12" is rolled. And if you play a "Place Bet," that is, select one of the big numbers "4," "5," "6," "8," "9," or "10," you're betting that one of those numbers will turn up before a "7" is rolled. This bet lasts only for one roll, and the numbers pay off differently than their actual odds—"4" or "10" pays 9 to 5, "9" pays 7 to 5, "6" or "8" pays 7 to 6.

"Hard Way" bets have some of the worst odds (9%–11% house edge) and involve the numbers "4," "6," "8," and "10." A Hard Way wins if the number that a player picked comes up as a pair (two "4"s make "8") and loses if a "7" is rolled or if the number you bet on is formed without a pair (a "5" and "3" make "8"). This bet sticks—it's not just on a single roll.

The Craps Layout

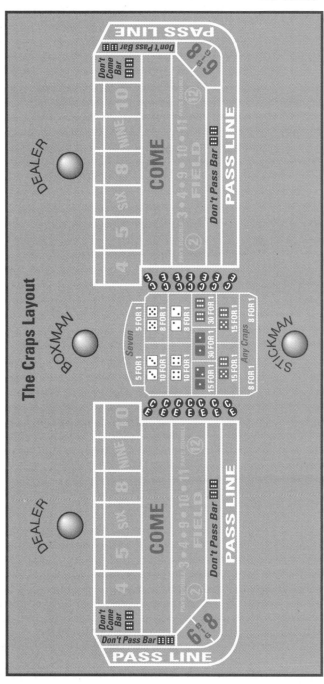

In general, experienced craps players only bet on the Pass, Come, and Odds line because the house advantage is lowest. But riskier players looking for bigger and quicker payoff often can't resist indulging in the other available bets.

In crapless craps, rolls of "2," "3," "11," and "12" count as point numbers.

Here's How the 36 Craps Combinations Stack Up			
Number Rolled	**How Many Ways to Roll the Numbers?**	**True Odds**	**Winning Combinations**
Two	1	35 to 1	⚀⚀
Three	2	17 to 1	⚀⚁ • ⚁⚀
Four	3	11 to 1	⚀⚂ • ⚂⚀ • ⚁⚁
Five	4	8 to 1	⚀⚃ • ⚃⚀ • ⚁⚂ • ⚂⚁
Six	5	6.2 to 1	⚀⚄ • ⚄⚀ • ⚁⚃ • ⚃⚁ • ⚂⚂
Seven	6	5 to 1	⚀⚅ • ⚅⚀ • ⚁⚄ • ⚄⚁ • ⚂⚃ • ⚃⚂
Eight	5	6.2 to 1	⚁⚅ • ⚅⚁ • ⚂⚄ • ⚄⚂ • ⚃⚃
Nine	4	8 to 1	⚂⚅ • ⚅⚂ • ⚃⚄ • ⚄⚃
Ten	3	11 to 1	⚃⚅ • ⚅⚃ • ⚄⚄
Eleven	2	17 to 1	⚄⚅ • ⚅⚄
Twelve	1	35 to 1	⚅⚅

KENO

An ancient Chinese game, legend holds that keno was used to get reluctant taxpayers to free up their yuan for their country's defense. The money was eventually used to build the Great Wall of China, they say. Chinese immigrants later brought the game to America, where residents took to it like, well, like a gambler to Las Vegas.

Keno is basically the lottery of casino games and is about the most loser-friendly bet you can make, with a house advantage of 25% to 40%. Why do people play, then? Because of the slim chance that you may win, and win big—$50,000 and more with a ticket that cost a buck or two.

Not too dissimilar from bingo, it can be a social game, where players sit around and chat as they're waiting to hear the numbers. It's also a very accessible game, both in ability to understand and also places to play. Many casino coffee shops and lounges offer keno runner services (people who'll put your bet in for you), or you can fill out your card directly at the keno counter. (Casinos provide either crayons or these cute little pens that some of us take advantage of more than we should.)

Once you receive your card, which consists of 80 different numbers, select up to 15 (though some casinos allow up to 20) by marking an "x" over your choices. If you are feeling less than decisive, there's also an option to have the computer do a "Quick Pick" for you. Then, mark your bet on the card and return the keno card to the counter or a keno runner, pay them, and they'll hand you a computerized card with your picks. Wait for the numbered balls to begin flying.

As 20 of the balls fly out of the hopper (one at a time), the numbers are called and light up the keno boards around the casino. The payout changes depending on the casino, so consult one of the keno brochures that each casino provides.

Gambling Etiquette

- ◆ Understand the rules of the game and know the minimum bet.
- ◆ Only buy and cash in chips between hands.
- ◆ If you hold your cards, do so with one hand. Always handle dice with one hand.
- ◆ When cards are dealt face-up, don't touch them.
- ◆ Respect the dealer and other players.
- ◆ If you leave a table game for a bathroom break, you can ask the dealer to watch your seat. But if you're going to be gone longer than a few minutes, free up your spot so that others can play. **Note:** Some casinos will take responsibility for your chips when you're on a break, but many won't. If the casino in which you are playing won't guard chips, never leave the table without taking them along. Ask the dealer to "color up" (converting your chips into the highest denominations possible) and take them along with you.
- ◆ Stack your chips with the highest denomination on the bottom and the lowest on top. The dealer can calculate your wager more quickly and potential chip thieves (it can happen) won't be able to get at your more expensive chips.
- ◆ Don't give advice unless someone asks for it.
- ◆ Don't use your cellphone or other electronic devices while playing.
- ◆ Some slot players use more than one machine at a time. Make sure no one's playing at a machine before sitting down.
- ◆ Remember to tip the dealer and the cocktail waitress. Note that many players choose to place bets on behalf of the dealer as a form of tip. If you want to do that, just let the dealer know.
- ◆ Never hand the dealer money or touch the dealer in any way. Wagers are placed on the table, never handed to the dealer.
- ◆ When playing table games, always signal to the dealer your wishes with your hands as well as your voice. It's required so that casino security can record player decisions to avoid accusations of misconduct or collusion.

Generally, the more numbers you hit, the higher the return; though the total amount you can win will depend on the ratio of how many numbers you hit versus the amount you selected overall. For example, if you hit seven numbers out of the 15 you selected, you'll get to collect, but what you win may not even cover breakfast. If you hit seven numbers, however, and you only picked seven numbers, winnings will be substantial—sometimes in the thousands. The fewer numbers you pick, the more you need to hit in order to win anything. For example, if you only picked three to seven numbers, then generally at least three of those numbers need to be called in order to win. If you marked 13 to 15 numbers, at least

The Frugal Gambler

Dan Rather nicknamed Jean Scott "The Queen of Comps." She's spent 2 decades pitting her frugal (to put it nicely) nature against casinos and taking from them whatever she can. Slow and steady like the tortoise, she and her husband, Brad, realized early on that slot club cards and casino hosts were their tickets to paradise—free meals, free shows, free vacations, and jackpots galore, all for doing what they already enjoyed: gambling. They once stayed 191 days out of a year in hotels, eating, playing, being entertained—and outside of their consistent gambling, they didn't pay a dime. And they had more money when they left than when they began.

That's nothing compared to a recent win. Brad Scott won first prize in a slot tournament at Caesars Palace, bringing home $500,000. "One thing I say is you put yourself in the path of luck, stay there long enough, you're going to run smack dab into Lady Luck with a wallop," says Jean, the author of *The Frugal Gambler, More Frugal Gambling,* and *Frugal Video Poker,* all published by Huntington Press.

She offers the following tips to get more bang for your gambling buck:

1. Choose the good games so you don't lose much while you're earning the comp. That means selecting the video poker machines with better odds and more return. (See the box on Anthony Curtis on p. 248 for the best video poker recommendations.)
2. Always sign up for slot cubs. What's the point in gambling if the casino doesn't know you're doing it? And don't be afraid to ask for a comp.
3. Sign up for promotions and drawings.
4. Play in slot tournaments. Entry fees can be high (the entry fee Brad paid for the Caesars tournament was $10,000, and he won $500,000). But so is payoff.

---

six need to come up. The odds of hitting all 20 numbers are 3.5 quintillion to 1. Still want to play?

Be sure and find out how much time you have to claim your winnings. Some places will give you 48 hours to an entire year; others want you to claim them before the next game begins. Most casinos also offer video keno, which can often be found on video poker machines that offer multiple games. The video version allows for quicker play at smaller denominations and has a higher return than live keno.

While researching this section, I came across a wonderful website (**www.big empire.com/vegas/oldlady.html**) that devotes a page strictly to "Old Lady Playing Keno" jokes. I shrugged it off at first, thinking they'd be dumb—but then I started reading them and had trouble controlling my laughter: Why do old ladies playing keno in Las Vegas fix up their kids with each other? Answers: A. To create a breed of super-keno babies. B. To get more birthday numbers.

5. Concentrate your play at one place so you can accumulate enough points to get comps. Jean suggests playing in the smaller casinos "where it's easier to be a big frog in a small pond." The bigger the resort, she says, the more you have to play to get the comp. Spend your money in places such as the Riviera, Slots-A-Fun, and Casino Royale, if you're on the Strip. If you're willing to venture off, try anyplace Downtown, or neighborhood casinos such as Arizona Charlie's, Sam's Town, and any of the Station casinos (Texas Station, Palace Station, Sunset Station, Green Valley Resort, Red Rock Resort, and so forth). But don't go around spending $20 at this spot and $100 at that one. It could take forever to accumulate enough points to get a comp. It's important to note that when multiple casinos are owned by one corporation, like MGM MIRAGE, Harrah's, and Station Casinos, a single slot club card can generally be used at all of those properties.

6. Be value conscious. Each slot club has a different system for point exchange rates. Take that into consideration, along with the expected loss on a game and the value of your time. If you're playing 9/6 Jacks or Better video poker (the 9/6 means it pays nine coins for a full house and six for a flush, which will be noted on the pay table on the machine) and you spend $20,000 on the game (which has a return of 99.54%, if played perfectly), you can expect to lose about $100, if played perfectly. Let's say the comp is $200. Was it worth the time spent?

7. Be smart and know your limits. If you're a beginning gambler who's not paying attention to strategy, you may manage to earn that free steak. But will it really taste that good if you spent $5,000 to get it?

The site also offers some good cheapo advice, so even old ladies who play keno may find something useful here.

POKER

If any game could ever take over the world, it's poker. Imagine if our leaders would sit down to a nice game of Texas Hold 'em to determine outcomes, rather than falling back on the old missile standby. It would take strategy, patience, a fair amount of acting, and a shake of luck—or would that be manifest destiny?—to win.

But in the meantime, the game just rules television, casinos, private parties, and has even infiltrated the celebrity world. Online poker games helped spike its draw (pun intended) as did the hole-card camera, which suddenly turned the game into a spectator sport.

Though its origins are questionable, tournament play became more popular when the **World Series of Poker (WSOP)** began in Las Vegas in the 1970s and was held Downtown at Binion's Horseshoe for 35 years, until the financially struggling casino was forced to shut down. At that point, Harrah's purchased Binion's and the WSOP, and moved the annual event to the Rio, where it continues to up the ante with poker talent.

When it comes to Las Vegas poker, players are actually playing against one another rather than the casino, so everyone stands a higher chance of winning. Of course, the casino still takes its share (they're not providing a room and a dealer free of charge) through what's called the rake, which is either a percentage of the pot or a set fee paid for each game played.

Poker rooms are where the skilled prey upon the unskilled. Emotional people who can't keep a straight face are their own worst nightmare and their competitors' dream. Though in most areas of gambling the locals avoid the Strip, knowing they stand a better chance in locals' casinos, the rules shift when it comes to poker. Here, they're after the fish, meaning people new to the game. That frat boy in from Minnesota looking to scrounge up a few bucks at the tables? Consider him battered and fried. Professional gamblers go for the poker rooms that draw the least skilled, and that means the low- to mid-buy-ins at large Strip properties—particularly at the casinos that offer poker lessons. That way, they can get 'em when they're fresh. (And it doesn't hurt that some of the nicer poker rooms, such as the one at the MGM Grand, feature tableside massage services.)

Let's move on to the game. Most of the large casinos have poker rooms (and most of them are actually nonsmoking, believe it or not) and tournaments, inspired, again, by the WSOP. Buy-ins range from around $20 and go into the thousands. You can find out when they're held by going to the "Gaming" section of each individual casino's website, or checking out the useful website www.all vegaspoker.com, which not only lists tournaments, but also buy-ins, administrative fees, returns, and reviews.

The first step to getting in on a game is approaching the floor supervisor. Tell him what you'd like to play (and how much you're willing to stake—you don't want to get caught in a high-limit game if you have a small budget), and he will lead you to an open spot at a table, or have you wait until a spot opens. The most common game is Texas Hold 'em, and you can often find an Omaha/8 tournament going on. The goal in all poker games is to get the highest hand at the table. (Or, at least bluff everyone into thinking you do.) The game surrounds a communal pot of chips, which accumulate as players bet on whether their own hand will win. To the victor go the spoils.

THE BASICS

To play poker (and other card games) you first should know that every deck of cards consists of four different suits: clubs, diamonds, hearts, and spades, and no suit is higher in value than the other. There are 13 cards of each suit: "2" through "10," jack, queen, king, and ace—with ace being the highest and "2" the lowest. Aces can also be used as low cards when it comes to what's called a "wheel straight": A 2-3-4-5. In most poker games, a hand consists of five cards.

A **royal flush** is the highest hand. This consists of an A-K-Q-J-10, all of the same suit.

A **straight flush** comes next. Unlike the royal, this can be any ordinal series of the same suit: 2-3-4-5-6.

Poker Hands

Four-of-a-kind is just as it sounds—a hand where four of the five cards have the same value. If more than one player has four-of-a-kind, the one with the higher hand wins (four "9"s beats four "3"s).

A **full house** is three-of-a-kind plus a pair, for example three "4"s and two queens. If more than one player has a full house, the one with the higher three-of-a-kind wins (K-K-K-2-2 beats 8-8-8-A-A).

A **flush** is a hand where all five cards are of the same suit. Cards don't have to be in any numeric order, for example, 9-2-5-Q-10 of spades. If more than one player has a flush, the one with the high card wins. If that's a tie, then the next high card wins, and so on.

The **straight** is a hand where all five cards are in numerical order, for example 5-6-7-8-9. An ace can be high (10-J-Q-K-A), or low (A-2-3-4-5). If more than one person has a straight, the highest card wins.

Three-of-a-kind is a hand in which three cards have the same numeric value, and two cards don't match, such as Q-Q-Q-5-9. If more than one player has a three-of-a-kind the highest card wins.

A **two-pair** hand consists of two sets of two cards with the same numeric value, for example 4-4 and K-K. If more than one player has two-pair then the highest pair wins. If there's a high-card tie, then the second highest pair wins.

A **pair** is a hand with a single pair of matching cards, such as 9-9-4-3-2. If more than one player has a pair, the high pair wins. If two players have the same numerical pair, then the one with the highest unmatched card wins (Q-Q-K-4-2 beats Q-Q-10-8-7).

When all hands consist of five unmatched cards, the hand with the highest card wins.

Now that you have the combinations down, let's talk about playing. Because the dealer is provided by the casino, there is a dealer "button" that's passed around to ensure the game varies as it would were the players doing the dealing. Note that poker games always require one or more players to make a forced bet in order to start off the pot that players will be contesting. Once the cards have been dealt, players can fold, bet, raise, or check. Folding means that your cards aren't worth investing money in. If you fold, place your cards on the table face-down. If you think your cards are worth an investment, you can bet. Another option is to "call," which means matching the bet another player has made. If you're confident in your cards, you can "raise," or bet more than the original bet. If, when it's your turn in a betting round, no one has called or raised, you also have the option of "checking." This means you're neither raising nor folding, but want to remain in the game. Once someone at the table puts money in the pot during a betting round, however, everyone must match or raise that amount. If, when the betting rounds have concluded, there is only one person left, that person is the winner; if two or more people remain, the remaining players must show their cards to all to determine who won.

Let's look at two popular poker games.

Texas Hold 'em

You can't throw a poker chip in Las Vegas without hitting a Texas Hold 'em game. "Hot" is an understatement when it comes to Hold 'em.

The basic goal is to get the best five-card hand while operating off two cards that only you see (the hole), along with five community cards that the rest of the table is also using. It sounds simple, but once you begin playing you'll realize it's anything but. Try to keep in mind the lyrics of the great Kenny Rogers: "You've got to know when to hold 'em. Know when to fold 'em."

The game starts with the blinds, which are basically forced bets placed by two designated players to get things going. The two players to the left of the dealer button post the blinds—the one closest to the dealer posts the **small blind** (equal to half of the minimum bet) and the next one over posts the **big blind,** which is equal to the minimum bet. The blinds count toward the total bet, meaning once betting begins the players who posted the blinds simply have to make up the difference between what they put in and the current bet to stay in the game. The dealer then deals two cards to each player, face-down. These are called the "hole" or the "pre-flop."

Then there's a round of betting. The amount bet is determined by the kind of game you're playing. If it's a 2–4 fixed-limit game, then the wager is the lower stake—in this case, $2. If it's a no-limit game, then it can be anything. When the round is completed, the dealer discards the top card (called "the burn") and deals "the flop": Three community cards are dealt face-up in the center of the table. The table bets again. Following another burn, the dealer deals a fourth card, face-up. This is called the "turn." The table bets, and if it's a fixed-limit game they bet the high stake, meaning the player in our hypothetical 2–4 game must now wager a minimum of $4 to stay in. The dealer burns another card and then deals the fifth card, face-up. This one is called the "river." By now you should really know whether or not it's time to bet or fold. The last round of betting takes place (in fixed-limit games the higher stake must still be wagered). If you're still in, show your cards to see who's made the best five-card hand and wins the pot. This is called "the showdown."

Omaha Hi/Lo

Also known as "Omaha 8-or-better" or "High-Low Split Poker," this game shares quite a few similarities with Texas Hold 'em. Depending on who you talk to, you'll hear that it's far more complicated or far less complicated than the latter. Which is the case? That's up to you to decide.

Better hands are needed at Omaha than they are at Hold 'em, because each player has four hole cards meaning nine cards total from which to select the best five—and therefore more options. Omaha is a split-pot game, meaning the high hand and the low hand will split the pot. So each player has two different chances to win each hand—high or low.

Just as in Texas Hold 'em, there are blinds and betting, a three-card flop, a turn card, and a river. The difference is that you must use two (and only two) of your four hole cards in making your five-card hand (though two different combinations can be used for your high and your low hands). Because you can only use two, there's no advantage to getting three- or even four-of-a-kind, or three or four cards of the same suit in the hole. When making your low hand, you want to avoid pairs (and anything higher than a pair) and the rules in many places hold that your highest number must be "8" or less. Straights and flushes don't count against the low. And for high hands, general poker rules apply. When it's time for the showdown, the best high hand and the best low hand split the pot.

The Advisor

Vegas success stories don't get much better than Anthony Curtis, who funded his own publishing company through his blackjack winnings. Curtis publishes the *Las Vegas Advisor* (www.lasvegasadvisor.com), which is a website and monthly newsletter chockablock with information on Vegas, deals, and a heavy emphasis on gambling. He's also the owner of Huntington Press, which publishes books on gambling and an assortment of locally themed tomes.

Once recognized as one of the world's top gamblers, Curtis has been studying Las Vegas since he moved here in 1979. His insight into the industry is perhaps unrivaled. But that doesn't mean he can just tell you how to hit the jackpot. "Everyone wants the magic pill," says Curtis. "Well, it really doesn't work like that. You literally have to study like you would study for a doctorate."

According to Curtis, the games to master are the four that are potentially beatable: Blackjack, video poker, poker, and sports betting (and he reserves the right to also add race betting to the list). He weighs in on each:

Blackjack

I would look for a game that deals as few decks as possible, a handheld deck, either a single or a double deck, that pays traditional 3 to 2 for blackjack. You can hardly find these anymore, especially on a single deck. Most Las Vegas single decks are now paying 6 to 5 for a natural. That seems insignificant, but it's devastating. It crushes you, a point-and-a-half percent.

Recommendation: Play Downtown. Particularly at El Cortez and the Plaza.

Video Poker

You've got to have a little bit of knowledge. It's all about pay schedules (at least, at the entry level). Look for the standard "Jacks or Better" game that returns nine for a full house and six for a flush. That game played perfectly by a computer will earn less than a half penny for every $100 you put through it. That's a very small tax to pay. Also, look for a place that has a slot club.

Recommendation: Find a quarter-level Jacks or Better game at the locals' casinos. Good choices here are the Fiestas (Rancho and Henderson), Station properties (Palace Station, Boulder Station, Texas Station, and

POKER OUTSIDE THE POKER ROOM

Poker played in poker rooms differs from the brand played against the house. The latter is found in casinos at tables that look similar to blackjack tables and are located among the table games, while the poker described above is isolated in others), Coast properties (Gold Coast, Suncoast, and others), Arizona Charlie's (Decatur and Boulder), and Palms.

Poker

With poker you want to be playing with more tourists than locals. You don't really want to go away from the Strip and sit down at a poker game with Johnny Omaha over here, who plays this game 6 out of 7 days a week. You really want to look for situations to be playing in the bigger, better-known poker rooms on the Strip.

Recommendation: Look for small- to midlevel limits, on and off the Strip. Look out for no-limit games, which have become popular (and can start with a $2 bet only to shoot up to $200). Some of Curtis's favorites are the Palms, Flamingo, Excalibur, and Texas Station.

Sports books

Sports books are a matter of taste. Your sports books are really the kind of place where you're going to find a generic product. And at almost all sports books you're betting $110 to win $100 on the base value, and that doesn't change very much. Where you're likely to find deals are in the places such as the Coast casinos or the Station casinos (both chains of locals' joints) during big events. They will change it so you pay $105 to win $100 instead of $110 to win $100. It makes a significant difference, and just about cuts the house edge in half.

Recommendation: The Hilton offers good deals and is the original super sports book. The director is a guy named Jay Kornegay, who's very innovative. This is the place you go during the Super Bowl, and you'll see 192 different proposition bets—"Will Ben Roethlisberger throw more passes than Kobe Bryant makes three-point shots?" He's really good at that kind of stuff.

Beyond these tips, joining Curtis's *Las Vegas Advisor* is one of the smartest things you can do before your trip to Las Vegas. For the $50-a-year membership fee (or $37 for online membership), you'll receive a monthly newsletter, gain access to online forums, and receive a coupon book full of offers for free game play, increased slot club points, free drinks, meals, show tickets, hotel rooms, and more. The value of these coupons alone may well pay for the membership. Sign up online at www.lasvegasadvisor.com or call ☎ 800/244-2224.

poker rooms located in a different part of the casino. When you play a table game version, you're no longer playing against the other people at your table, you're playing against the dealer (and, therefore, the house).

The house advantage is much higher in the following table-style poker games.

Caribbean Stud

If you know how to play five-card-stud poker, Caribbean Stud will be easy to pick up. This is a game where you play your hand against the dealer, not against the players around you. Once everyone places a bet in the ante box (and you also have the option of placing a $1 bet in the progressive box), the dealer deals five cards face-down to each player, and four face-down, and a fifth face-up. There's no draw, so your hand won't change. Players are then given the option of folding or calling, by making an additional bet that is double their original ante. The dealer then shows his hand. He must have at least an ace/king combination or higher to qualify, meaning the lowest qualifying hand is A-K-4-3-2, or the players win even money on the ante and the call bet is returned. If the dealer qualifies and defeats the player, the player loses the ante and the call bet. If the dealer qualifies and loses, the payout scale ranges from even money for a pair, to 100 to 1 on a royal flush, although there is usually a cap on the maximum payoff, which varies from casino to casino. Progressive bets pay off when the player has at least a flush, and you can win on this bet even if the dealer ends up with a better hand than you do. Most veteran gamblers will tell you the progressive is a bad bet (the math agrees with them), but Caribbean Stud already has a ridiculous house advantage, so if you're going to play, you might as well toss in the buck and pray.

Let It Ride

Another version of five-card-stud, Let It Ride involves three bets, and each bet must be the same amount, and equal to at least the minimum posted (for example, if the minimum bet is $5, players will be betting at least $15 per hand). Players can also pay $1 to a progressive pot (it has an obscene house advantage, but that's why it's called gambling!). The object of this game is to get a pair of "10"s or better by combining your cards with the community cards. The dealer deals two community cards and the three cards to each player, all face-down. Once a player has consulted her cards, she can take back one of her original bets or can stay in and let it ride. The dealer then turns over another community card. The player has another chance to take back one of her bets or let it ride. The dealer then turns over the second community card. At this stage, the dealer checks all players' hands and collects losing wagers and pays out winning hands. The typical payoff ranges from even money for a pair of "10"s to 1,000 to 1 for a royal flush. Note that if you're holding a pair of "10"s or better in your first three cards, you're a guaranteed winner and want to let your bets ride the whole way through.

Pai Gow Poker

Originally an Asian game played with tiles, *Pai Gow* has been adapted to playing cards and morphed into a form of poker. There's a lot going on in *Pai Gow.* The dealing is elaborate and complicated, involving dice and counting off counter-clockwise who gets the first set of cards. This is also a game where players can opt to be the bank, further complicating the rules. Like many games, *Pai Gow* is difficult to describe and more difficult for a novice to picture, but once you're sitting at the table it's fairly easy to pick up.

The game consists of making two hands out of a single seven-card hand dealt to you. The dealer starts out with a deck of 53 cards—a normal deck plus a joker, which can be used as an ace or to complete a straight, a flush, or a straight flush.

Players place bets and the dealer hands out sets of seven cards to everyone, including himself. Players cannot discuss their hands. Each player then divides his seven cards into two hands, one with two cards and the other made up of five cards. The goal is to make each hand the highest possible, with the caveat that the five-card hand must always be ranked higher than the two-card hand or you automatically lose. Poker rules apply when it comes to card value, with one exception: A-2-3-4-5 is the second-highest straight, between A-K-Q-J-10 and K-Q-J-10-9. The lowest possible pair is a set of "2"s, and the highest is a pair of aces. But remember, if you have a pair of aces in your two-card card set, you must have something higher in your five-card set.

Once players have arranged their cards they put them face-down on the table. The dealer then reveals what he has and proceeds to go around exposing the cards of the players, comparing them with his own. If the player wins both hands, he gets paid even money on the amount bet, minus a 5% commission. If the dealer wins one hand and the player wins one hand, it's a push and no money is exchanged. If the dealer wins both hands, he or she takes the player's wager. Ties go to the house, giving it an advantage.

ROULETTE

This game involves nothing more complicated than selecting a number or group of numbers and betting that a ball traveling around a circle will land on it. Roulette is a great place to start in a casino if you're an unsure gambler and want to get used to the interaction of a table game. Though the house has a distinct advantage (5.26% if there are double zeros on the wheel, 2.7% if it's a single zero), the game is fun and can be fairly social with the right crowd.

Players each get their own color of chips to distinguish them from each other. The dealer (or croupier) spins the wheel one way and sends a surprisingly loud ball on a track above the wheel in the opposite direction, which swirls around and eventually bounces into one of the slots marked by green zeroes or the red or black numbers. There are usually 38 slots—numbered "1" through "36," plus "0" and "00."

Before the ball settles, players have the option of placing bets on the outside of the table or requesting that the dealer place them on the inside, where the individual numbers are. Bets for both areas are straightforward. On the inside, you can select a single number to bet on (called a straight bet) or straddle your bet between two, three, or four numbers.

Your outside options are to bet on red or black, or to choose odd or even numbers. You can also select the inside numbers by placing your bet on "1 to 18," or the outside numbers by placing it on "19 to 36." The numbers are also divided in thirds, if you'd prefer to pick the first 12, second 12, or third 12. On the right side of the table are the "2 to 1" boxes, which place wagers on the entire column and pay accordingly.

As with all games, the lower the odds of winning, the higher the payout. The payout for straight bets is 35 to 1 (despite the fact that the actual odds are 38 to 1); split bets (placed between two numbers) pay out at 17 to 1; street bets, which cover one of the 12 columns pay 11 to 1; corner bets cover four numbers and pay 8 to 1; odd/even, red/black and low/high are all pay even money. But keep in mind that the presence of the green "0" and "00" throw those odds off, skewing them towards the house.

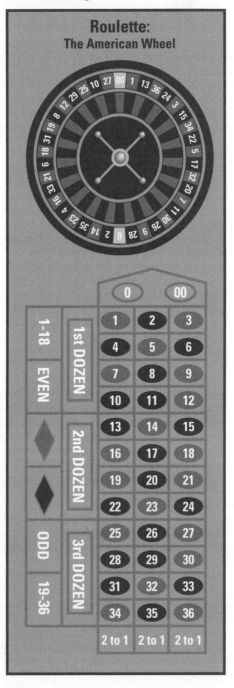

SLOT MACHINES

If you don't venture off the Strip you'd never know it, but slot machines are everywhere in Vegas: grocery stores, convenience stores, bars, restaurants, laundromats. Just about anywhere that there might be money—though they've managed to keep them out of churches . . . so far.

The slot machine has actually been around for more than 100 years and was invented in the 1890s by Charles Fey, a San Francisco car mechanic. The machine had three spinning reels with hearts, diamonds, spades, and a cracked Liberty Bell on them, and the jackpot was 50¢. The machines and technology have, of course, come a long way since then.

It's no surprise that this is now one of the most popular casino games, bringing in about 70% of their revenue. Players simply select a machine, let it suck in their bills, decide how many credits they want to play (credit just means coin, but the synonym is meant to distance the player from the fact that he's actually spending money), hit the "Spin" button, and the machine tells them if they won. No thinking or social interaction required. Keep in mind that slot machines fit in the gambling category called "negative expectation" games, which means that, over time, you will lose money.

Regardless, it's a game where players can make the most of the escapism that Vegas delivers, getting lost in the sounds and lights that signify the possibility of riches. Plus, slot machines offer choices. You can choose the denomination you want to play (from pennies to $500 a spin in the high roller areas), and how many coins you want to bet each time. And when you're done, you simply hit the "Cash Out" button (if there's any cash left) and take your ticket. Tickets have replaced coins, as most machines are now "paper only," meaning bills go in and paper comes out. The ticket can then be exchanged for cash or put into another machine to keep playing. Gone are the days of the winnings clanging on the metallic trays below (though there's often a simulated version of that sound played when you do cash out). It may seem like a convenience not to have to wait for all of the coins to be dispensed, but the casinos just aren't that concerned with helping make your life easier. They like it because this method is much quicker than the former, resulting in bonus time for—you guessed it—more gambling.

How do the machines work?

Slot machines are all computerized, and the outcome of each spin depends on what's called a Random Number Generator (RNG), which selects a different series of numbers that translate to the machine the moment you've pushed the "Spin" button whether you've won or lost. In the few seconds before you push "Spin" again, that random generator has already gone through thousands of combinations, one of which could have been a jackpot. Or will that come on your next spin? There lies the enticement.

That said, one thing to note is that each number is independently generated. Despite players' superstitions, strategies, and theories, there's no "hot" machine or machine operating on a streak. It's all a matter of timing on the part of your finger.

While the table games have set odds, meaning you know the house advantage before you play, slot machines are variable, depending on the casino, the denomination, maybe even the location of the machine. Generally, the house has an advantage of somewhere between 3% and 15%, meaning that over time, on average, $100 played in a machine will pay back $85 to $97. But that's over the long

slot machine pay lines

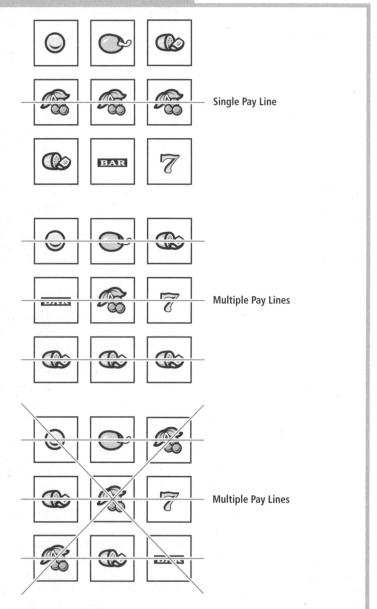

Single Pay Line

Multiple Pay Lines

Multiple Pay Lines

haul. Short-term play can be far better or far worse (see **www.wizardofodds.com** for specific casino average pays), and quarter and dollar machines tend to have better records than nickel machines.

Nevada law requires that slots pay back at least 75%. If you pick up publications such as *Casino Player* or talk to any seasoned gambler, you'll find that payback percentages are higher in Downtown and in locals' casinos than they are on the Strip. But to further break it down, frequent players on the Strip will tell you that the smaller casinos there have higher paybacks (and better comps) than do the large properties. Of course, that's on average. Because we're dealing with random numbers here, you could be just about anywhere and, thanks to perfect timing, hit it big.

Some people, however, insist that the machines in heavily trafficked areas, such as near the showroom or at the entrance to the casino, are looser (meaning the player is likely to win more). The theory goes that this method enables the casino to entice passers-by who might not have gambled to stay and play. It's likely true, but management at different casinos have different policies, and there's no definitive proof for or against it. Some gamblers think they can psychically detect a machine that's about to win. That's simply not the case. A machine doesn't have a "set" jackpot it's going to pay out after a player has invested a certain amount of money. And if you do win the jackpot, that doesn't preclude the machine from hitting it again soon after, as many players mistakenly assume. The numbers that determine the outcome are generated completely independently, so they're unaffected by what that machine already has or hasn't delivered.

To be an informed player, be sure to read the pay table at the top of the machine. This lets you know how much you can win from each combination of symbols, and the different amounts it will pay if you're betting one, two, three, four, or five (or more) coins at once. The more coins you play in a single machine, the more you increase your payoff should you hit the jackpot. Usually the increase reflects the number of coins: If you play two coins you win twice as much, and if you play five coins you win five times as much. But there are some machines that will only pay the maximum if you are betting the maximum. Meaning, if you're only playing one coin and you line up the symbols needed to get the jackpot, you won't win the entire jackpot because you didn't play the number of credits required to win. Take progressive slots, for example. These hold "linked" progressive jackpots (such as Megabucks, Quartermania, Nevada Nickels, and Fabulous Fifties), which allow the jackpot to build among a series of slot machines and can

The Tax Man

If you win a jackpot of $1,200 or more on a slot machine, you're required to pay taxes on it. When you're handed your winnings the slot attendant will also fill out a W2-G form to file with the government. Don't forget that you need to do the same. Table game tax reporting requirements vary; if you're worried about winning a large jackpot (lucky you!) at a specific game, ask any casino pit boss about possible IRS snafus.

Slot Tournaments

Cordoned off at Downtown's Main Street Station (and in many other casinos) is a group of zombie-eyed people, about the demographic of the bingo-playing set, staring at the screen of a slot machine and pounding the spin button, over and over and over again. This is not institutional field trip day—it's a slot tournament. And as silly as it looks (and sounds), it's surprisingly fun.

For years, I dismissed the concept as just plain weird. Should the words "slot" and "tournament" even be used together? Then I popped in one afternoon to the Downtown casino just to try it. To see what it felt like, competing against total strangers on a randomly selected machine to see who could earn higher points by repeatedly pushing a button.

At the "Go!" command, a group of about 20 of us started playing, hitting the button in rapid-fire motion, staring at the screen. This slot machine is called "The Big Kahuna," and everyone tries to line up three surfer guys. Players watch as their credits go up and the 20-minute timer goes down, switching from hitting "spin" with the left hand to the right as they tire, eyeing their neighbors to see where they stand. The participants are competing against each other for the highest number of points.

Once I got the trinity of matching surfers, I knew I was in. My score shot up quickly to 17,000, and with it, my confidence. It's sick, I know. It's purely a game of luck—but one in which I got third place and qualified for the finals.

"Beginner's luck," someone suggested. And maybe they were right. Because in the finals, I couldn't even make it over 7,000 points. I lost miserably and was helpless to do anything about it.

That injection of confidence? Gone. The intention to play in the future? Still there. My arm may be slightly sore from slapping a button for 40 minutes. But the mindless escape offered for only $10, and a shot at much more? Totally worth it.

Main Street Station hosts daily tournaments at 11am, 12pm, 2pm, and 3pm, with the finalists from each tournament returning for the championship at 4pm. It's $10 to play if you have a Player's Gold slot club card, or $15 without. And in this game, entry fees are divided among the top winners. In others, casinos charge higher entry fees and award larger prizes. For a list of slot tournaments go to **www.vegas.com/gaming/tournaments.html**.

pay in the millions. With these machines, you must play the maximum amount of coins to win the jackpot. Progressive machines make fewer small payments over time, so if you're a player who gets bored or frustrated when your credits aren't constantly climbing, they're not a good bet for you. But if you don't care about the process and you're just going for gold, progressive slots are the answer.

The bottom line: Choose a machine with a pay table that will pay the most according to what you're willing to spend.

Note: Beware of signs that advertise the machines pay "up to 97%." Take note of the words "up to," and keep in mind that the 97% (if it indeed pays up to it) is paid back over a period of time. And that period of time is bound to be longer than it takes to sink $20.

Endless varieties

Slot machine varieties have grown about as quickly as jackpot appreciation. There are those that still have reels, such as the well-known Triple 7 and fruit machines, and there are the video slot machines. Before you play, note how many pay lines each machine has. A pay line reveals where on the reels certain symbols must fall in order to win. In the old days there was only one: If you lined up three symbols across the screen you won. Now it's far more involved, with pay lines flowing across multiple rows and going up, down, diagonal, and zigzagging, producing a scene more elaborate than some subway maps. To further complicate matters, you can bet multiple amounts on each pay line. Experts recommend that you do bet on multiple pay lines if you have that option, but you should also remember that betting 1 or 20 credits on each line won't affect your odds of winning.

Game technology has also expanded to become more interactive and amusing, with such cartoon themes as *Little Green Men, The Addams Family, Monopoly, Wheel of Fortune, I Dream of Jeannie, The Beverly Hillbillies,* an Elvis machine that plays various hit songs for each jackpot payout, and countless others. When the proper combination lines up on the screen, a player is taken to a bonus round, where he can touch the screen to select a character (or other different options) and embark on a quick bonus game that's more complex and plot-driven than the spinning reels. For example, in the bonus round to "Reel 'em In" you select a character, who then sits on a boat, fishing. You also decide which fish the character should go for, and the points earned depend on what the fish was worth. It's a way of making a player really feel involved in their game.

VIDEO POKER

Unlike slots, video poker is a positive expectation game, meaning good strategy and the right machine can actually make you a consistent winner. Yes, here's a game where it's possible to beat the house. There are a number of different kinds of video poker, including Bonus, Double Bonus, Deuces Wild, Jacks or Better, and more. Some machines offer a multiple-play option, meaning you're playing between 3 and 50 games at once. (It sounds confusing, but it's actually quite simple. You're

Machine Databases

Need to know where to find certain video poker machines? Consult the video poker database at **http://members.cox.net/vpfree/LV.htm**. Looking for a particular slot machine? There's a searchable database for all of Harrah's-owned casinos (including Caesars Palace, Paris, Bally's, Flamingo, Horseshoe, and Harrah's) at www.harrahs.com.

dealt a single hand and you select the cards to hold. Those cards are held in every hand on the machine. So if you were dealt a three-of-a-kind of "3"s originally and you're playing 50 hands, you now have 50 different threes-of-a-kind. But when you hit "deal," the cards dealt to each hand are again randomized. So some hands could get another "3" and have a four-of-a-kind. Others could be dealt two of another card, for a full house. Or you could be dealt trash on every hand—highly unlikely, statistically speaking—in which case you'll still receive a nice payout for 50 threes-of-a-kind.) And it's not uncommon for a single video poker machine to offer different versions of video poker, in addition to video blackjack, slots, and keno.

Video poker is different from the poker game you play at the dining room table in that you're the only one playing. The goal is to get the best card combination possible.

The premise is simple enough: Once you insert money into the machine of your choice and bet, you're dealt five cards. To hold the cards you like, press the button directly beneath that card or touch the screen over those cards, and you will see the word "Hold" on the screen. Once you've chosen all of your cards to keep, hit "Deal/Draw," and the cards you didn't hold are replaced with new ones. This is the hand that determines how much you win.

Like in slots, you should always read the pay table printed on each machine in order to determine which machine will give you the most return. On average, returns vary from about 90% to over 100%.

Comparing pay tables on video poker machines is very important if you want the best chance of winning. If you put a quarter into a Jacks or Better machine and it pays nine coins for a full house and six coins for a flush, while another Jacks or Better machine pays eight coins for a full house and five for a flush, you should obviously opt to play for the one with the better pay table. The difference can mean a significant amount of money in the long run, and, as you've hopefully picked up on by now, the long run is what gambling's all about. So you can feel comfortable in choosing the "9/6" Jacks or Better machine, which has a payoff of 99.5%. But you'll only see this kind of payback if you play the game perfectly, and that takes time and skill.

Another informed choice is the "10/7 Double Bonus" machine, meaning if you put one quarter in and get a full house the machine pays 10 coins and if you get a flush it pays seven coins. This game actually pays back 100.7%, meaning that if you play perfectly, over time you ought to be making money.

Of course, as with the other games, entire books have been written about video poker and summing up the strategies here is simply impossible. One good book is Jean Scott's *Frugal Video Poker*. Another good option is a software program, Bob Dancer's *WinPoker*, which alerts you to mistakes as you play video poker on the computer. With the combination of the software and Dancer's strategy cards, which can accompany you into the casino and give advice on myriad hands, you should be on the path to positive poker. All of these products are available through Huntington Press and www.lasvegasadvisor.com.

WAR

Yes, you read it correctly. This child's game is now being played in Las Vegas casinos. And it's as easy as you may remember it. The game is played with six decks. Cards are ranked as they are in poker, but with aces always high. Players place

Gambling Lessons

It's an odd concept, learning a game from the entity that will, in time, be your rival. But many of the casinos offer gambling lessons so their clients are well informed and prepared (and, perhaps, enticed to gamble more?). The following is a list of some of the on-Strip options for lessons; keep in mind that schedules often change so be sure and call in advance.

Bally's: Poker noon Mon–Fri

Bill's Gamblin' Hall: Roulette 10am daily

Circus Circus: Roulette 10am–12:30pm; blackjack 10:30am–11am; craps 11am–2pm; all Mon–Fri only

Excalibur: Roulette 11am; blackjack 11:30am; craps noon; all daily

Imperial Palace: Craps 11am and 3pm Mon–Thurs, 11am Fri; blackjack 9am Mon–Fri; roulette 10am Mon–Fri

Mandalay Bay: Poker 2pm Mon–Thurs

Monte Carlo: Craps 11am daily

New York, New York: Craps 11am daily

Palazzo: Craps 11am; roulette noon; blackjack 12:15 pm; all Mon–Fri only

Paris: Poker noon Mon–Fri

Stratosphere: Craps 10:30 am; roulette 11:30 am; all Mon–Fri only

Tropicana: All games Wed–Sat 10am

Venetian: Craps 11am and 5pm; roulette noon; blackjack 12:15pm; all Mon–Fri only

their bets and the dealer hands out one card to each player and one to himself. If the player's card is higher than the dealer's, he gets even money. If the dealer's card is higher the player loses. If there's a tie the player can either surrender and give up half of his bet, or go to war. In the case of the latter, he must raise his bet by an equal amount to his initial wager. The dealer will then burn three cards and deal one to the player and one to himself. High card wins. This is another card game with a high house advantage. Be advised that the house advantage climbs even higher if you surrender, so this is one place where going to war is always the better option.

Vegas Shopping (Such as It Is)

Though it's extensive, it's not terribly varied or unique

by Kate Silver

I NEVER DREADED CHRISTMAS SHOPPING UNTIL I MOVED TO LAS VEGAS. It's not that this town doesn't have stores; it does, dozens upon dozens of them (as the town's PR hacks proclaim with glee). Problem is, they're the same sorts of stores you'll find everywhere else. Vegas primarily consists of chains, franchises, and corporate domination in all aspects of its existence, and shopping is no different. But what do you expect from a city where, year after year in local "Best of" surveys, Taco Bell wins best Mexican food and The Olive Garden wins best Italian? In shopping, Las Vegas caters to the median.

The malls distract us from their uniformity and high prices by throwing in the bells and whistles that this town of illusions is known for—giant Roman statues, boat rides, animatronic figures, and painted blue skies. Oddly enough, it's rare to see the word "mall" around town. Instead, expect to find semantics like shopping "destination" within the "shopping mecca" of Las Vegas.

But that doesn't help locals like me or visitors looking for more unique goods. I've resorted to doing my Christmas shopping online, looking for gifts that my family (who are spread out across the country), can't just go around the corner and buy for themselves. And buy for themselves more cheaply than I can get it here: Because retail rents are so high, you generally will pay more for the same goods in Las Vegas than elsewhere. The exception may be the outlet malls; and the odd, distinctly Vegas shops where items from feather boas to wigs to gambling stuff are for sale. I'll discuss these sorts of stores as well as the malls and strip malls, for those of you who will excuse the high prices in the name of convenience. Unless indicated, you can expect the stores and malls to accept most major credit cards.

MALLS ON THE STRIP

As this is where you'll likely be looking to spend your cash, I'll discuss malls on the Strip first, moving next to discount outlets and off-Strip malls. At the end of this chapter, you'll find information on the only-in-Vegas stores where you can buy wigs, feathers, and commemorative chips galore.

SOUTH STRIP

Mandalay Place (at Mandalay Bay; ☎ 877/632-7800 or 702/632-7777; www.mandalaybay.com; Sun–Thurs 10am–11pm, Fri–Sat 10am–midnight) has a fun and unique mix of shops—particularly by Vegas standards. The layout is simple, open, theme-free, and actually fulfills a dual purpose: In addition to retail space, it also provides a sky-bridge to the Luxor.

Coupon Clipping at the Mall

Coupon clipping works at home, and it also works in Vegas, so be sure to pick up the free coupon books that are available at each of the malls and outlet malls and offer savings at individual stores. Each mall has 'em (they generally have some variation of the word "passport" in the name: VIP Passport, Premier, and so forth) and along with discounts to both stores and restaurants, they often entitle the bearer to free gift offers with certain purchases. Here's the rub: To get the coupon book, you must first print out a coupon and take it to the customer service desk at each location. The coupons for the coupon can be found at various websites, including **www.destinationcoupons.com**. It's worth printing them out before you leave home, or seeing if the concierge at your hotel will do the deed for you.

Start on the first floor with the **Reading Room** ★ (☎ 702/632-9374), one of Vegas' few independent bookstores, with an impressive variety of offerings (including an extensive array of Vegas-themed publications) for its size. Located next to the **Chocolate Swan** (p. 84), it's not a bad place for relaxing with a guidebook and a snack or people-watching. Or continue up the elevators, and you'll find a primo wine shop (and tasting bar) to the right, called **55 Degrees Wine + Design** ★ (☎ 702/632-9355). They really know their vino here, and the salespeople don't get snotty when you tell them you're looking for something inexpensive. My favorite part about 55 Degrees is the (free) packaging they provide: Your bottle is suspended in an inflated plastic bag, so you don't have to worry about breaking it as you walk around, and it looks space-age and snazzy.

Other highlights among the 41 shops and restaurants are **Urban Outfitters** (which specializes in clothing, but also carries some fun and funny trinkets for semicheap); **Lush Puppy** and all of its dog-centric accouterments; and **The Art of Shaving,** a metrosexual's HQ. For easy access and exit there's a valet parking lot that few people know about right at one of the first-floor entrances to Mandalay Place.

CENTER STRIP

For sheer entertainment value, **The Forum Shops** ★★★ (at Caesars Palace; ☎ 702/893-4800; www.forumshops.com; Sun–Thurs 10am–11pm, Fri–Sat 10am–midnight; statue shows held hourly beginning at 10am) are by far the best. From the giant replica of Michelangelo's statue of David to the imported Italian marble, the winding escalators, and the painted ceiling that changes in brightness according to the time of day, it almost feels like a living museum of sorts, as costumed gladiators, Cleopatras, and assorted toga-wearers circulate among shoppers. On the eastern and western ends of the mall, animatronic statues act out nonsensical dramas (p. 118).

Navigating this mall can be a challenge. Because of the moving figures and ornate fountains, tourists are more focused on photo-ops than power shopping. It would take a horse-drawn chariot to make good time getting through here.

Still, the idea of mall entertainment clearly works, as this is one of the highest grossing malls, per square foot, in the nation. And we're talking a lot of square feet, with Caesars having recently opened an additional 175,000-square-foot area, bringing the Forum Shops' grand total to about 675,000 feet with an assortment of Rodeo Drive–caliber emporiums such as **Gucci, Dolce & Gabbana, Versace,** and more. A whimsical three-story **FAO Schwartz** ✪✪ and the "world's largest" **Tourneau** add some variety to the mix, and there are many standard midrange options, such as **Banana Republic** and **Anthropologie,** where prices are actually no higher than their non-tourist-trap siblings, and their sales racks are almost as good.

There's a valet parking lot just downstairs from the shops. So you can park, take an elevator up, and put that extra energy the valet saved you into hunting for bargains. And avoiding overly buff gladiators.

Though Caesars has more shopping options and a 175,000-square-foot advantage, The Venetian has stepped up to the plate to rival its architecture and mall entertainment with **The Grand Canal Shoppes** ✪✪ (at The Venetian; ☎ 877/883-6423 or 702/414-4500; www.grandcanalshoppes.com; Sun–Thurs 10am–11pm, Fri–Sat 10am–midnight). Modeled after Venice, the mall is lined with cobblestone walkways, so you'll want to avoid wearing high heels here. The tiles may be charming, but walking over them can be a painful challenge in stilettos.

Shops are framed to look like the exteriors of old homes built along a replication of the Grand Canal. The meandering little river splits the mall in two; gondolas float on canals through and around the building (p. 120). The gondolas are rowed by gondoliers, dressed in traditional black-and-white-striped shirts with red kerchiefs, who'll serenade you in Italian as you drift pass shops and under bridges and through St. Mark's Square—a large, open space filled with what the casino likes to call "Streetmosphere."

This is actually a great place to take a break with a cup of gelato and watch the *carnivale* performers, singers, mimes, and other acts. You won't find any hokey animatronics here, but before you sidle up to one of those gray sculptures for a photo op, be prepared that it might actually move. Many of the statues here are people painted to look like granite.

The surrounding shops and restaurants, all 500,000 square feet of them, are touted by PR gurus as "world class," which in layman's terms translates as pricey (that desert canal doesn't pay for itself, you know), and trendy. You'll find 80 standard to high-end restaurants and shops, including **Burberry, Kenneth Cole, St. John Sport, Pal Zileri, Mikimoto, Lior, Ca' d'Oro, Jimmy Choo,** the award-winning **Canyon Ranch Spa,** and many more.

The Shoppes at Palazzo (☎ 877/883-6423 or 702/414-4525; www.theshoppes atthepalazzo.com; Sun–Thurs 10am–11pm, Fri–Sat 10am–midnight) are the mature, richer sibling to the neighboring Grand Canal Shoppes. This isn't your run-of-the-mill Banana Republic/Gap/Ann Taylor depot (you'll get your fill of those at The Grand Canal Shoppes). The options are more rare and refined, and there's no theme here, aside from an ornate decor that's more reminiscent of shopping at Wynn or Bellagio. There's also never a crowd—the ruling's still out on just how ready the masses are for expensive, chichi, and theme-free, at least, in Vegas.

The crown jewel of the 60-plus-store retail plaza is **Barneys New York** ✪✪. The 81,000-square-foot anchor is one of 10 Barneys nationwide and is the third to bring its trendiest of trendy designers to Sin City. Barneys is one of nearly 30 stores at Palazzo that's a "first" to Las Vegas, including **Annie Creamcheese Designer Vintage, Diane von Furstenberg, Christian Louboutin, Piaget,** and more. But the store that has even locals doing a double-take is **Bauman Rare Books.** Sure, it seems counterintuitive to see a store selling a first edition of James Joyce's *Ulysses* at 10:30pm on a Friday night at a casino property. But it turns out it's not just too good to be true—the store demographic intersects with the theater-going demographic and is known to be a fun browsing stop following the *Jersey Boys.*

Over at Planet Hollywood, the transformation from the Shops at Desert Passage into the **Miracle Mile Shops** ✦ (at Planet Hollywood; ☎ 888/800-8284; www.miraclemileshopslv.com; Sun–Thurs 10am–11pm, Fri–Sat 10am–midnight) has been a positive albeit partial one. They've gotten rid of those dreadful, cobblestone-like tiles and added some modern touches, like circular bars in places, but the cloud-filled blue skies and Middle Eastern–style building facades still remain for half the "Mile." A few changes have also been made to the store selection, which now caters to a younger demographic, with **Urban Outfitters, Bettie Page** (a shop based on that '50s-era model's sexy style), and **H&M.** Still, many of the 168 retailers are tried-and-true holdovers from the Aladdin days, like **FCUK, Bebe,** and **Betsey Johnson.** The mall, as it stands, remains a kind of locals' secret. It's not as well traversed as Fashion Show and The Forum Shops, so it's rarely crowded and often has great sales. But those benefits don't come without a downside. Just walking through the Miracle Mile Shops can be a challenge, thanks to the aggressive salespeople manning the many carts selling wares such as jewelry, lotion, and curling irons. (And my skin is not too dry, nor my hair too straight, thank you very much!)

Located in the esplanade that also leads to Bally's, **Le Boulevard** (at Paris; ☎ 877/796-2096 or 702/946-7000; www.parislv.com; daily 9am–11pm) is yet another cobblestone walk down a quaint cityscape designed to imitate the Rue de la Paix. It's dotted with living statues and lined by the exteriors of Parisian buildings that actually serve to frame the French boutiques in this shopping area. You'll find 31,500 square feet of primarily specialty stores, peddling jewelry, art, and home accessories. The stores have French names and actually sell French items. **Les Enfants** is a children's store selling French apparel and toys; for provincial French home and garden items there's **Les Elements; La Cave** peddles French wine and cheese; and the list goes on. Watch out for the bikers that ride through the area toting bread. They're here to add ambience, but could cause a collision if you get too sidetracked by the stand that sells frozen drinks in Eiffel Tower shaped cups.

The Avenue Shoppes (at Bally's; ☎ 702/967-4111; www.ballyslv.com; daily 9am–11pm) are small by Vegas standards, with just 20 stores and no theme or even cobblestones (gasp!). But there's okay variety here, from fresh flowers to Harley Davidson's clothing boutique and rental referral service, as well as different clothing and gourmet food options. It's actually a sensory relief to be able to focus on shopping rather than "shoppertainment" (it's amazing that term has yet to be trademarked and claimed).

The shops of **Via Bellagio** (at Bellagio; ☎ 888/987-3456 or 702/693-7111; www.bellagio.com; daily 10am–11pm) target the same clientele as the hotel—and there's nothing "budget" about them. If ever you've wondered what people with

Seasonal Differences

Las Vegas has a unique climate, so even if the stores here are the same as back home, the clothes are more suited towards our seasons, or lack thereof. What this means in short is that what you'll find on the Banana Republic sales rack (and regular rack) in the desert in the winter—light wools and thin jackets—is going to be different from what you'll find on the Banana Republic sales rack back home in New York or Minnesota—heavy wools and thick coats. The same goes for summer, which lasts from about May through September.

more money than God do with it, look no further than the floors here, paved with imported Italian tile that takes on designs of flowers and bugs as it winds around the designer boutiques.

The stores are limited in number, of course. Why go for quantity, sniff, when you can have such quality as **Tiffany & Co., Giorgio Armani, Chanel, Dior, Fendi, Gucci, Hermes, Fred Leighton, Prada,** and **Yves Saint Laurent?** Think there's nothing you can afford here? C'mon, now. There's bound to be a keychain or cuff link for less than $100 somewhere. And even if there's not, just being inside the Bellagio gives you the perfect excuse to wander over to the (free) conservatory and see what designs the floral architects have come up with this season (p. 119). While you're there, be sure and gaze into the 27-foot-tall chocolate fountain, flowing with three kinds of chocolate at **Jean-Philippe Patisserie** (p. 85). Oh, and one thing you can afford is the free parking at the far entrance to Via Bellagio, which saves you a walk through the casino, and that can be priceless.

The Hawaiian Marketplace (3743 Las Vegas Blvd. S.; ☎ 702/795-2247; daily 10am–10pm; musical entertainment hourly 1–9pm; bird show Fri–Sun 2:30pm) is an open-air, island-targeted tourist trap. Las Vegas is Hawaii's No. 1 destination for tourism, and also a hot spot for relocating. It used to be that the downtown casinos were the ones who took advantage of the demographic (as you'll see by the number of restaurants there with Spam on the menu), until developers took notice and built a shopping area on the Strip devoted to Hawaiian culture—well, some parts of it. The 80,000-square-foot outdoor island-styled plaza located between the MGM Grand and Planet Hollywood is filled with Polynesian-themed huts selling overpriced leis, T-shirts, art, but, oddly enough, no Hawaiian food. It's unclear exactly who it's meant to cater to, as Las Vegas tourists typically aren't looking for a "Hawaii" T-shirt—and neither are tourists from Hawaii. But there's an outdoor bar with live bands playing, and for fans of winged creatures, there's a free bird show featuring The Birdman of Las Vegas (formerly of the Tropicana).

NORTH STRIP

Though it's free of moving statues and waterways, **Fashion Show** ✪✩ (3200 Las Vegas Blvd. S.; ☎ 702/369-0704; www.thefashionshow.com; Mon–Sat 10am–9pm, Sun 11am–7pm) still has a couple of gimmicks that set it apart from other more pedestrian malls. Externally, it's distinguished by "The Cloud"—a giant, bright, and incredibly distracting futuristic-looking thing that shades the mall during the day and projects advertisements at night. Internally, there's an 80-foot retractable runway at one wing of the property where fashion shows are held each weekend and models flaunt the latest and greatest to gathering crowds.

It's also different in that it's not attached to a casino and is darn big, at almost 2 million square feet. That's about half the size of Mall of America, though the folks who run the place bragged to me that their shopping space is actually just as large . . . since 2 million feet at Minneapolis's famous mall are taken up by roller coasters, aquariums, and the like. (Ah, ya gotta love the reflexive one-upmanship of Vegas!) Walking the entire mall could take an entire afternoon and counts as your anaerobic exercise for the day, as you'll be trekking into and out of over 200 stores and restaurants. **Neiman Marcus, Saks Fifth Avenue, Nordstrom, Bloomingdale's Home,** and **Macy's** are the flagship anchors and then there are all of the usual suspects squatting in the middle: **Diesel, Zara, Betsey Johnson, Banana Republic,** and **J. Crew**—along with dozens of other clothing and specialty shops. There's a dearth of "only in Vegas" stores (so what else is new), with the fashion forward **Talulah G** and the Scandinavian clothing chain **Sandwich** (chic and affordable) the best exceptions to that rule. Eighteen million people visit Fashion Show on a yearly basis, which averages out to about 40,000 a day, so if you hate crowds, avoid Fridays, Saturdays, and Sundays, when the fashion shows go on— seven times throughout the day—and shopping here can be elbow to elbow.

The Wynn Esplanade (at Wynn Las Vegas; ☎ 888/320-WYNN or 702/770-7000; www.wynnlasvegas.com; Sun–Thurs 10am–11pm, Fri–Sat 10am–midnight) caters to the same demographic as Via Bellagio and exudes a similar stateliness— as does pretty much everything in Wynn, considering Steve Wynn is the force behind both properties (though MGM MIRAGE now owns Bellagio). Again, you may as well go on a treasure hunt for the most affordable item (and then not buy it) so it at least feels like you're doing something other than staring at price tags, aghast, in stores such as **Dior, Oscar de la Renta, Louis Vuitton, Jean Paul Gaultier,** and even the "home-grown" **Wynn & Company Jewelry.** Another highlight that you won't lose sleep over avoiding? The Wynn Penske Ferrari/ Maserati dealership that charges a $15 entry fee (p. 133). It's not clear whether that fee is returned to you should you purchase a vehicle. When I asked, they answered with a laugh. And a blank stare.

WEST OF THE STRIP

Suburbanites love their shopping, too, and they're served well with options. **The Fashion Village at Boca Park** ✮ (750 S. Rampart Blvd., at the intersection of Charleston Blvd. and Rampart Blvd.; individual store hours vary) is a hot spot on the far west side that's located in Summerlin, a tony part of town, and its average patron tends to be blonde, bronze, and buxom. Less than 10 miles from the Strip, this enormous white strip mall caters to that look with trendy boutiques such as **Talulah G, C-Level,** and **Pink;** along with home decorating extravaganzas such as **The Great Indoors** and the higher-end **Design Within Reach** (funky mod furniture); and a spot for the bare necessities, **Amore European Lingerie.** There are a lot more shops, plus restaurants such as the trendy **Kona Grill** and **The Cheesecake Factory.**

One nice touch: There are a few reserved parking spots for expectant mothers. And some fun trivia—Boca Park is one of the few places in town away from the

Strip that actually has fountains in use. A couple of years ago, the county and city passed ordinances restricting fountain use (unless it could be proven to directly impact the business of a place, which is how the Strip gets away with it) because of the local water shortage. Triple Five, the developers of Boca Park, continue skirting the issue by importing their fountain water from Canada and other places.

Just west of Boca Park is another strip mall with the **Gap, Banana Republic, Ann Taylor, Williams-Sonoma,** and **Pottery Barn.** South of these stores, in yet another strip mall, is a **Whole Foods.** Add to that **Nora's Wine Bar & Osteria,** a local favorite for wine and small Italian plates, which is also located in the vicinity, and you've got the ingredients for an extensive shopping spree, with lunch.

SOUTH OF THE STRIP

At Vegas' newest shopping complex, **Town Square** ✪✪ (6605 Las Vegas Blvd. S; not too far from Mandalay Bay; ☎ 702/269-5001; www.townsquarelasvegas.com; Mon–Thurs 10am–9:30pm, Sat–Sun 10am–10pm, Sun 11am–8pm), wandering around and playing "name that architecture" is as enjoyable as actually shopping. Let me explain: Town Square is a 117-acre conglomeration of shops that's meant to look like a prosperous small town, down to a village green in the center with a playground. It feels a bit like a movie set—*The Truman Show,* perhaps?—but the 22 buildings all reference different international styles. **California Pizza Kitchen** was inspired by the architecture of an old Spanish mission, while **H&M** is based on the neoclassical design of many American train stations, and **Ann Taylor** is in modern mission style. It's aesthetically quite successful, a nice mix of influences, which may be why the restaurants here are doing a booming business; people just enjoy hanging out here.

But if you do choose to shop, the stores run the gamut, with quite a few first-in-Vegas options, like **Michael Stars** and **Robb & Stucky Interiors.** There's even a stylish locally owned boutique (a rarity in this chain-loving town), **Blend,** that brings in trendy clothes from new designers in Europe, New York, and Los Angeles. And then the old reliables: **Banana Republic, Gap, A|X Armani Exchange, J. Crew** (to save a few dollars be sure and visit the concierge for a Rewards brochure, which offers discounts to certain retailers). Non-shoppers in the group can also check out the 18-screen **Rave Motion Pictures,** or just sit in one of the many benches near the tranquil pond and less-than-tranquil playground. Parking is even convenient here, thanks to the metered spaces in front of individual stores.

One thing to note, for those of us who lack a sense of direction there's a maze-like feel among the varying buildings, and it's easy to get lost. I've been tempted more than once to fire up the "GPS" feature on my Blackberry.

The District at Green Valley Ranch (2240 Village Walk Dr.; ☎ 877/564-8595 or 702/564-8595; www.thedistrictatgvr.com; Mon–Sat 10am–9pm, Sun 11am–7pm) is part of the more vertical and efficient trend in southern Nevada. Located in Henderson (in a posh area referred to as, you guessed it, Green Valley) it's a mixed-use space (or a "metropolitan lifestyle center," as they call themselves) that's done what most cities do from their start—urban planning. The combination of suburban sprawl and rising real estate costs have finally inspired developers to place living spaces on top of businesses, resulting in places such as The District. Of course, in other cities the shops, restaurants, and businesses below tend to have

Souvenir Shopping: Beyond the Fuzzy Dice

Clotheshorses and fashionistas be damned: The most characteristic shopping that Las Vegas has to offer, hands-down, lies in its souvenir shops. Here, products are representative of the true Vegas economy, which revolves around entertainment; indulgence; kitsch; and you, the tourist.

Each show and major attraction also has a gift shop. Where else will you ever find a Cher pencil but at the **Cher store,** inside Caesars Palace? Where could you find a Barry Manilow purse, or a BM beach towel, aside from the **Barry Manilow store** at the Las Vegas Hilton? From the teddy bear gondoliers at The Venetian to the red, white, and blue hot pants Liberace Beanie Bears of the **Liberace Museum** (p. 129), it's easy to find unique, themed trinkets in Las Vegas that you never knew you wanted—such as the "Radioactive" patches and Einstein action figures at the **Atomic Testing Museum** (p. 125).

But the mother of all gift shops is **Bonanza Gifts** ★★★ (2440 Las Vegas Blvd. S.; ☎ 702/385-7359; www.worldslargestgiftshop.com; daily 8am–midnight). This place heralds itself as "The World's Largest Gift Shop," and though they're likely building something to rival it in Dubai, it's certainly the biggest and the best in Las Vegas. I actually avoided this place for years, assuming it would be just another cheap fuzzy dice outlet. When I finally submitted, I learned it certainly is a cheap, fuzzy dice outlet—and so much more. Aside from the T-shirts and postcards, there's also the lighted and iconic miniature "Welcome to Fabulous Las Vegas" sign, witty and crass T-shirts that even locals buy, an enormous collection of Archie McPhee toys (if you haven't yet discovered the wonders of McPhee, with its Avenging Unicorn set and an entire line of Jesus collectibles, now is the time: www.archiemcphee.com), and enough gag gifts to make you choke. The selection goes on forever, and one thing is more funny/kitschy/useless and stupid than the next. It's a delight!

character and a sense of place. Here, it's really just an outdoor mall that sprouted in the middle of the parking lot of a casino. (Green Valley Ranch Resort, to be more specific.)

Now, locals have the chance to purchase a loft (Vegas vocabulary for an expensive, airy apartment) above **Ann Taylor Loft, Williams-Sonoma, Anthropologie,** and **Along Came A Spider;** or above restaurants such as **La Salsa** (now, there's a smell to awaken to). The local response has been overly enthusiastic, as though intelligent utilization of space is a fresh concept. It's a smart-looking area—don't get me wrong. But the prestige (and there truly is prestige attached) of living above a mall is simply bizarre.

The District's second phase—known as "The District Expansion"—is across the street. Here, you'll find shopping options such as **Coach, West Elm** (furniture and housewares), and some small boutiques, in addition to a gorgeous **Whole Foods Market, The Cheesecake Factory,** and a **carousel.** To transport guests from one side of the street to the other, The District offers a free trolley service.

OUTLET MALLS

Unlike many cities that ship their outlets to the remote outskirts of town, two of the discount malls here are easily accessed. **The Las Vegas Premium Outlets** ★★ (875 S. Grand Central Pkwy.; ☎ 702/474-7500; www.premiumoutlets.com; Mon–Sat 10am–9pm, Sun 10am–8pm) offer more chichi options than are customary in such malls, and they actually have some good bargains. A part of the Chelsea Premium Outlets Group, the shops are located downtown, bringing much-needed business to the area. An expansion in 2008 brought even greater variety to the already impressive mall, and now the 150 shops include outlet rarities like **Ed Hardy, Juicy Couture, Salvatore Ferragamo, True Religion,** and more. The mall is open-air, and a refreshing change from the indoor shopping experience. And aside from our unbearable but limited slew of 115°F (46°C) days, it's even pleasant for much of the summer, with misters fighting off the triple digits, making for a vitamin-D filled, suntanning shopping experience.

As you may know, outlet malls have received unwanted attention in the media of late for their pricing and practices. Some journalists have pointed out that the prices at certain outlet malls are no longer lower than they are at regular malls. There's also been talk of the fact that many brands are now producing lower quality goods for distribution only at outlet malls. What's the situation here? With Premium Outlets you'll find a mixed bag. There are stores such as **Calvin Klein** and **Ann Taylor Factory Store** that do indeed have their own outlet line (you be the judge of the quality). Others have a mixture of off-season and discounted retail along with their own outlet line (**Banana Republic Factory Store, Theory,** and **Tommy Hilfiger**). Then there are the few gems that are adamant about quality, selling the same types of clothing you'd find at their retail outlets, such as **Dolce & Gabbana** and **White House/Black Market.**

For additional savings, register online (it's free) to receive coupons as part of the VIP Shoppers Club and the 50-plus shoppers club. The latter awards shoppers 50 and older with an additional 10% discount at participating stores on Tuesdays.

If you're staying in the downtown area, the malls provide low cost transportation for shoppers in the form of a white and blue shuttle printed with the words "city ride." It runs daily 10am to 5:15pm, with stops every 20 minutes, and costs $1 per ride. You can catch it at the Downtown Transportation Center, the California Hotel & Casino, the Plaza Hotel & Casino, and the Golden Nugget.

Except for its **Calvin Klein, Sean John,** and **Perry Ellis** stores, the offering at **Las Vegas Outlet Center** (7400 Las Vegas Blvd. S.; ☎ 702/896-5599; www.lasvegas outletcenter.com; Mon–Sat 10am–9pm, Sun 10am–8pm) are far more generic and typical of standard outlets. Narrow and bland, the smell of popcorn wafting throughout, window shoppers will see this mall for its orthopedic shoes and Corning Ware. Truly determined outlet scavengers, on the other hand, are bound to find some great bargains here, from china to silverware to unbeatable prices on clothing. It just takes some rummaging. But the best reason to visit is **Saks Fifth Avenue Off 5th** ★ (7680 Las Vegas Blvd. S.; ☎ 702/263-7692; Mon–Sat

10am–9pm, Sun 10am–7pm), which is conveniently located in an annex completely separate from the mall, so you can park and go in and not have to deal with crowds, walkways, or mall food smells. Saks sells a combination of lines bought specifically for the outlet, as well as off-season and clearance stock from Saks, with shoes, clothes, accessories, gourmet treats, and more. And, as a bonus, Nine West is its neighbor.

Nordstrom Rack ✪ (9851 S. Eastern Ave., at Silverado Ranch Plaza #376; ☎ 702/948-2121; www.nordstrom.com; Mon–Fri 10am–9pm, Sat 10am–8pm, Sun 11am–7pm) began in 1975 as a clearance store in the basement of the Downtown Seattle store. It's since come into its own, and there are now 50 Nordstrom Racks in 18 different states. With the growth, the store has gotten further away from its strict Nordstrom's devotion, but you'll still find some actual Nordstrom overflow at savings of 50% to 75%. And if it's not from the store, it comes directly from the different labels, so there are brands such as DKNY, Kenneth Cole, Lucky, Juicy Couture, Marc Jacobs, and more at solid clearance prices. In addition to men's and women's clothing, Nordstrom Rack has an impressive shoe department (with variety even for the Bigfoots among us), bath and beauty products, accessories, and home accents. You may have to dig through racks of varying styles and sizes, but it's worth it.

OLDIES BUT GOODIES (ANTIQUES & VINTAGE CLOTHES)

For antiques, head downtown. East Charleston Boulevard and the area just south of it, on Casino Center Boulevard and Colorado Avenue, is where you'll find heirlooms, relics, and the dust from past decades. The following are some of my favorites:

The Funk House ✪ (1228 S. Casino Center Blvd.; ☎ 702/678-6278; www.the funkhouselasvegas.com; Mon–Sat 10am–5pm) is what happens when antique shop meets curiosity shop meets Las Vegas. Located in the heart of the Arts District, the boxy store is covered in wacky murals and has large, metallic bugs hanging off the sides. From the lamps designed to look like women's torsos to the local artists' exhibits that change each month, The Funk House caters to hipsters, antiquers, and anyone looking to while away a few hours amid the stacks, piles, and heaps of slightly dusty furniture and adornments that line the walls, shelves, and aisles from the floor to the ceiling.

Some oddities from the past (that make this store as much a wacky museum as anything else) include two coffins with skeletons inside that can be seen through a window; a two-headed baby from an early 1900s freak show (it was actually made of papier-mâché and wood); showgirl-shaped lamps; and so much more. Of course, there are also myriad collectibles, wall hangings, art, jewelry, gambling collectibles, and other finds. The varied contents reflect the schizo nature of Las Vegas and owner Cindy Funkhouser (who's actually one of the forces behind First Friday; see p. 170) who can tell you just about anything you want to know about Downtown.

Red Rooster Antique Mall ✪✪ (1109 Western Ave.; ☎ 702/382-5253; Mon–Sat 10am–6pm, Sun usually 11am–5pm, though sometimes they don't open until 1:30pm) has no relation to the Red Rooster Swingers Club in the nightlife chapter (p. 222)—though both certainly feature older items looking for someone to take them home. The mall consists of dozens of different vendors, some of which are more theme-oriented than others. You'll find your share of midcentury modern, antique china, vintage Las Vegas items, Tiki-themed goods, and all kinds of old(ish) memorabilia, such as California Raisin figurines, Pez dispensers, and packs of Garbage Pail Kids cards (I hate to think that those who can remember such things are actually considered antiques). It's easy to get lost here, but the friendly staff is sure to help you find your way out. This place sets you on a mazelike treasure hunt through rooms and rooms of classic, vintage, and just plain old stuff.

For less expensive (but certainly not cheap) vintage (and "vintage") items with a more casual style, stop by **The Attic** (1018 S. Main St.; ☎ 702/388-4088; www.atticvintage.com; Mon–Thurs 10am–5pm, Fri 10am–6pm, Sat 11am–6pm, closed Sun), which bills itself the "Largest Vintage Clothing Store in the World." That

Zoot Suit Junction

A zoot suit was once as much a statement as it was a fashion, and **Valentino's Zootsuit Connection** ✪ (907 S. 6th St., Ste. 103; ☎ 702/383-9555; www.valentinoszootsuitconnection.com; Mon–Sat 11am–5pm) is no different. Zoot suits, which were first made popular in Harlem jazz culture in the late 1930s, consist of wide-legged trousers with tight cuffs and a long, matching coat with wide lapels and padded shoulders. The style was once poetically described by an unknown observer as "A killer-diller coat with a drape shape, reet pleats, and shoulders padded like a lunatic's cell." The zoot suit's popularity spread, and it quickly became popular among young Latinos and African-Americans in Los Angeles.

The outfits were actually banned by the War Production Board in 1942, which called the suit a waste of valuable material during wartime. As is always the case when a ban goes into effect, the style became even more popular, and in 1943 it was the cause of L.A. riots between groups of military men and Mexican-Americans—the servicemen claimed they'd been assaulted by a group wearing zoot suits. That led them to attack every Mexican American they could find wearing the fashion, and the subsequent violence became known as the Zoot Suit Riots. It was somehow later deemed that racism was not a factor.

With a history like that, there should be more stores dedicated to the get-up. Valentino's is owned by a husband and wife team (both former fashion models) and carries clothing from zoot to gabardine and Western wear to evening gowns; they also have hats of all varieties, shiny shoes, and a small but quality collection of vintage women's clothing. The exquisite lamps and charming pillows, purses, and other accouterments add character and grace to this savvy shop.

says to us most vintage clothing stores must be pretty small. Not that The Attic lacks in space. It's just that its size is less impressive than its funky selection, with two floors overflowing with groovy threads, some of which are from the '60s and '70s, and others, like The Attic's own brand of custom clothing, created to reflect such styles, which makes its self-proclaimed status even more questionable.

The clothes are surrounded by an array of furniture, shoes, accessories, and a little bit of everything else (including a "wiping rags" division that claims to ship rags to every country on the planet). It's neither dusty nor musty, managing to avoid the disheveled thrift-shop overtones that often cling to vintage (and vintage-inspired) duds. The fact that you have to pay $1 to enter is frustrating, especially considering that, if you're driving, you also have to put money in the parking meter (this area is one of the only spots in Vegas where you actually have to pay for parking). But that $1 is deducted from any purchases and seems to serve as a way to keep the area's more sketchy characters from entering.

Consignment and thrift stores in Las Vegas occasionally hold some hidden surprises, but finding them seems to take far more effort here than in other cities. The best spot for stylish used clothes is **Buffalo Exchange** (4110 S. Maryland Pkwy., Ste. 1; ☎ 702/791-3960; www.buffaloexchange.com; Mon–Sat 10am–8pm, Sun 11am–7pm), which is one in a chain of consignment stores found primarily in the Western and Southwestern states. There are definite hipster overtones to the clothing that Buffalo Exchange sells, so you won't have to hunt as you would in a thrift store, but you'll also be paying quite a bit more for the convenience.

VEGAS SPECIALTY STORES

When most people think of Vegas, they think of gambling, showgirls, and sex, among other things. Where there is demand, there is also supply. An array of retail stores help fuel our fulfillment of those industries.

BOOKS

The Gambler's Book Shop (630 S. 11th St.; ☎ 800/522-1777 or 702/382-7555; www.gamblersbook.com; Mon–Sat 9am–5pm) is to Las Vegas what Powell's is to Portland and what the Tattered Cover is to Denver. Though a fraction of the size of the aforementioned shops, its mission is similar: to serve and reflect the community where it roosts. It's been doing that since 1964, when it was opened by a couple named, appropriately enough, Luckman. Back then, men would gather to discuss gambling in a nonjudgmental, clublike atmosphere. Times have changed and gambling is more accepted, attracting men and women to the store who are interested in beating the casinos, intellectuals who are devising new games to play, Hollywood producers in need of a crash course in gambling for their next project, and more. Now the shop is owned by Howard Schwartz, who's a local gambling expert. As he should be, considering he's surrounded by more than 400,000 volumes, from *The Handicappers Condition* to *Dice Collecting*, and just about everything else gambling related.

And for more gambling lore, **The Gambler's General Store** ☆ (800 S. Main St.; ☎ 800/322-2447 or 702/382-9903; www.gamblersgeneralstore.com; daily 9am–6pm) claims to be the largest gambling superstore in the world, at 8,000 square feet. We'll go ahead and take their word for it—these aren't the type of people to bet against. It has a massive collection of chips, cards, slot machines, table games, and even a line of gambling-themed jewelry. There's also a wide selection of books and videos to help you sharpen up your game and, hopefully, gain some kind of advantage over the house.

Contrary to clichés, just as residents of Las Vegas don't live in hotels, they actually do have bookstores in no way related to gambling. We're home to a whole host of the old reliable bookstore giants. For books, and such special events as author appearances, there's **Barnes & Noble** (3860 Maryland Pkwy.; ☎ 702/734-2900; www.barnesandnoble.com; Mon–Sat 9am–10pm, Sun 10am–9pm) and **Borders** (at McCarran Airport; ☎ 702/261-5805; www.borders.com; daily 5am–1am). You'll find other Barnes & Noble and Borders outlets listed on their website (there are a bunch of them).

FEATHERS

True to its name, the **Rainbow Feather Company** (1036 S. Main St.; ☎ 702/598-0988; www.rainbowfeatherco.com; Mon–Fri 9am–4pm, Sat 9am–1pm) sells feathers—in every color of the rainbow, at that. In fact, if you need a boa or a headdress to match that zoot suit your man just bought from Valentino's (p. 270), the Rainbow Feather Company can do it. Show them a sample color and they'll show you the (dyed) feathers—from turkeys, chickens, geese, ducks, pheasants, ostriches, and peacocks. Never knew there was such a market for such fluff? This is where the showgirls go, along with fishermen, archers, and those in needs of boas, costumes, or fans made of feathers. Aside from the colorful plumes, the store is bare bones (or would that be quills?) and no frills.

FOR M&M'S FANS

M&M's World (in Showcase Mall, 3785 Las Vegas Blvd. S.; ☎ 702/736-7611; www.mymms.com; Sun–Thurs 9am–11pm, Fri–Sat 9am–midnight) managed to take just about everything that's ever been emblazoned with any kind of logo in the history of capitalism and chocolified it. The smiling chocolate-encrusted circles fill up four floors and take the form of hats, magnets, statuettes, NASCAR items—and oh so much more. Aside from the souvenirs and trinkets they also sell colors of M&Ms that you won't find in your local supermarket—gray, pink, black, and so forth—and allow customers to match at will. (*Warning:* A line tends to form at purple.) The place gets mobbed with tourists, so bring your patience, and while you're here check out the rest of the Showcase Mall—there's a **movie theater; Gameworks** (p. 132); and the **World of Coca-Cola,** where you can view and buy all things Coke.

SPORTING GOODS

Bass Pro Shops ✰✰ (in the Silverton, 8200 Dean Martin Dr.; ☎ 702/730-5200; www.basspro.com; Mon–Sat 9am–10pm, Sun 10am–7pm) takes you over the river (and under the waterfalls!) and through the woods, and face-to-face with an enormous dead moose. Wait, make that four of them, standing amid rocks and grass in as realistic a setting as you can get within a sporting goods store. And this is the Paul Bunyan of sporting goods stores. Consider its multiple aquariums (one even has fishing demonstrations), an indoor archery range, a shooting arcade for kids that has targets on animals that used to be alive, mounted deer heads at every turn—and we haven't even gotten started on the retail aspect. There are boats, guns, camo, fishing gear, camping gear, ATVs, and even a display for jerky. All set in a realistically outdoorsy habitat, with rocky precipices, streams, grass, and carved wood—even the non-sporty will be entertained here. And there are enough products for indoors lovers—clothes, shoes, dog toys, candy, and more jerky—that they won't be leaving empty-handed either.

WIGS

Though showgirls are far outnumbered by today's strippers, their iconic status remains, and so do at least a few traditional shows. **Serge's Showgirl Wigs** (953 E. Sahara Ave.; ☎ 702/732-1015; www.showgirlwigs.com; Mon–Sat 10am–5:30pm) keeps their bad hair days away. It's tucked away in Commercial Center, an old, run-down strip mall filled with such unexpected finds as Lotus of Siam (p. 100) and Serge's. Owner Steve Serge has been in the wig business for more than 20 years and has a clientele ranging from showgirls to dancers to housewives and chemo patients. Here you'll find just about any style of wig, from synthetic to $3,000 wigs made from real hair, plus hair clip-ons and accessories needed to take your coiffing to the next level. And for an added bonus, Serge also has a wig outlet for lower cost wigs located just across the strip mall.

SEX SHOPS

What Las Vegas shopping guide would be complete without the sex shops? Yes, they sell sex here—well, the concept of it, anyway. (Prostitution isn't legal in Clark County.) And they also sell sex accouterments—lots of them.

The largest chain in town, with five locations, is **The Adult Superstore** (3850 W. Tropicana Ave.; ☎ 702/798-0144; daily 24 hr.). They sell the fairly standard selections of pleasuring devices, in addition to gags (as in jokes), clothing, DVDs, user-friendly dolls, and pasta that resembles different body parts. Clean and large, it's less creepy than your standard adult joint but still has that awful fluorescent lighting; straight, low aisles; and a slight smell of bleach, wafting in from the "arcade" next door.

Déjà Vu Love Boutique ✪ (3275 Industrial Rd.; ☎ 702/731-5655; www. dejavu.com; daily 10am–4am offers a much different, more comfortable shopping experience. For one thing, carpet works wonders within a sex shop. So do display cases that vary in size, color on the walls, and outgoing and friendly saleswomen. With lotions and potions, salves and ointments, there's a little bit of everything here—bustiers, T-shirts, books, gag balls, and clamps. Though if you're looking for something fairly standard, the prices are high (packages of 12 Trojan condoms go for $20 and up). It's like an X-rated Spencer Gifts, with more class and with-out the mall. Located next to Déjà vu strip club, whose motto is "1,000s of beau-tiful girls and three ugly ones," this is a good place to catch dancers when they're not working. They need toys, too. If you're looking for higher brow erotic mem-orabilia, like art, the **Erotic Heritage Museum** (p. 139), located just across the parking lot from the Love Boutique, has a, yes, titillating gift shop.

Paradise Electro Stimulators ✪ (1509 W. Oakey Blvd.; ☎ 702/214-2851; www. peselectro.com; Mon–Fri 10am–6pm, Sat noon–6pm) is a small, nondescript shop within a Downtown strip mall. In fact, it's so nondescript it almost screams "beard!" Walk through the reflective doors into the front office where you must get approval for entry into the actual shop, which is best described as a fetishist's fantasy. There's everything you've never dreamed of here—it's a reminder of just how imaginative our species is when it comes to our favorite pastime. There are tubes, masks, rings, inserts, stimulators, locks and keys, leather (or rubber!) outfits, liquid latex, medical devices, gas masks, collars, shockers, blockers, and sharp objects that look like they'd hurt, no matter where they were placed. Despite the taboo offerings, there's nothing deviant about the ambience of this sadist boutique, and the open-minded staff is more than happy (and qualified) to answer your questions, or leave you alone.

12 Get Out of Town

Take a 2-hour drive (or less) out of Vegas, and you'll see mountains, lakes, and maybe even an alien

by Kate Silver

WHEN THE DINGING OF THE SLOT MACHINES, RESTLESS CROWDS, AND swirling eccentricities of Cirque du Soleil start to get on your nerves, it's time to alter the scene. Las Vegas is a great place for a couple of days, but you may soon be craving sunlight, fresh air, and blue skies that aren't painted on a casino ceiling. Head to the hills, the rivers, the mountains, the canyon, or even the mysterious hinterland of alien lore and I guarantee you a memorable, rewarding time.

Because it sits smack in the middle of the Mojave Desert, visitors are often surprised to find that the Las Vegas Valley is actually quite colorful and the outlying areas aren't just flat, dry, and dull stretches of sand and bleached bones (as the term "desert" implies).

When you flew into town, you may have noticed the mountains that surround the Las Vegas Valley. The area was actually shaped over the millennia by the eroding effects of water that once flowed through these mountains. The Spring Mountains and Red Rock Canyon lie to the west, Frenchman Mountain is to the east, the McCullough Range is to the south, and the Sheep and Las Vegas ranges border the north. Each area offers different outdoor opportunities, making it possible to spend your entire vacation amusing yourself in Las Vegas without setting foot in a casino. And people do. According to the Las Vegas Convention and Visitors Authority, more than one-fifth of Las Vegas visitors take some kind of side-trip during their stay here.

We applaud them for doing so. One of the reasons that this town has grown so quickly is its proximity to so many other adventures—places where you can downhill ski, water ski, raft, hike through multicolored canyons, and more . . . all in the middle of the desert.

With the exception of the Grand Canyon, I've limited this chapter to places that are less than 2 hours away. And if you're looking to go further, Los Angeles is 280 miles south by car, and San Diego is about 330 miles. To the northeast, Zion National Park is just 160 miles away, and Bryce Canyon National Park is 260 miles.

HOOVER DAM & BOULDER CITY

Hoover Dam ✫✫✫ (☎ 702/494-2517; www.usbr.gov/lc/hooverdam; visitor center daily 9am–5pm) is the first man-made structure to actually exceed the masonry mass of Egypt's great pyramids. A kind of inverted pyramid itself, the Dam has been named one of the Top Ten Construction Achievements of the 20th Century, one of Seven Engineering Wonders of the Modern World, and the Civil Engineering Monument of the Millennium. Though the dam is first and foremost a public works project, it's also a masterpiece. And it's what enables us to comfortably spend any amount of time in Southern Nevada. Let me explain . . .

The men and women who built Hoover Dam succeeded in altering Mother Nature. They actually changed the path of the Colorado River, which flows through seven states, by trapping its waters and converting what was essentially snow runoff from the Rockies into electricity and irrigation for the entire southwest portion of the United States, including the Las Vegas Valley. Desert land that was once barren and sparsely populated was converted into lush cities and thriving metropolises that could farm their own fruits and vegetables.

The timing couldn't have been better: Construction began in 1931 at the height of the Depression. The project was originally set to begin later, but hundreds of unemployed Americans caught wind of the plans, and before there were even living quarters set up, they flocked to southern Nevada to wait, and hope, for employment.

A total of 21,000 workers came to the area to create this colossal concrete structure, working 24 hours a day, 363 days a year at an average wage of $4 per day in hellish conditions. And they started from scratch. Before they arrived, this was a barren spot with no electricity and no clean water, just craggy mountains

Hoover Dam Facts

- Hoover Dam is 726 feet tall and weighs 6.6 million tons.
- It holds 18 million pounds of steel and 840 miles of pipe.
- The concrete at the base of the dam is two football fields thick.
- Construction employed an average of 3,500 workers a day.
- There's enough concrete in the dam to pave a two-lane road 3,300 miles long (about the distance from San Francisco to New York City).
- 17 generators power the dam; each is taller than a seven-story building and contains 60 train-cars full of parts.
- The intake towers were built to look like torches as a symbol of the energy the dam produces.
- Contrary to legend, there are no bodies buried within the dam. The closest anyone ever came was a man who was covered by concrete during construction. It took 16 hours to remove his body.
- The dam was completed in 5 years, 2 years ahead of schedule and vastly under budget.
- By 1986, enough energy was sold to pay for the dam's construction costs. Today, it continues to pay for itself and operates at no cost to taxpayers.
- Fifty-six percent of the energy produced goes to southern California, 25% remains in southern Nevada, and 19% is used by Arizona. Las Vegas receives only a small percentage of the dam's power because when the water rights were allocated its population was only 5,000. Re-allocation will occur in 2017.

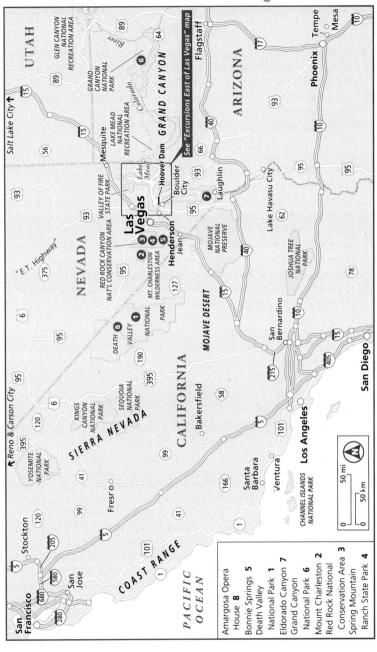

See "Excursions East of Las Vegas" map

Amargosa Opera House **8**
Bonnie Springs **5**
Death Valley National Park **1**
Eldorado Canyon **7**
Grand Canyon National Park **6**
Mount Charleston **2**
Red Rock National Conservation Area **3**
Spring Mountain Ranch State Park **4**

That Dam Tour

For years following 9/11, the tour formerly known as the Hard Hat Tour was off-limits. Today, called the **Dam Tour** ★★ (☎ 866/730-9097; $30; no children under 8 permitted, not wheelchair accessible; 9:30am–3:30pm), it's nearly identical to the old one, down to the yellow hard hats participants wear, and highly recommended. An educational walk within the bowels of the dam, it provides a more concrete understanding—pun intended—of the Dam's place in history, its engineering advances, its importance, and its sheer size and depth.

The tour starts out along the same path as the less-involved Power Plant Tour, which takes you into the belly of the earth, down more than 500 feet into the ground, where you walk through tunnels of exposed rocks eerily dripping with water. You end up in a room where you can actually feel the rumbling of 80,000 gallons of water per second rush in a pipe right below you. Then, after a brief tour of the power plant, Dam Tour participants break from the group, down a dark, narrow cement hallway to an even narrower ventilation shaft (if you're taller than 5 ft. 10 in. prepare to slouch). About 100 feet down the horizontal shaft, natural light streams in through metal shutters. Walk down and peer out: The river sits below and the road is above. You are now right smack in the middle of the dam. (It's a spot you may recognize from the movie *Vegas Vacation,* when Clark Griswold breaks through those shutters and climbs the scaffolding.) The tour then leads you further into the dam, but this view, alone, is worth the cost of admission.

and arid, 120°F (49°C) temperatures. Living out of their cars and hastily constructed shanty towns, the workers built the roads to bring in concrete and pipes, dug tunnels to divert the river, and even built manufacturing plants to create pipes and other large materials too big to transport. The housing they built for themselves eventually became Boulder City, a wholly government-owned enterprise.

And construction crews weren't the only vital elements. Artists and architects were hired to frame the project in the popular 1930s Art Deco style. From the 4-ton *Wings of the Republic* statues, to the star map indicating the location of the planets when the dam was dedicated, to the terrazzo tile in and around the plant, the dam has always been as much a work of art as a thick slab of concrete.

If you choose not to take the tour (see the box), there are still ample points of interest at the dam, and the views from the pedestrian sidewalks are always memorable. Inside, displays open to the public pay tribute to the thousands of workers, giving them a face and a name, while attesting to the harsh times. Obituary postings line another display, announcing some of the 96 deaths during construction: "A falling jumbo yesterday crushed every spark of life from the body of Victor K. Auchard, 25," and "Peter Savoff, 44, powder man, plunged to instant death this morning when he fell off the cliff," among others.

If you opt for the tour, arrive early. The Dam Tour is limited to 20 people per tour, and it's first-come first-served. Tours last about an hour and begin every 30 minutes, but the tour center gets crowded as the day progresses. Do note that it's not recommended for people with claustrophobia, pacemakers, or defibrillators. That's for good reason. During my tour two people made it to the bottom of the 70-second elevator ride only to realize their claustrophobia got the best of them, and they immediately returned to the surface. Though I've never had issues with claustrophobia, every time I've gone into the depths of the dam I've felt a bit woozy, myself.

But if you really want to get your toes wet, the closest you can get to being in the structure (without jumping) is **Black Canyon River Adventure** (in the Hacienda Hotel on Hwy. 93, just outside of Boulder City; ☎ 800/455-3490; www.blackcanyonadventures.com; $83 adults 16 and older, $80 children 13–15, $51 children 5–12 if you drive yourself, $44 extra per person for round-trip transportation from Las Vegas). A motor-assisted raft departs from the base of Hoover Dam and makes its way along the Colorado River through majestic, fiordlike Black Canyon, as guides discuss the history and geology of the landscape. Every now and again the raft is moored to allow passengers to swim or splash around (so important when the weather is steamy). Though pricey, the tour includes lunch, lasts about 3 hours, and involves no white water (so it's friendly even to the weaker of heart). It ends on Willow Beach, where a tour bus waits to return you to your hotel or to the Hacienda Hotel.

In 2004, another gigantic project began: Construction of the Hoover Dam bypass bridge. Because the roads that wind above the dam simply aren't equipped to handle the 14,000 vehicles now passing through daily, the Federal Highway Administration began focusing on an alternative route. Slated to be complete in 2010, the bridge is a massive effort and yet another engineering feat by the states of Nevada and Arizona to complete a 3½-mile corridor that begins in Nevada, bypasses the dam, and crosses over the Colorado River about 1,500 feet downstream from the Dam. It ends in Mohave County, Arizona.

On the way to Hoover Dam, you'll drive through Boulder City, the former government-owned reservation that was built to house the dam workers. Now a town of about 15,000, Boulder City is the only town in Nevada where gambling is illegal—a law harkening back to the days of government control that residents have opted to keep.

A drive through the town's main drag is a trip through history. Here, hotels named for the large, popular casinos of Las Vegas' past—hotels long since imploded—still stand. Places such as The Dunes, El Rancho, The Desert Inn, and The Hacienda, create a satirical ghost walk through the state's history.

While in town, check out the **Boulder Dam Hotel** (1305 Arizona St.; ☎ 702/293-3510; www.boulderdamhotel.com), a relic of days past built in Dutch Colonial

Excursions East of Las Vegas

style, that's made it onto the National Register of Historic Places (and is said to have more than a few interesting ghost stories within its creaky doors). And be sure to stop by **Milo's Best Cellars** (538 Nevada Hwy./Arizona St.; ☎ 702/293-9540; www.miloswinebar.com; daily 11am–10pm, Fri–Sat bar open until midnight;) for wine, cheese, and charm.

To get there: Take U.S. 93/95 (also known as I-15) south about 30 miles, following signs to Boulder City. To get to Hoover Dam, continue on U.S. 93, 7 miles past Boulder City. Garage parking is $7, but there are also free lots on each side of the dam. **Gray Line** (☎ 800/634-6579; www.graylinelasvegas.com; daily [except Thanksgiving, Christmas, and New Year's] at 8:30am and 11:30am, and takes about 4½ hrs.; Internet fare is $48 and doesn't include admission to The Power Plant or Dam Tour; hotel pick-up is available) offers a mini–Hoover Dam bus tour from Las Vegas.

Tourist info: Boulder City Visitors Center (100 Nevada Hwy.; ☎ 702/294-1252; www.bouldercity.com/visitors; daily 8am–4:30pm).

LAKE MEAD

Lake Mead (☎ 702/293-8906; www.nps.gov/lame; $5 per car; daily 24 hr.) abuts Hoover Dam and is the fruit of the massive structure's operation. At 1.5 million

acres, the Lake Mead National Recreation Area is home to the largest man-made lake in the Western Hemisphere—and a welcome sight amid the sandy brown desert hues of southern Nevada. Because the water fills a canyon rather than a basin, the lake is deeper than most, with an average depth of 225 feet and a maximum depth of 500 feet. That translates into enough water, at 1 foot deep, to cover the entire state of Pennsylvania. But in recent years, the water levels of the lake have decreased because of drought conditions, which is immediately evident with the lake's ring-around-the-bathtub type effect marked clearly on surrounding rocks.

The first stopping point is the **Alan Bible Visitor's Center** (☎ 702/293-8990; www.nps.gov/lame/planyourvisit; daily 8:30am–4:30pm), where park rangers can answer any questions you might have, and you can buy maps, books, souvenirs, and water, and admire the cactus gardens that surround the center.

One of my own favorite area hikes is the Historic Railroad Trail, located next to this Visitor's Center. This 5-mile out-and-back hike takes you through crude tunnels blasted out of the volcanic ridges above Lake Mead to deliver concrete, pipes, food, and other supplies during the construction of Hoover Dam. The trail traces around mountains and canyons that border the lake, and the views of Boulder Basin are unbeatable, particularly when the area's wildflowers are in bloom. Because the hike is before the park entrance, you can soak in some of the most beautiful lake views without paying the $5 per vehicle fee.

Of course, the Lake itself is the main draw here, beckoning nine million boaters, water skiers, and other activity seekers. But don't come expecting a serene beach experience. The shore areas are generally rocky or muddy, and the water near the shore sometimes carries a less-than-pleasant odor. You're better off swimming at your hotel pool.

Plenty of fish have a home in the lake, the most visible of which are the enormous carp, which flock around **Lake Mead Marina** (490 Horsepower Cove; ☎ 702/293-3484; www.lasvegasboatharbor.com; summer 7am–6pm, winter 7am–5pm). Tourists pelt them with popcorn. This is NOT recommended, and not good for the fish, but the feeding frenzy of carp-on-carp action is like watching some sick mutated fish horror movie. Just try and look away.

The marina also has a floating restaurant, a small grocery store, and a shop that rents fishing boats, ski boats, personal watercraft, and patio boats to help navigate around 550 miles of shoreline. Rentals aren't cheap, though. Personal watercraft start at $130 for 2 hours; boat rentals range from $50 to $70 per hour.

A less expensive way to explore the lake at Lake Mead is by taking a cruise on the *Desert Princess* or *Desert Princess II* (☎ 702/293-6180; www.lakemeadcruises. com; rates and amenities change according to time of cruise; $22–$58 adults, $10–$58 kids; cruises leave 10am–7:30pm). Both are charming, Mississippi-style paddle-wheel vessels that make a leisurely jaunt out to Hoover Dam and back, and passengers can get a gander at the area from on deck or from the air-conditioned cabins.

To get there: Take U.S. 93/95 (also known as I-15) 4 miles past Boulder City. Entrance to Lake Mead is on your left.

ST. THOMAS

One side effect of the region's ongoing drought is that visitors can view areas of the lake that haven't been seen in decades—and not just watermarks on canyon walls. These days, you can walk among the **ruins of the city of St. Thomas** (for info, call the Lake Mead Visitors Center; ☎ 702/293-8990), an Atlantis-style ghost town.

A former salt mine used by the American Indians, the area that is now St. Thomas was transformed, in 1865, into a settlement by the Mormons. Important enough to become a railroad stopping point in 1912, the town prospered from its salt and copper mines and was home to orchards, vineyards, and a thriving community life, with the residents united by their strong religious beliefs. Of course, the federal government tends to emphasize development over an established sense of community. So as the plans for Hoover Dam were set in motion and the Colorado River's course was forever changed, the government began buying property in St. Thomas in an attempt to get everyone out. Some residents relocated to nearby cities, such as Overton, but not everyone could afford to. Some simply stuck it out until 1938, when the waters of newly forming Lake Mead began to engulf the town. A man named Hugh Lord was the last one out, actually rowing away from his house on June 11, 1938.

Today, the water's going in the opposite direction. As levels decrease, more and more of the city has been exposed. Remnants of eroded homes are clearly visible, some having retained no more than their foundation, or parts of walls that are now just knee high. Others are better preserved, and you can still see pieces of wood attached to the concrete window cut-outs. Wells were caged over with rebar, presumably to keep divers out. Dark waters remain deep down in the holes.

It's an easy walk down and around the ruins. The 2½-mile loop leads you on a sandy trail marked by seashells and other lake refuse—broken bottles, rusting cans, unidentified metallic parts—through the tall tamarisk weeds that sway in the wind, like cornfields.

For more archaeology-themed stops, continue on Lakeshore Drive to the town of Overton and stop at the **Lost City Museum** (721 S. Moapa Valley Blvd.; ☎ 702/397-2193; www.comnett.net/~kolson; $3 adults, $2 seniors, free for kids under 18; daily 8:30am–4:30pm, closed Thanksgiving, Christmas, and New Year's Day), which is a quaint but informative pueblo made from sun-dried adobe brick. Here, the Park Service maintains exhibits of excavated items from the "Lost City" of Pueblo Grande de Nevada, where the Anasazi Indians once lived in subterranean pits sometime after the 1st century A.D. The area was later occupied by the Puebloans, who, as their name implies, lived in pueblos from A.D. 700 to 1150. As the waters of Lake Mead began to rise, the sites were excavated, ironically, by the Civilian Conservation Corp—the very same people who helped build the dam.

To get there: If you're coming from Lake Mead, you can access St. Thomas from Northshore Road; it's opposite S.R. 167, which leads to the Valley of Fire. Follow the dirt road to its end—St. Thomas Point. There are signs leading you to the town of St. Thomas; which is visible from the parking area. From Las Vegas, take I-15 north about 35 miles to S.R. 169. Go east on S.R. 169, which becomes S.R.167 for about 25 miles (past Valley of Fire). When you come to the intersection of Northshore Road, S.R. 167 becomes a dirt path. Drive down it about 1½ miles, and there will be spots to park and a path down to St. Thomas. To get to the Lost City Museum, return to Lakeshore Drive and continue towards Overton.

ELDORADO CANYON

If you brought your 10-gallon hat along, now is the time to wear it. A trip to Eldorado Canyon is a journey back in time to the Old West, a swagger through the famous Techatticup Mine and around the dusty soon-to-be-ghost-town of Nelson, Nevada. Ask around Las Vegas and you may get some blank stares when you mention Eldorado Canyon. You know you've stumbled onto something, well, underground when even the Las Vegas natives haven't heard about it.

A **Pink Jeep tour** (☎ 888/900-4480; www.pinkjeep.com; $99; 8am and 1pm daily) introduces you to places you might not otherwise find. A Pepto-colored vehicle picks you up at your hotel and then transports you about an hour southeast of Las Vegas to a dusty, mountainous area studded with Joshua trees. As the tour guide maintains a steady stream of history and trivia you'll drive through Nelson, a town of about 50 residents (plus a trailer park of about 30), where more than a few houses are made of tin and outhouses still exist. From there, the jeep stops at the Techatticup Mine. This area was home to one of the biggest gold and silver mining booms in Nevada history, beginning in the early 1860s and continuing for about 4 decades. Now the mine and the 50-plus acres surrounding it belong to the Werly family, who have restored the old buildings and cleaned up the mine for tours.

Don't expect Disney-fied panning-for-gold stations and touristy sarsaparilla sales. This is the real deal. The outside is surrounded by rusted mining equipment, antique signs, and even the carcass of an old airplane. Inside is a 600-foot-deep mine with 3 miles of cool, windy tunnels over rocky terrain. Look closely and you can still see the traces left by the miners' drills, and even drippings of wax from their candles. Traces of quartz, amethyst, gold, and silver shine in the mine, and wooden ladders dangle from ropes along the hard-rock walls, which reach 200 feet over your head, and 400 feet below. As Bobbie Werly guides you through the area she weaves stories about the history of the town and the backbreaking logistics of mining. The spooky highlight comes when you're deep within the mine and Bobbie turns off the lights. The meaning of pitch black has never been quite so vivid. After the tour enjoy a cold soda in the main office, which is a restored General Store, and check out the many movies (such as *Eye of the Beholder, 3,000 Miles to Graceland, Breakdown*) and photos/videos/commercials that have been set in Eldorado Canyon. Like all well-kept secrets, this canyon is hiding a heap of drama.

RED ROCK CANYON
NATIONAL CONSERVATION AREA

Red Rock Canyon National Conservation Area ✪ (☎ 702/515-5350; www. nv.blm.gov/redrockcanyon; $5 per car; Nov–Feb daily 6am–5pm, Mar daily 6am–7pm, Apr–Sept 30 daily 6am–8pm, Oct daily 6am–7pm; visitor center hours 8am–4:30pm) is one of the area's closest awe-inspiring sights. Just 17 miles from the Strip, you'll suddenly find yourself away from the endless housing developments and gated neighborhoods, surrounded by hardy mountains of deep red and white sandstone, intercut with tufts of green and even waterfalls and springs. Though the park seems like a well-kept secret, it has for years beckoned to rock climbers with its tantalizing rock formations and more than 2,000 climbing routes, making it one of the top five rock-climbing destinations in the country.

The canyon is a part of the Navajo Formation, which is a particular kind of sandstone believed to be what's left of 150,000 square miles of desert that existed 178 to 192 million years ago. The bright orangey-red and white rocks began as grains of sand, transported by the wind. With time and more sand, giant dunes formed, solidified by their own weight and cemented together, resulting in these mounts of rock. It's one of the world's largest wind-deposited formations. You may note similarities to the Valley of Fire, Redstone in Lake Mead, Zion National Park, Canyonlands National Park, and Arches National Park, all of which are also part of the Navajo Formation. But I think Red Rock is particularly striking, with the dissonance of the Strip as a glittering afterthought in the background.

One of the area's unique geologic features is the Keystone Thrust Fault. It formed about 65 million years ago, when two of the earth's plates collided, shoving gray limestone through red sandstone. You can't miss the striped contrast as you drive past the park on State Route 159 or through the park on a scenic 13-mile loop. The paved road leads vehicles through the 197,000-acre expanse and is also popular with bikers, thanks to the numerous hills and valleys and changing scenery.

Of course, Red Rock Canyon is not all, well, rocks. Listen to the trickle of water and look for the wildlife it draws at the White Rock–Willow Springs area (one of the most popular stops for hikes and picnics). Take a hike on the Pine Creek Canyon trail (3 miles round-trip), past an old homestead and into the canyon. You can then branch off along a short, figure-eight-style trail where a controlled burn of Ponderosa Pine took place and learn about fire ecology. Throughout the park, you'll see kit fox, bighorn sheep, coyote, burros, lizards, snakes, and petroglyphs and pictographs left by the American Indians, who once lived here.

Safety note: Be sure to take plenty of water (1 gallon per person is recommended). The desert just seems to wick that water right out of you. And be sure to pick up a trail map at the visitor center, because the signs on the trails themselves can be misleading.

How to get there: Head west on Charleston, which becomes S.R. 159. Red Rock is less than 20 miles from Las Vegas.

SPRING MOUNTAIN RANCH

Spring Mountain Ranch State Park (☎ 702/875-4141; www.parks.nv.gov/smr. htm; $5 per car; daily 8am–dusk; tours daily noon, 1pm, 2pm, Sat–Sun additional tour at 3pm; ranch house 10am–4pm) is an idyllic setting, rich in history as a working ranch and luxury retreat. Nestled within Red Rock National Conservation Area, the ranch sits at the base of Wilson Cliffs. Volunteer docents show guests around the property, while families picnic in the green grass, all enjoying the cool breezes that come with a higher elevation (the park is consistently 10–15° cooler than Vegas). With six springs, the ranch has a constant water supply, which helped make it an oasis for the Paiute Indians, the Mormons, and for travelers using a nearby Cottonwood Valley route as an alternative to the Spanish Trail. It later became a cattle ranch and passed through the hands of the famous and the furriers—as in, chinchilla, thanks to a man named Willard George, who was a prominent figure in the fur-coat-wearing community of Hollywood. Other residents included Chet Lauck (Lum of the Lum and Abner radio show); German actress Vera Krupp, who owned the famous Krupp diamond (now owned by Elizabeth Taylor); and later, the odd but venerable movie producer, aviator, and casino owner Howard Hughes, before it was sold to the Nevada Division of State Parks.

In the summer, the park remains open at night for **Super Summer Theatre** (☎ 702/895-2787; www.supersummertheatre.com; $15 at the door, $10 in advance; plays begin at 8:05pm). Theatergoers usually bring a picnic dinner and a glass of wine which they enjoy on the lawn while watching the show under the stars, surrounded by mountains and fresh air. Don't expect to find Strip-quality shows out here. It's more like community theater, but the night sky, stars, and warm desert breezes make it worth the trip. Be sure and bring a sweater. Even if it's near triple digits in Las Vegas it can get chilly out here.

How to get there: Head west on Charleston Boulevard, which becomes S.R. 159. The entrance to Spring Mountain Ranch is about 3 miles past Red Rock.

BONNIE SPRINGS OLD NEVADA

The Nevada of days' past is brought back to life—sort of—at **Bonnie Springs Old Nevada** 🧒 (☎ 702/875-4191; www.bonniesprings.com; $20 per carload; summer daily 10:30am–6pm, winter daily 10:30am–5pm). In truth, this replica of a mining town is as campy as they come, with gunfights breaking out in the streets, villains being hanged, and outhouses exploding (musta been some chili!). It's like an unintended satire of a John Wayne movie but one that kids sure do love.

This despite the fact that this Old West imitation is pretty darn dirty and run down: It's amazing ducks can swim around the thick, scummy pond here and the animals roaming around the "petting zoo" (pigs, goats, chickens) are about a step away from the big glue factory in the sky. Still, who am I to knock it? Families enjoy the off-the-beaten-path kitsch and the ability to take the mini-train around the property, have a beer in the old-fashioned saloon, and roam through the replica Main Street with its theater, blacksmith shop, shooting gallery, and more.

One note: If you're just there to eat at the restaurant the parking attendants will waive the fee, though I wouldn't come all the way out here just for the restaurant.

How to get there: Head west on Charleston Boulevard, which becomes S.R. 159. The entrance to Bonnie Springs is after Spring Mountain Ranch.

VALLEY OF FIRE

Valley of Fire State Park ★ (☎ 702/397-2088; http://parks.nv.gov/vf.htm; $6 per car; visitor center daily 8:30am–4:30pm; park daily 24 hr.) is Nevada's oldest and largest state park, and one of the strangest looking. Mounds of iron-tinged dunes seem to bubble up out of nowhere, like sandstone rocks . . . on LSD. The mounds were formed 150 million years ago and have been eroded by the wind and water ever since. Though the Valley of Fire is similar in appearance to Red Rock, the main difference is that here, the sandstone hasn't changed as it has at Red Rock, where limestone was uplifted and thrust through the layers on top of it. The only force that's shaped the Valley of Fire's formations is erosion.

Hikes out here are generally pretty short and won't pose much of a challenge, making this an ideal day trip for those traveling with children. Trails lead past petrified logs and petroglyphs, which were etched in the stone some 3,000 years ago by the Basketmaker people and the Anasazi Pueblo farmers.

One of the easiest trails, Mouse's Tanks, was the hideout for a rowdy Paiute Indian named Mouse in the 1890s who, legend has it, shot up an Indian camp, killed a couple of prospectors, and fled to the Valley of Fire. He supposedly chose this area because it's a well-hidden maze within Petroglyph Canyon, where the "Tanks," or depressions in the sandstone, catch and act as a storage spot for rainwater. But eventually his hiding place became his trap; he was tracked down and, after refusing to surrender, was killed in the subsequent gunfight. On this and other trails, the petroglyphs mark the rocks everywhere you look, guiding you through what feels like an ancient storybook.

The White Dome trail is also popular, leading hikers through a slot canyon and past the stone ruins of the abandoned movie set for *The Professionals,* starring Burt Lancaster, which was filmed back in the '60s. The park no longer allows filmmakers to leave traces, and for good reason: It's a popular filming spot. You may recognize the scenery from *Star Trek: Generations, Total Recall, Iron Eagle, Heldorado,* and more.

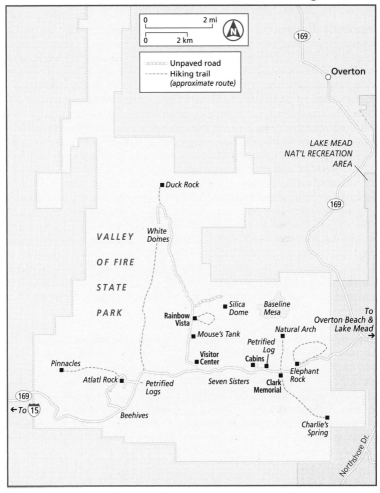

From the road within the park you'll be able to see formations that carry such apt names as Bee Hives and Elephant Rock, along with another called the Seven Sisters. But it's just as enjoyable to discover and name your own shapes within the structures. As this is the unabashed desert, summertime temperatures can top 110°F (43°C). Visits are easier at other times of the year, but if you really must see it then, arrive here as early in the day as possible, carry at least a gallon of water per person, and plan to get out before noontime.

To get there: Take I-15 north about 35 miles to S.R. 169. Drive east on S.R. 169 east for about 15 miles. That will bring you to the Valley of Fire's west entrance.

MOUNT CHARLESTON

Mount Charleston (☎ 702/872-5486; www.fs.fed.us/r4/htnf/recreation/wilderness/mt_charleston.shtml) is the Kilimanjaro of Las Vegas. Sure, it's not 19,000 feet tall, like the great African peak, but at nearly 12,000 feet, it's the tallest point in southern Nevada. Just a 45-minute drive from the Strip transports visitors from a sweltering 110°F (43°C) at the base to a beautiful 80°F (27°C) at the top of the mountain. Located in the Toiyabe National Forest and part of the Spring Mountain Range, Mount Charleston remains a cool 25 to 30° less than Las Vegas, and the landscape reflects the change. At the lowest elevations, Joshua trees dot the land like malformed characters straight out of Dr. Seuss. As you climb to greater heights, you'll find cedar trees, and then finally, towards the top of the mountain, you reach alpine territory.

Mount Charleston is part of the Spring Mountain Range, which is known for its babbling springs, and also for the plants and animals found here. There are wild horses and burros, songbirds, birds of prey, hummingbirds, desert tortoise, deer, elk, coyote, fox, and bobcat. Trees include juniper, ponderosa pine, white fir and bristlecone pines—all growing within a majestic setting of waterfalls, caves, canyons, and trails. It's easy to forget you're still in the desert. That's especially true if you hike along the popular Mary Jane Falls trail, which is 3 miles round-trip and ascends to two tall but not very watery waterfalls. Hikes range from 1 mile (various) to 17 miles (Charleston Peak), and this is a good place to bring kids, as you'll be able to find a good trail for about every skill level.

The mountain is also popular in the winter, even though its very name sounds like an oxymoron: **Las Vegas Ski and Snowboard Resort** (Hwy. 156, in Lee Canyon; ☎ 702/385-2754; www.skilasvegas.com). Lift ticket prices are subject to change, but as of this writing they are $50 full-day adults, $45 half-day, $30 full-day children 12 and under/seniors 65 and older and $25 half-day. The lifts are open daily November through April, conditions permitting (resort open 8:30am–4:30pm, lifts open 8am–4pm). Though it's no Tahoe or Mammoth, the mountain is still a regional delight and home to 11 trails, all bearing such fitting names as Keno, Blackjack, and Slot Alley. There is also a cafe and bar up here as well as rentals for equipment and clothing.

The mountain has two options for lodging: **The Mount Charleston Lodge** (1200 Old Park Rd.; ☎ 800/955-1314 or 702/872-5408; www.mtcharlestonlodge.com; AE, DISC, MC, V) has 24 individual cabins that aren't exactly rustic, with their whirlpool tubs, and some even come equipped with satellite TV. It's quite popular, and you'll want to reserve well in advance. The restaurant here is a standard hamburger/sandwich-type outfit, but they have a patio with gorgeous views for summer dining, and an inviting fireplace perfect in winter. At the **Mt. Charleston Hotel** (2 Kyle Canyon Rd.; ☎ 702/872-5500; www.mtcharlestonhotel.com; AE, DISC, MC, V), rooms have a woodsy motif and come equipped with artificially lighted fireplaces. The restaurant offers options that are more gourmet than those at the Lodge. Six campgrounds with more than 100 camping units are also available around the mountain, and in the summertime reservations are recommended (☎ 800/280-2267 or 702/515-5400). Some are more bare bones than others; if you plan on showering opt for Hilltop Campground, which has coin-operated showers.

To get there: Take U.S. 95 north and turn left on Highway 157 at the Kyle Canyon cutoff. To get to Las Vegas Ski and Snowboard Resort, once you're on the mountain, turn right on State Highway 156 going to Lee Canyon. The highway ends at the ski resort.

Tourist Info: For more information about Mount Charleston call the **Kyle Canyon Forest Service Station** (☎ 702/872-5486). For snow reports and winter road conditions call the **Snow Phone at Las Vegas Ski and Snowboard Resort** (☎ 702/593-9500).

THE EXTRATERRESTRIAL HIGHWAY

In the mood for some real-life X-Files (or possibly a really long and boring drive)? Then take a trip down the "E.T Highway," where alien buffs have been spotting strange lights, UFOs, and other supernatural phenomena for longer than we rooted for a love connection between Mulder and Scully. (Skeptics, realists, and those prone to motion sickness should stay home.)

Extraterrestrial Highway, also known as Nevada Highway 375, is the closest public-access point to Area 51, a top-secret military base located within the Rhode Island–sized Nevada Test Site. That complex was a major player in the Cold War, and nuclear bombs were detonated here from 1945 to 1992. (See p. 172 for details on tours of the facility.) Also known as Watertown, Dreamland, Paradise Ranch, and Groom Lake, Area 51 is said to be where the military develops and tests new planes, such as the Stealth Bomber. But ask anyone who's currently in the military what goes on here, and they'll either avoid the question or roll their eyes and tell you, "Nothing."

That's the opposite answer you'll hear from former Test Site workers, who insist the government actually possesses dead aliens, and performs experiments on them. Some extremists also claim that this area, with its rocky, lunarlike geology, is where Neil Armstrong and Buzz Aldrin's moon landing was filmed. Meaning, yes, that our country was duped into believing we'd actually landed in space, when it was really just a sound stage in the Mojave desert.

Conspiracy theorists are a determined lot, and a trip here is essentially the pinnacle of their alien obsession, which is why the long and lonely stretch of road was renamed "Extraterrestrial Highway" and given a road sign with an alien-like font by Nevada Governor Bob Miller in 1996. It's a publicity stunt that seems like something more brazen than the government would allow, if there actually were otherworldly activity still going on at Area 51. Considering how well known the place is (for a top-secret facility), you'd think—you'd hope—that any real secret testing has been moved someplace more, well, secret.

Conspiracies aren't helped by the signs surrounding the area that trespassers will be shot. The military doesn't mess around here. You may think of it as an adventure, but they're doing their job. If you venture off the road and actually try to enter Test Site territory, which is lined with cameras, speeding government vehicles will be on the scene before you can say, "phone home," and armed guards will escort you off the property (or shoot you or take you to jail, depending on how far you've crossed and how suspicious you look). Truly, this is no laughing matter.

Nevertheless, the road draws a steady stream of UFO seekers each year, who drive up to Rachel, Nevada, stopping at the **Little Al'e Inn** (located right off Hwy.

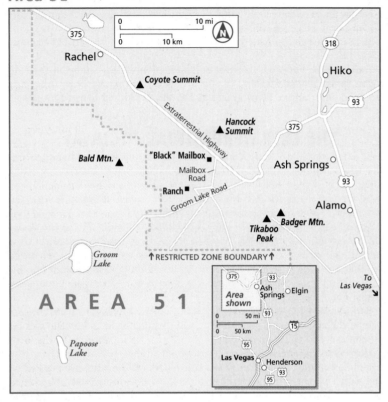

375; ☎ 775/729-2515; www.littlealeinn.com; daily 8am–10pm [the grill is turned off at 9pm]; AE, DISC, MC, V) for an "Alien" burger (described as "out of this world") and chat with some of the kooky locals, only to turn around for the long drive home. Some report sightings along the way, whether it's black things zooming through the sky, or mutilated cows along the side of the road. (In the conspiracy world, dead cows are possibly connected to alien abductions; in the rational world, free-range cattle regularly are hit by cars.) All I saw on my last drive were oversized rabbits diving in front of my bumper, seemingly bent on being removed from this alien tourist trap forever.

How to get there: Be sure and gas up before heading out because gas stations are few and far between. Take I-15 north to U.S. 93 North, which is exit No. 64 (it's easy to miss, especially if your eyes are on the sky), for 85 miles to Nevada S.R. 375, heading west. After about 20 miles you'll reach the road that leads towards Area 51—you'll know it by the white mailbox (referred to by those-in-the-know as "the black mailbox," because that's the color it used to be). Turn left, and follow any of the dirt roads to the border of Area 51. To get to the most popular entrance, veer right at the fork in the road.

But before going to Area 51, I recommend going past the white mailbox turnoff and on about 20 miles further on S.R. 375 to Rachel. Once you're in the proper mood and have purchased the appropriate alien earrings, turn back and look for the Little Green Men.

Tourist info: Call the **Nevada Commission on Tourism** (☎ 800/NEVADA-8).

AMARGOSA OPERA HOUSE

The town of Death Valley Junction has as many opera houses as it does residents: exactly one. And though the closest town to the **Amargosa Opera House** (☎ 760/852-4441; www.amargosa-opera-house.com; $15 adults, $12 children 5–12; Oct 7–May 12 Sat only, doors open 7:45pm, shows start 8:15pm) is 30 miles away, it manages to pack the house every Saturday it's open. The show is unlike any you've ever seen, and considering its creator and star, Marta Beckett, is 84 and growing more feeble every season, there's no telling how much longer it will be around.

Located on the edge of Death Valley, the opera house is the culmination of a dream of the bizarre Beckett, who arrived here by accident in 1967 and hasn't left yet. A dancer, Beckett had been touring in California. She and her husband were driving back east when they discovered their car had a flat tire. The closest garage was in Amargosa, which at the time was a company town run by the Pacific Borax Company. While the tire was being fixed, Beckett poked around the old adobe structures and instantly fell in love with the opera house. "As I looked into that hole, into this empty building, I had this distinct feeling I was looking into the other half of my life," Beckett recalls.

Though the floors and ceilings were falling apart and there were rats living in the space, it symbolized freedom and independence. So she did it. She and her husband abandoned their lives in New York City to move out here, at the intersection of nowhere and nothing.

The opera house itself is a work of art—and so is the hotel it's attached to. Before she began performing, Beckett wanted to guarantee herself an audience. She spent 4 years painting its walls to resemble the inside of a theater, with level upon level of character-filled balconies. There are whimsical nuns, prostitutes, court jesters, and royalty. Two years were spent on the blue ceiling, illustrated with cherubs flying amid clouds. The people she painted were a silent guarantee, to her anyway, that she'd never be performing to an empty house. Since the beginning, she's performed whether there was an actual audience or not.

Often, there wasn't, and her painted characters sufficed. An unexpected stroke of luck befell the opera house 6 years into its run, when a writer from *National Geographic* stumbled upon the show. He loved it, wrote about it, and the place has been packed ever since.

The Opera House is more than just a roadside attraction. It's a labor of love, and showcases the true (though slowing) talent of Beckett, whose husband left a few years after they moved here. For 23 years she took on a partner, a maintenance man with a flair for comedy. He passed away in 2005, and now she performs the shows alone, to sold-out crowds. Be sure and call in advance for tickets and to book a hotel room.

How to get there: Amargosa is located about 90 miles from Las Vegas. Take I-15 South, exit Blue Diamond Road/Highway 160, and drive 55 miles to Pahrump. In Pahrump you'll pass through two stoplights. The second stoplight is Basin Road. About 3 miles beyond Basin Road, you'll come to Bell Vista. Turn left and continue on Bell Vista another 25 miles to Death Valley Junction.

DEATH VALLEY

The names say it all: Devil's Golf Course. Dante's Ridge. Desolation Canyon. Here is a land of extremes, a story of tenacious beauty and survival: **Death Valley** ✮✮ (☎ 760/786-3200; www.nps.gov/deva; $20 per car; visitor center open daily in summer from 8am to 5pm, 9am to 5pm in summer). Straddling Nevada and California, at 282 feet below sea level, Death Valley boasts (if you can call it that) the second hottest temperature in the world, recorded at 134°F (57°C). The weather begins cooling off (meaning temperatures drop below 100°F/38°C) in October and start heating up again in April. But people do, indeed, visit year-round. Whether you're intending to stay in your car or get out and walk around, be sure and bring plenty of water—at least 1 gallon per person.

From salt deposits to rolling hills to stark mountains, Death Valley is a mural of changing scenery, and in the spring is known to even grow a stunning array of wild-flowers, if the fall and winter rains were heavy enough. Stop in at the **Furnace Creek Visitor Center and Museum** (☎ 760/786-3200; $20 park entrance fee; 9am–5pm daily) to learn more about the park and see a slide show. From November through April, rangers lead walks, talks, and presentations about Death Valley's history.

My favorite spot here is a place called Devil's Hole. It's an outlet for a series of underground streams that run so deep into the earth they've actually never been measured (the deepest anyone has gone is about 400 ft., and the floor was nowhere in sight). Another choice stop is Devil's Golf Course, where fields of chunky salt deposits make it look as though you've made a lunar landing. You can walk along the crunchy plane and see up close the salt "pinnacles," which look like intricate, lacy sculptures.

About an hour north of Furnace Creek is **Scotty's Castle** ✮ (☎ 760/786-2392; $11; summer daily 9am–4:30pm, winter daily 8:30am–5pm), named after the flamboyant but beloved "Death Valley Scotty," who grifted money out of investors, convincing them he'd discovered gold in Death Valley. One was so charmed by Scotty and Death Valley that he ordered construction of this castle but died before its completion. Tours of the property are led by guides dressed in clothing straight out of 1939 and operate every 10 minutes during peak season.

To get there: Take I-15 South, exit Blue Diamond Road/Highway 160, and drive 55 miles to Pahrump. In Pahrump you'll pass through two stoplights. The second stoplight is Basin Road. About 3 miles beyond Basin Road, you will come to Bell Vista. Turn left and continue on Bell Vista another 25 miles to Death Valley Junction. Turn right on Highway 190 and drive 13 miles to the eastern entrance of Death Valley. Scotty's Castle is located at the north end of Death Valley National Park, 53 miles from Furnace Creek. If you don't want to drive through the park, take U.S. 95 North 154 miles to Nevada State Route 267, then drive 26 miles to the Castle.

Although there are good choices for staying within Death Valley, the most charming and colorful accommodations are one valley east, at the **Ranch House Inn** ✮ (2001 Old Spanish Trail Hwy.; ☎ 760/852-4360; www.ranchhouseinn.com; AE, MC, V) in the tiny trailer-filled town of Tecopa, California. Nestled in a ver-dant valley, surrounded by hundreds of acres of date trees, guests stay in giant tepees that accommodate up to six. Don't expect your cellphones or Internet to

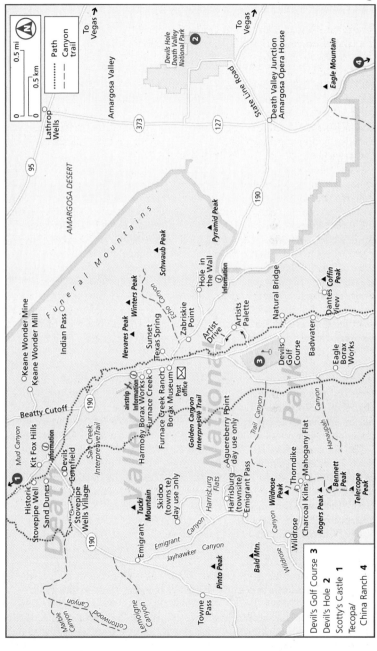

work; instead rely on shooting stars, the howls of coyotes, and the crackling of the campfire to serve as entertainment. Be sure and stop in at the gift shop next door and buy an unforgettable date shake and homemade date cookies. They're the perfect sugary pick-me-up for your drive home.

To get there from Death Valley: Take Highway 190 east to Death Valley Junction. Turn right on Highway 127. Drive approximately 8 miles past Shoshone and turn left on Old Spanish Trail Highway. The Ranch House Inn is about 5 miles further.

To get there from Las Vegas: Take I-15 South to west Highway 160. Head west on Tecopa Road (which turns into Old Spanish Trail Hwy.) to Furnace Creek Road. Turn left and follow the signs to China Ranch.

THE GRAND CANYON

The Southern Paiute tribe's name for the **Grand Canyon** ★★★ (☎ 928/638-7888; www.nps.gov/grca; $25 per vehicle; the South Rim is open all year, the North Rim from mid-May to October) was *Puaxant Tuyip,* or "Holy Land." And even without knowing the ins and outs of their religion, we tend to see it in much the same way. It's a deeply spiritual place, with a transcendent beauty and an intense sense of mystery.

That mystery is partially scientific. Though 40 layers of rock have been identified in the striated, multicolored walls of the canyon, with the Vishnu schist at the bottom dating back an astounding 2 billion years (which is half the age of Earth itself), scientists have long been unable to pinpoint when the Grand Canyon was carved.

Until recently, the educated guess had been that the canyon was 5 or 6 million years old. But a recent study, published in the journal *Science,* posits that the Canyon probably started to form some 15 to 16 million years ago (snowmelt from the Rockies formed the Colorado River, which began eroding its own windy path through what had become the Canyon). So it's likely that the first tourists to the canyon were the dinosaurs.

Whether you're the first or the 500 millionth tourist, however, one thing is certain: There are few sights in the United States, or the world, as awe inspiring. Or as worthy of repeat visits. A mile deep and 18 miles wide in places, you're always going to find something new to explore. Now considered one of the Seven Wonders of the Natural World, the Canyon is so large that it's visible from outer space and grand enough to attract nearly 5 million visitors annually.

The Grand Canyon's South Rim is located about 280 miles from Las Vegas and is the most famous portion of the Grand Canyon, thanks to its elevation, sheer enormity, and bright colors that change with the sun and clouds throughout the day. It draws nearly 4 million visitors annually.

The West Rim is about 120 miles from Vegas and is growing more popular thanks to the SkyWalk, which is a glass-bottomed horseshoe-shaped bridge that's suspended 4,000 feet above the canyon and juts out 70 feet. The SkyWalk cost more than $31 million to construct and they say it has the strength to hold 71 fully loaded Boeing 747s (or 71 million pounds), and winds in excess of 100 miles per hour. But will your wallet be able to withstand the $32 tickets and the $30 souvenir photos (no cellphones, cameras, or bags are allowed on the SkyWalk)? While the SkyWalk is a curiosity, I think the views are actually better from nearby Eagle Point, which doesn't cost extra and you can take all the photos you want.

Getting to the Grand Canyon: Your Options

Method of Travel	Price Range	Pros	Cons
Plane	$200–$300	Spectacular views, less travel time	Can feel rushed
Helicopter (West Rim)	$300–$500	Spectacular views, interesting tour guides, less travel time	Cost
Bus	$100–$150	Cost	10–14-hour trip
Rental car	$80–$100 per carload	Cost, independence	7–10-hour drive

One interesting fact about the West Rim is it's owned by the Hualapai Indians, instead of the National Park Service, which means it's regulated by different rules than the South Rim. Most notably, helicopters are allowed to actually land within the canyon (to the chagrin of environmentalists and Las Vegas residents whose homes lie along the noisy helicopter's flight paths).

PLANNING YOUR VISIT

Because of the different scenery, price points, and distances, I've listed tours for both the South and the West rims. Sorting through the available travel options is overwhelming, but I'll try to simplify. If you're not planning on driving yourself and staying for a couple of days (which is, in truth, the ideal way to "do" the Canyon), you'll probably be looking at a 1-day tour. If you choose to visit the South Rim (which is further away and pricier but worth it, in my book, as there's more to see and do) airplane and bus trips are available. No helicopters fly from Las Vegas to the South Rim (it's too far and would be too expensive), but helicopter rides above the Canyon are available once you land. I won't be getting into details here but **Grand Canyon Helicopters** (702/835-8477; www.grandcanyonhelicoptersaz.com; $130 plus fees) offers 30-minute flights with knowledgeable pilots.

If you prefer the closer West Rim option, there are helicopters, planes, and buses. Additions are also available for each package, ranging from rafting trips to Hummer rides to mule adventures and more (which I also won't be getting into here).

PLANES

Two airlines fly from Las Vegas to the South Rim: Grand Canyon Airlines and Vision Air. The tour routes are very similar and include air transportation to the canyon and bus transportation upon arrival. The descriptions below highlight the differences.

South Rim

The Canyon Connoisseur ★★ (☎ 866/235-9422; www.grandcanyonairlines.com; $299; times vary) flight offers about the best perspective available on the overwhelming volume of the canyon. About half of the flight is spent directly over it,

Grand Canyon National Park

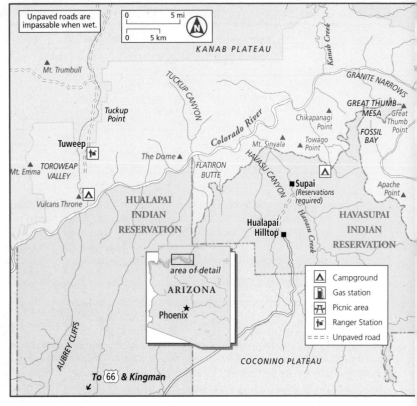

and there's nothing else to see in any direction except the canyon, with its reds, browns, purples, and greens. Its beauty is fully visible through the panoramic windows of the 20-seat Vistaliner plane (though that view takes some getting used to, as the ground seems alarmingly close at first). Another selling point for these tours is the quality of their staff. The guides are remarkably personable and knowledgeable, and cover, in an entertaining fashion, every aspect of the canyon: its history and size as well as the flora and fauna—they even stop to let you smell a ponderosa pine tree, which actually has a delicious vanilla scent.

Nitty gritty: The tour lasts about 7 hours and never manages to seem rushed. That includes shuttle rides from your hotel out to Boulder City (about a half-hour away from Vegas) where the plane takes off, flying over the Hoover Dam and Lake Meade en route. Other inclusions:

- An informative, 45-minute IMAX movie about the canyon.
- A bus ride along the rim, which spends nearly 45 minutes at both Mather Point and Bright Angel Lodge.
- Headsets onboard the plane presenting a basic audio narrative (in different languages) of facts about Las Vegas, the dam, and the Grand Canyon.

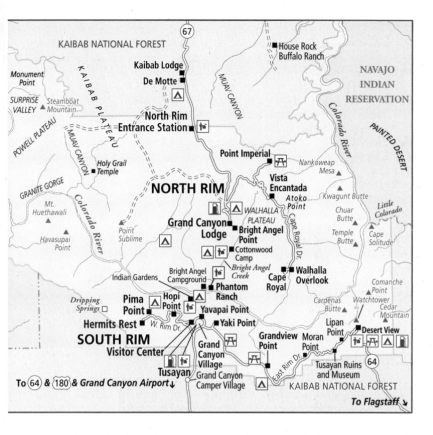

- A buffet lunch at the Best Western (if you arrive before 2pm) or a boxed lunch (sandwich, crackers, and cookies) if you get there later.

The South Rim Tour offered by **Vision Airlines** (☎ 800/256-8767; www.visionholidays.com; $304; times vary) offers a faster-paced option. Vision's planes seat 19 or 32 and are the size of commuter planes. Their primary purpose is transportation, not sightseeing, so there's no narrative as you fly out of the North Las Vegas Airport (which is about 20 min. closer than Boulder City) and over Lake Mead, Hoover Dam, and parts of the Grand Canyon. Rather than taking a tour it feels like you're on a regular flight to Anywhere, USA, in which passengers seem more likely to nap or talk than look out the window. But once you land, the basics here are similar, albeit more rushed—you get a boxed lunch (sandwich, chips, cookie, and an apple) and a bus takes you to Mather Point and Bright Angel, stopping for about 30 minutes at each, which is exactly enough time for your tour guide to take your picture in front of the canyon, before re-boarding the bus and returning to the airport. No IMAX movie on this one.

West Rim

Despite the fact that the West Rim is closer to Las Vegas (a 45-min. flight versus a little over an hour to the South Rim) the airplane tours here are nearly the same length of time—about 7 hours. Five airlines offer flights to the West Rim. I've profiled the two I think are the best.

Sightseeing is as much a priority as transportation on the 20-seat Vistaliner plane, thanks to its panoramic windows, which are used by **Scenic Airlines' Indian Adventure Tour** ★ (☎ 800/634-6801; www.scenic.com; $199; times vary). The planes offer nerve-wracking but beautiful views of the desert en route to the canyon. Though you may experience a sudden fear of heights upon take-off (I know I did), if you can get over it the scenery is truly breathtaking (however close it may be). The tour starts in Boulder City (about 30 min. from Las Vegas) and includes a 45-minute plane ride, passing over Hoover Dam and Lake Mead en route. Headsets present a basic audio narrative (in multiple languages) that shares facts about Las Vegas, the dam, and the Grand Canyon. Upon arrival you'll board a bus run by the Hualapai Indian reservation, which takes you to the two main stops: Eagle Point and Guano Point. A light buffet-style lunch (barbecue beef, mac and cheese, beans and tortillas) is provided at Guano Point, where you can hike around to two small mountains for a 360-degree view of the canyon. The trip is about 7 hours, which gives you 3 to 4 hours to spend on the ground. That's a long time. Because the Hualapai are protective of their sacred land (helicopters and airplanes aside) there are no hiking trails or opportunities to really explore here. Let me put it this way: You might want to bring a book.

A similar but more expensive option is **Vision Airline's West Rim Tour** (☎ 800/256-8767; www.visionholidays.com; $304; times vary), which leaves from the North Las Vegas Airport (about 20 min. closer than Boulder City) and is on a larger, commuter-style plane with small windows. There's no narrative to tune into as you pass over landmarks and formations, and passengers tend to zone out during the flight. Other than that, its tour is identical to Indian Adventure Tours.

HELICOPTERS
West Rim

A helicopter ride gives you the best grasp on the size of the canyon. Comparatively, you'll feel about as big as a fly. These tours take about half as long as airplane tours (about 2 hr., plus ground transportation) and the pilots serve as your tour guide, educating and answering questions for the duration of the flight. Four companies offer helicopter flights to the West Rim, but the following two offer the best value.

Heli USA's Chariot of Fire Grand Canyon ★★ (☎ 800/359-8727; www.heliusa.com; $319 plus fees; see website for times/days) gets two stars because of the strength of its staff. The pilot I was assigned on my most recent flight was simply the best Grand Canyon tour guide I've encountered (and at this point, I've done *a lot* of these tours). In rapid-fire style, he painted a vivid picture of the history of Las Vegas, the geology of the area, how the physics of wind shaped the canyons, you name it. This was no canned pitch; the pilot was just as good at answering questions lobbed to him by the passengers.

As for the nitty-gritty: This tour is not for large groups as the helicopter can hold only five passengers. Over the course of the tour, it zips over Hoover Dam and Lake Mead, past an extinct volcano and old mines and into the western part of the canyon. It takes about 40 minutes to fly to the West Rim, and then about 10 minutes are spent 1,000 feet below the rim of the canyon getting a close-up view of the rocks, as the tour guide discusses the Canyon and the Hualapai Indians who call it home (for about $50 more you can land at the bottom of the canyon and ride a horse-drawn carriage and have a Western-style meal). The trip finishes with a jaunt through the red-rocked Bowl of Fire before heading around Downtown Las Vegas and up the Las Vegas Strip. The urban developments and expanding skyline are an excellent contrast to the starkness of the canyon. Just make sure you pick a day that's not windy, as the helicopters are pretty sensitive to air currents. Taking Dramamine ahead of time is a safe bet.

  Maverick Helicopter's Silver Cloud ★ (☎ 888/261-4414; www.maverick helicopter.com; $339 plus fees; see website for times/days) offers a similar flying tour in terms of route and timing. The sightseeing spiel given was adequate though not as colorful and in-depth as Heli USA. In fact, the narration doesn't begin until about 15 minutes into the flight, once you're over Hoover Dam. Although this trip is described as "air-only" there is a brief stop for fueling up, at a fuel tank located in the middle of the desert, which is an unexpected and inconvenient delay. On a more positive note, the helicopter is slightly larger (it can seat up to seven) and a more comfortable ride.

BUS TOURS

Bus trips are the least expensive mode of travel aside from renting a car, but do entail a 10- to 13-hour day (only 3 of which are spent at the Canyon). I'd think carefully if that's how you really want to use your time on vacation (this may be one case where a splurge on a helicopter or plane ride makes sense). Nearly 300 buses drive through the South Rim entrance per day (they come from all over, with just a handful coming daily from Las Vegas). Six coach companies drive to the West Rim daily and four generally head to the South Rim. Here are my picks should you decide to bus it:

South Rim

Grand Canyon Coaches (☎ 702/577-9056; www.grandcanyoncoaches.com; $91 if you order tickets online; 7:30am daily) provides a buffet lunch at Max and Thelma's in Williams, Arizona, before you hit the park for your 3 hours there, during which you stop at both Mather Point and Bright Angel. During the long, long rides to and from the Canyon, movies are shown and the bus driver gives information about some of the sights you'll pass along the way.

  Grayline (☎ 800/634-6579; www.graylinelasvegas.com; $155 but book online for discounts; 7:30am daily) offers a similar tour—same lunch stop, same sorts of entertainment while on the road, same viewing points at the canyon. But since it's significantly more expensive, we only include it in case the Grand Canyon Coach has sold out.

West Rim

Grand Canyon Coaches (☎ 702/577-9056; www.grandcanyoncoaches.com; $104; 7:30am daily) trek out to the West Rim. The bus trips include narrations about the history of Las Vegas and Hoover Dam, and are about 3 to 4 hours each way (although the West Rim is just 120 miles away, travel is slow because of traffic going over Hoover Dam and a 14-mile unpaved road to the Canyon). Upon arrival, a bus run by the Hualapai Indians transports visitors to Eagle Point (and the SkyWalk) and Guano Point. A light buffet lunch is provided at Guano Point (barbecued beef, mac and cheese, beans and tortillas). You'll have about 3½ hours to spend here, which is quite a long time, considering the limited areas open to visitors. I think the South Rim is a better option for bus tours.

GOING IT ALONE

Renting a car and driving yourself, as we said above, is a terrific option (and certainly the most affordable way to go, especially if you have several people traveling together). Four to five hours each way (or about 3 hours each way if you're headed to the West Rim) is quite a trek for a side trip, but it's not impossible. It's quicker than a slow and unwieldy bus, you're in control of your own schedule, and once you get there and realize that the Grand Canyon pretty much trumps everything in Vegas, you'll have the option of staying longer and exploring under the Rim of the canyon, if you have your own set of wheels (it's relatively easy to find accommodations at the last minute except during key school vacation periods, that is, the summer and spring break/holidays).

To get there: If you drive, take U.S. Highway 93 South (over the Hoover Dam) to Kingman, Arizona, then east on I-40 to Williams. At the Arizona Highway 64 junction, turn left (north) and proceed to the south entrance of Grand Canyon National Park. To get to the West Rim take Highway 93 south to I-40. Take I-40 east to Kingman, north on Stockton Hill Road to Pierce Ferry Road. Take Pierce Ferry Road north to Diamond Bar Road, go east on Diamond Bar Road.

13 The Essentials of Planning

THE HIGHLIGHTS OF A VISIT TO LAS VEGAS—THE TOP SIGHTS AND activities, the hotels, restaurants, shops, and spectacles that best serve your needs—have accounted for the bulk of this book. But almost as important is the miscellany that doesn't fit into broader categories. Those nitty-gritty details—from trip-planning essentials to perks to tips for travelers with special interests and needs—are what you'll find in this chapter.

The good news is that tourism is Las Vegas' largest industry and much of its infrastructure is devoted to catering to the needs of visitors. It boasts the most powerful tourist board in the nation, the **Las Vegas Convention and Visitors Bureau** (☎ 877/VISIT-LV or 702/892-7575; www.visitlv.com), which works with a budget that is four times as large as any other tourist board in the United States. It's a well-run, efficient organization staffed by real experts who love their jobs; and its website offers a wealth of information and discounts for the traveler. Anything that you can't find in this book—and hopefully that won't be much—you should be able to find through the tourist office.

WHEN TO VISIT?

The key to a successful vacation is timing. If you visit when the city is in the throes of a major convention, you can end up paying four times as much for your holiday as you would at any other time. Las Vegas now leads all of the other major cities in the U.S. for most conventions per year; there are weeks when literally 150,000 visitors can descend on the city. That translates to half-hour waits at the food courts, sold-out shows, mighty expensive hotel rooms, and often (let's lay it all on the table) more prostitutes on the streets. I've charted the major conventions for 2009–10 on p. 302—avoid these dates at all costs. For more convention dates—and some will land on the calendar after this book goes to press—check the website of the tourist board (**www.lvcva.com**) and click on "Meeting Planners." I'd think twice about visiting during any period when more than 50,000 conventioneers are scheduled to arrive, as that means that almost a third of the city's 153,000 rooms will be gone.

Conventions won't be the only item to consider when choosing the date for your Vegas vacation. Set in the heart of the driest desert in the United States, Las Vegas also experiences extremes of temperature that can, to put it mildly, detract from its appeal. In the summer months of June, July, and August, the mercury regularly hits 115°F (46°C). I've heard boosters say that because the heat is the dry kind it's not that bad; if you'd like to decide for yourself, heat up your oven, open the door and stand right in front of it for 20 minutes. That's dry heat too, and none too pleasant, to my mind. Just as summer gets hot, you'll want to avoid Vegas from November to early April if your fantasy vacation includes lounging by the pool. The vast majority of pools are outdoor ones here, and many simply shut down in these months, as the desert can get quite chilly in winter (see the chart

Major Convention Dates 2009–10

Convention	Dates	Number of attendees
National Assoc. of Broadcasters	Apr 10–23, 2009	115,000
National Hardware Show	May 5–7, 2009	50,000
RECon	May 18–20, 2009	50,000
Assn of Woodworking & Furniture Suppliers	July 15–18, 2009	45,000
World Show Association	July 27–29, 2009	30,000
ASD/AMD Show.	Aug 5–14, 2009	64,000
PACK Expo	Oct 5–7, 2009	30,000
Automotive Aftermarket Industry	Nov 3–6, 2009	130,000
Int'l Assoc of Amusement Parks & Attractions	Nov 17–20, 2009	30,000
G2E Global Gaming Expo	Nov 17–19, 2009	33,000
Consumer Electronics Show	Jan 7–10, 2010	150,000
Int'l Builders Show	Jan 19–22, 2010	105,000
World of Concrete	Feb 2–5, 2010	85,000
ASD/AMD Trade Show	Mar 1–4, 2010	64,000
Int'l Hospitality Week	Mar 9–10, 2010	31,000
Infocom	June 9–11, 2010	45,000
ASD/AMD Show	Aug 4–12, 2010	64,000
Int'l Baking Industry Expo	Sept 26–29, 2010	35,000
Photo Marketing Assoc	Feb 1–3, 2011	35,000

below). Those that don't close compensate by heating the water, but the moment you climb out of the pool you'll feel like you've unwittingly joined the Polar Bear Club. Despite that problem, I like Vegas in the winter, but you should bring layers, as you may need to bundle up.

In terms of holiday periods, Vegas no longer slows down to any great extent over Easter, Thanksgiving, Christmas, or any of those holidays that people traditionally spend with their families. More and more are choosing to eat turkey at the buffet so that they can get right back to baccarat. Early December, however, is traditionally slow, as is January and many periods during the summer (except when there's a convention in town or a major sports event worth betting on), so if you're looking to save money, those are good times to go. Be aware, however, that some shows go on hiatus in December and over Christmas week, so if going to the theater is a big reason for your visit, there may be better times to arrive.

The table below charts seasonal weather shifts. Look at them when planning your trip.

Las Vegas' Average Temperatures (°F/°C)

	Jan	Feb	Mar	Apr	May	June	July	Aug	Sept	Oct	Nov	Dec
Average Temp. (°F)	47	52	58	66	75	86	91	89	81	69	55	47
(°C)	8	11	14	19	24	30	33	32	27	21	13	8
Avg. High Temp. (°F)	57	63	69	78	88	99	104	102	94	81	66	57
(°C)	14	17	21	26	31	37	40	39	34	27	19	14
Avg. Low Temp. (°F)	37	41	47	54	63	72	78	77	69	57	44	37
(°C)	3	5	8	12	17	22	26	25	21	14	7	3
Average Precip. (in.)	.59	.69	.59	.15	.24	.08	.44	.45	.31	.24	.31	.40

Las Vegas' Visit-Worthy Events

There actually aren't all that many special events in Vegas—in a town this unusual, do you really need food fests and parades?—though people certainly come to Vegas to bet on special events elsewhere (such as the March Madness college basketball playoffs). But there are a handful of options that are worth a special visit. As the complete schedule is unpredictable, I can't include all of the nifty happenings. To get a fuller picture, surf over to **www.lasvegasevents.com**, which tracks events, shows, and more.

March

NASCAR/Winston: For NASCAR fans, March Madness has nothing to do with basketball. It's the Winston Cup races at the Las Vegas Motor Speedway (7000 Las Vegas Blvd. N.; ☎ 800/644-4444; www.lvms.com), which draw an estimated 150,000 race fans to Vegas for the Sam's Town 300 race and the UAW-Daimler Chrysler 400. Two of the most important races of the year, these are the events at which sporting legends are born.

June

CineVegas International Film Festival: It just makes sense that the L.A. Film community would support its nearby "playground" and its budding film festival. With nearly as many celebs as Cannes or Sundance, CineVegas has lately become a major launching pad for new films and is a must-do for film fans. June 11 to 20 are the dates for 2009. Learn more at www.cinevegas.com (or call 702/992-7979).

July

The World Series of Poker: In 2008, this premier poker championship tried to shake things up by breaking up its tournament play. The 6,800 competitors vying for the title and $9.1 million prize started their play on July 3 knowing that the final tables of the event wouldn't occur until a nail-biting 5 months later in November. As I write this, the common consensus was this new schedule was a bust, driving down (not up) interest in the event. I'm assuming it will go back to its former scheduling of play all within 1 month, but that's just a guess. Stay tuned to www.worldseriesofpoker.com for more info. However this shakes out, know that attending the matches is a kick. Bystanders can get right up to the action, standing around the tables and watching the action for the usual weeks of play. No admission is charged to watch, though you could be in for death threats if you tried to tip off any of the players.

September

Oktoberfest: As in many parts of the U.S., the German Oktoberfest is a big deal—or at least an excuse to listen to oompah music without embarrassment and drink copious amounts of beer. It's celebrated with verve at the **Hofbräuhaus** (p. 103), a perfect re-creation of the famous Munich beer hall of the same name, where the motto is "Every Day's Oktoberfest." When the actual holiday rolls around they ramp up the merriment a notch, with keg-tapping festivals, folk art celebrations, music performed by groups brought over from Germany, and, of course, beer. Lots and lots of beer. In nearby **Mount Charleston** (p. 288) there are similar festivities but with the bonus of a spectacular view.

October

Halloween: Vegas has dozens of other special events for Halloween itself, including multiple haunted houses at the Orleans Arena, and the Adventuredome (p. 131); costume parties at all the major dance clubs; the Fetish and Fantasy Halloween Ball; and a number of other events. Any excuse for a party is welcomed in Vegas, of course, and Halloween is no exception. The website www.halloweenlasvegas.com lists all of the various happenings.

December

The National Finals Rodeo: Yee-haw! This 12-day event, which usually starts the first 2 weeks of the month, is the be-all and end-all in everything cowboy, a must for those who take their roping, wrangling, and bull riding seriously. Nearly 170,000 people show up to watch the competitions, with $5 million in prize money distributed over the course of the events. For the top 15 male rodeo stars there are six events—calf roping, steer wrestling, bareback riding, saddle bronco riding, team roping, and bull riding—that might net them the title of "Cowboy of the Year." The top 15 women compete in barrel racing. All of Vegas goes Western for the event, with a cowboy gift show at

the Convention Center, and there's an invasion of country music stars who might include Vince Gill, Tanya Tucker, Brooks and Dunne, and Charlie Daniels. To order tickets (you'll need reservations long in advance) or find out more, go to www.nfrexperience.com or call ☎ 702/895-3900.

The Las Vegas Marathon: A relatively new event but growing in popularity, the marathon attracts about 15,000 participants, some of whom sweat their way through a jog-through wedding at the **Special Memory Chapel** (p. 151). Beyond the brides and grooms a select number run in showgirl regalia and there are a growing number of Elvi who race as well. A loop run, the marathon starts in front of Mandalay Bay, where the hotel blasts the song "Viva Las Vegas" as a starting gun, and indulges in a major laser light show. Go to www.lvmarathon.com for complete information.

New Year's Eve: By some estimates, more people are now crowding the Strip in Las Vegas to ring in the New Year than in Times Square. I personally think both groups are nuts; standing around in the cold, crowded together with hundreds of drunk people, is not my idea of a good time. But if the idea appeals to you, know that a large swatch of the Strip is closed for the festivities and to erect a large stage, on which some major rock star gives a concert. The evening is capped off with something called "America's Party," basically a gargantuan fireworks display in which firecrackers are blasted from the roofs of 10 Strip hotels in succession, leading to a finale in which all of them turn the sky into one massive crackling, glowing, glittering canvas. You'll find information on special New Year's activities at the tourist board's website (see p. 301).

ENTRY REQUIREMENTS FOR NON-AMERICAN CITIZENS

Be sure to check with the U.S. embassy or consulate for the very latest in entry requirements, as these continue to shift since 9/11. Full information can be found at the **U.S. State Department's** website, **www.travel.state.gov**.

VISAS

As of this writing, citizens of western and central Europe, Australia, New Zealand, Brunei, Mexico, Canada, South Korea, and Singapore need only a valid passport and a round-trip air ticket or cruise ticket to enter the U.S. Canadian citizens can also enter without a visa; you simply need to show proof of residence.

Citizens of all other countries will need to obtain a tourist visa from a U.S. consulate; depending on your country of origin, there may or may not be a charge attached (and you may or may not have to apply in person). To get the visa, you must have a passport valid to at least 6 months from the end of your scheduled U.S. visit, and you'll need to complete an application and submit a 1½-inch square photo. It's usually possible to obtain a visa within 24 hours, except during holiday periods or the summer rush.

For information about U.S. visas, go to **www.travel.state.gov** and click on "Visas."

PASSPORTS

To enter the United States, international visitors must have a valid passport that expires at least 6 months later than the scheduled end of your visit.

For Residents of Australia: You can pick up an application from your local post office or any branch of Passports Australia, but you must schedule an interview at the passport office to present your application materials. Call the **Australian Passport Information Service** at ☎ **131-232**, or visit the government website at **www.passports.gov.au**.

For Residents of Canada: Passport applications are available at travel agencies throughout Canada or from the central **Passport Office,** Department of Foreign Affairs and International Trade, Ottawa, ON K1A 0G3 (☎ **800/567-6868**; www.ppt.gc.ca). *Note:* Canadian children who travel must have their own passports.

For Residents of Ireland: You can apply for a 10-year passport at the **Passport Office,** Setanta Centre, Molesworth Street, Dublin 2 (☎ **01/671-1633**; www.irlgov.ie/iveagh). Those under age 18 and over 65 must apply for a 123€ 1-year passport. You can also apply at 1A South Mall, Cork (☎ **021/272-525**), or at most main post offices.

For Residents of New Zealand: You can pick up a passport application at any New Zealand Passports Office or download it from their website. Contact the **Passports Office** at ☎ **0800/225-050** in New Zealand or 04/474-8100, or log on to **www.passports.govt.nz**.

For Residents of the United Kingdom: To pick up an application for a standard 10-year passport (5-year passport for children under 16), visit your nearest passport office, major post office, or travel agency; or contact the **United Kingdom Passport Service** at ☎ 0870/521-0410. You can also search its website at **www.ukpa.gov.uk**.

MEDICAL REQUIREMENTS

No inoculations or vaccinations are required to enter the United States, unless you're arriving from an area that is suffering from an epidemic (cholera or yellow fever, in particular). A valid, signed prescription is required for those travelers in need of syringe-administered medications or medical treatment that involves narcotics. It is extremely important to obtain the correct documentation in these cases, as your medications could be confiscated; and if you are found to be carrying an illegal substance, you could be subject to significant penalties. Those who are HIV-positive may also need a special waiver in order to enter the country (as you will be asked on your visa application whether you're a carrier of any communicable diseases). The best thing to do is contact **AIDSinfo** (☎ 800/448-0440 or 301/519-6616; www.aidsinfo.nih.gov) for up-to-date information.

CUSTOMS REGULATIONS FOR INTERNATIONAL VISITORS

Strict regulations govern what can and can't be brought into the United States—and what you can take back home with you.

WHAT YOU CAN BRING INTO LAS VEGAS

Every visitor more than 21 years of age may bring in, free of duty, the following: (1) 1 liter of wine or hard liquor; (2) 200 cigarettes, 100 cigars (but not from Cuba), or 3 pounds of smoking tobacco; and (3) $100 worth of gifts. These exemptions are offered to travelers who spend at least 72 hours in the United States and who have not claimed them within the preceding 6 months. It is altogether forbidden to bring into the country foodstuffs (particularly fruit, cooked meats, and canned goods) and plants (vegetables, seeds, tropical plants, and the like). Foreign tourists may carry in or out up to $10,000 in U.S. or foreign currency with no formalities; larger sums must be declared to U.S. Customs on entering or leaving, which includes filing form CM 4790. For details regarding U.S. Customs and Border Protection, consult your nearest U.S. embassy or consulate, or U.S. Customs (☎ **202/927-1770;** www.cbp.gov/xp/cgov/travel/).

WHAT YOU CAN TAKE HOME FROM LAS VEGAS

For a clear summary of **Canadian** rules, write for the booklet *I Declare,* issued by the **Canada Border Services Agency** (☎ **800/461-9999** in Canada, or 204/983-3500; **www.cbsa-asfc.gc.ca**).

For information, **U.K. citizens** contact **HM Customs & Excise** at ☎ **0845/010-9000** (from outside the U.K., 020/8929-0152), or the website at **www.hmce.gov.uk**.

A helpful brochure for **Australians**, available from Australian consulates or Customs offices, is *Know Before You Go.* For more information, call the **Australian Customs Service** at ☎ **1300/363-263,** or log on to **www.customs.gov.au**.

Most questions regarding **New Zealand** rules are answered in a free pamphlet available at New Zealand consulates and Customs offices: *New Zealand Customs Guide for Travellers, Notice no. 4.* For more information, contact **New Zealand Customs,** The Customhouse, 17–21 Whitmore St., Box 2218, Wellington (☎ **04/ 473-6099** or 0800/428-786; www.customs.govt.nz).

FINDING A GOOD AIRFARE TO LAS VEGAS

In 2008, Las Vegas lost a good 20% of the flights that used to service the city, but you can still find a good fare if you look. Here are some ways in which you may be able to save money on airfares but note that in some cases you'll find yourself paying higher rates than you have in the past (and there's little recourse for that):

- **Consider the low-fare carriers:** Airlines such as **Allegiant Air, JetBlue, Frontier Airlines, Southwest, Spirit, Virgin America,** and **AirTran** will sometimes have better fares than the larger airlines, but they may not appear on such major search engines as Expedia. So use a broader tool such as **Sidestep.com, Kayak.com, Momondo.com,** or **Mobissimo.com,** which search airline sites directly, adding no service charges and often finding fares that the larger travel sites miss. The only airline these sites don't search is Southwest, which doesn't allow its fares to be accessed by any outside entity. If you're flying from Europe into the United States, take a look at the fares from bmi, Continental, Delta, United, and Virgin Atlantic, as these carriers tend to have the lowest rates for international travel. I've always found that Mobissimo.com and CheapFlights.uk.com are best for searching fares that don't originate in the U.S.

- **Fly when others don't.** Las Vegas is a weekend destination, so you'll find the lowest airfares (and hotel rates) on Monday, Tuesday, and Wednesday flights.

- **Book at the right time.** Sounds odd, but you can often save money by booking on a Tuesday or Wednesday. That's because most airfare sales are announced on Mondays and it will usually take a day or so for other carriers to match. Since the sales will be pulled by Thursday, you don't want to book too late in the week. Be sure to monitor such sites as **Frommers.com** and **SmarterTravel.com,** which highlight fare sales.

- **Try booking through a consolidator:** Persons traveling to Las Vegas from another country may wish to use a consolidator or "bucket shop" to snag a ticket. These companies buy tickets in bulk, passing along the savings to their customers. If you reside in Europe, the best way to find one that services your area is to go to the website **www.cheapflights.co.uk,** which serves as a clearinghouse for bucket shops both large and small. Many will also advertise in the Sunday papers. Be careful, though: Some charge outrageous change fees, so read the fine print before you purchase your ticket. Bucket shops will not be useful for those flying within the U.S., as they are not generally able to undercut standard pricing on domestic travel.

- **Don't be particular about airports:** Sometimes by driving an extra hour and flying out of such so-called "secondary" airports as, say, Oakland instead of San Francisco, or Providence in lieu of Boston, you'll pay far less. Cast a wide net when you search for fares and prepare to be flexible.

Booking Hotel Rooms

There's an art to getting the best price on hotel rooms in Las Vegas and it's discussed in chapter 3. For tips on booking online, go to p. 25; for tips on bargaining, go to p. 25; and for information on renting an apartment or staying in a private home, go to p. 18.

PACKAGE DEALS VS. BOOKING INDEPENDENTLY

Las Vegas is a prime packaging destination simply because it has such a vast number of hotel rooms that it needs to keep filled year-round. Go to p. 25 for my complete write-up on the companies that specialize in packages and tend to get the best rates.

A key to deciphering packages is to remember that their prices are always based on double occupancy, so be sure to double the costs and then subtract the airfares to get the lowdown on what you're actually paying for your room. The one exception to this rule may be packages that you create using such sites as Travelocity, Expedia, and Orbitz. Very occasionally, if you have a specific hotel in mind, you can save money on those websites. But it's a long shot.

TRAVEL INSURANCE—DO YOU NEED IT?

When purchasing a big-ticket travel item—a guided tour, a cruise, a safari—it's essential to buy travel insurance. Many unforeseen circumstances can interrupt or cause you to cancel a trip, and with these types of trips, those events can lead to a large financial loss. But do you need such a policy for your trip to Las Vegas? Not necessarily. If you're purchasing the insurance to cover unforeseen medical expenses, lost luggage, or a cancelled flight, you may already be covered by your regular insurance if you're an American citizen. And hotel stays should never be insured, as hotels will usually allow you to cancel 24 hours in advance with no penalty (the only exception being if you book through a website such as Priceline or other Web discounters that require payment upfront for your stay).

So what might you want to insure? If you've booked a **condo or home rental** and have had to put down a large deposit, that should be insured. If your homeowners insurance does not cover lost luggage, you may want to insure any **valuables you may be carrying with you** (as the airline will only pay up to $2,800 for lost luggage domestically, less for foreign travel). If you're an **international visitor** coming to Las Vegas, you should probably invest in insurance that will **cover medical expenses.** Unlike most European nations, the United States does not have any form of socialized health care, meaning that hospitals and doctor visits can be extremely expensive. In non-emergency situations, both doctors and hospitals have the right to refuse care without advance payment or proof of coverage. (***Note:*** We're not utter barbarians; if you're in a life-or-death situation you won't be denied health care. But as with non-emergency care, the uninsured pay dearly for any services rendered—you'll just get the bill a bit later.) American citizens usually find that their regular insurance will cover them in Las Vegas, making additional health insurance unnecessary (the exception being certain HMOs, so check first).

If you do decide to buy insurance, you can easily assess the different policies by visiting the website **InsureMyTrip.com,** which compares the policies of all of the major companies. Or contact one of the following reputable companies directly:

- ◆ **Access America** (☎ 866/807-3982; www.accessamerica.com)
- ◆ **Travel Guard International** (☎ 800/826-4919; www.travelguard.com)
- ◆ **CSA Travel Protection** (☎ 800/873-9844; www.csatravelprotection.com)

TRAVELING FROM LAS VEGAS TO OTHER PARTS OF THE UNITED STATES

Las Vegas, as a major travel hub, is a convenient hopping-off point for other areas of the United States, even those located across the continent. Competition among carriers has kept fares from Sin City to most of the major gateways of the U.S. relatively cheap. To book airfares from Vegas to points west, north, and south take a look at "Finding a Good Airfare to Las Vegas," above. Unfortunately, Las Vegas does not currently enjoy rail service, so that's not an option for travelers.

If you're renting a car to get around Las Vegas, you may want to consider simply keeping that car for travel around the region. This will give you the most freedom, but there are almost always one-way drop-off fees involved in renting a car in one locale and dropping it in another, so be sure to calculate these costs before you book. Priceline and Hotwire do not allow one-way rentals, but you can calculate them using the website of any of the major car-rental companies (see p. 10 for more info on car rentals).

For bus travel, an International Ameripass for international visitors is offered by **Greyhound/Trailways** (www.greyhound.com). Greyhound buses cover the United States, and the company's prices, both for individual trips and for the passes can be the cheapest form of transportation if you don't have a car. The conditions aboard these buses aren't particularly pleasant, however—cramped conditions, smelly bathrooms, and delays when traffic hits—making this a less pleasant option than driving or flying. I recommend looking at car rentals or a plane first.

If you simply want to hop the bus from Vegas to LA, Anaheim, or San Diego, you have the option of using Greyhound (average rate $39) or one of its new competitors, the so-called "Chinatown buses." These simple but clean vehicles stop at the Riviera, Harrah's, and the Tropicana (as well as the city's Chinatown Mall on Spring Mountain Rd.) and then make their way to a series of locales in the cities listed from their Chinatowns to Los Angeles Airport. The Chinatown bus companies—**US Asia, Dragon Tours, and Bravo Travel**—use one central location for their bookings, a website called **www.gotobus.com**. There you'll find prices (on average the cost to get to LA is $30) and pick up and drop off locations for the various buses. Travel time between LA and Vegas is listed as being 5 hours on the GoToBus.com, and 6 hours with Greyhound (I have no idea whether that has to do with the number of stops made or the speed these buses go).

HOW DO I GET TO (& FROM) THE AIRPORT? LET ME COUNT THE WAYS . . .

Unlike other major world cities, the McCarran International Airport, Las Vegas' major hub, is in the very center of the city itself. In fact, the nighttime approach to Vegas is one of the most dramatic in aviation today: a steep bank directly above the twinkling buildings of the Strip. You'll literally hear first timers gasping with fright, sure that the pilot is going to crash the plane right between the MGM Grand and New York–New York. Beyond the spectacular introduction that the landing affords (book a night flight if you can, especially if you're a Vegas virgin), the fact that the runway is so close to the Strip means that it's surprisingly easy to get into town. No, there's no train direct from the airport to the Strip (though there is talk that the Monorail will one day extend that far), but there are a raft of affordable, quick options, such as:

◆ **Bell Trans** (☎ 702/739-7990; www.bell-trans.com). This company sends a steady parade of minibuses (seating 20) to the airport from 7:45am to midnight. Buses then go to all the major Vegas hotels and motels. If you don't see a Bell Trans bus, use one of its competitors. They're all reliable, leaving every 10 minutes or so and charging $6.50 to the Strip Hotels, $8 for Downtown (book round-trip and you'll save a buck on the overall costs). If you're arriving after midnight, you can arrange for special pick-up. Go out door #9 at the airport to get to the pick-up spot for the minibuses.

◆ **Citizens Area Transit** or **CAT** (☎ 702/CAT-RIDE; www.rtcsouthernnevada. com). The public bus system also loops out to the airport. Take Bus 109 if you're staying Downtown; otherwise, Bus 108 will take you to the Stratosphere, from which you can transfer to Bus 301 making a number of stops along the Strip. Fares are just $2 for adults, 60¢ for seniors and children, but weigh whether that $2 is worth the hassle of the buses. Truth be told, many won't stop near the hotel you've booked and you could end up lugging your

The Airport Waiting Game

After you factor in travel time, do a bit of research to learn how long it will take you to get through security lines at the airport. The government maintains a helpful website at **http://waittime.tsa.dhs.gov** that displays average and maximum waiting times at all U.S. airports, terminal by terminal, during a 4-hour time frame, based on data collected in the previous few weeks at each airport.

It's also a good idea to call a day before your flight to confirm your seat. Be sure to inquire at that time if your flight is overbooked. If that's the case, tack an extra 20 minutes onto your "getting to the airport" time just to make sure you get a seat on the plane. You may also want to go online and check in using the Web. All domestic airlines now allow passengers to check-in online within 24 hours of their flight. The advantages? You'll be much less likely to be bumped (usually the last to check in is the first to be bumped).

What Things Cost

Small unexpected costs can add up. To help you better budget for your vacation, here are the average costs or range of costs for some of the items and services you may need to purchase in the course of your trip.

Bus ride	$2
Monorail	$5
Cup of regular coffee	$3–$4
Diner breakfast	$6
Lunch in cheap restaurant	$5–$8
Lunch in moderate–expensive restaurant	$12–$30
Dinner in cheap restaurant	$7–$12
Dinner in moderate–expensive restaurant	$13–$50
Bottle of domestic beer in a Strip bar	$6
Bottle of imported beer in a Strip bar	$9
Cocktail in a Strip bar	$14
Bottle of water (off the Strip)	$1
Bottle of water (on the Strip)	$2–$3 (up to $9 in a club)
Average museum entrance fee	$15
Full-price evening show ticket	$44–$204
Discount evening show ticket	$11–$65
Souvenir T-shirt	$10
Tube of toothpaste	$3
Contact lens solution (12 oz.)	$4

bags a long distance along the crowded Strip before you get to your hotel. Vans go right up to hotel entrances and are thus a good option for those with a lot of luggage.

◆ **Car rentals.** These are a terrific option, not only for getting around Vegas but for tootling out to Red Rock Canyon, or taking an eating excursion off the Strip. For my complete advice on saving on rental cars, please turn to p. 10.

◆ **Taxis.** Taxis are the costliest option, but not by all that much. A taxi will cost between $9 and $20 to most Strip hotels (depending on traffic and location) and $30 to Downtown. Add $1.25 airport tax to those costs.

MONEY MATTERS

Every casino in town—which in Vegas means about half the buildings in the tourist areas—scatter **ATM** or **bank machines** alongside the slots. They are ubiquitous—the casinos want you to have easy access to your cash, after all (that's why local casinos deviously offer locals check-cashing services with lottery drawings; you'll see the lines every Fri). Because thievery is the norm here, the ATMs charge the highest fees I've seen anywhere: as much as $5 in a casino, and $4.50 in local banks. It's frustrating, but for those changing a foreign currency, ATMs are the name of the game: Banks are located far from the tourist areas, and the few Change Bureaus on the Strip (also hard to find) charge even higher fees.

Traveler's checks will elicit a confused stare from many waiters and shop clerks. With ATMs so common, hardly anyone uses these little slips of paper anymore, and there can be significant fees attached to their exchange at some banks.

Credit cards are widely accepted and can be used in hotels, restaurants, shops, and even Monorail ticket vending machines. In some cases, a $15 minimum will be required for credit card use, but this is such a plastic-happy town, that even that minimum is often waived. Do ask first, though.

HEALTH & SAFETY

One of the most dangerous things you can do in Las Vegas is to cross the street. No joke, Vegas has one of the highest rates of pedestrian deaths in the United States. To combat this, police in this town take jaywalking seriously and will issue tickets to those dodging between cars, refusing to wait for the light, or otherwise bucking the traffic laws.

Jaywalking isn't the only law that's strictly enforced, so if you're coming here because you feel this is an "anything goes" type destination, you're in for a rude surprise (and possibly a stint in the clink). Prostitution is illegal in Las Vegas (despite all evidence to the contrary) and soliciting risks heavy fines and possible jail time, as does the use of narcotics and other illegal substances. Recently, the law was changed to outlaw open containers of liquor on the streets, so though you may be tempted to parade with your Eiffel Tower–shaped drink down the Boulevard (and many do), know that you are risking a fine.

To steer clear of those who are breaking the law—and with a city where this much cash is floating around, there will be pickpockets and other thieves—be sure to guard your valuables. When gambling, keep your pocketbook in sight at all times, and consider carrying your wallet in a jacket pocket rather than on your fanny. Speaking of that, avoid fanny packs altogether: They're extremely easy to lift. If you win big at the machines or at a table, ask the pit boss or slot attendant to cut you a check; much safer than carrying around cash. You may also want to ask security to escort you to your car or taxi.

Beyond the casinos, the shopping malls and large outdoor spectacles (the fountains at the Bellagio, the pirate show at Treasure Island, and so forth) are prime stomping grounds for pickpockets, so stay aware of who's around you and where your valuables are being kept. To foil these types altogether, try not to carry too much cash on your person. Store your valuables in your in-room safe, and if you don't have one of those, ask to use the one behind the counter in the lobby.

Along with pickpockets, scam artists remain a problem. The most common scams involve a stranger asking for the use of your ATM card, briefly they say, until they can access their funds. Don't fall for it. You will also possibly be approached by panhandlers asking for money. These unfortunate souls are rarely dangerous, and if you want to be generous, the best thing to do is to buy them a bit of food, because gifts of cash may go to feed a drug or gambling habit.

HEALTH CONCERNS

If you develop any kind of illness while in Las Vegas, your best bet is to talk with the desk clerk at your hotel and ask him or her to recommend a dentist or a doctor. You'll probably receive better care that way than calling a toll-free number for referrals. Doctors in Las Vegas almost never make house calls; most only work between 10am and 6pm, but an increasing number are keeping office hours on Saturdays and evenings to handle the overload of patients. You can get referrals for dentists through the **Southern Nevada Dental Society** (☎ 702/733-8700); for physician referrals call the **Desert Springs Hospital** (☎ 702/388-4888). In addition, the **Imperial Palace Hotel & Casino** (☎ 702/309-5144), of all places, also houses an urgent care facility and is an option for those with problems not serious enough to require a hospital visit. It's open Mondays through Fridays from 9am to 5pm only and walk-ins are welcome.

If you have an acute need to see a doctor at a time of day when regular physicians aren't seeing patients, and you're worried that your condition may be too serious for the Nevada Resort Medical Center, you'll have to go to a local hospital for care. Again, ask the clerk at your hotel for the nearest emergency room or, if you cannot make it there under your own steam, call ☎ **911,** which is also the number to call in the United States for emergency help from the police and fire department.

One word on prescription medications: It is crucial that you pack your prescription medications in their original containers and bring them in your carry-on luggage. Be sure, also, to bring along copies of your prescriptions in case you run out or misplace your pills. If you need a prescription filled during your stay, **Walgreens** (3763 Las Vegas Blvd. S., across from the Monte Carlo; ☎ 702/739-9638) is open 24 hours a day, right on the Strip. Two other 24-hour options include **Sav-On** (1360 E. Flamingo Rd.; ☎ 702/731-5373) and **White Cross Drugs** (1700 Las Vegas Blvd. S.; ☎ 702/382-1733).

PACKING

The most important item in your suitcase will be a pair of very, very comfortable shoes because your dogs are gonna be barking! Distances are deceptive on the Strip and what seems like a short stroll can quickly become a strenuous hike. Even the distances within certain casinos can be daunting, with a walk from the parking garage to a restaurant eating up a good quarter of an hour. A springy, supportive pair of shoes is essential (you may want to bring two pairs to increase your foot comfort).

Second most important items: sunscreen and hats, particularly in summer. Unless you plan to spend every waking moment in the casino, it's important to protect yourself from the sun in this often steamy, desert city. Other than those items, feel free to fill your suitcase with what pleases you most at home. Very few actual Las Vegans have the budget or time to dress like the actors on the TV show *Las Vegas,* and unless you plan on going to a very fancy restaurant, casual clothes should suffice. If you want to go clubbing, turn to p. 202 to read our advice on the specialized "club clothes" you're going to need to get past the velvet ropes.

Dressing appropriately for the weather is also key, so be sure to check the chart at the top of this chapter for the average temperatures at various times of the year.

Those visiting in the fall, winter, and early spring months (mid-Oct to mid-Apr) are advised to bring clothes that you can layer, as a balmy afternoon can turn chilly once the sun goes down. Summer will be mighty sultry, so be sure to pack sandals, bathing suits, shorts, and shirts in fabrics that breathe. But even in the summer, you'll want to pack a light sweater, as the air-conditioning in the casinos can get downright arctic.

SPECIALIZED TRAVEL RESOURCES

With its emphasis on tourism and its tolerance for all sorts of naughty behavior, Sin City is welcoming to persons of all types. But because certain visitors have special needs (and also get special perks), I want to address these groups directly with a few choice words of advice.

ADVICE FOR FAMILY TRAVELERS

Remember that advertising campaign touting Vegas as a family destination? They ditched it in favor of the far more salacious "What happens in Vegas, stays in Vegas" tagline . . . as well they should. Yes, there are activities for children here, but there are also many things that you may not want your children to see: prostitutes soliciting Johns, reeling drunks, billboards of nearly naked women, and gambling, of course. Lots and lots of people playing games that make bells go off and lights flash . . . a glamorous scene for a little kid, which leads me to my next question: With the widespread problems we have in the U.S. with gambling addictions, do you really want to imprint these images on those sensitive little brains? It's something I struggled with when I brought my kids to Vegas and went so overboard talking about the dangers of gambling that my daughter ended up harrumphing her way through each casino, muttering loudly how "stupid these people are for throwing away their money like this" (which got us more than one annoyed look from an insulted gambler).

As for restaurants, many in town are friendly to families, providing appropriately bland food and high chairs. There are some, however, that make it abundantly clear they don't want the little dears around. How can you tell that a restaurant wants your kids? Call in advance and ask about highchairs and kids' menus; those that have them are saying, "Come on in." Those that don't should be visited only by parents with exceptionally well-behaved offspring. You should also check out those restaurants that I've marked with a 🧒 icon in chapter 4.

Hotels are a tricky topic. Many have elaborate pools that will appeal to youngsters but require long treks through smoky casinos whenever you have to leave or enter your room. And almost all the Strip hotels charge extra for children (something off-Strip hotels do not), making these glamorous properties a pricey proposition for parents. Consider renting a house rather than staying in a hotel. It may afford you more privacy, as you may not have to share a room with the kids; and you'll have access to a kitchen so you'll save on restaurant meals (that may also save your sanity if your child is a picky eater).

DISCOUNTS: Remember that children under 12 receive discounted or free admission to nearly every museum and attraction in the city and can get discounted movie tickets. They ride the public buses here for half-price as well. The only place your kids will not get a discount is at the shows, some of which do not admit children under the age of 5 (and aren't appropriate for young kids). I've attached our 🐾 symbol in the show chapter (p. 175) to those productions that are appropriate for families.

If you're hoping for a night or afternoon away from the kids, ask at the front desk if your hotel can provide a babysitter or has a list of reliable babysitters (better yet, ask before you book). Those staying in an apartment or a hotel without such a service should contact **Around the Clock Childcare** (☎ 800/798-6768 or 702/365-1040; www.aroundtownchildcare.com). The service is not cheap ($75 for the 4-hr. minimum, $15 for each additional hour, and extra if you have more than two kids), but the sitters from this organization are veritable Mary Poppinses (they'll even take your kids out on the town, if you wish), and are licensed, insured, and bonded. These short-term nannies are on call 24 hours and even work holidays (for an additional fee, of course). Be sure to call at least 3 hours ahead to book.

ADVICE FOR TRAVELERS WITH DISABILITIES
Hotels/Casinos

Because Las Vegas is constantly remaking its hotels (imploding some, upgrading others), it's done a better job than many older cities in complying with the Americans with Disabilities Act. All of the major hotels have accessible rooms, with roll-in showers, ramps, and the like. Problems arise, however, on the casino floors, which can be quite cramped. Machines and tables are often set one next to the other, with little room for negotiating in between; and the constant crowds, particularly in the evening hours, makes getting around even more difficult, particularly for those who use scooters or wheelchairs. This is especially true for the smaller Downtown casinos.

Visitors who choose to stay on the Strip should inquire where their room is located before booking. Las Vegas has seven of the largest hotels in the world and the distances within these hotels are often vast. Try to book a room as close to the elevator as possible, and on an elevator bank that serves the center of the casino.

For insider advice on casino accessibility, visit the website **www.access-able.com**, which has a poorly organized but still useful database of accommodations reviews for Las Vegas. You can also e-mail **SATH** (Society for Accessible Travel and Hospitality; www.sath.org) with any questions on hotels, and the staff there will get back to you . . . eventually (it's understaffed) with what they know about the accessibility of the hotel in question. In addition the **Nevada Commission on Tourism** (☎ 800/638-2328; www.travelnevada.com) distributes free accommodations guides that include information on access.

Veterans with disabilities should contact the **American Wheelchair Veterans Association** (5355 Medre Mesa; ☎ 702/631-1900) and ask for permission to stay in the fully accessible apartment complex it has created in Las Vegas. The apartments come with fully equipped kitchens and rooms large enough to maneuver a wheelchair. A pool on-site has a wheelchair lift. Veterans can apply to stay here for up to a week; amazingly, there is no cost whatsoever for this housing.

Theaters

Every Strip show now has spaces set aside for persons in wheelchairs. These are limited in number, however, so it's important to book well in advance to ensure that you get a spot at the show you wish to see.

Transportation

Because of the distances involved in navigating the Strip (and other parts of Vegas), visitors with disabilities are well advised to rent a car or van. Many of the major car rental companies now offer cars with hand controls. For this service Avis (www.avis.com) requires 48-hour advance notice; Hertz (www.hertz.com) requires between 24 and 78 hours at most of its offices. Full accessible vans, with hand controls, automatic ramps and lifts, remote controls, and tie down systems, can be rented from **Wheelchair Getaways of Nevada** (☎ 888/824-7413; www. wheelchairgetaways.com).

ADVICE FOR GAY & LESBIAN TRAVELERS

Vegas is not as "live and let live" as its reputation suggests. In truth, this is a conservative city, meaning that the gay and lesbian scene is much smaller than in other cities its size. There's but one gay hotel, and a small district, called the "Fruit Loop" (p. 215), of gay bars. Until very recently there were no gay clubs on the Strip. That has changed with the arrival of Krave. And I've had gay friends tell me that they've been made to feel uncomfortable when publicly displaying affection. Despite this lack of facilities designed solely for gay men and women (and, perhaps, tolerance), Vegas is nevertheless one of the most popular gay and lesbian destinations in the country, with many choosing the Mandalay Bay as their home base, along with the gay resort Blue Moon (p. 63).

For more complete listings of bars and special events than you'll find in this tome, pick up a copy of *Q Vegas* (www.qvegas.com), available at LGBT nightclubs and bookstores, Borders, Tower Records, most libraries. There's also a calendar of events at www.gaylasvegas.com.

ADVICE FOR SENIORS

Age has it privileges, even in Vegas, with seniors eligible for a raft of discounts—you just have to ask (and show a picture ID if you look particularly spry). Many of the large hotel chains offer discounts to persons over 60, and movie theaters and museums do as well. Seniors can also get half-price rides on the city buses (60¢).

Those who belong to **AARP** (601 E St. NW, Washington, DC 24009; ☎ 888/687-2277; www.aarp.org) get even more discounts, especially at hotels, so start waving around that card if you have it. Anyone over 50 can join.

In terms of meals, Las Vegas does not have the same abundance of "early bird specials" that you'll find in cities largely populated by seniors. What it does have are heaping portions, and my father, Arthur Frommer (now 80), insists that with age comes a diminishment in appetite. His advice to seniors, which I pass along here, is to share food: One appetizer and one entree are what he and Roberta, his wife, have when they go out to dine, and they leave perfectly satisfied.

STAYING WIRED

Like everything else in this town, the philosophy seems to be: Why give it away for free when we can make a buck off it? So while a handful of hotels offer free Internet access, most charge $9.95 per day for the privilege. Depending on the hotel, this will be Wi-Fi, dial-up, or a choice of either.

Hot Zones, where Internet access is free, are almost nil in the tourist areas (an odd exception are the lobbies of both The Venetian and Palazzo). However, you will have access to computers and the Internet at any of the business centers at the large Strip hotels; or at the **Cyber Stop Internet Café** (200 Fremont St. at the Fitzgerald Hotel, Downtown; ☎ 702/736-4782; open 7am–2:30am). The many free-standing **Starbucks** (www.starbucks.com) sprinkled about town also offer Internet access for a price to those carrying their own laptops. Those Starbucks located inside casinos never have Wi-Fi.

One warning: You should not carry a computer or anything resembling a computer into a casino, unless you have a yen to meet the security guards (briefly, as they'll boot you out swiftly, with accusations of cheating).

RECOMMENDED BOOKS & FILMS

From Mormons to miners to mobsters, Las Vegas boasts a colorful, intriguing history. The books that have best captured its idiosyncratic nature and past are:

- *Casino* by Nicholas Pileggi. A rollicking, detailed, almost novel-like account of the rise and fall of mob-controlled Vegas that was later turned into a movie by Martin Scorsese (see p. 318).

- *Super Casino* by Pete Earley. Starts where *Casino* left off, telling the story of how corporations took over Vegas after the mob was pushed out by the Feds. Filled with insightful and ultimately moving portraits of a wide gallery of characters who called Sin City home in the late '90s.

- *A Short History of Las Vegas* by Barabara Land, Myrick Land, and Guy Louis Rocha. This is just what it says it is: a concise but sweeping tale of the area, from the Native American settlements here through the Hoover Dam construction days, and all the way up to the millennium.

- *Fear and Loathing in Las Vegas.* Okay, Hunter S. Thompson's masterpiece is not a history *per se,* but it captures better than any other book out there the surreal soul of the city, its excesses, and hideous underside (actually, it could be said it does the same for the author). Briefly, Thompson recounts his drug-addled adventures in Las Vegas while covering a national police convention and desert race.

And if you'd like a more in-depth introduction to the various casino games, try one of the following top how-to books:

- *The Frugal Gambler* by Jean Scott is a how-to manual on how to get free meals, stays, and other privileges from the casinos. It also covers basic strategies for video poker and many other games. *More Frugal Gambler* is Scott's helpful follow-up to the first.

- *Beat the Dealer* by Ed Thorp is possibly the most influential book on gambling. It introduced the rudiments of card counting.

- *The Theory of Blackjack* by Peter Griffin is considered by many to be the bible of that game. It's not an easy read, but it will give you strategies for every type of play possible.

- *The Theory of Poker* by David Sklansky does what the *Theory of Blackjack* does, for this popular game.

For good movies and TV series that focus on the city, rent the PBS television show *Las Vegas* (available at some video stores), a 3-hour epic featuring extensive interviews with historians, politicos, casino owners, and average Joes. It offers a compelling portrait of Las Vegas, throughout its history, with particular emphasis on the odd period when Howard Hughes was buying up every hotel in sight. Other movies that will teach you a bit about the town include Martin Scorsese's masterpiece *Casino,* which takes on mob Las Vegas; and *The Cooler,* which goes into the behind the scenes running of a casino. Just for the fun of it, you might also want to view *Viva, Las Vegas* (with Elvis, of course), *Diamonds Are Forever* (Bond in Vegas!), *Indecent Proposal, Honeymoon in Vegas, Leaving Las Vegas, Swingers, Oceans Eleven* (either version), and *Showgirls.* Rent one before you come, and then look for locations as you wander round the city. TV shows *Las Vegas, Vega$* (for classic Vegas), and the original *CSI* are also good for a peek at the city before you arrive. Or turn on the Travel Channel any time of the day or night: It seems like half their programming nowadays is dedicated to Sin City (and poker, for that matter).

The ABCs of Las Vegas

Area Codes The 3-digit area code for Las Vegas is **702.** When dialing within Vegas to a Vegas number you do not have to use the area code—simply use the 7-digit telephone number. To dial anywhere else in the United States or Canada, you'll need to use the prefix 1 and then add the 3-digit area code. To dial outside of the United States or Canada, dial 011 before the telephone number.

ATMs & Currency Exchange See "Money Matters," earlier in this chapter.

Business Hours Offices are generally open on weekdays between 9am and 5pm, while banks tend to close at 3pm. A scattering of banks throughout the city are now open between the hours of 9am and 1pm on Saturday. Typically, stores open between 9am and 10am and close between 7 and 8pm Monday through Saturday, with a number of pharmacies extending their hours until midnight. Stores within casino-hotels usually have longer hours, some staying open until midnight on weekends. On Sunday, stores generally open at 11am and rarely stay open later than 6pm.

Drinking & Gambling Laws The legal age for the purchase and consumption of any sort of alcohol is 21; that's also the

age minimum for casino gambling. Proof of age is often requested at liquor stores, bars, clubs, casinos, and restaurants, so be sure to carry photo ID with you at all times. Recently, Vegas changed its open container laws to make carrying alcoholic beverages on the street illegal (so empty that Eiffel Tower margarita before you leave Paris Las Vegas!).

Electricity The United States uses 110–120 volts AC (60 cycles), compared to the 220–240 volts AC (50 cycles) that is standard in Europe, Australia, and New Zealand. If your small appliances use 220–240 volts, be sure to buy an adaptor and voltage converter before you leave home, as these are very difficult to find in the United States.

Embassies & Consulates All embassies are located in the nation's capital, Washington, D.C. Some consulates are located in major U.S. cities, and most nations have a mission to the United Nations in New York City. If your country isn't listed below, call for directory information in Washington, D.C. (☎ 202/555-1212) or log on to **www.embassy.org/ embassies.**

The embassy of **Australia** is at 1601 Massachusetts Ave. NW, Washington, DC 20036 (☎ **202/797-3000;** www.usa.embassy.gov.au.org). There are consulates in New York, Honolulu, Houston, Los Angeles, and San Francisco.

The embassy of **Canada** is at 501 Pennsylvania Ave. NW, Washington, DC 20001 (☎ **202/682-1740;** www.canadian embassy.org). Other Canadian consulates are in Buffalo (New York), Detroit, Los Angeles, New York, and Seattle.

The embassy of **Ireland** is at 2234 Massachusetts Ave. NW, Washington, DC 20008 (☎ **202/462-3939;** www.ireland emb.org). Irish consulates are in Boston, Chicago, New York, San Francisco, and other cities. See website for complete listings.

The embassy of **New Zealand** is at 37 Observatory Circle NW, Washington, DC 20008 (☎ **202/328-4800;** www.nz embassy.com). New Zealand consulates are in Los Angeles, Salt Lake City, San Francisco, and Seattle.

The embassy of the **United Kingdom** is at 3100 Massachusetts Ave. NW, Washington, DC 20008 (☎ **202/588-7800;** www.britainusa.com). Other British consulates are in Atlanta, Boston, Chicago, Cleveland, Houston, Los Angeles, New York, San Francisco, and Seattle.

Emergencies Call ☎ **911** for the police, to report a fire, or to get an ambulance. If you have a medical emergency that does not require an ambulance, you should be able to walk into the nearest hospital emergency room (see "Hospitals," below).

Holidays Banks close on the following holidays: January 1 (New Year's), the third Monday in January (Martin Luther King, Jr., Day), the third Monday in February (Presidents Day), the last Monday in May (Memorial Day), July 4 (Independence Day), the first Monday in September (Labor Day), November 11 (Veterans Day), the fourth Thursday in November (Thanksgiving Day), and December 25.

The handful of museums that are open on Monday tend to stay open on holidays, though almost all museums in the city close for Thanksgiving, Christmas, and New Year's. Do note that the casinos close for nobody and nothing—they stay open round-the-clock, year-round.

Hospitals The following hospitals are well regarded and have emergency rooms that are open 24 hours:

University Medical Center (1800 W. Charleston Blvd., at Shadow Lane; ☎ 702/383-2000); **Sunrise Hospital and Medical Center** (3186 Maryland Pkwy., between Sahara Ave. and Desert Inn Rd.; ☎ 702/731-8080).

Mail As of May 2009, domestic postage rates are 28¢ for a postcard and 44¢ for a letter. For international mail, a first-class letter of up to 1 ounce costs 98¢ (75¢ to Canada and 79¢ to Mexico). For more information go to **www.usps.gov** and click on "Calculate Postage."

Always include ZIP codes when mailing items in the U.S. If you don't know your zip code, visit **www.usps.gov/zip4**.

The post office most convenient to the Strip is in the Forum Shops at Caesars; there's also one at 3100 Industrial Rd., between Spring Mountain Road and Sahara Avenue. It's open 8:30am to 5pm. All hotels will post mail for you at no additional charge.

Newspapers & Magazines There are two major daily newspapers in Las Vegas: *The Las Vegas Review Journal* and *The Las Vegas Sun,* though the national paper *USA Today* is widely available as well. Each comes out in the morning. The *Review Journal* is an excellent source for listings of concerts, performances, parties, and other special events that might be happening around town. You'll probably find one of the free local magazines in your hotel room as well—*Vegas Visitor, What's On in Las Vegas, Where to Go in Las Vegas,* and others. Don't bother reading the reviews in these publications—they're all paid advertising. These periodicals can, however, be a good source for coupons, show times, and event listings.

Pharmacies See p. 313 for a listing of 24-hour pharmacies.

Smoking Las Vegas used to be the haziest American city, though that haze is now lifting a bit thanks to a stringent ban on smoking in places where food is served. Poker rooms were already smoke-free, but now bars and restaurants are as well. The casinos however are still quite smoking.

Taxes When guestimating your expenses for the trip, you should always factor in a **sales tax** of 7% on goods and many services, and the **hotel tax** of 9%.

Telephone & Fax Generally, hotel surcharges on long-distance and local calls are astronomical, so you're better off using your **cellphone** or a **public pay telephone.** Many convenience stores sell **prepaid calling cards** in denominations up to $50; for international visitors these can be the least expensive way to call home. Many public phones at airports now accept American Express, MasterCard, and Visa credit cards. **Local calls** made from public pay phones in most locales cost either 25¢ or 35¢. Pay phones do not accept pennies, and few will take anything larger than a quarter.

Most long-distance and international calls can be dialed directly from any phone. For calls within the United States and to Canada, dial 1 followed by the area code and the 7-digit number. For other international calls, dial 011 followed by the country code, the city code, and the number you are calling.

Calls to area codes **800, 888, 877,** and **866** are toll-free. However, calls to area codes **700** and **900** (chat lines, bulletin boards, "dating" services, and so on) can be very expensive—usually a charge of 95¢ to $3 or more per minute, and they

sometimes have minimum charges that can run as high as $15 or more.

For **reversed-charge** or **collect calls,** and for **person-to-person** calls, dial the number 0, then the area code and number. An operator will come on the line, and you should specify whether you are calling collect, person-to-person, or both. If your operator-assisted call is international, ask for the overseas operator.

For **local directory assistance** ("information"), dial ☎ **411;** for long-distance information, dial 1, then the appropriate area code and 555-1212.

Most hotels have **fax machines** available for guest use (be sure to ask about the charge to use it). Many hotel rooms are even wired for guests' fax machines. A less expensive way to send and receive faxes may be at stores such as The UPS Store (www.theupsstore.com).

Time The continental United States is divided into four time zones: Eastern Standard Time (EST), Central Standard Time (CST), Mountain Standard Time (MST), and Pacific Standard Time (PST). Las Vegas is on Pacific Standard Time, so when it's noon here, it's 3pm in New York (ET), 2pm in Chicago (CST), and 1pm in Phoenix. Daylight saving moves the clock an hour ahead of standard time. A new law went into effect in 2007, extending daylight saving time; clocks now change the second Sunday in March and the first Sunday in November.

Tipping Tips are customary and should be factored into your budget. Waiters should receive 15% to 20% of the cost of a meal (depending on the quality of the service), bellhops get $1 per bag, chambermaids get $1 to $2 per day for straightening your room, valets get $2 to park or retrieve your car, and cab drivers should get 15% of the fare. Casino dealers should receive a tip that's the equivalent of 5% of your average bets that evening (which can either be given on an hourly basis or at the end of your run). As an alternative, it's also perfectly appropriate to place a bet on behalf of the dealer (especially if you're losing!) in lieu of a direct tip. Just tell the dealer what you're planning if you go this route. Slot attendants don't have to be tipped.

Toilets Every casino, restaurant, and hotel in the city has public toilets and they never check to make sure you're a customer at the establishment in question before letting you use the facilities.

Index

See also Accommodations and Restaurant indexes, below.

NOTES

NOTES

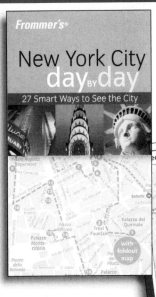

A Guide for Every Type of Traveler

Frommer's Complete Guides

For those who value complete coverage, candid advice, and lots of choices in all price ranges.

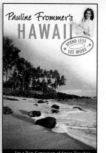

Pauline Frommer's Guides

For those who want to experience a culture, meet locals, and save money along the way.

MTV Guides

For hip, youthful travelers who want a fresh perspective on today's hottest cities and destinations.

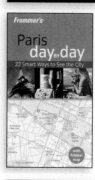

Day by Day Guides

For leisure or business travelers who want to organize their time to get the most out of a trip.

Frommer's With Kids Guides

For families traveling with children ages 2 to 14 seeking kid-friendly hotels, restaurants, and activities.

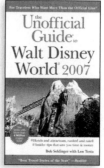

Unofficial Guides

For honeymooners, families, business travelers, and others who value no-nonsense, *Consumer Reports*–style advice.

For Dummies Travel Guides

For curious, independent travelers looking for a fun and easy way to plan a trip.

Visit Frommers.com

WILEY
Now you know.

Limerick County Library

Now hear this!

FREE download of Frommer's Top Travel Secrets at
www.audible.com/frommers*

Download **Frommer's Audio Tours**
into your MP3 player and let **Pauline Frommer**
be your personal guide to the best sights in
cities around the world.

Get your Frommer's Audio Tours plus Frommer's
recommended language lessons and other great
audiobooks for the trip ahead at:
www.audible.com/frommers

The One-Stop Travel Audio Solution.

audible.com®

*Offer valid through May 2009

Frommer's®

A Branded Imprint of ⊛**WILEY**
Now you know.

Frommers.com

travels where you do—anywhere, anytime.

Wherever you go, Frommers.com is there with online, mobile, and audio travel resources you can depend on 24/7. Frommers.com travels where you do—anywhere, anytime.

Frommer's®
A Branded Imprint of WILEY